the whitney guide

THE LOS ANGELES PRESCHOOL GUIDE

By Fiona Whitney

www.thewhitneyguide.com

4TH EDITION

THE WHITNEY GUIDE:
THE LOS ANGELES PRESCHOOL GUIDE
4th Edition
by
Fiona Whitney

© Copyright The Whitney Guide - 2010

All rights reserved.
This book may not be reproduced, stored in a retrieval system, or
transmitted, in any form or by any means, electronic, mechanical,
photocopying, recording or otherwise in full or part
without written permission from the publisher.

978-0-9825304-1-2

Published by :
The Whitney Guide, Los Angeles, California

Cover Design :
Fitch Creative, Pacific Palisades, Calirfornia

THE WHITNEY GUIDE
Los Angeles, California

Email: FionaWhitney@me.com

www.thewhitneyguide.com

DEDICATION

THIS EDITION IS DEDICATED
WITH LOVE AND THANKS TO THE FOLLOWING PEOPLE:

To Mona Holmes-Nisker for her help in updating both books this year.
I couldn't have done it without her!

To my Mum and Dad, who gave me the gift of a wonderful
private school education and who continue to be my biggest supporters.

To my children, Bevan and Charlotte, who inspire me
with their love of school and learning.

To Marnie and her kids.

TABLE OF CONTENTS

Dear Parents 7
Top Ten Things When Considering A Preschool 9
NAEYC 10
Teaching Methods 12
Bird's Eye View 16
10th Street Preschool 19
Adat Ari El Rose Engle Early Childhood Center 22
All Children Great and Small 26
Bel Air Presbyterian Church Preschool 29
Berkeley Hall Preschool 32
Beverly Glen Playgroup 36
Beverly Hills Montessori School 39
Beverly Hills Presbytetian Preschool 42
Canyon Cooperative Nursery School 46
Children's Circle Nursery 49
Children's Creative Workshop 53
Christopher Robin Nursery School 56
Circle of Children Preschool 59
Clairborn School 62
Crestwood Hills Cooperative Nursery School 66
Delaney Wright Fine Arts Preschool 69
Doheny School 73
Ecole Claire Fontaine 76
First Lutheran Circle of Love Preschool 79
First Presbyterian Nursery School 83
Flintridge Montessori 86
Fountain Day School 89
Glendale Montessori 93
Highland Hall Waldorf School 96
Hogg's Hollow 99
Hollywood School House 102
La Cañada – Flintridge Community Center Preschool 106
La Cañada Preschool 110
L.A. Family School 114
La Playa Cooperative Preschool 119
Little Village Nursery School 122
Malibu Methodist Nursery School and Infant Toddler Center 126
Malibu Presbyterian Nursery School 130
Manhattan Academy 134

Mann Family Early Childhood Center	139
Montessori of Manhattan Beach	144
Montessori Shir-Hashirim	148
Oakdale School	151
Pacific Oaks Childrens School	154
Parents and Children's Nursery School	158
Pilgrim Preschool	162
Play Mountain Place	165
The Plymouth School	170
Rabbi Jacob Pressman Academy of Temple Beth Am Early Childhood Center	173
Rustic Canyon Cooperative Preschool	176
Sand Tots Parent Participation Nursery School	179
The Sherman Oaks Nursery School	183
Silverlake Independent Jewish Community Center Preschool	187
St. George's Preschool	190
St. Mark's Preschool	194
St. Matthew's Preschool	199
St. James' Preschool	203
Sunset Montessori	208
Sunshine Preschool	211
Temple Isaiah Preschool	214
Temple Israel Nursery School	217
The Center for Early Education	221
The Country School	225
The Early Years School	230
The Growing Place Preschool and Kindergarten	233
The Neighborhood School	237
The New School West	242
Topanga Cooperative Preschool	245
Turning Point School	249
UCLA Early Care and Education	254
University Parents Nursery School	258
Wagon Wheel	262
Walden School	266
Westminster Child Center	270
Westminster Presbyterian Church Preschool	274
Westside Jewish Community	277
Westside Waldorf School	281
Map	286
Accreditation/Membership Codes	287

Dear Parents:

Many of you may be familiar with my other book, "The Whitney Guide: The Los Angeles Private School Guide," which is now in its' seventh year under my name. Well, my first book gave birth to a darling baby preschool guide and here we are turning three! I know that most of you are just starting out on this adventure. Don't worry – it's not as daunting as you might think. Keep focused and clear on what it is that you are looking for, and read this book with an open mind. You may find that there are schools in here that you never would have considered but now, as you read the review, you may feel more inclined to go visit the school and see for yourself.

I have changed the format of this book and asked the schools to participate more by answering a very detailed questionnaire, which I believe is the sort of information that you want to know. Some schools answered every question while others chose not to, and I have noted that in the Q&A section. I tried to keep my reviews short and to the point, but wanted to give you a taste of each school from a parent's perspective. This year I have added a number of new schools that I wanted you all to know about.

Please forgive me if I have left out a school that one of your children went to, or a school that you've heard good things about. I would love to know about it for a future edition. I have tried to keep the information current. Each year I do my best to update information in the body of each review, but this is not always possible, so feel free to e-mail me at: **fionawhitney@me.com** with any comments, suggestions or information that you feel would make this a more useful guide for you as parents. You can also find information about my **School Guide Consultation Service**, which I offer to parents by visiting **www.thewhitneyguide.com** or call me at **(323) 309-3521** to make an appointment.

In the meantime, please use this book as if it were a school workbook. Don't worry about writing in it or even tearing out a page or two. I want you to get as much out of it as I put into it. I do hope that this guide will help to illuminate the path that lies ahead.

Best of luck in your search!

Fiona Whitney

* The reviews given are based solely on my opinions and the information given to me by the schools.

TOP TEN THINGS WHEN CONSIDERING A PRESCHOOL

10. **CONSIDER AN NAEYC-ACCREDITED SCHOOL.** This tells you that the school had to meet strict criteria regarding teacher credentials, teacher/student ratios, updating learning materials and high standards of safety. Visit www.naeyc.com for more information on accreditation. Do not pass over a school if it doesn't have NAEYC accreditation—it may be applying for it, or it could be a religious school which is exempt from the process. (See more about NAEYC on page 10).

9. **RELIGIOUS OR NOT?** Ask yourself this question before you begin your search.

8. **DECIDE WHICH SCHOOL'S TEACHING METHOD BEST SUITS YOUR CHILD'S TEMPERAMENT.**

7. **DECIDE ON WHAT SCHOOL'S PHILOSOPHY BEST SPEAKS TO YOU.** Please put your kids' needs first, since they are the ones spending all their time there.

6. **TRAVEL TIME.** How far are you willing to go each day? You may have heard about a fabulous preschool over the hill, and then find yourself battling traffic, wildfires, landslides and stray lions just to get your child to school for a couple of hours each day!

5. **HOW MUCH DO YOU WANT TO SPEND?** Do you want to spend a lot of money on preschool? A little? Or somewhere in the middle? How much preschool do you want for your money? Do you want your child enrolled for a full day, a half-day or every-other-day classes, or just on some days?

4. **CAN THE SCHOOL LOOK AFTER YOUR CHILD?** There may be times when you can't be there to pick up your child on time. Will the school accommodate your needs? Is there some flexibility or do you get fined every time that you're a few minutes late?

3. **ASK ABOUT TEACHER TURNOVER.** If a school is constantly losing their staff, there must be a reason and you need to know. Are the teachers trained and certified? Are they required to obtain continuing education? Do they conduct background checks on the teachers before they are hired?

2. **ASK WHAT SCHOOLS THE KIDS WILL GO ON TO ATTEND.** See if those schools are ones that you are interested in for the future.

1. **AND THE NUMBER ONE THING TO LOOK FOR IN A PRESCHOOL: HOW DOES THE PLACE FEEL WHEN YOU WALK AROUND AND OBSERVE IT?** Do the kids look happy and interact well with each other and with their teachers? You will know instinctively if the environment suits your child. Don't listen to anyone else about this. Follow your instincts! Your antennae will be picking up all sorts of interesting information for you to think about at 3 a.m.

Remember if you want to, go back and visit for a second and third time. Don't be shy. You may see something on subsequent visits that you didn't see before.

Good luck!

NAEYC

WHAT IT MEANS AND WHAT TO LOOK FOR

The National Association for the Education of Young Children (NAEYC) is the nation's largest organization of early childhood professionals. In September 1985, the NAEYC established a national, voluntary independent accrediting system called the National Academy of Early Education Programs. It helps to set professional standards for early childhood education programs across the country and to assist families in identifying high-quality programs. There are currently more than 10,000 NAEYC accredited programs in the country, serving 800,000 children and their families.

An early education program is defined as: a child care center, a before-school program, an after-school program, preschool and/or kindergarten.

In order for a school or learning center to achieve accreditation, the program goes through an extensive self-study based on the Academy's "Criteria for High Quality Early Childhood Programs," which involves visits to the sites by a team of trained volunteer validators. This validated self-study includes the program director's responses to the validation visit, followed by a review conducted by a three-member national commission made up of early childhood education and child care experts. The childhood program is then judged to be in substantial compliance with the Academy's criteria and is granted accreditation for a period of three years.

During that three-year period, any early childhood program who achieves accreditation agrees to act upon the commission's suggestions regarding areas of marginal compliance within the Criteria. Annual written reports are then submitted, documenting improvements that have been made to their program as well as providing notification about major changes and evidence of continued compliance.

What is a high-quality early education program? According to the NAEYC, it is a program that "provides a safe and nurturing environment while promoting the physical, social, emotional, and intellectual development of young children." Here are some things that you should ask yourself when looking for a preschool:

Do the children appear relaxed and happy as they engage in play and other activities? Parents should look around and ask themselves if their child would enjoy that particular setting. There should be frequent and positive interactions going on between teachers and students.

Are there enough adults present who are trained in early childhood development and education? For effective administration, the Academy's Criteria recommends at least two teachers for all groups. Infants should be in groups of 6-8 children, 2-and 3-year-olds should be in groups no larger than 14, and 4-and 5-year-old groups should be around 16-20 children. Adults with specialized training in early education and childhood development are usually more effective both as instructors and caregivers.

Do adult expectations vary for children in different age groups and with different interests? Toys and activities should vary by age, as should the instructors' expectations for the children under their care.

Is equal time and attention devoted to the child's cognitive development as well as their social, emotional and physical development? Good inclusive programs, according to the NAEYC, "help children learn how to learn," to use their developing skills in a way that allows them to get along with others, to question why and to discover alternative answers to their questions.

Are there regular staff meetings to plan and evaluate the program? There should be a balance between vigorous outdoor play and quiet indoor play, with activities that allow children to work and play individually or in small groups. The staff should also be flexible enough to meet a child's individual needs and interests, with activities that are both child-initiated and teacher-directed.

Does the school welcome parents in and allow them to observe, discuss policies, make suggestions and participate? There should be regular two-way communication between parents and the teachers regarding the child's experiences. The staff should show respect for families of cultural diversity and different backgrounds.

Are the teachers conscious of the health and safety of the children and themselves? Good hygienic practices should be in place (with both the teachers and children washing their hands between activities), nutritious and varied foods should be served at appropriate times, and the facilities and play areas should be safe with well-maintained equipment. There should be up-to-date medical and emergency records, with emergency procedures in place that are familiar to both the staff and students.

But what if a program is not accredited? The accreditation process takes anywhere from nine months to three years to complete, so some programs may already be involved in a self-study. You should ask whether or not a school is involved in the process and if not, why not.

According to the NAEYC website, "Significant growth in and demands on the accreditation system led the NAEYC Governing Board to establish a project to reinvent accreditation by developing new program standards, criteria, and assessment procedures and by taking immediate steps to improve the reliability and accountability of the system while better managing the demand for accreditation. The transition to the next era of NAEYC accreditation is now underway, with the full implementation currently in process.

For more information on the NAEYC, accreditation, and for the latest news and information on early childhood issues, visit www.naeyc.org or contact them at:

National Academy of Early Childhood Programs
NAEYC
1509 16th Street, N.W.
Washington, D.C. 20036-1426
Phone: (202) 232-8777 or (800) 424-2460 (extension 360)
Fax: (202) 328-1846
www.naeyc.org

TEACHING METHODS

The National Center for Education Statistics reports that almost sixty percent of children, ages three to five, are involved in center-based childcare programs. But what kind of early education should your child receive? If you've decided on preschool, then there are a number of different teaching methods available. See which one of these philosophies best suits your needs and then visit as many schools as you can.

TRADITIONAL SCHOOLS

Traditional preschools are the most common in the United States, and have teachers and directors that uphold a time-tested and research-based curriculum. Teachers are the ones in charge, and the focus is on direct adult instruction rather than child-initiated learning.

Common materials used in the classroom include puppets, blocks, puzzles, art supplies including clay and crayons, rhythm instruments, and dress-up costumes. There are story times and songs which help to teach children about colors, numbers, shapes, animals and the letters of the alphabet. This environment provides a place for children to socialize and begin their studies.

Academics (reading, writing and arithmetic) play a big part in the traditional preschool environment. Homework assignments and worksheets are used to measure achievement, and to help children adjust to an academically-focused curriculum so they can make a solid transition into conventional grade schools.

Traditional preschools will often incorporate other teaching applications such as Montessori, Waldorf, Reggio and/or other methods that will help supplement the traditional system.

COOPERATIVE PRESCHOOLS

Cooperative preschools are also called developmental or parent-participation nursery schools, and rely heavily on parental involvement. The first co-op preschools began in 1916, and were organized by faculty wives at the University of Chicago.

These schools are often started by a group of families who share similar viewpoints when it comes to early childhood education. Co-ops are similar to traditional preschools, except that there are more adults in the classroom. This helps in two ways: the children get individualized attention, and parents have an opportunity for direct interaction as they watch their children learn and grow. This helps children learn by doing and to develop at their own rate and using their own interests, with adults assisting but not dictating the information to be learned.

Most cooperatives have at least one professional teacher but include heavy (and sometimes mandatory) involvement from the parents, who are involved in every aspect of the school from instruction to janitorial services.

Tuition is often lower at cooperative preschools than at traditional schools. The only drawbacks are that parents are required to be involved (making this unsuitable for parents who work outside the home), and parents must enjoy being around other people and their children.

THE MONTESSORI METHOD

The History

Maria Montessori (1870-1952) was Italy's first female physician, specializing in psychiatry and pediatrics. After developing a methodology to work with disabled children, she opened a daycare center for children aged four to seven called "Casa dei Bambini" (Children's House) in 1907, in a slum housing project in Rome.

Montessori utilized manipulative puzzles and other hands-on tools—a system which she'd found successful for her mentally handicapped patients.

Montessori believed in the natural intelligence of children and viewed their development as a series of six-year periods, like repeating triangular waves, and presented the idea that each "wave" had its own area of focus for the child.

Her first book came out in 1915 and her unique approach to education became known as the "Montessori method." There are close to 1,000 schools affiliated with the American Montessori Society, although there are nearly 8,000 schools in the U.S. that call themselves Montessori Schools. An American teacher, Nancy Rambush, helped to promote the Montessori education in the United States. The movement intensified in the 1960s, when parents pushed for Montessori teaching methods to be used in public schools, and since then the Montessori method has been applied from toddler and preschool ages up to the high school level.

The Statistics

Out of the 5,000 schools in the United States that use the name "Montessori" in their title, about 20% of them are accredited with either the Association Montessori Internationale (AMI) or the American Montessori Society (AMS). The AMI promotes the original Montessori ideas, while the AMS supports a less rigid Montessori education against a backdrop of American culture.

The Method

The Montessori Method wants children to develop a love of learning and to advance at their own pace. The system utilizes mixed-age classrooms that span three years. The Method teaches that the "unconscious absorbent mind" is from birth to age three (infant-toddler years), and from ages three to six (primary years) is the time of the "conscious absorbent mind." During these periods, it is believed that children seek order, sensory input, and the freedom to choose their activities and explore without limitations.

Students work alone or in small groups, and they learn from one another as they engage in a variety of activities. This helps older children to develop leadership potential, while the younger children have role models for more mature behavior. The classrooms are arranged with different areas and materials that encourage the children to use their abilities to practice practical life skills, sensorial, mathematics, language, science, geography, art and music. Following Montessori's "writing to read" method, some children may master reading and writing before the age of six.

Several teachers guide the children in their play, but also encourage independence. Teachers give demonstration lessons when an individual or a group shows that they are ready to advance and learn, and the curriculum is put together based on classroom observations. The Montessori teaching methods are used in the morning, and typical child play, including fantasy play, is done in the afternoon.

The Criticism
In this environment of self-discovery, some experts believe that the teachers are too passive in their instruction. Children may have adjustment problems when they shift to a traditional classroom environment.

THE WALDORF APPROACH

The History
In 1919, Austrian scientist and educational theorist Rudolf Steiner visited the Waldorf Astoria cigarette factory in Stuttgart, Germany. He was asked to establish a school there for the factory's employees, and the first independent Waldorf School opened later that year.

Steiner's vision was that this new kind of school would help to create a fair and peaceful society. He went against many of the conventions of the day—the classrooms were coeducational (teaching boys and girls at the same time), he opened the school to families of any background, made it accessible without entrance exams, and developed a comprehensive system that could be used from preschool through high school.

Steiner believed that good education could restore balance between thinking, willing and feeling. His theory was that child development went through three cycles of seven-year stages, each with its own learning needs in an ascending spiral of knowledge.

The Statistics
There are currently around 800 Waldorf Schools in 53 countries, and the Waldorf method is also used by those involved with home schooling. The Association of Waldorf Schools of North America (AWSNA) has more than 140 schools affiliated with it. More information on AWSNA can be found at www.awsna.org.

The Method
The school stresses the importance of unity when it comes to educating children, focusing on the body, mind and spirit as a whole. The heart is as important as the head. Instead of academics, the Waldorf method provides opportunities for the children to involve themselves with creative play, which is considered important "work" and the main activity where they can grow. Bodily exploration, constructive and imaginative play, dance, music, and oral (not written) language, story and song are a large part of the curriculum.

In Waldorf schools, students rarely sit at desks. Computers and television are discouraged. A large part of morning activities is devoted to uninterrupted play, artwork using watercolors or beeswax, cooking, going outdoors for nature walks or to work in the garden, using wooden blocks, or hearing a story told with puppets. Teachers follow a schedule of activities that shifts depending on the day, week and year, and include festivals and foods. This cyclical teaching method is to help children understand the importance of "rhythm" and of balancing energetic and restful play. The Waldorf instructional method emphasizes the relationship between the teacher and child. The teacher stays with the same group of children for up to eight years, and a familial bond is created.

The Criticism
The Waldorf method might cause adjustment problems for students who move to a traditional school, as they must shift their focus from creativity to the standard academic cur-

riculum. Preschoolers are more likely to play dress-up, cook, paint or sing than learn phonics. In preschool and kindergarten, students are not exposed to academics; reading is not often taught until the second or third grade.

REGGIO SCHOOLS

The History
After World War II, parents and teachers in northern Italy began to work together to build quality preschools for their children in a city called Reggio Emilia. The city took over funding for the schools and opened municipal preschools (ages three to six years old) in 1963, followed by infant-toddler centers (ages three months to three years) in 1970.

The Reggio method emphasizes the physical environment, and often refers to the classroom as "the third teacher." The programs are family-centered. Children, parents and teachers are seen as equal partners in the education process.

The Statistics
Reggio Children/USA is the North American arm of the Reggio Children SRL, which distributes publications as well as educational information about the Reggio method. The U.S. contains about 55 Reggio preschools.

The Method
A Reggio curriculum is also seen as an "emergent" curriculum, because it emerges from the ideas and interests of both the teachers and students. It emphasizes art, because teachers believe that children use "100 languages" and spoken language is just one form of expression. Artistic creations—forming letters in clay or wire, for example—is one unique way in which children may learn the alphabet.

Aesthetics are important, and the classroom reflects the need for beauty and space. They are organized in an architectural and functional way to support the interweaving of relationships and encounters between adults and children, between children, and among adults. Play, discovery and research are the essential elements of learning.

The Criticism
Reggio is not right for every family. Parental involvement is expected on everything from school policy to child development concerns. Some children (depending on their personalities) might be better off in a more structured classroom.

A BIRD'S EYE VIEW
Reading the Graph

The following categories are the key to reading the graph which you can find at the bottom of each school. Each letter corresponds to a different element of education, and the quality is measured on a scale of 0-5:

A. Learning to Read • B. Dress-up • C. Hand-Eye • D. Building Blocks
E. Arts and Crafts • F. Body Coordination • G. Meeting Time • H. Weights and Measures •
I. Beakers and Bunnies • J. Counting 1-2-3 • K. Outdoor Play

A. Learning To Read: This category rates how the school introduces children to the world of books. This could be through story time, using art and music to introduce children to the alphabet, listening games, puppetry and conversation.

B. Dress-Up: This indicates how much a school lets children experiment with different roles through play, using items such as a play stove, dishes, baby dolls, and dress-up. Children learn to share, work with one another and make compromises.

C. Hand-Eye: This category measures the amount of manipulative play provided to children. Manipulative play helps children learn about the size, shape, weight, length and height of objects, as they gain knowledge about the objects and develop coordination of eye, arm, hand and finger muscles.

D. Building Blocks: This indicates that an adequate amount of space, storage and flooring is provided for children to use blocks (made of a variety of materials—plastic, wood, cardboard) in the development of their math skills. Blocks can be used to create enclosures, make rows, create artistic patterns, and work on physical skills.

E. Arts and Crafts: This category measures the level of art involvement in classroom activities. Does the school provide a wide range of materials and craft projects? Some tasks might include making collages, using play dough or clay, painting and coloring with crayons or markers.

F. Body Coordination: This indicates the amount of physically active play that the school encourages among its students. Agility, coordination and balance are developed as children gain increasing control over both the large and small muscles in their bodies. Exercises and play equipment might include such items as climbing structures and tunnels.

G. Meeting Time: Also sometimes known as "Circle Time," this category indicates if children gather with their instructor to take attendance, read a story together, and learn about the day's plans.

H. Weights and Measures: Water and sand tables are often provided for children to improve their sensory abilities—hand-eye coordination in particular, with lifting, pouring and controlling the elements at hand. It also helps children to explore early math and science concepts, to develop concentration and problem-solving, and to develop social skills as they play with others.

I. Beakers and Bunnies: This category addresses items that may be around, such as class pets (fish, bunnies, hamsters, snakes), aquariums, and plants may be some of the elements involved. Others might include recycling, food preparation and nature walks.

J. Counting 1-2-3: Does the school have computers available for the students? Does their philosophy support the use of computers in the classroom? Is there enough equipment available, and is there beginner software for the children to learn from? If there are no computers, are phonics and/or counting games present?

K. Outdoor Play: This refers to the kind of outdoor environment that is provided by the school. There might be swings, balls of different sizes to play with, paved areas for bicycles, outdoor craft areas, sand and/or grass areas, etc.

preschool

10TH STREET PRESCHOOL

1444 10th St.
Santa Monica, CA 90401
Phone: (310) 458-4088
See Map D on page 286

Contact: Cindy Wasson, Director

- ACCREDITATION: NAEYC
- FOR-PROFIT
- FINANCIAL AID IS AVAILABLE
- NUMBER OF KIDS: 80
- TUITION: $11,000 YEAR
- WE HAVE KIDS WITH SPECIAL NEEDS

WHEN TO APPLY: CONTACT SCHOOL FOR MORE DETAILS AND TO TAKE A TOUR.

Cindy Wasson, the Director of the 10th Street Preschool in Santa Monica, is a master at communication and at making people feel at ease. Even as we perched on child-size chairs, and the pregnant moms shared the sofa in the school's library, there was a sense of warmth, ease and grace as she spoke frankly about early childhood education. The first thing you see, literally, upon entering the school are the amazing murals by painter Jurrer-Alvet that are on every wall, fence, and available flat surface. It creates a magical Disney-esque quality to the school. Then, each room is an individual "bungalow." For example, there is the "Art Bungalow" and a "Building Bungalow." The incredibly organized wall structure that houses all the wooden blocks in the building bungalow, was the envy of every parent on the tour! There are also Polaroid pictures everywhere, taken by the children.

The 10th Street Preschool is a mixed-age grouping school. They believe in mixed age, the same way they believe in mixed humans, and extreme diversity. In families, there are different ages, the same as here at school. Children learn communication and to get along. Answering a young father's question of the schools philosophy, Wasson replies, "I'm too old to follow one practice! That boxes you in. And I feel it's incredibly presumptuous to assume how your child will learn. The goal is to reach the children." The staff of teachers at 10th Street must be empathetic, loving human beings (besides having credentials, of course). They must have unwavering kindness and patience to not rush in and "fix it." In the area of conflict resolution, Cindy Wasson and her teachers never force a child to apologize. "A child doesn't really understand right from wrong at that age. You have to have a moral conscience to be sorry," says Wasson. Basically, there is a conversation to assess what happened, children can express what they felt, and discuss what appropriate actions might have been made instead. The teacher, of course, guides all this but it is the child who provides the solution. And (I loved this) there are teething rings in the fridge that are "magic rings," according to Wasson, where a child has the opportunity to participate in the healing of the "injured" child, and the situation.

Cindy Wasson completes the tour in her down-to-earth, no-nonsense manner by stating, "Kindergarten is the new first grade. If children don't have the social skills and tools, they can't attend to the task of learning. You don't need to go to preschool. It is a huge gift. Here, they learn kindness, self-esteem and practice social skills. You simply can't give them the social experience at home."

BACKGROUND

Established in 1982 by Cindy Wasson.

BIRD'S EYE VIEW

	Non-existent	Poor	Fair	Good	Excellent
Learning to Read Children learn to explore the world of books					✓
Dress-Up Children experiment with different roles and imagination					✓
Hand-Eye Children develop fine motor skills by using fingers and hands					✓
Building Blocks Children practice symbolic representation. They are developing an understanding of the relationships between size and shape, and the basic math concepts of geometry and numbers					✓
Arts and Crafts Children are developing small muscle control as well as creativity					✓
Body Coordination Children crawl through tunnels, climb and balance					✓
Meeting Time Gathering place to listen to the teacher and to stories					✓
Weights and Measures Water and Sand tables					✓
Beakers and Bunnies Classroom pets, aquariums....planting...					✓
Counting 1-2-3 A good preschool will stock basic early-learner software such as phonics or counting games					✓
Outdoor Play Encourage large muscle control and coordination					✓

Q & A

HOW THEY LEARN

What is your school's teaching philosophy? No feedback received.

How do you implement the philosophy? No feedback received.

What specialty teachers are brought into the school? We bring in a music specialist.

What is the teaching method? Developmental.

At what age do the children start? To what age is the school licensed? 18 months & up.

HOW TO GET IN

Are there open house dates? When are tours given? It varies, typically once a month. Tour dates are always stated on our answering machine.

Is there an interview? With the child or without? Yes, we require meeting prospective parents and child.

Is preference given to applicants whose siblings are alumni? Yes.

Are letters of recommendation encouraged?

From what types of people? Letters are encouraged from school family and friends.

How many applications do you receive each year? 150.

How many open spots are there each year? Varies.

What are some of the schools that children go on to after finishing their education at your preschool? No feedback received.

PIGGY BANK

Apart from tuition, what other fees do you charge? There is a preschool/new student enrollment fee. Contact school for details.

How is tuition broken down? $11,000/year.

What are the different payment plans available? Call for information.

What is the fee schedule? 1-3 payments.

Is there a contract? Yes.

Do you have a tuition insurance program? No.

HELPING HANDS

What accreditation is necessary for the teachers to work at your school? Credential – ECE.

How many teachers are there? Six teachers, three per group.

How many aides are there? None.

IN THE 'ROOM

What's the adult-to-child ratio? 1:7.5

What are the policies for initial separation between parent and child? Separation period of one to two weeks. Each child has a specific separation teacher.

Can you visit any time unannounced? Yes, if your child is on campus.

What are the hours? 9 a.m.-12 p.m., 1-4 p.m.

Do you offer early bird or after-hours pick-up? If so, is there an extra fee? There is an extra fee from 12-1 p.m.

Please describe a typical day for a child at your school. No feedback received.

What kinds of academic activities are offered? We believe in an emergent academic curriculum.

What kinds of art activities are offered? A wide variety.

Is the child's time structured or unstructured, or a mixture of both? Balance of both.

If a child is not interested in a particular activity, does he/she have other choices or is he/she encouraged to try it anyway? Children are always encouraged to try everything but always have other choices.

How are disputes handled when they occur between the children? No feedback received.

When and for how long is nap time? No nap times.

What kinds of beds do you use? None.

What do you do when a child is dropped off in the morning and is obviously not well? What do you do when a child becomes sick during the day? Parent is called. Child goes home.

Can you accommodate children with special needs? Yes.

KEEPING IT SAFE

Please describe your security measures for arriving and leaving the school. All children must be signed in and out by a parent or known entity.

What medical supplies do you have on hand, and what medical experience does your staff have? Is your staff trained in CPR? Every staff member is Red Cross/First Aid/CPR trained. We are right next door to 10th Street Pediatrics in case of emergency.

Please describe your earthquake-preparedness plan, and what special equipment do you have on hand in the event of a disaster? Earthquake kit is provided for every child and updated yearly.

SWINGS 'N THINGS

Please describe your playground. Does it have plenty of shade? Awnings and tents provide shade during sunny times.

Do you put sunscreen on the children? Sunscreen is applied as needed.

What kind of toilet training is available? None.

HELPING OUT

What kinds of fundraising events are at your school each year? Scholarship Drive, Parent Party, raffles, etc.

How much participation is required by each parent? No feedback received.

KEEPING IN TOUCH

How do you communicate with parents? Is there a newsletter or phone tree? Newsletters (both school and parent association), phone tree, open assemblies, two parent/teacher conferences per year, staff and parents in daily communication.

Does the school publish an address book with all the parents' information in it? Yes.

preschool to 6th grade

ADAT ARI EL ROSE ENGEL EARLY CHILDHOOD CENTER

12020 Burbank Blvd., Valley Village, CA 91607
Phone (818) 766-9426
www.adatariel.org
See Map A on page 286

Contact: Beryl Strauss

- ACCREDITATION: NAEYC
- NOT-FOR-PROFIT
- FINANCIAL AID IS AVAILABLE
- NUMBER OF KIDS: 180
- TUITION: $3,835-$11,556 YEAR
- WE HAVE KIDS WITH SPECIAL NEEDS

WHEN TO APPLY: APPLY ANY TIME, BUT MOST APPLICATIONS ARE RECEIVED LATE WINTER/EARLY SPRING.

According to the school's statement, "Adat Ari El Early Childhood Center offers a warm, integrated and developmentally appropriate general and Judaic program that promotes the creative and intellectual development of each child, in an atmosphere where each child's uniqueness is valued and nurtured." The integration of this philosophy into the practical preschool environment is remarkable.

It should be noted that this school is large and has 175 students per day, ranging in age from the "Parent and Me" two-and-a-half-year-olds to the five-year-old Gesher Class. In spite of its size, the teacher-to-student ratio is 7:1, with two teachers per classroom and, at times, an aide as well. The school is on the same campus as, but separate from, the Adat Ari El Elementary School. The shared parking lot has a security guard station and strict security, as well as a gated, secured entrance to the actual preschool with camera surveillance.

Once inside the gates of the preschool, kids can run and play in the playground, which has a garden to one side of the play area. All of the classrooms face the playground. The art studio stands out in particular. Students go there once a week to weave, trace, play with clay, paint, and learn that art is a language. Each of them is prodded to express all that they can through this medium. Student writing—taken by dictation—is found in the classrooms, posted on projects hanging on the walls. As part of the Reggio Emilia philosophy, "Their words are just as important as library books." "Respect and communication between children," and learned problem-solving, are mainstays here as well.

Art, creativity and individuality are the focus of the rooms during the tour. Many photos of both the children and their families adorn the spaces to create the "extension of the home in the school" ideology. The curriculum here is Reggio-inspired emergent curriculum, and in many cases the interests of the students becomes the focus of activity. Another behemoth of individuality is that the children are learning to time manage and tune into their own bodies, and accordingly may snack when deemed appropriate by the hunger impulse in each of them. In other words? No group snack time. A non-profit, parochial school, Adat Ari El's admissions process gives priority to Synagogue members, children currently enrolled in Infant/Toddler programs and siblings of children enrolled in the Early Childhood Center and Day School.

BACKGROUND

The school was established in the early 1950s by Rose Engel. The Early Childhood Center began over 60 years ago and many of today's students are second or third generation attendees.

BIRD'S EYE VIEW

	Non-existent	Poor	Fair	Good	Excellent
Learning to Read Children learn to explore the world of books				✓	
Dress-Up Children experiment with different roles and imagination				✓	
Hand-Eye Children develop fine motor skills by using fingers and hands				✓	
Building Blocks Children practice symbolic representation. They are developing an understanding of the relationships between size and shape, and the basic math concepts of geometry and numbers					✓
Arts and Crafts Children are developing small muscle control as well as creativity					✓
Body Coordination Children crawl through tunnels, climb and balance				✓	
Meeting Time Gathering place to listen to the teacher and to stories					✓
Weights and Measures Water and Sand tables					✓
Beakers and Bunnies Classroom pets, aquariums....planting...					✓
Counting 1-2-3 A good preschool will stock basic early-learner software such as phonics or counting games				✓	
Outdoor Play Encourage large muscle control and coordination					✓

Q & A

HOW THEY LEARN

What is your school's teaching philosophy? Adat Ari El Early Childhood Center offers a warm, integrated and developmentally-appropriate general and Judaic program that promotes the creative and intellectual development of each child, in an atmosphere where each child's uniqueness is valued and nurtured.

How do you implement the philosophy? The integration of the philosophy into the practical preschool environment is remarkable.

What specialty teachers are brought into the school? All children have music with a specialist once a week.

What is the teaching method? The curriculum here is Reggio-inspired emergent curriculum, and in many cases the interests of the students become the focus of activity. For example, in one classroom there's been a sudden "wow" regarding spiders, and boom! There's a handmade large web hovering over one of the reading areas, complete with (plastic) spiders.

At what age do the children start? To what age is the school licensed? Children start at 2.6 years of age. The school is licensed from 2-5.

HOW TO GET IN

Are there open house dates? When are tours given? There are no open house dates. Prospective parents may book individualized tours.

Is there an interview? With the child or without? Parent interview is part of the tour process, and the tour can be with or without the child.

Is preference given to applicants whose siblings are alumni? The admission process gives priority to Synagogue members, children currently enrolled in Infant Toddler programs, and siblings of children enrolled in the Early Childhood Center and Day School.

Are letters of recommendation encouraged? From what types of people? No.

How many applications do you receive each year? No feedback received.

How many open spots are there each year? 35-40.

What are some of the schools that children go on to after finishing their education at your preschool? Adat Ari El Day School, The Buckley School, Campbell Hall, Oakwood School, Westland, Los Encinos, Emek Hebrew Academy, Stephen S. Wise Elementary School, Children's Community School, Heschel Day School, Viewpoint School, Curtis School, public elementary schools such as Carpenter, Riverside, Sherman Oaks.

PIGGY BANK

Apart from tuition, what other fees do you charge? There is a one-time entrance fee of $50.

How is tuition broken down? Two mornings is $3,835, and five full days is $11,556.

What are the different payment plans? We offer three different payment plans—full payment in cash or check, three credit card payments using Visa or Master Card, or ten equal consecutive monthly installments from a checking/savings account.

What is the fee schedule? It depends on the number of days or half-days.

Is there a contract? No.

Do you have a tuition insurance program? No.

HELPING HANDS

What accreditation is necessary for the teachers to work at your school? Minimum of 12 child development units. Most have A.A. or B.A. degrees.

How many teachers are there? Thirty-four teachers.

How many aides are there? Three.

IN THE 'ROOM

What's the adult-to-child ratio? It varies between 5:1 and 9:1.

What are the policies for initial separation between parent and child? Our separation policy requires a gradual introduction to school. The teacher, parent and director will determine the time allotted for separation on an individual, as-needed basis.

Can you visit any time unannounced? Yes, unless the child has trouble separating.

What are the hours? Open from 8 a.m.-5:30 p.m. (4:30 p.m. on Fridays).

Do you offer early bird or after-hours pick-up? If so, is there an extra fee? Early drop-off is from 8-8:30 a.m. and is included in the full day fee. There is no after hours pick-up. School closes at 5:30 p.m.

Please describe a typical day for a child at your school. It varies by age. All children have inside playtime (dramatic play, manipulatives, science discovery, art, block building, etc.), meeting/circle time (discussion, stories, finger plays, songs, movement), snack, outside time, and lunch in the mornings. The younger children nap in the afternoon, eat snack, play outside and inside. Older children rest or participate in a quiet activity but do not nap. Older children also go to the school library once a week. Children work in the art studio with the art teacher at least once a week.

What kinds of academic activities are offered? Children are exposed to shapes, numbers, letters and words through their daily activities. Children are encouraged to dictate their thoughts and stories. A variety of writing implements are available for student experimentation. Problem solving and higher level critical thinking skills are encouraged. Most children recognize numbers and letters and are able to write their names by the time they finish pre-kindergarten.

What kinds of art activities are offered? The art studio especially stands out. All students go once a week to weave, trace, play with clay, paint, and learn that art is a language. Each of them is prodded to express all that they can through this medium.

Is the child's time structured or unstructured, or a mixture of both? Combination.

If a child is not interested in a particular activity does he/she have other choices or is he/she encouraged to try it anyway? There are usually many options to choose from in the classroom. Sometimes, a child may be guided into another activity. Other times, he may be encouraged to try an activity. This is dependent on the individual child's needs.

How are disputes handled when they occur between the children? Children are listened to and encouraged to express their feelings. Children (with adult help when needed) learn to problem-solve their conflicts.

When and for how long is nap time? For the two-and-a-half to four-year-olds, nap time is from 12:45-2:15 p.m.

What kinds of beds do you use? The beds are Angeles cots. Each child brings his/her own blankets, sheets and pillow.

What do you do when a child is dropped off in the morning and is obviously not well? What do you do when a child becomes sick during the day? Children are not permitted in the school if they are not well. The parent would be asked to take the child home.

Can you accommodate children with special needs? Definitely. At present, we have about twelve children on the autism spectrum with therapeutic companions. We welcome diversity.

KEEPING IT SAFE

Please describe your security measures for arriving and leaving the school. The school is on the same campus as, but separate from, the Adat Ari El Elementary School. The shared parking lot has a security guard station and strict security to enter, as well as a gated, secured entrance to the actual preschool with camera surveillance.

What medical supplies do you have on hand, and what medical experience does your staff have? Is your staff trained in CPR? We have basic First Aid supplies. All staff is trained in CPR and we have two teachers who are advanced life saving/first aid certificates, and there is a teacher with EMT training.

Please describe your earthquake-preparedness plan, and what special equipment do you have on hand in the event of a disaster? There is a Synagogue plan that we participate in and supplies are available for each child in the event that they must remain at school beyond their normal hours. We are linked with a school out of state so in the event of local communication problems, information can be disseminated.

SWINGS 'N THINGS

Please describe your playground. Does it have plenty of shade? Once inside the gates of the preschool, kids are running and playing in the wide-open playground. There is a garden located to one side of the play area where different classrooms are harvesting their choice of plants. The classrooms all face the playground, which is shaded and spacious, and when walking through them, the outdoor area seems a mere extension of the indoor areas.

What kind of toilet training is available? Children do not have to be potty trained upon admittance. Parents and teachers work together to determine readiness. Teachers are supportive and encouraging of parents' decisions.

HELPING OUT

What kinds of fundraising events are at your school each year? Hot lunch program, Bowl-a-Thon, Make-a-Plate, morning coffee cart sales, children's art auction, Ladies' Night Out (in conjunction with other Synagogue departments), Kadima Quartet.

How much participation is required by each parent? Volunteering is strongly encouraged. Room representatives for each class, driving on field trips, cooking with a class, etc.

KEEPING IN TOUCH

How do you communicate with parents? Is there a newsletter or phone tree? Monthly newsletter written by a parent volunteer, flyers about programs or events as needed sent via student folders and/or e-mail, each classroom writes a weekly newsletter for parents, room representatives have a phone tree.

Does the school publish an address book with all the parents' information in it? An updated student/parent roster with addresses, phone numbers and email addresses is distributed several times a year.

preschool

ALL CHILDREN GREAT AND SMALL

4612 Welch Place
Los Angeles, CA 90027
Phone: (323) 666-6154
www.allchildrengreatandsmall.com
See Map C on page 286

Contact: Yolanda Ruiz

- ACCREDITATION: NONE
- TUITION: $300-$500 MONTH
- WE HAVE KIDS WITH SPECIAL NEEDS
- NUMBER OF KIDS: 48
- NOT-FOR-PROFIT
- FINANCIAL AID IS NOT AVAILABLE

WHEN TO APPLY: APPLICATIONS ARE YEAR-ROUND.

Through this door walk the greatest kids in the world," says the sign on the Craftsman house on a side street in the very hip Franklin and Vermont/Los Feliz area. And All Children Great And Small does, indeed, remind you of someone's house—taken over by a gaggle of incredibly energetic, very hip looking children. What immediately impressed me was the way that director Yolanda Ruiz gave me a big welcome and then told me to "make myself at home" before going up in the loft to read to some of the children. There were no anxious looks my way, no attempt to impress me with facts and figures—while she was happy to have me there, her main priority was the kids…as it should be.

The facility isn't very big, which gives it even more of that little gem feel. The ceiling is painted to resemble the sky, and various quotes adorn the walls, "The pressure to achieve constricts," and "You must be the change you wish to see in the world," among them. The large room is stuffed with board games, a play restaurant, art supplies, blocks and costumes, all of which were being utilized. When one of the teachers suggested, "Let's fix the problem" to one of the kids who was dumping sand in the play sink, he promptly did—earning him a warm acknowledgement from two of the teachers.

As one of the mothers told me, "It's the kids' school. They're the community and everything is about, 'How do we work together to do whatever it is we're doing?' So they learn responsibility and respect for others and, in doing that, they learn a sense of self, integrity and respect for themselves. But they don't know that's what's happening, they just think they're having fun." What more could a parent ask for? One thing to keep in mind—All Children is a co-op, so involvement by parents is mandatory. However, compared to some of the other co-ops in town, the parameters of this involvement aren't as time-consuming.

BACKGROUND

Founded in 1983 by a group of dedicated parents and teachers who dreamed of a special place where young children could be respected for who they are.

BIRD'S EYE VIEW

	Non-existent	Poor	Fair	Good	Excellent
Learning to Read Children learn to explore the world of books					✓
Dress-Up Children experiment with different roles and imagination					✓
Hand-Eye Children develop fine motor skills by using fingers and hands					✓
Building Blocks Children practice symbolic representation. They are developing an understanding of the relationships between size and shape, and the basic math concepts of geometry and numbers					✓
Arts and Crafts Children are developing small muscle control as well as creativity					✓
Body Coordination Children crawl through tunnels, climb and balance				✓	
Meeting Time Gathering place to listen to the teacher and to stories				✓	
Weights and Measures Water and Sand tables					✓
Beakers and Bunnies Classroom pets, aquariums....planting...				✓	
Counting 1-2-3 A good preschool will stock basic early-learner software such as phonics or counting games					✓
Outdoor Play Encourage large muscle control and coordination				✓	

Q & A

HOW THEY LEARN

What is your school's teaching philosophy? We believe that children are individuals. Therefore, the process by each child develops is unique. Our classroom is designed so that children can learn through active involvement in a variety of experiences. We seek to create a balanced environment that simulates curiosity, develops imagination and encourages self-knowledge through interactive play.

How do you implement the philosophy? Children learn through play. They learn through active involvement in a variety of types of experience.

What is the teaching method? We emphasize hands-on learning, where one's intellectual, social and emotional self is engaged. We are a child-centered school.

At what age do the children start? To what age is the school licensed? We are licensed for ages 3-5.

HOW TO GET IN

Are there open house dates? When are tours given? We have an open door policy.

Is there an interview? With the child or without? No.

Is preference given to applicants whose siblings are alumni? Yes.

Are letters of recommendation encouraged? From what types of people? No.

How many applications do you receive each year? No feedback received.

How many open spots are there each year? No feedback received.

What are some of the schools that children go on to after finishing their education at your preschool? No feedback received.

PIGGY BANK

Apart from tuition, what other fees do you charge? There is a $15 annual application fee if you wish to stay on the waiting list. Upon confirmation of enrollment, there is a $100 entrance fee per child. There is an annual membership fee of $50 per family.

How is tuition broken down? $300 for three days per week, and $500 for 5 days per week.

What are the different payment plans available? Tuition may be paid in one, two or 10 installments. A 10% discount on tuition will be applied to siblings attending school concurrently.

What is the fee schedule? One installment is due in September, two installments are due in September and February, or pay ten installments monthly (September-June).

Is there a contract? Yes.

Do you have a tuition insurance program? No. The school requires four weeks' notice prior to withdrawal or payment of four weeks of tuition.

HELPING HANDS

What accreditation is necessary for the teachers to work at your school? A minimum of 12 units in ECE.

How many teachers are there? Three teachers.

How many aides are there? One aide.

IN THE 'ROOM

What's the adult-to-child ratio? No feedback received.

What are the policies for initial separation between parent and child? Done on a case-by-case basis, when the child is ready.

Can you visit any time unannounced? Yes.

What are the hours? Do you offer early bird or after-hours pick-up? If so, is there an extra fee? No early-bird or after-hours pick-up.

Please describe a typical day for a child at your school. There is inside time and centers such as art, blocks, books, dolls, animals, instruments, and dress-up. This is followed by snack and outside time.

What kinds of academic activities are offered? Pre-math and pre-reading skills are practiced with all the different activities.

What kinds of art activities are offered? Painting, collage, blocks, etc.

Is the child's time structured or unstructured, or a mixture of both? A mixture of both.

If a child is not interested in a particular activity, does he/she have other choices or is he/she encouraged to try it anyway? They move to their interests.

How are disputes handled when they occur between the children? We are big on problem-solving skills, and giving children the tools (words) to use to help solve the problems.

When and for how long is nap time? No nap time.

What kinds of beds do you use? No nap time.

What do you do when a child is dropped off in the morning and is obviously not well? What do you do when a child becomes sick during the day? Children should stay home when sick.

Can you accommodate children with special needs? We have a ramp and handlebars in the bathroom.

KEEPING IT SAFE

Please describe your security measures for arriving and leaving the school. A locked front door.

What medical supplies do you have on hand, and what medical experience does your staff have? Is your staff trained in CPR? Our staff is trained in CPR.

Please describe your earthquake-preparedness plan, and what special equipment do you have on hand in the event of a disaster? School staff have participated in an earthquake awareness and preparedness programs. Emergency evacuation plans have been formulated and are posted in the teacher bathroom. We have an ample supply of food and water.

SWINGS 'N THINGS

Please describe your playground. Does it have plenty of shade? We have swings, a climbing structure, trees (for shade and climbing on), a children's garden, and water.

What kind of toilet training is available? There is no toilet training. However, it is not mandatory to be potty trained. We have lots of diapers, pull-ups and wipes.

HELPING OUT

What kinds of fundraising events are at your school each year? Each family is required to participate in and attend our annual fundraiser and may be asked to help in others. If the family does not, they will be assessed $250 as a value comparable to the money raised by those who did participate. If a family does not fulfill its two-hour work shift at the event, $25 an hour will be assessed.

How much participation is required by each parent? Varies.

KEEPING IN TOUCH

How do you communicate with parents? Is there a newsletter or phone tree? Newsletters, a phone tree and emails.

Does the school publish an address book with all the parents' information in it? We have a community roster with the child's name, parent's name, address and phone number.

preschool

BEL AIR PRESBYTERIAN CHURCH PRESCHOOL

16100 Mullholland Dr.
Los Angeles, CA 90049
Phone: (818) 990-6071
www.belairpres.org/preschool
See Map D on page 286

Contact: call office for any inquiry

- ACCREDITATION: NONE
- NOT-FOR-PROFIT
- FINANCIAL AID IS AVAILABLE
- NUMBER OF KIDS: 150
- TUITION: $3,940-$6,500 YEAR
- WE HAVE KIDS WITH SPECIAL NEEDS

WHEN TO APPLY: APPLICATIONS ARE AVAILABLE AT THE BEGINNING OF SEPTEMBER BEFORE THE SCHOOL YEAR THEY ARE APPLYING FOR, AND DUE IN FEBRUARY.

I began my tour of Bel Air Presbyterian Church Preschool in Miss Tina's class. There were floor mats, and over it were HUGE rolls of multicolored crepe paper that the children were leaping in like a pile of leaves: Two little girls were making dresses out of bright purple paper, and several children crumpled it up, tossed it around, and then landed in it! It called out to my inner child and made me wish I could leap in, too!

As a church-run preschool, Bel Air recognizes and validates the need for a creative, God-centered atmosphere where children can grow and learn in an environment of love, respect and discovery. The school was established to provide a Christian-oriented preschool program that will benefit the child, the family, the community, and the church. While it is not mandatory that parents be a member of Bel Air Presbyterian Church, Church members are considered first in accordance with their commitment to ministry and outreach in their communities.

Located at what used to be the Stephen Wise Temple Preschool, physical space is abundant. There are five to six playgrounds, including an occasional (weather permitting) outside classroom. There are five morning classrooms and two afternoon classrooms with two teachers in each classroom, making the adult/child ratio between 1:6 and 1:8. The ratio is even lower with adult volunteers (parents) or interns.

The Bel Air curriculum is planned so children can develop at their own rate of growth. They really understand that each child comes with their own individual style and rate of learning/growth. Miss Tina explained to me that they seek to constantly adapt the program to meet the individual needs of each child. The emphasis is that central emotional growth is more important than academic, and there are no computers present, "because they have computers at home!" You could tell that education really excites Miss Tina, and she loves being a teacher, and the children adore her. Bel Air has been accredited by the NAEYC for seven years, and they keep active in current research and what is going on in the community.

BACKGROUND

The school was founded by Ruth Gusting.

BIRD'S EYE VIEW

	Non-existent	Poor	Fair	Good	Excellent
Learning to Read Children learn to explore the world of books					✓
Dress-Up Children experiment with different roles and imagination					✓
Hand-Eye Children develop fine motor skills by using fingers and hands					✓
Building Blocks Children practice symbolic representation. They are developing an understanding of the relationships between size and shape, and the basic math concepts of geometry and numbers					✓
Arts and Crafts Children are developing small muscle control as well as creativity					✓
Body Coordination Children crawl through tunnels, climb and balance					✓
Meeting Time Gathering place to listen to the teacher and to stories					✓
Weights and Measures Water and Sand tables				✓	
Beakers and Bunnies Classroom pets, aquariums....planting...				✓	
Counting 1-2-3 A good preschool will stock basic early-learner software such as phonics or counting games				✓	
Outdoor Play Encourage large muscle control and coordination					✓

Q & A

HOW THEY LEARN

What is your school's teaching philosophy?
To provide a full-day Christian-oriented preschool program that will benefit the child, family, community and church.

How do you implement the philosophy?
Our purpoe is to provide a safe, loving, nurturing environment that preserves the experience of childhood through a carefully planned Christian program.

What is the teaching method? Christian-oriented.

At what age do the children start? To what age is the school licensed? From 2.5-6 years of age.

HOW TO GET IN

Are there open house dates? When are tours given? Tours are scheduled two-three times a month, from October to February. Call the office for specific dates. Applications are given to families who come on tours.

Is there an interview? With the child or without? There is a parent tour only, no interview process.

Is preference given to applicants whose siblings are alumni? Yes.

Are letters of recommendation encouraged? From what types of people? No, but they will be read if they are sent.

How many applications do you receive each year? No feedback received.

How many open spots are there each year? Varies.

What are some of the schools that children go on to after finishing their education at your preschool? Curtis, John Thomas Dye, Berkley, Westland, Brentwood, Roscomore Road, and Warner.

PIGGY BANK

Apart from tuition, what other fees do you charge? There is a $50 application fee, $12 one-time emergency kit fee, and a $150 per year registration fee.

How is tuition broken down? Tuition ranges from $394-$650 per month over nine months (most preschools are 10 months).

What are the different payment plans available? One yearly payment, trimester, monthly. Due on the 15th of every month.

Is there a contract? Yes.

Do you have a tuition insurance program? No.

HELPING HANDS

What accreditation is necessary for the teachers to work at your school? ECE units, and the amount varies based on the level of teaching.

How many teachers are there? There are seven lead/co-teachers and two administrative staff members.

How many aides are there? Three associate teachers and one resource teacher.

IN THE 'ROOM

What's the adult-to-child ratio? For the 2.5 to 3.5-year-olds, it is 6:1. For the 3 to 6-year-olds, it is 8:1.

What are the policies for initial separation between parent and child? Please consult the school handbook.

Can you visit any time unannounced? No.

What are the hours? Do you offer early bird or after-hours pick-up? If so, is there an extra fee? The morning program is from 9 a.m. to noon. Students must attend the morning program to attend in the afternoon. Afternoon Enrichment is from 12-3 p.m. There is an early morning drop-o (Morning Enrichment) from 5:25- 9 a.m.

Please describe a typical day for a child at your school. Open center, circle time, outside team snack.

What kinds of academic activities are offered? Only those which emerge from play—nothing teacher-initiated.

What kinds of art activities are offered? No feedback received.

Is the child's time structured or unstructured, or a mixture of both? No feedback received.

If a child is not interested in a particular activity, does he/she have other choices or is he/she encouraged to try it anyway? Children are encouraged to try things but never forced.

How are disputes handled when they occur between the children? No feedback received.

When and for how long is nap time? There is a 45-minute nap for Afternoon Enrichment classes.

What do you do when a child is dropped off in the morning and is obviously not well? What do you do when a child becomes sick during the day? Generally, we only treat with soap, water and Band-Aids unless the parent has given us other medications.

Can you accommodate children with special needs? Yes.

KEEPING IT SAFE

Please describe your security measures for arriving and leaving the school. No feedback received.

What medical supplies do you have on hand, and what medical experience does your staff have? Is your staff trained in CPR? Staff is trained in CPR and First Aid certification.

**Please describe your earthquake-preparedness plan, and what special equipment do you have on hand in the event of a disaster? No feedback received.

SWINGS 'N THINGS

Please describe your playground. Does it have plenty of shade? Big with plenty of shade.

Do you put sunscreen on the children? Yes.

What kind of toilet training is available? Children must be toilet trained upon attending.

HELPING OUT

What kinds of fundraising events are at your school each year? There is a parent-run fundraiser once a year, a selective auction and event.

How much participation is required by each parent? No feedback received.

KEEPING IN TOUCH

How do you communicate with parents? Is there a newsletter or phone tree? We put a flyer in the child's mailboxes.

Does the school publish an address book with all the parents' information in it? Yes, unless parents specifically request to be left out.

BERKELEY HALL PRESCHOOL

preschool to 8th grade

16000 Mulholland Drive
Los Angeles, CA 90049
Phone: (310) 476-6421
www.berkeleyhall.org
See Map D on page 286

Contact: Jacque Hammar

- ACCREDITATION: WASC, CAIS
- NON-PROFIT
- FINANCIAL AID IS AVAILABLE FOR K-8
- NUMBER OF KIDS: 34 (Pre) 226 (K-8)
- TUITION: $7,200-$18,200 YEAR
- WE HAVE KIDS WITH SPECIAL NEEDS

WHEN TO APPLY: FALL. THE CUT-OFF DATE IS IN JANUARY.

The first impression of Berkeley Hall is space, and lots of it. Built on 66 acres (yes, 66) there are wide-open areas to be filled by invention, discovery, and play. The spaciousness includes the classrooms, playground, and library. Everywhere there is room to move, and the classrooms have different "centers" where children rotate throughout the day, allowing for individual attention. There is also a large, multi-purpose room (cafeteria style) used for snacks, gymnastics/tumbling, and drama. Music is a daily activity as well.

In the library, there is a large fireplace, and a sort of sunken living room, for telling stories. Children each pick out a book per week that comes back to the classroom for story time. Another unique day is "Family Heritage Day" where each child (and their parents) gets to share what is special about their family and their display board goes up in the room. There is also a wall-sized map that has yarn linking the student to their origin. This is the beginning concept of "global." I was impressed by the incredible diversity in the classroom. "Our teachers, all of whom are active Christian Scientists, cherish each child as inherently intelligent, good, inquisitive, and uniquely talented. They help students exceed expectations and encourage exploration and discovery, while supporting and nurturing them."

Berkeley Hall is not a church-supported or parochial school. The Christian Science religion is not taught in the classrooms, but spiritual principles of love, respect, and self-esteem underlie all aspects of school life. The school offers a balanced learning environment that includes the development of intellectual, moral, social, artistic, and physical capabilities. Security and safety is not a question, with a roadside gate, and sign-in/and sign-out for every student. I also loved the idea that each of the older classes has a younger "buddy" class, to incorporate age diversity and interaction. So, yes, I was pretty darned impressed with this school. Berkeley Hall has created a nurturing, caring learning environment in a non-competitive way, on a stunning campus. Oh, and did I mention the view?

BACKGROUND

Berkeley Hall was founded in 1911 by two dedicated educators, Leila and Mabel Cooper. Their approach to education was rooted in their study of Christian Science, which recognizes that God-given qualities are a part of each child's nature.

BIRD'S EYE VIEW

	Non-existent	Poor	Fair	Good	Excellent
Learning to Read Children learn to explore the world of books					✓
Dress-Up Children experiment with different roles and imagination					✓
Hand-Eye Children develop fine motor skills by using fingers and hands					✓
Building Blocks Children practice symbolic representation. They are developing an understanding of the relationships between size and shape, and the basic math concepts of geometry and numbers					✓
Arts and Crafts Children are developing small muscle control as well as creativity					✓
Body Coordination Children crawl through tunnels, climb and balance					✓
Meeting Time Gathering place to listen to the teacher and to stories					✓
Weights and Measures Water and Sand tables					✓
Beakers and Bunnies Classroom pets, aquariums....planting...					✓
Counting 1-2-3 A good preschool will stock basic early-learner software such as phonics or counting games					✓
Outdoor Play Encourage large muscle control and coordination					✓

Q & A

HOW THEY LEARN

What is your school's teaching philosophy? To develop active thinkers in a balanced learning environment that inspires children of diverse backgrounds to fulfill their unlimited, God-given potential.

How do you implement the philosophy? Our teachers, all of whom are active Christian Scientists, cherish each child as inherently intelligent, good, inquisitive, and uniquely talented. They help students exceed expectations and encourage exploration and discovery, while supporting and nurturing them.

What is the teaching method? Letting the children's interests be the engine, academic investigation in the Nursery and JK is self-paced and fun. The program is designed to nurture and highlight the children's individual talents. Teachers balance a schedule with activities appropriate for the maturity and readiness of each child and cover social, emotional, academic, artistic, moral and physical. Respect, responsibility, honesty and compassion are the four core values governing every aspect of school life.

At what age do the children start? To what age is the school licensed? Children need to be 3 prior to July 1 for Nursery, and 4 prior to July 1 for the JK. The preschool is licensed to age 5.

HOW TO GET IN

Are there open house dates? When are tours given? There are two admission information meetings in October and November on Sunday afternoons. Regularly scheduled tours are also available.

Is there an interview? With the child or without? Part of the application process is a parent interview. Children applicants come to a special "play date with other children to be observed and assessed for school readiness.

Is preference given to applicants whose siblings are alumni? Yes, preference is given to siblings and alumni children but is dependent upon meeting qualifications for admissions.

Are letters of recommendation encouraged? From what types of people? A character reference from a non-relative who knows the family and child well and, if the child has already attended a preschool, a confidential preschool recommendation from a teacher or director.

How many applications do you receive each year? 30 to 40.

How many open spots are there each year? 16 to 20.

What are some of the schools that children go on to after finishing their education at your preschool? Most continue at Berkeley Hall School through 8th grade.

PIGGY BANK

Apart from tuition, what other fees do you charge? A $2,000 deposit.

How is tuition broken down? $7,200 for three morning classes, up to $18,200 for five full days.

What are the different payment plans available? One, two and ten payments.

What is the fee schedule? A $1,500 new family fee.

Is there a contract? Yes.

Do you have a tuition insurance program? Yes. The Tuition Refund Plan is required for the two-payment and ten-payment plans. The insurance premium is 1.5% of total tuition and is due on July 15.

HELPING HANDS

What accreditation is necessary for the teachers to work at your school? Teachers and assistants maintain all requirements mandated by the State of California Department of Social Services.

How many teachers are there? There is a lead teacher in each class.

How many aides are there? There is an aide in each class as well as one shared by the Early Childhood classes.

IN THE 'ROOM

What's the adult-to-child ratio? Nursery: 1:8, and JK: 1:9.

What are the policies for initial separation between parent and child? Each child can come with their parent to a visitation day prior to the start of school. Teachers facilitate a happy and harmonious separation taking into account the maturity, personality and independence of each child.

Can you visit any time unannounced? Yes.

What are the hours? Do you offer early bird or after-hours pick-up? If so, is there an extra fee? Half days are from 8:30-11:30 a.m., and full-day students end at 3:15 p.m. Children may be dropped off as early as 7:15am at no extra cost. After-school care for Nursery/JK students until 5:30 p.m.

Please describe a typical day for a child at your school. Character education is a part of every daily assembly. Art, music, movement, and dramatic play are also important activities. Daily outdoor play and movement instruction help the development of gross muscle skills, and a daily nap. Gymnastics is included in the weekly program.

What kinds of academic activities are offered? Although Berkeley Hall believes that the "work" of young children is play, the teachers support early cognitive development through thematic units: early literacy, math, science, and social studies. Music, art and story time are daily activities. The full-time librarian meets weekly for story time, learning library usage, book talks, and borrowing books.

What kinds of art activities are offered? There is a rich arts program. Children are provided with a wide variety of materials to use in painting, modeling clay, and collage.

Is the child's time structured or unstructured, or a mixture of both? Mixture.

If a child is not interested in a particular activity, does he/she have other choices or is he/she encouraged to try it anyway? Children are given choices and encouraged to try new things.

How are disputes handled when they occur between the children? Children learn to settle differences by using verbal skills, to respect others and their property rights, and to be courteous.

When and for how long is nap time? The Nursery class naps for 1.5 hours, and JK for 1 hour.

What kinds of beds do you use? Cots for the Nursey and JK have tri-fold mats.

What do you do when a child is dropped off in the morning and is obviously not well? What do you do when a child becomes sick during the day? The parent is always the first one called. If the illness or injury is life-threatening, Emergency Assistance will be provided by our local fire station, and a parent (or the alternate person) will be notified. In other situations, First Aid will be administered by a Red Cross-trained faculty member, if required, and the parent will be called for guidance on follow-up actions.

Can you accommodate children with special needs? Each situation is considered individually. Although we do differentiated instruction, a child with special needs is better served in a school with appropriately-trained teachers.

KEEPING IT SAFE

Please describe your security measures for arriving and leaving the school. Each child must be signed in and out daily. There is a security guard drop-off and pick-up times. Once the students are in class, the campus gates are closed during school hours.

What medical supplies do you have on hand, and what medical experience does your staff have? Is your staff trained in CPR? Our faculty and staff are trained in First Aid/CPR.

Please describe your earthquake-preparedness plan, and what special equipment do you have on hand in the event of a disaster? The school can fully sustain 300 students/adults for three days with food, water, sanitation, First Aid, communications and other necessary supplies and services. There is a detailed emergency disaster procedure which is practiced by staff and students and is distributed to parents, with a central evacuation location and staff committees are responsible for security, supplies, sweep and rescue, and First Aid. The school will be under direction of the police and fire departments in extreme cases.

SWINGS 'N THINGS

Please describe your playground. Does it have plenty of shade? The school facility provides well-equipped play yards for preschoolers with ample shade, climbing equipment, sandboxes, slides, wheel toys, a playhouse and gardening planters. Much of the secure, 66-acre Santa Monica mountain campus overlooks the San Fernando Valley.

What kind of toilet training is available? All students are expected to be toilet-trained prior to starting school in September.

HELPING OUT

What kinds of fundraising events are at your school each year? The school holds an Annual Gala Dinner/Silent Auction in the fall and a Country Fair in the spring.

How much participation is required by each parent? We ask that all parents participate in the Annual Fund to the best of their ability. Volunteer activities range from the Country Fair to the library to the Hot Lunch program, to room moms or dads.

KEEPING IN TOUCH

How do you communicate with parents? Is there a newsletter or phone tree? There is a monthly classroom newsletter. Parents are encouraged to contact teachers by phone or e-mail. In an effort to go "green", the all-school detailed weekly schedule is published on the website and available for downloading. E-mail blasts and automated telephone notifications are used to convey important information and reminders.

Does the school publish an address book with all the parents' information in it? A searchable family directory is available in the "private" password-protected area of the website.

preschool

BEVERLY GLEN PLAYGROUP

10409 Scenario Lane
Los Angeles, CA 90077
Phone: (310) 470-0992
www.bgplaygroup.com
See Map D on page 286

*Contact: Zeke Rippy, Asst. Director
or Shadi Bakhtiari, Assistant Director*

- ACCREDITATION: NONE
- NOT-FOR-PROFIT
- FINANCIAL AID IS NOT AVAILABLE
- NUMBER OF KIDS: 37
- TUITION: $3,703-$8,464 YEAR
- WE HAVE KIDS WITH SPECIAL NEEDS

WHEN TO APPLY: BY DECEMBER.

Beverly Glen Playgroup is aptly named. Located in woodsy Beverly Glen, you feel like you're at a relaxed summer camp rather than preschool, which is exactly how they want you to feel. Out of all the co-ops I visited, this one definitely demanded the most participation. During the tour, the membership chair said "If you're looking for a school where you can just drop your kid off and leave, this isn't it. As part of a co-op, you're always on call." Not fulfilling those obligations (which come about to about four to five days a month of your time) result in fines.

The school is located in a wooden community center with hardwood floors, cozy rugs, and beamed ceilings. It's full of books, puzzles, and blocks but, as director Julie Patel says, "If you're at all interested in an academic school, we're not it." That being said, she's assembled what she proudly calls "the best teachers in L.A., all of whom are extremely overqualified." The kids were all outside in the big playground while the tour went on, playing on the climbing equipment and doing art. However, when one of the little girls saw the membership chair surrounded by about 40 parents, she asked "Sharon, are you alright in there?" And with the drama that accompanies picking the right school for your child, was a perfectly legitimate question to ask!

Getting in is difficult, there's only about seven or eight spots available each year. Some of the schools that the kids go on to include Roscoe and Warner (public) as well as John Thomas Dye, Curtis, Buckley, Willows, Crossroads, and Wildwood. If you're looking for an opportunity to be intimately involved with your child's preschool, Beverly Glen Playgroup might be a great place for you. However, if you're somewhat ambivalent about getting paint on your clothes and being a substitute teacher once a month, don't bother!

BACKGROUND

The Beverly Glen Playgroup was established by friends and neighbors in 1946, and is a parent cooperative preschool.

Bird's Eye View

	Non-existent	Poor	Fair	Good	Excellent
Learning to Read Children learn to explore the world of books				✓	
Dress-Up Children experiment with different roles and imagination				✓	
Hand-Eye Children develop fine motor skills by using fingers and hands				✓	
Building Blocks Children practice symbolic representation. They are developing an understanding of the relationships between size and shape, and the basic math concepts of geometry and numbers				✓	
Arts and Crafts Children are developing small muscle control as well as creativity				✓	
Body Coordination Children crawl through tunnels, climb and balance				✓	
Meeting Time Gathering place to listen to the teacher and to stories				✓	
Weights and Measures Water and Sand tables				✓	
Beakers and Bunnies Classroom pets, aquariums....planting...				✓	
Counting 1-2-3 A good preschool will stock basic early-learner software such as phonics or counting games				✓	
Outdoor Play Encourage large muscle control and coordination					✓

Q & A

HOW THEY LEARN

What is your school's teaching philosophy? Our focus is on the process of education versus the end product. It is important to recognize the uniqueness of each child and respect his or her real work. It is through play that children integrate and understand the world around them.

How do you implement the philosophy? We have a morning program with 24 kids, four teachers and one parent, and an afternoon program with 15 kids, four teachers and one parent.

What is the teaching method? We endorse a developmental approach to learning, and believe that children learn by doing.

At what age do the children start? To what age is the school licensed? Children must be 2 by September 1st to begin our afternoon program. We are licensed for ages 2-5.

HOW TO GET IN

Are there open house dates? When are tours given? From October to May 19th.

Is there an interview? With the child or without? We interview the parents without the child.

Is preference given to applicants whose siblings are alumni? Yes, if they are present families or have left Playgroup in good standing.

Are letters of recommendation encouraged? From what types of people? We only accept letters of recommendation from present or past Playgroup families.

How many applications do you receive each year? No feedback received.

How many open spots are there each year? No feedback received.

What are some of the schools that children go on to after finishing their education at your preschool? No feedback received.

PIGGY BANK

Apart from tuition, what other fees do you charge? There is a $50 application fee, but no entrance fee.

How is tuition broken down? Call school for details.

What are the different payment plans available? We bill on a monthly basis.

What is the fee schedule? No feedback received.

Is there a contract? Yes, a membership contract is required.

Do you have a tuition insurance program? No tuition insurance.

HELPING HANDS

What accreditation is necessary for the teachers to work at your school? All teachers and assistants have at least a Bachelor's degree in Early Childhood or a related field.

How many teachers are there? In both the morning and afternoon programs, there are two teachers.

How many aides are there? There are two assistants.

IN THE 'ROOM

What's the adult-to-child ratio? In the Morning Program, 24 kids/4 teachers/1 parent (3-5 year olds); in the Afternoon Program, 15 kids/4 teachers/1 parent (2-3 year olds).

What are the policies for initial separation between parent and child? Each child is different, so we handle the separation on an individual basis.

Can you visit any time unannounced? Present families can, yes.

What are the hours? Do you offer early bird or after-hours pick-up? If so, is there an extra fee? The Morning Program is from 9-1 p.m. on Monday, Wednesday and Friday. The Extended Day Program is from 1-3 p.m. The Afternoon Program is from 1:45-4:45 p.m. on Tuesdays and Thursdays. No additional hours.

Please describe a typical day for a child at your school. For the Morning Program, we begin at 9 a.m. with circle time, have free time, a snack, music, art, clean-up, story time, lunch, and pick-up for the kids. The Extended Day and Afternoon Program children have story time, free time, a snack, art outside, circle time inside and pick-up.

What kinds of academic activities are offered? We work with children in their last year on kindergarten readiness skills such as cooperative play, staying on task and follow-through.

What kinds of art activities are offered? Various.

Is the child's time structured or unstructured, or a mixture of both? Both. Children have a choice in everything.

If a child is not interested in a particular activity, does he/she have other choices or is he/she encouraged to try it anyway? No.

How are disputes handled when they occur between the children? Children are given words to use. Redirected. Choices are possibly limited for older children. There are no time outs. We try to have children resolve their own conflicts, with teacher supervision if needed.

When and for how long is nap time? No feedback received.

What kinds of beds do you use? No feedback received.

What do you do when a child is dropped off in the morning and is obviously not well? What do you do when a child becomes sick during the day? We don't have a sick room, so sick children are sent home.

Can you accommodate children with special needs? Yes.

KEEPING IT SAFE

Please describe your security measures for arriving and leaving the school. No feedback received.

What medical supplies do you have on hand, and what medical experience does your staff have? Is your staff trained in CPR? No feedback received.

Please describe your earthquake-preparedness plan, and what special equipment do you have on hand in the event of a disaster? We have an earthquake shed, with supplies for each child for up to 48 hours. We can evacuate either up the canyon to Briarwood Park, or leave the canyon to Holmby Park. Teachers have equipment to take during any evacuation. We practice both earthquake and fire drills with children.

SWINGS 'N THINGS

Please describe your playground. Does it have plenty of shade? There is both in sun and shade, a sun deck with cushioning and a sand surface. Water is always out and available for drinking.

What kind of toilet training is available? We ask that parents let us know when they start potty training so we can help, but children do not have to be potty trained to attend. There is a unisex children's bathroom (two potties).

HELPING OUT

What kinds of fundraising events are at your school each year? We have two major fundraisers—a yard sale in the fall and an auction/dinner in the spring.

How much participation is required by each parent? Basically all parents donate auction items, time and sweat to raise money for our kids.

KEEPING IN TOUCH

How do you communicate with parents? Is there a newsletter or phone tree? We have a newsletter, monthly calendar, a phone tree, email, and notes in the cubbies.

Does the school publish an address book with all the parents' information in it? For present parents only.

---

preschool-kindergarten

BEVERLY HILLS MONTESSORI SCHOOL

1105 N. Laurel Avenue
Los Angeles, CA 90046
Phone: (323) 650-2922
See Map C on page 286

Contact: Linda Kaufman

- ACCREDITATION: NONE
- FOR-PROFIT
- FINANCIAL AID IS AVAILABLE
- NUMBER OF KIDS: 60
- TUITION: $300-$1,083 MONTH
- WE HAVE KIDS WITH SPECIAL NEEDS

WHEN TO APPLY: YEAR-ROUND. THERE IS NO CUT-OFF DATE TO APPLY.

"The blue school with the bunny," as it's been called by children over the last 25 years, is actually located in West Hollywood, just east of Crescent Heights and Santa Monica Boulevards. The inside has seen better days, but it's obvious that the children who attend Beverly Hills Montessori will go on to kindergarten with much more than improved socialization skills. Beverly Hills Montessori makes academics a huge part of the program, taught through a very creative, Montessori-based philosophy. But what makes the school even better is the lack of rigidity about the adherence to the Montessori method—meaning that director Linda Kaufman and her teachers will use everything at their disposal that they can (both inside and outside) to teach. So during the 2004 Olympics, they studied about Greece, the Greek gods, ate Greek food, and took a field trip up the street to watch the torch go by! The classrooms in the school all flow into each other, giving it a pleasant, open feeling, and every room was filled with a variety of wonderful learning aids such as Montessori beads, step boards and puzzles. When the kids were learning about the solar system, the walls were filled with the kids' renditions of the various planets, and it was fascinating to see each child's uniqueness in action. Some of the kids played outside while others quietly worked on art projects, and then later on they all got ready for lunch.

The school is now a LA Universal Preschool, and you should check out the information at www.LAUP.net. If you're not hung up on aesthetics, and instead are looking for a school where your child will be assured of truly learning in a creative way, then Beverly Hills Montessori is definitely worth a visit.

BACKGROUND

Established 1979. Linda Kaufman has been the director for 25 years.

BIRD'S EYE VIEW

	Non-existent	Poor	Fair	Good	Excellent
Learning to Read Children learn to explore the world of books				✓	
Dress-Up Children experiment with different roles and imagination			✓		
Hand-Eye Children develop fine motor skills by using fingers and hands					✓
Building Blocks Children practice symbolic representation. They are developing an understanding of the relationships between size and shape, and the basic math concepts of geometry and numbers					✓
Arts and Crafts Children are developing small muscle control as well as creativity					✓
Body Coordination Children crawl through tunnels, climb and balance				✓	
Meeting Time Gathering place to listen to the teacher and to stories				✓	
Weights and Measures Water and Sand tables				✓	
Beakers and Bunnies Classroom pets, aquariums....planting...			✓		
Counting 1-2-3 A good preschool will stock basic early-learner software such as phonics or counting games				✓	
Outdoor Play Encourage large muscle control and coordination				✓	

Q & A

HOW THEY LEARN

What is your school's teaching philosophy? A modified Montessori.

How do you implement the philosophy? Through themes, projects and materials in the classroom. "Let's bring in as much from L.A."

What is the teaching method? Montessori.

At what age do the children start? To what age is the school licensed? No feedback received.

HOW TO GET IN

Are there open house dates? When are tours given? Mondays, Tuesdays and Thursdays between 9 a.m. and 11 a.m.

Is there an interview? With the child or without? No. There is a "visit" where parents and children get to know the school and vice versa.

**Is preference given to applicants whose siblings are alumni? Yes.

Are letters of recommendation encouraged? From what types of people? No.

How many applications do you receive each year? 20.

How many open spots are there each year? Varies.

What are some of the schools that children go on to after finishing their education at your preschool? Mirman, L.A. Unified, Beverly Hills, Culver City, Echo Horizons, Curtis, Campbell Hall, Berkeley Hall, Temple Israel.

PIGGY BANK

Apart from tuition, what other fees do you charge? A $200 registration fee, $500 enrollment fee, $220 materials fee, $50 a month diaper fee (if needed).

How is tuition broken down? Call school for breakdown.

What are the different payment plans available? Monthly payments. Discount, if you pay the whole year up front. Financial aid.

What is the fee schedule? No feedback received.

Is there a contract? No feedback received.

Do you have a tuition insurance program? No feedback received.

HELPING HANDS

What accreditation is necessary for the teachers to work at your school? All have had 24 units – Master's degrees.

How many teachers are there? Four teachers.

How many aides are there? No aides.

Do they come from other preschools? Yes.

IN THE 'ROOM

What's the adult-to-child ratio? 1:8.

What are the policies for initial separation between parent and child? Depends on what the parents need and what the child's needs are. New parents can call every 20 minutes.

Can you visit any time unannounced? Yes.

What are the hours? Do you offer early bird or after-hours pick-up? If so, is there an extra fee? 7:30 a.m.-5:45 p.m.

Please describe a typical day for a child at your school. Students arrive and are on the playground until 9 a.m., followed by snack and circle time attendance, the Pledge of Allegiance, a work period until 11 a.m., outside time and art projects, lunch, music, story time, a nap, and a snack outside with arts and crafts.

What kinds of academic activities are offered? Pre-reading, math, phonics, cooking, social studies, science.

What kinds of art activities are offered? No feedback received.

Is the child's time structured or unstructured, or a mixture of both? Freedom within the structure of computers, art, blocks, home living, dramatic play, music, math, language and science.

If a child is not interested in a particular activity, does he/she have other choices or is he/she encouraged to try it anyway? Yes.

How are disputes handled when they occur between the children? We encourage them to talk it out. If they can't, they will have time out appropriate to their age, then we have them come together again to talk it out.

When and for how long is nap time? Nap time is 2:30-4 p.m.

What kinds of beds do you use? We use cots, and children bring their own bedding.

What do you do when a child is dropped off in the morning and is obviously not well? What do you do when a child becomes sick during the day? Call the parents right away. If they look like they are coming down with something, will call parents to alert them.

Can you accommodate children with special needs? Yes.

KEEPING IT SAFE

Please describe your security measures for arriving and leaving the school. The front door is locked at all times.

What medical supplies do you have on hand, and what medical experience does your staff have? Is your staff trained in CPR? Staff is First Aid and CPR-trained. First Aid kits are located around the building.

Please describe your earthquake-preparedness plan, and what special equipment do you have on hand in the event of a disaster? If an earthquake hits, there is food and water for three days, we would go to Laurer Elementary or Fairfax High. Earthquake supplies are in four areas of school.

SWINGS 'N THINGS

Please describe your playground. Does it have plenty of shade? Digging area, swings, slide, and playhouse. Plenty of shade.

Do you put sunscreen on the children? Sunscreen is applied if they provide it.

What kind of toilet training is available? Children must be toilet trained.

HELPING OUT

What kinds of fundraising events are at your school each year? Scholastic book fair, e-script, U-Promise accounts.

How much participation is required by each parent? Voluntary.

KEEPING IN TOUCH

How do you communicate with parents? Is there a newsletter or phone tree? Written notes, verbally, email and at parent meetings.

Does the school publish an address book with all the parents' information in it? No.

preschool to 1st grade

BEVERLY HILLS PRESBYTERIAN PRESCHOOL

505 N. Rodeo Drive
Beverly Hills, CA 90210
Phone: (310) 271-5197
www.bhpc2.org/preschool/index.html
See Map D on page 286

Contact: Sheila Hogan, Director

- ACCREDITATION: NAEYC
- NOT-FOR-PROFIT
- FINANCIAL AID IS NOT AVAILABLE
- NUMBER OF KIDS: 68
- TUITION: $395-$535 MONTH
- WE HAVE KIDS WITH SPECIAL NEEDS

WHEN TO APPLY: APPLICATIONS ARE AVAILABLE AT ANY TIME.

Director Linda George took the opportunity to step away from her busy desk for a moment to give me a tour of this lively, warm (and huge!) preschool. She is extremely proud of her school, and I can see why. Most of the teachers at the school have been there eight to twenty years! The student body is incredibly and surprisingly multi-cultural. The focus around the holidays is about family, and Beverly Hills Preschool has a very diverse community of families, including many single parent families, and several children with same-sex parents. I found this exposure to the variation of what constitutes a family very open minded for a church based school! The school does hold chapel, but does not push religion, which I also found remarkable.

The children are also exposed to other cultures through weekly cooking of different ethnic cuisine, lots of seasonal field trips, Spanish classes (two days a week), and for Thanksgiving, a performance by local Native American dancers, including songs for Thanksgiving and necklaces and headdresses made by the children. The children are currently learning to tell time, through a play, in which each child represented a different time. There is also a science exploration area, two play yards and computer time available starting at age three.

There are Parent Education Workshops once a month, to increase parent training and development, and strengthen community. Located smack-dab in Beverly Hills, there are quite a few celebrity parents. These parents who can afford to send their children anywhere, and choose here, speaks volumes to me. "We are very fortunate to have funding from the church, so we are not about money, but about outreach. Our focus is quality, not quantity," says George. Her office and desk, however, are covered in preparation for the schools' silent auction fundraiser. Linda George smiled and said, "Silent auctions seem to be the thing everyone is doing for fundraising these days." Many children will go on to Curtis, The Center, Warner and Saint Matthews.

BACKGROUND

Beverly Hills Presbyterian Preschool provides a Christian-based educational experience for the greater Beverly Hills community through a program of developmentally-appropriate activities, care and supervision.

BIRD'S EYE VIEW

	Non-existent	Poor	Fair	Good	Excellent
Learning to Read Children learn to explore the world of books					🦉
Dress-Up Children experiment with different roles and imagination					🦉
Hand-Eye Children develop fine motor skills by using fingers and hands					🦉
Building Blocks Children practice symbolic representation. They are developing an understanding of the relationships between size and shape, and the basic math concepts of geometry and numbers					🦉
Arts and Crafts Children are developing small muscle control as well as creativity					🦉
Body Coordination Children crawl through tunnels, climb and balance					🦉
Meeting Time Gathering place to listen to the teacher and to stories					🦉
Weights and Measures Water and Sand tables					🦉
Beakers and Bunnies Classroom pets, aquariums....planting...				🦉	
Counting 1-2-3 A good preschool will stock basic early-learner software such as phonics or counting games					🦉
Outdoor Play Encourage large muscle control and coordination					🦉

Q & A

HOW THEY LEARN

What is your school's teaching philosophy? A balance of developmental and academics. We touch on social, emotional, cognitive, spiritual and physical with each individual child.

How do you implement the philosophy? All teachers are uniquely qualified and compliment each other. The philosophy is implemented through music, movement, chapel time, etc. Each child works at their own pace, and lots of one on one time available. They are able to use their own creativity.

What specialty teachers are brought into the school? No feedback provided.

What is the teaching method? Hands-on, auditory, visual and natural. The curriculum is modified so that every child can succeed at their own level.

At what age do the children start? To what age is the school licensed? At eighteen months for Mommy and Me, the age of three by October for pre-school. The school is licensed to six years old. We now have first grade!

HOW TO GET IN

Are there open house dates? When are tours given? Tours are the last Wednesday of every month.

Is there an interview? With the child or without? No interview.

Is preference given to applicants whose siblings are alumni? Church members, then siblings and legacies.

Are letters of recommendation encouraged? From what types of people? Not really.

How many applications do you receive each year? About 100.

How many open spots are there each year? About 28 for brand-new students.

What are some of the schools that children go on to after finishing their education at your preschool? Curtis, The Center, Warner, St. Matthew's, John Thomas.

PIGGY BANK

Apart from tuition, what other fees do you charge? There is a $315 registration fee, and a $65 a month fee for security.

How is tuition broken down? Tuition is three days for $395, and five days for $535. There is a 15% discount for church members.

What are the different payment plans available? Parents can pay yearly, twice a year, or monthly.

What is the fee schedule? See above.

Is there a contract? There is an agreement, but not a contract.

Do you have a tuition insurance program? No insurance.

HELPING HANDS

What accreditation is necessary for the teachers to work at your school? State requires credits, and some are working towards their master's degrees.

How many teachers are there? Three lead teachers, and five teachers.

How many aides are there? No feedback received.

IN THE 'ROOM

What's the child-to-adult ratio? 6:1.

What are the policies for initial separation between parent and child? Parents are encouraged to stay for the first two weeks of September. Most preschool students have started in the toddler program and are ready to separate.

Can you visit any time unannounced? Yes, and we have observation windows, too.

What are the hours? 8:45 a.m.-12 p.m.

Do you offer early bird or after-hours pick-up? If so, is there an extra fee? Extended hours are until 2:30 p.m. The fee varies depending on the child's age and how many days.

Please describe a typical day for a child at your school. Morning meeting, outside play, snack, table activities, outside free play again.

What kinds of academic activities are offered? Letters of the Week, abecca curriculum, language experience, number and alphabet worksheets, cooking, science—all theme-based with the Letter of the Week.

What kinds of art activities are offered? Painting, coloring, Play-doh, lots of glue! Seasonal art activities.

Is the child's time structured or unstructured, or a mixture of both? A mixture of both.

If a child is not interested in a particular activity, does he/she have other choices or is he/she encouraged to try it anyway? Usually, there are three or four activities going on at one time. There are always choices.

How are disputes handled when they occur between the children? We have children use their words, resolving the problem themselves with guidance.

When and for how long is nap time? Nap time is for extended stay.

What kinds of beds do you use? We have cots, and the children provide pillows, blankets and comfort items.

What do you do when a child is dropped off in the morning and is obviously not well? What do you do when a child becomes sick during the day? There is a wellness check in the morning, or the parent is called for pick-up.

Can you accommodate children with special needs? We can accommodate special needs, but it is limited. Inquire at school.

KEEPING IT SAFE

Please describe your security measures for arriving and leaving the school. Full-time security guard at a locked gate. Parents/guardians walk children in and sign them in and out, or sign them in and out with a teacher at drop-off. There must be a written letter form the parent if an alternate person is picking up or dropping off.

What medical supplies do you have on hand, and what medical experience does your staff have? Is your staff trained in CPR? Staff is CPR and First Aid certified, and there are First Aid kits in every classroom.

Please describe your earthquake-preparedness plan, and what special equipment do you have on hand in the event of a disaster? The whole downstairs is like a bomb shelter. Each child has a kit. There are three to four days' worth of food and water, always current.

SWINGS 'N THINGS

Please describe your playground. Does it have plenty of shade? We have two play yards, good shade.

Do you put sunscreen on the children? Sunscreen is applied in the morning, and hats and extra sunscreen are encouraged in the summer months.

What kind of toilet training is available? Must already be toilet trained.

HELPING OUT

What kinds of fundraising events are at your school each year? There is a silent auction in December, t-shirt sales, and new ideas to be implemented in the new year.

How much participation is required by each parent? It is not mandatory, but participation is encouraged.

KEEPING IN TOUCH

How do you communicate with parents? Is there a newsletter or phone tree? Each class has its own newsletter that goes to parents. There is a room parent in each classroom. Open communication. Phone, email, newsletter, everything.

Does the school publish an address book with all the parents' information in it? Roster.

preschool to kindergarten

CANYON COOPERATIVE NURSERY SCHOOL

1820 N. Las Palmas Ave.
Hollywood, CA 90028
Phone: (323) 464-7507
www.canyonschoolhollywood.org
See Map C on page 286

Contact: Celia Williams or Adina Russ

- ACCREDITATION: NONE
- FOR-PROFIT
- FINANCIAL AID IS AVAILABLE
- NUMBER OF KIDS: 30/15
- TUITION: $215-$275 MONTH
- WE HAVE KIDS WITH SPECIAL NEEDS

WHEN TO APPLY: OPEN ENROLLMENT.

As I arrived at the Canyon School, I was greeted by a little boy who told me, "This is only for kids." While the kids at Canyon definitely have the energy to power a medium sized country and therefore seem to be calling the shots. He's wrong—it's not just for kids. Because it's a co-op, it's just as much for the parents. Canyon is by no means fancy. It's also not expensive. Situated next to a senior center in the heart of Hollywood at Las Palmas and Franklin, it consists of a very large play yard filled with a giant sandbox and a slide, a shed for art supplies, and a small building that houses a small kitchen and an area to read and do puzzles. And, as it's a co-op, parents are asked to work one class session a week. Every morning session there are two teachers and at least five parents present. Less parents in the afternoon, because there are fewer kids.

As Alex Horner, the down-to-earth and refreshingly candid Membership Chair took me on a tour, Celia Williams, the school's director, sat on the floor playing with a puzzle with one of the kids. While she was completely focused on the task at hand, it was obvious that she knew exactly what was going on everywhere in the building, giving me the strong impression that she's one of those people who was born with eyes in the back of her head. I'm also sure that while the atmosphere at Canyon might be a bit too chaotic for certain parents, Celia has the experience (20 years plus) and fortitude to get all 30 of those kids in a single silent line in five seconds flat.

From what I witnessed, and from what Alex told me, Canyon seems to be made up of young families who can't necessarily pay the huge tuitions of other schools. Nor do they want to. They look at preschool as a place for their kids to play and socialize rather than start prepping for Harvard or Yale. And they also want the experience of being able to share in that experience in a hands-on way. Some of the schools that Canyon kids end up going on to include Oakwood, Campbell Hall, Pilgrim School, St. James, Valley View, Rosewood Elementary, Wonderland Elementary and Willow.

BACKGROUND

The school was started in 1948 by mothers who weren't ready to put their children in daycare. The idea was started in the backyard of Canyon Drive.

BIRD'S EYE VIEW

	Non-existent	Poor	Fair	Good	Excellent
Learning to Read Children learn to explore the world of books				✓	
Dress-Up Children experiment with different roles and imagination					✓
Hand-Eye Children develop fine motor skills by using fingers and hands				✓	
Building Blocks Children practice symbolic representation. They are developing an understanding of the relationships between size and shape, and the basic math concepts of geometry and numbers				✓	
Arts and Crafts Children are developing small muscle control as well as creativity				✓	
Body Coordination Children crawl through tunnels, climb and balance				✓	
Meeting Time Gathering place to listen to the teacher and to stories					✓
Weights and Measures Water and Sand tables				✓	
Beakers and Bunnies Classroom pets, aquariums....planting...				✓	
Counting 1-2-3 A good preschool will stock basic early-learner software such as phonics or counting games				✓	
Outdoor Play Encourage large muscle control and coordination				✓	

Q & A

HOW THEY LEARN

What is your school's teaching philosophy? Love and understand each child individually. We pride ourselves in knowing our students and treating them as individuals.

How do you implement the philosophy? Our school has five parents and two teachers who bring their specialty to the school.

What specialty teachers are brought into the school? We have two specialty teachers (drumming and dancing) for one-hour sessions on Mondays and Fridays.

What is the teaching method? There is no set method, but we believe in children listening and following directions as given by the teachers and parents.

At what age do the children start? To what age is the school licensed? Our children start with the toddler program, which is 18 months, and parents stay with them. The morning and afternoon starting age is two years, nine months.

HOW TO GET IN

Are there open house dates? When are tours given? Tours are scheduled with the membership chairperson.

Is there an interview? With the child or without? There is a three-day work day with the children that gives parents a hands-on idea of how the school works.

Is preference given to applicants whose siblings are alumni? Yes, there is no need to complete the three-day process and they are allowed entrance without interviewing.

Are letters of recommendation encouraged? From what types of people? No, just a commitment from parents to volunteer and spend time at Canyon.

How many applications do you receive each year? Varies.

How many open spots are there each year? None in the morning program, and five to six in the evening program.

What are some of the schools that children go on to after finishing their education at your preschool? Oakwood, Campbell Hall, Pilgrim School, St. James, Valley View, Rosewood Elementary, Wonderland Elementary, Willows.

PIGGY BANK

Apart from tuition, what other fees do you charge? There is an application fee of $25 and an entrance fee of $25.

How does the tuition break down? $215-$275 per month.

What are the different payment plans available? Monthly or pay for the full year.

Is there a contract? Yes, there is a contract.

Do you have a tuition insurance program? No tuition insurance.

HELPING HANDS

What accreditation is necessary for the teachers to work at your school? SCAEYC, this can be completed while working or they can enroll.

How many teachers are there? Two teachers.

How many aides are there? There are five parents who assist as aides.

IN THE 'ROOM

What's the adult-to-child ratio? No feedback received.

What are the policies for initial separation between parent and child? Parents are allowed to stay until the child is comfortable with the school and teachers, then parents can leave for one hour, then release time as the child accumulates.

Can you visit any time unannounced? Yes!

What are the hours? Do you offer early bird or after-hours pick-up? If so, is there an extra fee? 8:30 a.m.-12:30 p.m. for working parents, 9 a.m.-12 p.m. for children. 12-3 p.m. for workday parents and children. There is after school for morning parents, for a fee of $12 each session.

Please describe a typical day for a child at your school. Circle time, art projects, bike riding, sand play, balls, creative play, dress-up.

What kinds of academic activities are offered? Book reading.

What kinds of art activities are offered? Painting, Play-doh.

Is the child's time structured or unstructured? Or a mixture of both? Mixture of both. The children must attend two circles during the day.

If a child is not interested in a particular activity, does he/she have other choices or is he/she encouraged to try it anyway? There are two choices given during the day. They are encouraged to look at the project but, if not interested, they can play on the play yard.

How are disputes handled when they occur between the children? We try working it out with the children involved and to use words to express themselves. If there are serious hits, bites, or sand throwing, that is handled with.

When and for how long is nap time? No nap time.

What kinds of beds do you use? No nap time.

What do you do when a child is dropped off in the morning and is obviously not well? What do you do when a child becomes sick during the day? We will call parents to pick up their child if the child becomes sick during the day. We have a cot in the office and a parent or teacher sits with the child until they are picked up.

Can you accommodate children with special needs? Yes.

KEEPING IT SAFE

Please describe your security measures for arriving and leaving the school. We have a combination gate that locks automatically when the gate is closed. We also have ADT security patrol.

What medical supplies do you have on hand, and what medical experience does your staff have? Is your staff trained in CPR? We have a Zee medical supply box with all the needed essentials. Teachers are Red Cross certified.

Please describe your earthquake-preparedness plan, and what special equipment do you have on hand in the event of a disaster? We are to exit on the west side of the school.

We have a Coleman stove with two weeks of food supplies and water for 50 children. Blankets, lights, batteries for an extensive stay.

SWINGS 'N THINGS

Please describe your playground. Does it have plenty of shade? Lots of shade on the sand area and over the eating site. We have grass on our yard also.

Do you put sunscreen on the children? Sunscreen is available upon request.

What kind of toilet training is available? We assist parents with all toileting and have wipes and changes of clothes for accidents.

HELPING OUT

What kinds of fundraising events are at your school each year? A Hop-Skip-Jump-a-Thon with donations from the families. Ralph's and Albertson's five percent give back for groceries purchased. A spring fundraiser dinner dance and silent auction.

How much participation is required by each parent? Each family is expected to participate and each event has different limits that each family must bring in.

KEEPING IN TOUCH

How do you communicate with parents? Is there a newsletter or phone tree? Newsletter and a phone tree by computer if there is a need (field trip, school closure, school meeting). Teacher/director will communicate all information needed directly.

Does the school publish an address book with all the parents' information in it? Yes. The director and teachers' phone numbers are included.

preschool

CHILDREN'S CIRCLE NURSERY SCHOOL

6328 Woodman Ave.
Van Nuys, CA 91401
Phone: (818) 782-9060
See Map A on page 286

Contact: Timothy J. Craig, Director

- ACCREDITATION: NONE
- FOR-PROFIT
- FINANCIAL AID IS AVAILABLE
- NUMBER OF KIDS: 85
- TUITION: $804-$1,061 MONTH
- WE HAVE KIDS WITH SPECIAL NEEDS

WHEN TO APPLY: APPLY YEAR-ROUND. THERE IS NO CUTOFF DATE.

Located along a busy strip of the Valley, this bungalow is all but hidden from the street and those passing by. The entrance of the school faces the alleyway parallel to Woodman Avenue which provides a calm and almost secluded feel from the rest of the world. I have to admit I drove back and forth a couple of times before finding it, as there is no signage facing the outside.

Tim Craig, director and founder of Children's Circle Nursery School, has been in business since 1975. He's now seeing "a second generation coming back," which is a clear indication of the solid experience these adults had in their own nursery days. Enough so that families from as far as Malibu have children enrolled here. The play-based, hands-on school with mixed-age groups in the classroom is, according to Tim, "much more open than a lot of schools. The environment sustains the children, this is not a teacher centered school." There seems to be less division and rigor and more of a free feel than in some other places I've visited. Puzzles, books, blocks and games are in abundance. Tim tells me there are 500 feet of storage on the premises, which is apparently put well to use as he boasts of having 2,000 books and 500 puzzles on hand and rotates them out as the days go by.

There are six teachers, two per classroom, as well as a floating teacher who serves as an extra pair of hands as needed—all of whom have their B.A. or an equivalent degree, to keep an eye on the 60 children enrolled. Kids on the playground, some barefoot, romp in the sand, swing on swings, climb and slide. The vibe here is very calm and subdued, while still active, much like the director, himself. Clearly an environment wherein families partake, there are yearly three-day camping trips. After leaving Children's Circle, about half of the students head on to public schools while the other half enroll in private schools such as; The Oaks, Westland, Children's Community, Foundation, Sequoyah, Oakwood, Curtis, Buckley, Westley, Campbell Hall, St. Francis and Adat Ari El.

Background

Children's Circle Nursery School was founded to integrate the family, the child, and the school community. Established in 1975 by Jim Craig, founder.

Bird's Eye View

	Non-existent	Poor	Fair	Good	Excellent
Learning to Read Children learn to explore the world of books					✓
Dress-Up Children experiment with different roles and imagination					✓
Hand-Eye Children develop fine motor skills by using fingers and hands					✓
Building Blocks Children practice symbolic representation. They are developing an understanding of the relationships between size and shape, and the basic math concepts of geometry and numbers					✓
Arts and Crafts Children are developing small muscle control as well as creativity					✓
Body Coordination Children crawl through tunnels, climb and balance					✓
Meeting Time Gathering place to listen to the teacher and to stories					✓
Weights and Measures Water and Sand tables					✓
Beakers and Bunnies Classroom pets, aquariums....planting...					✓
Counting 1-2-3 A good preschool will stock basic early-learner software such as phonics or counting games				✓	
Outdoor Play Encourage large muscle control and coordination					✓

Q & A

HOW THEY LEARN

What is your school's teaching philosophy? Promoting independence, initiative, and feelings of self-worth encourages the child's growth in self-understanding. The preschool years are a critical time for the development of attributes that will affect a child's entire life. During these years, it is important that a child develop: Trust, Independence and Competency.

How do you implement the philosophy? We implement the philosophy through the existing staff. If trust and independence have been established, the child has the foundation to experiment, develop new skills, and learn through discovery. The environment of the preschool community, which is geared toward success for the child and minimizes competition, creates the conditions for these attributes to flourish. In this setting, the child's self-concept is nourished. The child who feels good about him or herself can afford to feel good about others.

What specialty teachers are brought into the school? We do not bring in specialty teachers.

What is the teaching method? This is a progressive family-based nursery school. Infants and toddlers learn best, we believe, by doing, rather than by being shown or told. We do not so much "teach" them as we help them to learn.

At what age do the children start? To what age is the school licensed? Children start at 2 years, 1 month of age. There are two licenses—2 years, 9 months to 6 years; and 1-12 years.

HOW TO GET IN

Are there open house dates? When are tours given? Parents make appointments throughout the year.

Is there an interview? With the child or without? There is an interview, without the child.

Is preference given to applicants whose siblings are alumni? Yes.

Are letters of recommendation encouraged? From what types of people? No.

How many applications do you receive each year? 150.

How many open spots are there each year? 25.

What are some of the schools that children go on to after finishing their education at your preschool? The Oaks, Westland, Children Community, Foundation, Sequoyah, Oakwood, Curtis, Buckley, Westley, Campbell Hall, St. Francis, Adat Ariel.

PIGGY BANK

Apart from tuition, what other fees do you charge? There is a $400 non-refundable entrance fee deposit. No application fee.

How does the tuition break down? Tuition is three days for $804, four for $943, and five for $1,061.

What are the different payment plans available? Yearly, quarterly or monthly.

What is the fee schedule? No feedback received.

Is there a contract? Yes.

Do you have a tuition insurance program? No.

HELPING HANDS

What accreditation is necessary for the teachers to work at your school? B.A., B.S. or equivalent.

How many teachers are there? There are six teachers, all co-teachers.

How many aides are there? There are no aides.

IN THE 'ROOM

What's the adult-to-child ratio? No feedback received.

What are the policies for initial separation between parent and child? Parents stay with the child.

Can you visit any time unannounced? Yes.

What are the hours? Do you offer early bird or after-hours pick-up? If so, is there an extra fee? Hours are 8:30 a.m.- 2:15 p.m., and 1-4 p.m. There are early-bird hours are from 8:30-9 a.m.

Please describe a typical day for a child at your school. Early drop-off and quiet time to begin the day. The school day begins, outdoor playground time, transition to indoor time. Wash hands, bathroom. Group meeting time, kids taking turns talking about home and the world they live in. Teachers reflect and keep subject matter similar for several minutes, talk about our day (an upcoming holiday, feeling day, sharing day, kids' special events). Release to play inside. Table activities. Blocks. Dress-up, home and work themes. Second group meeting with clean up, review of day, read book consistent with theme of the day, child whose day it is marks calendar. Child whose day it is calls names for kids to get lunches. Lunch. Some lunch for every kid. Clean up and look at books. Go back outside to play and pick-up.

What kinds of academic activities are offered? None.

What kinds of art activities are offered? Varies.

Is the child's time structured or unstructured? Or a mixture of both The environment sustains the child.

If a child is not interested in a particular activity, does he/she have other choices or is he/she encouraged to try it anyway? It depends on the child.

How are disputes handled when they occur between the children? Disputes are handled in an individual basis in a way that supports community.

When and for how long is nap time? No nap time; half a day of school.

What kinds of beds do you use? None.

What do you do when a child is dropped off in the morning and is obviously not well? What do you do when a child becomes sick during the day? The child is not dropped off sick. If the child becomes ill during the day, we follow the state-mandated procedure for being picked up within 10 minutes by a parent or other emergency contact.

Can you accommodate children with special needs? Yes.

KEEPING IT SAFE

Please describe your security measures for arriving and leaving the school. Parent and child are greeted by a staff member.

What medical supplies do you have on hand, and what medical experience does your staff have? Is your staff trained in CPR? All staff has current CPR and First Aid training.

Please describe your earthquake-preparedness plan, and what special equipment do you have on hand in the event of a disaster? We have a trailer with supplies to support 150 people for a week's time. We practice this twice a year.

SWINGS 'N THINGS

Please describe your playground. Does it have plenty of shade? An adventure yard with a climbing structures, playhouse, and tricycles.

What kind of toilet training is available? Yes, we toilet train children.

HELPING OUT

What kinds of fundraising events are at your school each year? None.

How much participation is required by each parent? None. Parents are not required to help; they enjoy helping.

KEEPING IN TOUCH

How do you communicate with parents? Is there a newsletter or phone tree? In person, by phone.

Does the school publish an address book with all the parents' information in it? Yes.

...preschool to pre-k

CHILDREN'S CREATIVE WORKSHOP

6955 Fernhill Drive
Malibu, CA 90265
Phone: (310) 457-2937
www.childrenscreativeworkshop.org
See Map D on page 286

Contact: Shari Latta, Director

- ACCREDITATION: NAEYC
- NOT-FOR-PROFIT
- FINANCIAL AID IS AVAILABLE
- NUMBER OF KIDS: 57
- TUITION: $440-$985 MONTH
- WE HAVE KIDS WITH SPECIAL NEEDS

WHEN TO APPLY: A ONE YEAR WAIT-LIST ACCEPTED IN FOLLOWING ORDER: CURRENT-STUDENT SIBLINGS, ALUMNI FAMILIES, THEN NEW STUDENTS.

The Children's Creative Workshop, the preschool at Point Dume, has an incredible view where the children eat lunch daily al fresco, or play in one of the two playgrounds. Director Shari Latta, who has been with Children's Creative since 1983, guides me around the colorful classrooms and playgrounds. Children's Creative was the first Malibu preschool to be accredited by the NAEYC. They still implement many of the practices established, though because they really are too structured, they are currently not accredited.

The curriculum at Children's Creative is meant to give an awareness and curiosity of the wonders on the world. They are fortunate to be next to a marine science lab, and have access to the tide pools and extensive marine life. There are also two bunnies and a turtle, with roomy cages in the outdoor playground, and the children are quite involved in their care and upkeep. There is a Theme of the Week, and a Letter of the Week. Children bring in an item that begins with the letter of the week, and have an alphabet book in which they cut out pictures of things beginning with that week's letter, and have a page a week for each letter. The weekly theme is implemented through music, fun, games, and stories. The week right before Thanksgiving, the theme is Native American, and there are diverse and surprisingly well-crafted dream catchers covering the walls, and the art tables are set up with oatmeal containers to make drums for the day's craft activity.

Latta discusses the issue of problem-solving. "We really try to have kids come up with their own resolution, guided by the teachers. If we solve problems for them, how will they learn problem solving skills?" Latta's earthy, grounded demeanor and obvious love of children displays the nurturing, solid companion the students have in their teacher. Children's Creative accepts children between two-and-a-half and five-years-old. On average, a quarter of the students go on to elementary school at Point Dume. "When the kids go on to elementary school here, it's great because we get to continue to watch them grow up and develop," says Latta.

BACKGROUND

Children's Creative Workshop was created in 1982 by Shari Latta.

Bird's Eye View

	Non-existent	Poor	Fair	Good	Excellent
Learning to Read Children learn to explore the world of books					✓
Dress-Up Children experiment with different roles and imagination				✓	
Hand-Eye Children develop fine motor skills by using fingers and hands					✓
Building Blocks Children practice symbolic representation. They are developing an understanding of the relationships between size and shape, and the basic math concepts of geometry and numbers				✓	
Arts and Crafts Children are developing small muscle control as well as creativity					✓
Body Coordination Children crawl through tunnels, climb and balance					✓
Meeting Time Gathering place to listen to the teacher and to stories					✓
Weights and Measures Water and Sand tables					✓
Beakers and Bunnies Classroom pets, aquariums....planting...					✓
Counting 1-2-3 A good preschool will stock basic early-learner software such as phonics or counting games					✓
Outdoor Play Encourage large muscle control and coordination					✓

Q & A

HOW THEY LEARN

What is your school's teaching philosophy? Our goals at Children's Creative Workshop are to provide a safe and nurturing environment where children can explore, create and use their imagination to the fullest. Our unique science-based curriculum provides a starting place for the children to begin their explorations and adventures.

How do you implement the philosophy? Teachers will offer information and materials for the children to absorb and digest at their own level. Concurrently, the alphabet and phonics will be introduced weekly in a fun, creative manner through art, music and stories.

What is the teaching method? Thematic weekly topics are introduced through stories, art, science and music.

At what age do the children start? To what age is the school licensed? 2 1/2 years to school age.

HOW TO GET IN

Are there open house dates? When are tours given? Tours are set up as needed.

Is there an interview? With the child or without? There is no interview.

Is preference given to applicants whose siblings are alumni? Accepted in this order: siblings of current students, alumni families, then new students.

Are letters of recommendation encouraged? From what types of people? No.

How many applications do you receive each year? Between 50 and 100.

How many open spots are there each year? There is a one year wait list.

What are some of the schools that children go on to after finishing their education at your preschool? Viewpoint, Our Lady of Malibu, and Malibu Public schools.

PIGGY BANK

Apart from tuition, what other fees do you charge? There is a $10 application fee, a $100 annual entrance fee and a $300 tuition deposit which applies to the child's last month.

What are the different payment plans available? Tuition is due on the first of the month. Payments can be made in advance. Some special payment needs can be met.

How is the tuition broken down? $440-$985 per month.

Is there a contract? Yes, a parent signs a contract.

Do you have a tuition insurance program? No tuition insurance other than the $300 deposit.

HELPING HANDS

What accreditation is necessary for the teachers to work at your school? Teachers are chosen for their love for children and ability to handle them loved.

How many teachers are there? Four teachers.

How many aides are there? One aide.

IN THE 'ROOM

What's the adult-to-child ratio? 6:1 or better.

What are the policies for initial separation between parent and child? Case by case, but we encourage children to visit with their parents before they start.

Can you visit any time unannounced? YES!

What are the hours? Do you offer early bird or after-hours pick-up? If so, is there an extra fee? School hours are 8:45 a.m.-2:45 p.m. There is 8 a.m. early care and 3-5 p.m. after school care, each for a fee.

Please describe a typical day for a child at your school. Open-ended outdoor/indoor play, circle time/music/story, bathroom/hand wash/snack time, small group academics, outdoor play, art, lunch/story and pick-up.

What kinds of academic activities are offered? Open-ended and directed, paints clays and Play-Doh, collage, paper mache, crazy creative crafts.

What kinds of art activities are offered? Various.

Is the child's time structured or unstructured? Or a mixture of both? Structured, but what is done with the structured time is up to the child.

If a child is not interested in a particular activity, does he/she have other choices or is he/she encouraged to try it anyway? We do encourage children to participate in our activity. Minimal choices will be offered if the child does not want to participate.

How are disputes handled when they occur between the children? Case by case, safety first. Teachers try to let the children problem-solve, and assist when needed.

When and for how long is nap time? Nap time/rest time is 1-1:30 p.m Children can sleep as long as they want.

What kinds of beds do you use? Mats.

What do you do when a child is dropped off in the morning and is obviously not well? What do you do when a child becomes sick during the day? Ill children cannot stay. They are sent home.

Can you accommodate children with special needs? Usually, yes. A shadow may be needed, and the parent may need to provide that resource.

KEEPING IT SAFE

Please describe your security measures for arriving and leaving the school. We are on site of a locked-down elementary school. Identification must be shown to enter.

What medical supplies do you have on hand, and what medical experience does your staff have? Is your staff trained in CPR? We have one LA County fire-trained EMT. Most of the staff knows CPR and we have First Aid kits.

Please describe your earthquake-preparedness plan, and what special equipment do you have on hand in the event of a disaster? We are on site of an evacuation center and we have 50 earthquake kits.

SWINGS 'N THINGS

Please describe your playground. Does it have plenty of shade? We have trees and an EZ-Up tent.

Do you put sunscreen on the children? Children need to bring own sunscreen, parents apply in am (we can reapply).

What kind of toilet training is available? We assist, and will take children in diapers.

HELPING OUT

What kinds of fundraising events are at your school each year? Direct donation (approximately $250 per family suggested), and a small fun family event.

How much participation is required by each parent? None is required, but it is encouraged!

KEEPING IN TOUCH

How do you communicate with parents? Is there a newsletter or phone tree? Monthly newsletter, paper and email.

Does the school publish an address book with all the parents' information in it? A list is given out to parents.

preschool

CHRISTOPHER ROBIN NURSERY SCHOOL

815 N. Alta Vista
Los Angeles, CA 90046
Phone: (323) 934-6512
www.christopherrobinpreschool.com
See Map C on page 286

Contact: Susan Huber and Elizabeth de Roo

- ACCREDITATION: NONE
- FOR-PROFIT
- FINANCIAL AID IS NOT AVAILABLE
- NUMBER OF KIDS: 40
- TUITION: $7,200-$11,700 YEAR
- WE HAVE KIDS WITH SPECIAL NEEDS

WHEN TO APPLY: PARENTS CAN TOUR THE SCHOOL FROM FALL TO WINTER, THEN APPLY AFTER VISITING THE CAMPUS.

Set in-between apartment buildings just southeast of La Brea and Santa Monica Boulevard, the outside of the Christopher Robin Nursery School isn't all that remarkable. Nor, frankly, is the inside—it's not very colorful and the whole thing looks a little muted, like an Oakwood apartment. And yet while definitely more low-key than Wagon Wheel or the Hollywood School House, Christopher Robin is another name that comes up quite a lot when discussing preschools east of Beverly Hills.

On the wall when I first walked in were some 8x10 black and white close-up photographs of some of the students that looked like they could be hanging in a gallery. When I asked co-Director Elizabeth de Roo (the other is her mother, Susan Huber) about them, she told me that they were some of the more "contemplative" students and she had taken the photographs in an attempt to draw them out and find out more about what they were thinking, thus hopefully spreading light on some of their behavior. It's this sort of understated creative approach that seems to permeate Christopher Robin.

The older kids are housed in front, and the younger kids are in the back. Each room is divided up into different centers with areas for blocks, science, library, and dramatic play and the older group also has a writing area. I was there later in the day, so a lot of the kids were outside playing in the back. In addition to a sandbox, the outside play area also has an art area, easel painting, a bike area, and a climbing area, all nicely shaded with umbrellas. The teachers were all very attentive and obviously have good relationships with the kids. When finished there, the kids will go on to attend schools like Third Street School, Rosewood, and Wonderland Elementary.

BACKGROUND

Christopher Robin Nursery School was founded by Vera Sander in 1960.

BIRD'S EYE VIEW

	Non-existent	Poor	Fair	Good	Excellent
Learning to Read Children learn to explore the world of books			✓		
Dress-Up Children experiment with different roles and imagination				✓	
Hand-Eye Children develop fine motor skills by using fingers and hands				✓	
Building Blocks Children practice symbolic representation. They are developing an understanding of the relationships between size and shape, and the basic math concepts of geometry and numbers				✓	
Arts and Crafts Children are developing small muscle control as well as creativity					✓
Body Coordination Children crawl through tunnels, climb and balance				✓	
Meeting Time Gathering place to listen to the teacher and to stories				✓	
Weights and Measures Water and Sand tables				✓	
Beakers and Bunnies Classroom pets, aquariums....planting...				✓	
Counting 1-2-3 A good preschool will stock basic early-learner software such as phonics or counting games				✓	
Outdoor Play Encourage large muscle control and coordination					✓

Q & A

HOW THEY LEARN

What is your school's teaching philosophy? The philosophy is based on constructivist theories All these ages, kids are constructing theories of how the world works. So we present them with opportunities and experiences to do so.

How do you implement the philosophy? We present them with something that will interest them and go by observations of the children.

What specialty teachers are brought into the school? We don't bring in specialty teachers.

What is the teaching method? See philosophy listed above.

At what age do the children start? To what age is the school licensed? No feedback received.

HOW TO GET IN

Are there open house dates? When are tours

given? There are two hours a month through January.

Is there an interview? With the child or without? No interview, parent tour only.

Is preference given to applicants whose siblings are alumni? Yes.

Are letters of recommendation encouraged? From what types of people? No.

How many applications do you receive each year? 40-50.

How many open spots are there each year? 10.

What are some of the schools that children go on to after finishing their education at your preschool? 3rd Street School, Rosewood, Wonderland. Not a lot of our kids go off to private schools.

PIGGY BANK

Apart from tuition, what other fees do you charge? There is a $35 application fee and a $75 registration fee.

What are the different payment plans available? Payment is due on a monthly basis.

How is the tuition broken down? $7,200-$11,700 per month.

Is there a contract? Yes, there is a contract.

Do you have a tuition insurance program? No.

HELPING HANDS

What accreditation is necessary for the teachers to work at your school? Teachers need a minimum of 12 units. We look for teachers with some experience.

How many teachers are there? Five teachers.

How many aides are there? One aide.

Do they come from other preschools? Yes.

IN THE 'ROOM

What's the adult-to-child ratio? 8:1 for the younger kids, 10:1 for the older, and 12:1 for the oldest.

What are the policies for initial separation between parent and child? We want parents to come for a visit first. Parents stay for the first few days.

Can you visit any time unannounced? Yes.

What are the hours? Do you offer early bird or after-hours pick-up? If so, is there an extra fee? 8 a.m.-5:30 p.m. There are no early bird/late hours.

Please describe a typical day for a child at your school. Arrival at 9 a.m., 9:15 a.m. classroom meeting, 9:30 a.m. choice time in centers. There is a 10:30 a.m. snack. Transition to either outside or inside (there are four groups of children and two classrooms). Lunch, nap, less structured time, enrichment activities (people from the community come and participate in storytelling, movement, music and art).

What kinds of academic activities are offered? We try and work on longer term projects for a week and or month.

What kinds of art activities are offered? Clay, collages, painting and sculpture.

Is the child's time structured or unstructured? Or a mixture of both? A mixture.

If a child is not interested in a particular activity, does he/she have other choices or is he/she encouraged to try it anyway? Yes, they have choices but they also need to participate in group so they know what's going on.

How are disputes handled when they occur between the children? Positive redirecting (offering kids other options). We are big on expressing things. As they get older, we encourage them to solve problems without interference from teachers.

When and for how long is nap time? 12:30-2:30 p.m., although the older kids usually get up at 2 p.m.

What kinds of beds do you use? We use cots. They bring their own blankets.

What do you do when a child is dropped off in the morning and is obviously not well? What do you do when a child becomes sick during the day? We call parents right away to have them pick the kid up.

Can you accommodate children with special needs? We like to, if possible.

KEEPING IT SAFE

Please describe your security measures for arriving and leaving the school. There are coded doors.

What medical supplies do you have on hand, and what medical experience does your staff have? Is your staff trained in CPR? No feedback received.

Please describe your earthquake-preparedness plan, and what special equipment do you have on hand in the event of a disaster? There are two earthquake sheds. Kids must bring in a backpack with extra clothes and a family picture. The Parents Association puts together kits.

SWINGS 'N THINGS

Please describe your playground. Does it have plenty of shade? There is a sandbox, art area, easel painting, bike area and climbing area. There are umbrellas for shade.

Do you put sunscreen on the children? Yes, we put sunscreen on them.

What kind of toilet training is available? Children don't have to be potty trained. We will work with parents.

HELPING OUT

What kinds of fundraising events are at your school each year? None, but the Parents Association raises money for some of the enrichment activities and organizes a book fair.

How much participation is required by each parent? None.

KEEPING IN TOUCH

How do you communicate with parents? Is there a newsletter or phone tree? Newsletter. Every month there is a parent meeting for each group where the teacher tells them what is going on.

Does the school publish an address book with all the parents' information in it? Yes.

CIRCLE OF CHILDREN PRESCHOOL

1227 Montana Ave.
Santa Monica, CA 90403
Phone: (310) 393-7731
See Map D on page 286

Contact: Michele Gathrid

- ACCREDITATION: NONE
- FOR-PROFIT
- FINANCIAL AID NOT IS AVAILABLE
- NUMBER OF KIDS: 44
- TUITION: $7,300-$9,000 YEAR
- WE HAVE KIDS WITH SPECIAL NEEDS

WHEN TO APPLY: PARENTS MUST TAKE A TOUR BEFORE GETTING AN APPLICATION. NO CUTOFF DATE. IF THERE ARE TOO MANY APPLICATIONS, THEY WILL STOP HAVING PARENT TOURS.

Located on Montana Avenue in Santa Monica, Circle of Children Nursery School has many circles of children, each generating a lot of energy. The school is essentially one big room split into two with an outside play area, housing 48 kids. The energy was a bit chaotic when I was there (perhaps because it was raining) but even despite the weather, Circle of Children doesn't seem as organized as some of the other schools. What was rather endearing was how the dramatic play area had been turned into a doctor's office as one of the kid's mothers was about to go into the hospital.

The older children were having circle time when I visited, while the younger ones ate lunch. However, lunch was forgotten for the moment when one of their teachers from last year showed up for a visit and they all rushed up for hugs. Because of its location, Circle of Children attracts well-off kids, and most of them end up going on to schools in the area like Brentwood, John Thomas Dye, Crossroads and Curtis. The amount of open spaces a year varies, depending on sibling count. This year, there are 33 siblings enrolled.

If you're looking for a place for your child to socialize for three hours a day, then Circle of Children might work for you. However, if you're looking for a preschool with a strong vision, then I'd suggest looking elsewhere.

BACKGROUND

Established in 1981. Founded by Phyllis Klein.

BIRD'S EYE VIEW

	Non-existent	Poor	Fair	Good	Excellent
Learning to Read Children learn to explore the world of books			✓		
Dress-Up Children experiment with different roles and imagination				✓	
Hand-Eye Children develop fine motor skills by using fingers and hands				✓	
Building Blocks Children practice symbolic representation. They are developing an understanding of the relationships between size and shape, and the basic math concepts of geometry and numbers			✓		
Arts and Crafts Children are developing small muscle control as well as creativity				✓	
Body Coordination Children crawl through tunnels, climb and balance				✓	
Meeting Time Gathering place to listen to the teacher and to stories			✓		
Weights and Measures Water and Sand tables				✓	
Beakers and Bunnies Classroom pets, aquariums....planting...			✓		
Counting 1-2-3 A good preschool will stock basic early-learner software such as phonics or counting games				✓	
Outdoor Play Encourage large muscle control and coordination				✓	

Q & A

HOW THEY LEARN

What is your school's teaching philosophy? We are concerned with the development of the whole child—the physical, mental and emotional. Our primary concern is to create an environment for the child to explore with members of his/her peer group, to develop his/her facilities in dealing with a child's world and to promote his/her self-esteem.

How do you implement the philosophy? Through play.

What specialty teachers are brought into the school? None.

At what age do the children start? To what age is the school licensed? 2.9-5 years old.

HOW TO GET IN

Are there open house dates? When are tours given? Intimate tours for three to four families at a time.

Is there an interview? With the child or without? No.

Is preference given to applicants whose siblings are alumni? Yes.

Are letters of recommendation encouraged? From what types of people? No.

How many applications do you receive each year? Varies.

How many open spots are there each year? Depends on sibling count; this year, there are 33 siblings.

What are some of the schools that children go on to after finishing their education at your preschool? Brentwood, John Thomas Dye, Crossroads, Curtis.

PIGGY BANK

Apart from tuition, what other fees do you charge? There is an application fee of $50 and a registration fee of $75.

How is tuition broken down? $7,300-9,000 per year.

What are the different payment plans available? Flexible.

What is the fee schedule? Twice a year—half of tuition in September and half in January.

Is there a contract? Yes.

Do you have a tuition insurance program? No.

HELPING HANDS

What accreditation is necessary for the teachers to work at your school? Need to meet state requirements. The majority have As, some have Bs.

How many teachers are there? Six teachers.

How many aides are there? No feedback received.

IN THE 'ROOM

What's the adult-to-child ratio? 1:6 or 1:7.

What are the policies for initial separation between parent and child? We do have visits. We ask parents to clear their calendars for at least two weeks.

Can you visit any time unannounced? Yes.

What are the hours? Do you offer early bird or after-hours pick-up? If so, is there an extra fee? 9 a.m.-12 p.m., and 12:30-3:30 p.m. No.

Please describe a typical day for a child at your school. 1.5 hours inside for circle time and snacks, then 1.5 hours outside, then lunch.

What kinds of academic activities are offered? None.

What kinds of art activities are offered? No feedback received.

Is the child's time structured or unstructured? Or a mixture of both? Mixture of both.

If a child is not interested in a particular activity, does he/she have other choices or is he/she encouraged to try it anyway? Yes.

How are disputes handled when they occur between the children? Conflict resolution.

When and for how long is nap time? No nap time.

What kinds of beds do you use? No nap time.

What do you do when a child is dropped off in the morning and is obviously not well? What do you do when a child becomes sick during the day? Call parents right away.

Can you accommodate children with special needs? Yes, but no physical (no ramps).

KEEPING IT SAFE

Please describe your security measures for arriving and leaving the school. Gated facility. Children must be signed in and out.

What medical supplies do you have on hand, and what medical experience does your staff have? Is your staff trained in CPR? First Aid kit. Teachers have CPR training.

Please describe your earthquake-preparedness plan, and what special equipment do you have on hand in the event of a disaster? All children have earthquake kits, practice drills every two months.

SWINGS 'N THINGS

Please describe your playground. Does it have plenty of shade? Swings and climbing equipment.

Do you put sunscreen on the children? Yes.

What kind of toilet training is available? We prefer them to be potty trained but will work with parents.

HELPING OUT

What kinds of fundraising events are at your school each year? One fundraiser a year, put on by parents.

How much participation is required by each parent? None.

KEEPING IN TOUCH

How do you communicate with parents? Is there a newsletter or phone tree? Newsletter, phone, verbally. No email.

preschool to 8th grade

CLAIRBOURN SCHOOL

8400 Huntington Drive
San Gabriel, CA 91775
Phone: (626) 286-3108
www.clairbourn.org
See Map B on page 286

Contact: Admissions Director, Janna Windsor

- ACCREDITATION: NAEYC/CAIS/NAIS/WASC
- NOT-FOR-PROFIT
- FINANCIAL AID IS AVAILABLE
- NUMBER OF KIDS: 60
- TUITION: $10,000-$13,250 YEAR
- WE HAVE KIDS WITH SPECIAL NEEDS

WHEN TO APPLY: APPLICATIONS DUE LATE JANUARY.

Clairbourn has a beautiful campus, with eight tree-lined acres of rolling lawns, a swimming pool, both old and modern facilities all landscaped, manicured, and it is spread out like a college campus. There is a feeling of orderliness throughout—everything in its proper place. The school was strictly for Christian Scientist families from its inception in 1926 until the board of directors voted to open the enrollment to people of other religions in 1967. Today, while the school considers students of different religions and ethnic backgrounds for admission, the staff, faculty and administration remain active Christian Scientists, although note: there is NO religion taught.

According to Karen Paciorek, Early Childhood Director, "The teachers plan for and provide an environment rich with materials and experiences into which the children can get their hands, minds, and feelings. The role of the Clairbourn Early Childhood teacher is to challenge the child's thinking by doing and reflecting along with the child. Teaching practices with the young child go beyond the mere providing of toys and activities and, on the other end of the scale, beyond the mere "giving of information." In addition to facilitating meaningful, purposeful, and functional engagement, the teacher also observes, listens to, responds to, and documents the child's learning experiences."*

Clairbourn's goal is to assure that, without using undue pressure, each child is challenged to grow and develop his or her own special strengths and interests, to achieve a high level of competency in the essential skills and areas of knowledge, and to enter adulthood with confidence and high expectations.

In 2008, Clairbourn began it's final phase of construction for the west campus. The center includes a multimillion dollar preschool with three new classrooms, an age-appropriate play yard that will feature areas to bike, climb, swing and slide, sections for digging and planting, and an outdoor theatre area for dramatic play.

BACKGROUND

The school was founded in 1926 by Mr. & Mrs. Arthur Bourne, who opened a kindergarten for children of parents interested in Christian Science, but no religion is taught. After much growth and development, Clairbourn opened its' doors to students of other faiths, resulting in a social, religious, and ethnic mix in the student body, while the faculty, staff, and administration remains active Christian Scientists. The school has continued to thrive and expand and is an independent, coeducational day school currently enrolling approximately 425 students in preschool through eighth grade.

Bird's Eye View

	Non-existent	Poor	Fair	Good	Excellent
Learning to Read Children learn to explore the world of books					✓
Dress-Up Children experiment with different roles and imagination					✓
Hand-Eye Children develop fine motor skills by using fingers and hands					✓
Building Blocks Children practice symbolic representation. They are developing an understanding of the relationships between size and shape, and the basic math concepts of geometry and numbers					✓
Arts and Crafts Children are developing small muscle control as well as creativity					✓
Body Coordination Children crawl through tunnels, climb and balance					✓
Meeting Time Gathering place to listen to the teacher and to stories					✓
Weights and Measures Water and Sand tables					✓
Beakers and Bunnies Classroom pets, aquariums....planting...				✓	
Counting 1-2-3 A good preschool will stock basic early-learner software such as phonics or counting games					✓
Outdoor Play Encourage large muscle control and coordination					✓

Q & A

HOW THEY LEARN

What is your school's teaching philosophy? Clairbourn's Early Childhood program is based on developmentally appropriate practices based on the premise that children should be actively involved in the construction of their own knowledge.

How do you implement the philosophy? Activities that are meaningful and relevant to the child's life experiences provide opportunities to teach across the curriculum and assist children in seeing the interrelationship of things they are learning. The child-peer-teacher interaction that takes place on a daily basis helps put the child's construction of knowledge into a meaningful context and addresses equally the important issues of cognitive, emotional, physical, social, and spiritual growth and development.

What specialty teachers are brought into the school? The children meet with some specialist teachers throughout the school year.

What is the teaching method? The teachers plan for and provide an environment rich with materials and experiences into which the children can get their hands, minds, and feelings. The role of the Clairbourn Early Childhood teacher is to challenge the child's thinking by doing and reflecting along with the child. Teaching practices with the young child go beyond the mere providing of toys and activities and, on the other end of the scale, beyond the mere "giving of information." In addition to facilitating meaningful, purposeful, and functional engagement, the teacher also observes, listens to, responds to, and documents the child's learning experiences.

At what age do the children start? Students must be age 3 by September 1st.

HOW TO GET IN

Are there open house dates? When are tours given? Informational meetings and tours of the campus typically take place in November and January.

Is there an interview? With the child or without? Parents will schedule a brief office visit with a preschool official and the Admissions Director. There is an interview for students applying for Pre-Kindergarten. In addition, a special "play day" will be arranged on a Saturday morning when a group of children will be observed and assessed for school readiness.

Is preference given to applicants whose siblings are alumni? Yes – dependent upon applicant meeting qualifications for admission.

Are letters of recommendation encouraged? From what types of people? If the child has previous school experience, a teacher recommendation is required.

How many applications do you receive each year? Varies.

How many open spots are there each year? Varies.

What are some of the schools that children go on to after finishing their education at your preschool? It is expected that the majority will continue at Clairbourn through the eigth grade.

PIGGY BANK

Apart from tuition, what other fees do you charge? No.

How is the tuition broken down? $10,000-13,250 per year.

What are the different payment plans available? Single payments due July 1. Two payments, with 60% due July 1 and 40% due January 1.

What is the fee schedule? New applications are $75; a Reservation deposit (per child, non-refundable, due with contract; applied toward tuition of $1,000. Clairbourn Families' Association Dues (per child, required yearly) are $20.

Is there a contract? Yes.

Do you have a tuition insurance program? Tuition Refund Plan (TRP) insurance is mandatory for two payment plans and optional for single payment plans. The insurance premium is 1.0% of total tuition and fees. TRP insurance is due July 1.

HELPING HANDS

What accreditation is necessary for the teachers to work at your school? Teachers and assistants maintain all requirements mandated by the State of California Department of Social Services licensing board.

How many teachers are there? There is one junior pre-kindergarten teacher and one pre-kindergarten teacher per classroom.

How many aides are there? Each teacher has one assistant per class, plus one shared assistant.

Do they come from other preschools? None come from other preschools.

IN THE 'ROOM

What's the adult-to-child ratio? 2:16 for the junior pre-kindergarten, and 2.5:20 for the pre-kindergarten.

What are the policies for initial separation between parent and child? No policy.

Can you visit any time unannounced? Yes.

What are the hours? Do you offer early bird or after-hours pick-up? If so, is there an extra fee? Junior pre-kindergarten is from 8 a.m.-12 p.m., pre-kindergarten is from 8 a.m.-2:45 p.m. There is no before or after school care for preschool students.

Please describe a typical day for a child at your school. Preschool classrooms are filled with a variety of materials such as blocks, art tools, books, science displays and experiments and dramatic play, all of which are used on a daily or weekly basis. A typical day includes some structured and some unstructured time, indoor and outdoor time, snack and lunch times (for Pre-K), as well as a rest and quiet time.

What kinds of academic activities are offered? Academic activities are developmentally appropriate and integrated into the curriculum through various play, art, literature, and manipulative activities.

What kinds of art activities are offered? Various art activities are provided throughout the school year and integrated into the curriculum in a variety of ways.

**Is the child's time structured or unstructured? Or a mixture of both? Mixture of both.

If a child is not interested in a particular activity, does he/she have other choices or is he/she encouraged to try it anyway? Children are provided with a variety of activities and choices throughout the day. Keeping respect for the child in mind, they are never forced but always encouraged to challenge themselves and to try new things.

How are disputes handled when they occur between the children? Developmentally appropriate conflict resolution skills are addressed with all children on an ongoing basis.

When and for how long is nap time? Nap time takes place after lunch and is one hour long. Nap time is not part of the partial day program.

What kinds of beds do you use? Pre-kindergarten children are provided with soft mats on which they can rest or sleep during nap time.

What do you do when a child is dropped off in the morning and is obviously not well? What do you do when a child becomes sick during the day? Parents are advised to keep their child at home if they cannot participate fully or have obvious signs of an illness. If a child becomes ill or injured at school, parents will be contacted immediately. If the parents cannot be reached, the office will use the designated call list provided by the parents on an emergency information form.

Can you accommodate children with special needs? Determined per case.

KEEPING IT SAFE

Please describe your security measures for arriving and leaving the school. Parents/designated guardian sign child in/out of the school daily. Visitors during the day must check in with the receptionist at the front office and receive a visitor's pass.

What medical supplies do you have on hand, and what medical experience does your staff have? Is your staff trained in CPR? All staff are trained in CPR.

Please describe your earthquake-preparedness plan, and what special equipment do you have on hand in the event of a disaster? The school has a fully developed earthquake/disaster plan with regular drills performed.

SWINGS 'N THINGS

Please describe your playground. Does it have plenty of shade? A brand new developmentally-appropriate playground mainly shaded by large trees, umbrellas and canvas covers.

Do you put sunscreen on the children? Sunscreen is not applied unless specifically requested and provided by parents.

What kind of toilet training is available? No toilet training available.

HELPING OUT

What kinds of fundraising events are at your school each year? Several major and minor fundraising events/efforts take place. Call for more information.

How much participation is required by each parent? Participation is not required but enthusiastically encouraged mainly through the Clairbourn Families Association.

KEEPING IN TOUCH

How do you communicate with parents? Is there a newsletter or phone tree? Communication with parents includes a packet of information sent home weekly, which may include the Headmaster's weekly newsletter, Clairbourn Families Association information, and other school related materials. The classroom teachers each send home a weekly newsletter as well. Also, in addition to daily communication with the teacher as needed, two mandatory and one optional parent-teacher conferences are scheduled throughout the school year.

Does the school publish an address book with all the parents' information in it? A school directory is published each year, and parents indicate what personal information they want included.

preschool to 6th

CRESTWOOD HILLS COOPERATIVE NURSERY SHOOL

986 Hanley Ave.
Los Angeles, CA 90049
Phone: (310) 472-1566
www.crestwoodhillscoop.org
See Map D on page 286

Contact: Cathy Wagener

- ACCREDITATION: NONE
- NOT-FOR-PROFIT
- FINANCIAL AID IS AVAILABLE
- NUMBER OF KIDS: 68
- TUITION: $6,800 YEAR
- WE HAVE KIDS WITH SPECIAL NEEDS

WHEN TO APPLY: APPLICATIONS AVAILABLE YEAR-ROUND. GET APPLICATIONS IN EARLY.

When you arrive at Crestwood Hills Co-Op, which is tucked up inside the hills of an "architecturally controlled" community, you'd never know that you're just up the road from Brentwood's busy and chic San Vicente Boulevard. In fact, it feels more like you're in nearby Topanga Canyon minus the Birkenstocks! The school is one smallish wooden building with a good-sized playground located next to a huge grassy park. Crestwood Hills is known for having one of the best art programs in town, and one look around the classroom showed an abundance of art supplies. While I was there, some of the kids were on the playground, while some painted and did puzzles.

Crestwood takes its co-op status very seriously. When they say the school is "very parent and family-oriented," they mean it. Parents have to work in the class twice a month as well as a three-hour weekend shift four times a year, attend two evening parent meetings a year, and are billed $300 for the two yearly fundraisers whether they attend or not. As I watched the kids, what was great was how it was difficult to tell the parents from the teachers—the working parents knew and loved all of the kids and vice versa.

There's always a wait list to get in! Although many of the families are from the area, some come from as far away as West Hollywood or the Valley. Upon leaving, most of the kids go on to Crossroads, Brentwood, Willows, Echo Horizons, John Thomas Dye, Mirman, or Kenter Public.

BACKGROUND

The school was founded in the 1990s by Crestwood Hills residents.

BIRD'S EYE VIEW

	Non-existent	Poor	Fair	Good	Excellent
Learning to Read — Children learn to explore the world of books				✓	
Dress-Up — Children experiment with different roles and imagination				✓	
Hand-Eye — Children develop fine motor skills by using fingers and hands				✓	
Building Blocks — Children practice symbolic representation. They are developing an understanding of the relationships between size and shape, and the basic math concepts of geometry and numbers				✓	
Arts and Crafts — Children are developing small muscle control as well as creativity					✓
Body Coordination — Children crawl through tunnels, climb and balance				✓	
Meeting Time — Gathering place to listen to the teacher and to stories				✓	
Weights and Measures — Water and Sand tables				✓	
Beakers and Bunnies — Classroom pets, aquariums....planting...				✓	
Counting 1-2-3 — A good preschool will stock basic early-learner software such as phonics or counting games				✓	
Outdoor Play — Encourage large muscle control and coordination					✓

• • • • • • • **Q & A** • • • • • • •

HOW THEY LEARN

What is your school's teaching philosophy? We believe that children learn through play. It is a developmentally-based philosophy based on respect for the uniqueness and dignity of each individual.

How do you implement the philosophy? Teachers bring learning into the classroom and help children learn how to make their own choices.

What specialty teachers are brought into the school? A music teacher comes in every Friday.

What is the teaching method? It is a non-academic, non-directed curriculum.

At what age do the children start? To what age is the school licensed? 2.9-6 years of age.

HOW TO GET IN

Are there open house dates? When are tours given? Monthly, except in August.

Is there an interview? With the child or without? No.

Is preference given to applicants whose siblings are alumni? Crestwood Hills Homeowner's Association members get priority, then siblings, then alumni children, then toddler program participants.

Are letters of recommendation encouraged? From what types of people? No.

How many applications do you receive each year? 100.

How many open spots are there each year? There is always a waiting list.

What are some of the schools that children go on to after finishing their education at your preschool? Kenter Public, Crossroads, Brentwood, Willows, Echo Horizons, J.T. Dye, Mirman.

PIGGY BANK

Apart from tuition, what other fees do you charge? There is a $40 application fee and a $100 non-refundable entrance fee.

How does the tuition break down? $6,800 per year. Parents must pay for five days a week, but the child doesn't have to attend all 5 days. There is a morning or afternoon program, but the child can attend all day.

What are the different payment plans available? See below.

What is the fee schedule? Divided into one, four or ten monthly payments.

Is there a contract? Yes.

Do you have a tuition insurance program? No.

HELPING HANDS

What accreditation is necessary for the teachers to work at your school? State requirements.

How many teachers are there? Three teachers.

How many aides are there? One aide and two parents.

Do they come from other preschools? Yes.

IN THE 'ROOM

What's the adult-to-child ratio? 1:3 for three-year-olds; 1:4 for four; 1:6 for mixed ages.

What are the policies for initial separation between parent and child? We ask parents to clear their calendar for two weeks.

Can you visit any time unannounced? Yes.

What are the hours? No feedback received.

Do you offer early bird or after-hours pick-up? If so, is there an extra fee? Children can attend either the morning or afternoon sessions.

Please describe a typical day for a child at your school. 45 minutes of free play, then clean, circle time, snack, then outside time. As there are two classes, one group starts outside so they would end up inside.

What kinds of academic activities are offered? It is non-academic, but teachers are bring learning into the classroom.

What kinds of art activities are offered? Everything.

Is the child's time structured or unstructured, or a mixture of both? Mixture of both.

If a child is not interested in a particular activity does he/she have other choices, or is he/she encouraged to try it anyway? Yes.

How are disputes handled when they occur between the children? Conflict resolution. We help them use their words. If you tell a child "no," then you have to be able to give them an option—redirect them.

When and for how long is nap time? None.

What kinds of beds do you use? No beds.

What do you do when a child is dropped off in the morning and is obviously not well? What do you do when a child becomes sick during the day? Children have to stay home for the first three days of an illness and then be fever-free for 24 hours before returning.

Can you accommodate children with special needs? Yes.

KEEPING IT SAFE

Please describe your security measures for arriving and leaving the school. There is a locked gate.

What medical supplies do you have on hand, and what medical experience does your staff have? Is your staff trained in CPR? We have First Aid kits and CPR training.

Please describe your earthquake-preparedness plan, and what special equipment do you have on hand in the event of a disaster? We have enough food and water for three to five days. Each child has a comfort kit of family pictures, etc. The kids will be evacuated to a synagogue on Sunset Boulevard.

SWINGS 'N THINGS

Please describe your playground. Does it have plenty of shade? It has climbing equipment, a sand area, and is shaded.

Do you put sunscreen on the children? Yes.

What kind of toilet training is available? Children don't have to be toilet trained to attend.

HELPING OUT

What kinds of fundraising events are at your school each year? Full picnic ($100 spring auction).

How much participation is required by each parent? Parents are billed $300 for the spring and fall fundraisers.

KEEPING IN TOUCH

How do you communicate with parents? Is there a newsletter or phone tree?

Does the school publish an address book with all the parents' information in it? We publish a roster.

preschool to 6th grade

DELANEY WRIGHT FINE ARTS PRESCHOOL

6125 Carlos Avenue
Los Angeles, CA 90028
Phone: (323) 871-2470
www.fineartspreschool.org
See Map C on page 286

Contact: Nasrin Pez, Director

- NUMBER OF KIDS: 55
- ACCREDITATION: NONE
- WE DO NOT HAVE KIDS WITH SPECIAL NEEDS
- TUITION: $365-$795 MONTH
- FINANCIAL AID IS NOT AVAILABLE

WHEN TO APPLY: ANY TIME.

From the church parking lot, (no church affiliation) a big shady tree greets you upon entering the schoolyard. There is a shaded sandbox on the left, a large new pavilion with bikes and tables, a grassy area and an inviting climbing structure. For being so close to the 101 freeway, this school is surprisingly quiet.

Shelley Acton started this school a few years ago, but has been teaching since 1977, has a M.S. in psychology, as well as other teaching credentials. As a mother, she values the unique stages of a child's life which is clearly reflected in her developmental philosophy. Her philosophy is simple: provide a child with a learning environment that is filled with music, singing, dancing, enriched language, storytelling, creative expression and dramatic play - and that child will blossom intellectually, socially, emotionally and physically.

Nasrin Pez took me on a tour of the school and although Montessori trained, keeps to the schools' mission statement of an arts-based curriculum. The school has small but exciting classrooms filled with costumes, instruments and art, just the stuff any preschooler would want to play with. The children are well taken care of by seven teachers, plus music, theater, drama and dance specialists. Full day children have special interest teachers as well. Open 8:30 to 5:45p.m. for children ages 2 to 5 (children do not need to be toilet trained), options for half or full day, this school is a refreshing alternative to the "hurry up and grow fast" mentality that we see more and more in preschools today.

The teachers at DWFAP all emphasize caring, inclusive and nurturing behaviors, and model positive and happy relationships within the classrooms. Despite the artsy bent and the four classrooms, I observed clean bathrooms and great organization. Parents eagerly give their time to help in on-going activities of this school whether they are plays, art projects, fundraisers or get-togethers that all re-enforce this school as a community effort. If you're looking for a preschool where your child can act his or her age, then do take a look at this one!

BACKGROUND

As of October 2005, The Delaney Wright Fine Arts Preschool was founded to offer an early childhood alternative to the product-oriented, highly competitive, "hurry and grow up fast" mentality that permeates many of our educational arenas today. Children need to grow into who they will be at their own paces, develop in their unique styles, and take with them fun and wonderful memories of childhood.

BIRD'S EYE VIEW

	Non-existent	Poor	Fair	Good	Excellent
Learning to Read Children learn to explore the world of books			✓		
Dress-Up Children experiment with different roles and imagination					✓
Hand-Eye Children develop fine motor skills by using fingers and hands				✓	
Building Blocks: Children practice symbolic representation. They are developing an understanding of the relationships between size and shape, and the basic math concepts of geometry and numbers				✓	
Arts and Crafts Children are developing small muscle control as well as creativity					✓
Body Coordination Children crawl through tunnels, climb and balance				✓	
Meeting Time Gathering place to listen to the teacher and to stories					✓
Weights and Measures Water and Sand tables					✓
Beakers and Bunnies Classroom pets, aquariums....planting...				✓	
Counting 1-2-3 A good preschool will stock basic early-learnersoftware such as phonics or counting games				✓	
Outdoor Play Encourage large muscle control and coordination					✓

Q & A

HOW THEY LEARN

What is your school's teaching philosophy? We allow children to express their creativities through the use of different art materials, play and basic learning without the constraints of a rigid schedule/format.

How do you implement the philosophy? To round out our exciting environment, we offer a meaningful, cognitively and developmentally appropriate curriculum that sparks a child's natural curiosity and sense of wonder, while enhancing his or her motivation to learn.

What specialty teachers are brought into the school? We have teachers that are hired through art production company, who teach music, theatre/drama, and dance.

What is the teaching method? Our teachers are warm, nurturing, and loving. They recognize each child as an individual and strive to meet his/her needs.

At what age do the children start? 2 years of age.

To what age is the school licensed? Entry to the first grade.

HOW TO GET IN

Are there open house dates? When are tours given? No, however tours are given when when there is a scheduled opening available.

Is there an interview? With the child or without? Yes, but not with the child or his/her siblings.

Is preference given to applicants whose siblings are alumni? Yes.

Are letters of recommendations encouraged? From what types of people? No.

How many applications do you receive each year? 75-100.

How many open spots are there each year? It depends on the number of pre-k graduates.

What are some of the schools that children go on to after finishing their education at your preschool? Los Feliz Charter, Fountain Day School, Ribbett Academy, Little Red School House, Larchmont Charter.

PIGGY BANK

Apart from tuition, what other fees do you charge? For extracurricular activities like music, dance, theatre/drama.

How is tuition broken down? Five days/week: $795; MWF full-day: $685, MWF half-day: $550; T/TH full-day-$450, T/TH half-day: $365 per month.

What are the different payment plans available? No feedback received.

What is the fee schedule? Beginning of each month.

Is there a contract? No.

Do you have a tuition insurance program? No.

HELPING HANDS

What accreditation is necessary for the teachers to work at your school? A minimum of 12 units of ECE.

How many teachers are there? Seven.

How many aides are there? One.

IN THE ROOM

What's the child-to-adult ratio? 8-10:1.

What are the policies for initial separation between parent and child? We encourage parents to stay for not more than an hour for the first few days of enrollment.

Can you visit any time unannounced? Yes.

What are the hours? 8:30-5:30 p.m.

Do you offer early bird or after-hours pick-up? If so, is there an extra fee? Yes, $15 for the first 15 minutes and $5 for every minute after.

Please describe a typical day for a child at your school? "Greet the Day," snack, free play, lessons, lunch, naptime, snack, and finally afternoon program.

What kind of academic activities are offered? Varies with the age level.

What kinds of activities are offered? Music, theatre/drama, dance, art and crafts.

Is the child's time structured or unstructured or a mixture of both? Mixture of both.

If a child is not interested in a particular activity, does he/she have other choices or is he/she encouraged to try it anyway? Yes.

How are disputes handled when they occur between the children? Both children are pulled away from the group and talked to about what the dispute was about and if there was a way for them to resolve it without any injuries.

What and for how long is nap time? It is a time for the children to regain energies and nap time lasts from 1:00-3:00 p.m.

What kinds of beds do you use? Nylon cots.

What do you do when a child is dropped off in the morning and is obviously not well? What do you do when a child becomes sick during the day? We would ask for the parent to take their child home and make sure they come to school only when they are feeling well enough to participate with their classmates.

Can you accommodate children with special needs? No.

KEEPING IT SAFE

Please describe your security measures for arriving and leaving the school? We make sure that children are taken and dropped off only by people the parents have listed on their sign-up sheets.

What medical supplies do you have on hand, and what medical experience does your staff have? Is your staff trained in CPR? We have a semi-advanced first aid kit. Select members of the staff have taken child medical classes so they are able to assist in a situation. Most to all of our staff is trained for CPR.

Please describe your earthquake-preparedness plan, and what special equipment do you have on hand in the event of a disaster? Evacuate the building and head for the open playground. Each child has a "earthquake prepared" kit. There are mandatory monthly fire drills, and every three months, an earthquake drill is conducted.

SWINGS 'N THINGS

Please describe your playground. Does it have plenty of shade? We have a shaded sandbox, a partially shaded jungle gym, a non shaded grass section, and shaded area for bike play, art, lunch and various activities.

Do you put sunscreen on the children? Yes, though the parents are asked to bring special types (if needed) and then group types.

What kind of toilet training is available? Generally, toilet training is started at home, and continued here. We have frequent restroom breaks for those in the "potty training" stage.

HELPING OUT

What kinds of fundraising events are at your school each year? "Breakfast at Delaney" (bake sale), "Entertainment Night", "Silent Art Auction.

How much participation is required by each parent? It is voluntary, but preferred.

KEEP IN TOUCH

How do you communicate with parents? Is there a newsletter or phone tree? We communicate via email and phone calls. Monthly newletters are sent via email.

Does the school. Publish an address book with all parent's information in it? In each room, there is a parent in charge of a family roster, as well as a full list with the teachers.

preschool

DOHENY SCHOOL

968 Doheny Dr.
West Hollywood, CA 90069
Phone: (310) 275-3004
See Map C on page 286

Contact: Paula Carter, Director

- ACCREDITATION: NONE
- FOR-PROFIT
- FINANCIAL AID IS NOT AVAILABLE
- NUMBER OF KIDS: 33
- TUITION: $590-$840 MONTH
- WE HAVE KIDS WITH SPECIAL NEEDS

WHEN TO APPLY: WHEN A SPACE IS AVAILABLE, THEY REFER TO A WAIT LIST.

The Doheny School is camouflaged in many ways. Tucked in away from the street, and in the middle of condos and high-rises, you wouldn't know it is a school. There is an iron gate along the street, and a very discreet sign next to the door that states it is indeed the Doheny School. Its pale yellow façade, with bright red trim and door, make it a bright spot on the street. But other than that, it appears like just another house. Director Paula Carter states, "People find us if they are looking for us." The Doheny School is also deceptively small from the outside. Just as parents must walk their child into the school and sign in, I had to be admitted through the door and sign in. It being the day after Election Day, I walked in on a discussion of the candidates, between several three-year-olds, who shared that they had watched the election the night before. I was amazed, as always, how early opinions are formed and expressed!

I was given a tour by Paula Carter herself, who has worked at the school for 27 years (twenty of that with two-year-olds). It is evident how much she loves children, and takes great pleasure in witnessing their "first accomplishments." There is a different pet in each room, and the children all participate in their care and maintenance. The school is small and quite intimate. Every teacher knows every child's name and vice versa. The playground in back has rubber chips instead of wood, and Carter encouraged me to try it out. It has a bouncy, trampoline feel and softens the blow if a child were to stumble and fall. "Of course, when we first got the rubber chips, they went home with the children by the pocketful!"

There is a driveway for tricycles and miniature cars, and a converted garage that serves as a multi-purpose room, but primarily used for arts and crafts. Carter stopped mid-stride to respond to a cry from inside of, "That's my Thomas! He doesn't like his diaper changed." As she smoothed away the little boy's distressed tears, it was obvious that the children love Paula Carter as much as she does them, and that she undeniably embodies the warm, loving, comfortable atmosphere that is Doheny School.

BACKGROUND

No feedback received.

BIRD'S EYE VIEW

	Non-existent	Poor	Fair	Good	Excellent
Learning to Read Children learn to explore the world of books					✓
Dress-Up Children experiment with different roles and imagination					✓
Hand-Eye Children develop fine motor skills by using fingers and hands				✓	
Building Blocks Children practice symbolic representation. They are developing an understanding of the relationships between size and shape, and the basic math concepts of geometry and numbers				✓	
Arts and Crafts Children are developing small muscle control as well as creativity					✓
Body Coordination Children crawl through tunnels, climb and balance					✓
Meeting Time Gathering place to listen to the teacher and to stories					✓
Weights and Measures Water and Sand tables				✓	
Beakers and Bunnies Classroom pets, aquariums....planting...					✓
Counting 1-2-3 A good preschool will stock basic early-learner software such as phonics or counting games				✓	
Outdoor Play Encourage large muscle control and coordination					✓

Q & A

HOW THEY LEARN

What is your school's teaching philosophy? We believe that only a secure child learns at a pace approaching his full potential. Our first task is to provide an environment in which a child feels warm, comfortable and safe. We believe that a child must learn to identify and understand his feelings and to express those feelings appropriately. Our job is to teach them the words to use and those patterns of behavior which will allow them to express emotions in socially acceptable ways. It is our job to respond to achievements and failures in valid, supportive ways. Our teachers will be qualified by education, experience and commitment to carry out our program.

How do you implement the philosophy? Teachers are hired based on having similar philosophies, and to provide loving, caring, safe learning environments.

What is the teaching method? Learning through play, experience and we also offer academics.

At what age do the children start? To what age is the school licensed? Start at age two through entry into kindergarten.

HOW TO GET IN

Are there open house dates? When are tours given? Tours are available year-round by appointment.

Is there an interview? With the child or without? We ask the child to come on the tour also, or to come by for a visit.

Is preference given to applicants whose siblings are alumni? Yes.

Are letters of recommendation encouraged? From what types of people? No.

How many applications do you receive each year? We only take applications for spaces available.

How many open spots are there each year? No feedback received.

What are some of the schools that children go on to after finishing their education at your preschool? Echo Horizons, Wonderland Elementary, The Center for Early Education, or the local public schools in Beverly Hills and West Hollywood Hills.

PIGGY BANK

Apart from tuition, what other fees do you charge? There is a non-refundable annual registration fee of $150, a $25 late tuition fee that is due after the fifth of the month, and a $25 late fee for bounced checks.

How is tuition broken down? Tuition range is between $590-840.

What are the different payment plans available? No feedback received.

What is the fee schedule? Monthly, due on the first of the month.

Is there a contract? Yes, there is a contract.

Do you have a tuition insurance program? No insurance program.

HELPING HANDS

What accreditation is necessary for the teachers to work at your school? Must be fully qualified with ECE units and experience.

How many teachers are there? Three teachers.

How many aides? One aide.

Do they come from other preschools? No feedback received.

IN THE 'ROOM

What's the adult-to-child ratio? 12:1 in older two classes; 10:2 in younger classes with teacher and aide.

What are the policies for initial separation between parent and child? A couple of visits together, then separate.

Can you visit any time unannounced? Yes.

What are the hours? 8 a.m.-6 p.m.

Do you offer early bird or after-hours pick-up? If so, is there an extra fee? No.

Please describe a typical day for a child at your school. Arrival, morning snack, inside play, circle time, story, outside play, clean-up and lunch.

What kinds of academic activities are offered? The two-year-olds get a basic introduction to circle time. The four-year-olds get beginning reading, letter, math and sound recognition.

What kinds of art activities are offered? Art room in garage.

Is the child's time structured or unstructured, or a mixture of both? Structured.

If a child is not interested in a particular activity, does he/she have other choices or is he/she encouraged to try it anyway? Children are encouraged and offered the activity, but never made to do it.

How are disputes handled when they occur between the children? We try to have children resolve using their words, with guidance from teachers.

When and for how long is nap time? One nap time from 2:30-3 p.m.

What kinds of beds do you use? The children sleep on low cots.

What do you do when a child is dropped off in the morning and is obviously not well? What do you do when a child becomes sick during the day? Parents are called to come and pick up their child.

Can you accommodate children with special needs? Depends on the need.

KEEPING IT SAFE

Please describe your security measures for arriving and leaving the school. Parents must walk the child into the school and sign in.

What medical supplies do you have on hand, and what medical experience does your staff have? Is your staff trained in CPR? First Aid kits, everyone is CPR and First Aid trained.

Please describe your earthquake-preparedness plan, and what special equipment do you have on hand in the event of a disaster? We relocate to West Hollywood Elementary School in a disaster. Each child has an earthquake backpack. Fire drills and earthquake drills are done monthly.

SWINGS 'N THINGS

Please describe your playground. Does it have plenty of shade? The backyard has rubber chips underneath, a small play home, three swings, a play structure, and a driveway for tricycles and cars.

Do you put sunscreen on the children? We

do not use sunscreen.

What kind of toilet training is available? We toilet train using positive reinforcement and get everyone involved.

HELPING OUT

What kinds of fundraising events are at your school each year? There is a once-a-year fundraiser with the profits going to the school; usually something to be fixed.

How much participation is required by each parent? Voluntary.

KEEPING IN TOUCH

How do you communicate with parents? Is there a newsletter or phone tree? We see parents every day. We do send letters.

Does the school publish an address book with all the parents' information in it? No.

preschool to kindergarten

ECOLE CLAIRE FONTAINE

226 Westminster Ave.
Venice, CA 90291
Phone: 310-314 9976
www.laclairefontaine.org
See Map on page 286

Contact: Kristi Dick

- ACCREDITATION: NONE
- FOR-PROFIT
- FINANCIAL AID IS AVAILABLE
- NUMBER OF KIDS: 80
- TUITION: $600-$1,885 MONTH
- WE HAVE KIDS WITH SPECIAL NEEDS

WHEN TO APPLY: ONE YEAR IN ADVANCE RECOMMENDED.

Ecole Claire Fontaine is a bilingual French preschool serving children aged 2 to 6. The program they offer encourages a child's natural, holistic growth in a very nurturing environment. They engage children to develop habits of observation, questioning and listening through language, the exploration of nature, music and crafts. On any given week the kids can expect to have Dance & Movement, Music classes taught by professional adjunct instructors. Arts and crafts, sewing, baking, photography, gardening in the vegetable and flower gardens on the newer campus (a must-see), and walking field trips to a park or the beach for play and sports. There's even a French chef who cooks nutritious organic hot lunches for the children! Parents are invited to drop in and pay for their lunch (which helps raise funds for the school). Tuition ranges from $325 to $1735 per month. I loved both campuses for different reasons. Go see for yourself.

The school also offers music classes on Saturdays led by music instructor, Frederic Michot. Currently they have a Mommy and Me music class for very young children and a class for preschool age children. Children do not have to attend Ecole Claire Fontaine to enroll in these classes.

BACKGROUND

Established in 1988.

Bird's Eye View

	Non-existent	Poor	Fair	Good	Excellent
Learning to Read Children learn to explore the world of books				🦉	
Dress-Up Children experiment with different roles and imagination					🦉
Hand-Eye Children develop fine motor skills by using fingers and hands					🦉
Building Blocks Children practice symbolic representation. They are developing an understanding of the relationships between size and shape, and the basic math concepts of geometry and numbers					🦉
Arts and Crafts Children are developing small muscle control as well as creativity					🦉
Body Coordination Children crawl through tunnels, climb and balance					🦉
Meeting Time Gathering place to listen to the teacher and to stories					🦉
Weights and Measures Water and Sand tables					🦉
Beakers and Bunnies Classroom pets, aquariums....planting...				🦉	
Counting 1-2-3 A good preschool will stock basic early-learner software such as phonics or counting games				🦉	
Outdoor Play Encourage large muscle control and coordination					🦉

Q & A

HOW THEY LEARN

What is your school's teaching philosophy? Our developmental program encourages a child's natural, holistic growth in a nurturing environment.

How do you implement the philosophy? We engage children to develop habits of observation, questioning and listening, and foster their natural abilities through language, music, play, art activities, and the exploration of nature. Instruction is presented in French and English.

What specialty teachers are brought into the school? Music, dance, sculpture, art, woodworking and photography.

What is the teaching method? Developmental.

At what age do the children start? 2 years-old.

To what age is the school licensed? 6 years-old.

HOW TO GET IN

Are there open house dates? When are tours given? No. Tours are given five times a year.

Is there an interview? With the child or without? Yes. Without the child.

Is preference given to applicants whose siblings are alumni? Yes.

**Are letters of recommendations encouraged? No.

How many applications do you receive each year? Over 100.

How many open spots are there each year? Westminster Campus: 12-18. Abbot Kinney Campus: 10-16.

What are some of the schools that children go on to after finishing their education at your preschool? Lycee Francais of West Los Angeles, and public and private schools in the surrounding area.

PIGGY BANK

Apart from tuition, what other fees do you charge? New student processing fee: $275, and annual registration fee: $300.

How is tuition broken down? Tuition depends on schedule, from two morning sessions per week (8–1p.m.) to five full days per week (8-6p.m.).

What are the different payment plans available? One annual payment, three payments or monthly payments.

What is the fee schedule? Payments are due the first of every month.

Is there a contract? Yes.

Do you have a tuition insurance program? No.

HELPING HANDS

What accreditation is necessary for the teachers to work at your school? Bachelor's degree and/or ECE units as required by the state.

How many teachers are there? Westminster Campus: four, Abbot Kinney Campus: five.

How many aides are there? Westminster Campus: three, Abbot Kinney Campus: three.

IN THE ROOM

What's the child-to-adult ratio? Minimum is 1:5.

What are the policies for initial separation between parent and child? Parents stay until the child is comfortable.

Can you visit any time unannounced? Yes.

What are the hours? 8 - 6p.m.

Do you offer early bird or after-hours pick-up? No.

Please describe a typical day for a child at your school? Breakfast and free play, classroom activities, special classes, circle time singing and snack, free play, lunch, free play, storytelling, naptime or special classes, free play.

What kind of academic activities are offered? Nature study in the garden and science exploration, language, graphic skills and reading to the children.

What kinds of activities are offered? Music classes with guitar and piano, dance class, baking, gardening, art activities include painting, clay modeling and collage. The older children also have woodworking class, photography class, yoga and handicrafts.

Is the child's time structured or unstructured or a mixture of both? A mixture of both.

If a child is not interested in a particular activity, does he/she have other choices or is he/she encouraged to try it anyway? Children are encouraged to try all of the activities offered, and may choose from available choices.

How are disputes handled when they occur between the children? Teachers engage the children and guide them to resolve conflict using their words.

When and for how long is nap time? 1:30 - 3:00 p.m.

What kinds of beds do you use? Padded mats on covered floor, with individual linens for each child.

What do you do when a child is dropped off in the morning and is obviously not well? The parent is asked to take the child home. What do you do when a child becomes sick during the day? The child is provided with a quiet space to lie down away from the other children, and a parent is called to pick up the child.

Can you accommodate children with special needs? Sometimes.

KEEPING IT SAFE

Please describe your security measures for arriving and leaving the school? Parents enter through a secure designated entrance. Sign-in and sign-out sheets are posted, and children are released only to parents or a previously authorized caregiver.

What medical supplies do you have on hand, and what medical experience does your staff have? Basic medical supplies. All teaching staff is trained in First Aid and CPR.

Please describe your earthquake-preparedness plan, and what special equipment do you have on hand in the event of a disaster? We have school earthquake-preparedness supplies on each campus, and a detailed earthquake preparedness plan.

SWINGS 'N THINGS

Please describe your playground. Swings and a slide, a sandbox area and a garden area with playhouses, with plenty of room for riding trikes, shade trees and two covered decks serve as extra activity areas.

Do you put sunscreen on the children? Yes.

What kind of toilet training is available? When the child is ready, we work with the parents to assist the child in the process of toilet training.

HELPING OUT

What kinds of fundraising events are at your school each year? No feedback received.

How much participation is required by each parent? Opportunities are available for parent participation.

KEEP IN TOUCH

How do you communicate with parents? On campus on a daily basis, via email and telephone, and parents meetings twice a year.

Is there a newsletter or phone tree? Newsletter.

Does the school publish an address book with all parent's information in it? Yes.

FIRST LUTHERAN CIRCLE OF LOVE PRESCHOOL

1100 Poinsettia Ave.
Manhattan Beach, CA 90226
Phone: (310) 545-5653
www.first-lutheran.com
See Map E on page 286

Contact: Nancy Durkovic, Director

- ACCREDITATION: NONE
- NOT-FOR-PROFIT
- FINANCIAL AID IS AVAILABLE
- NUMBER OF KIDS: 165
- TUITION: $310-$780 MONTH
- WE HAVE KIDS WITH SPECIAL NEEDS

WHEN TO APPLY: APPLICATIONS AVAILABLE YEAR-ROUND. CUTOFF DATE FOR FALL ENROLLMENT IS MID-MARCH.

Driving up Manhattan Beach Boulevard, I was worried that I might miss the school. It is off a busy street, and I feared that I might drive right past it. Just when I thought I'd gone too far, I saw a huge playground with children playing. Some were riding bikes in a gated area, and others were playing on the slides and in the sand. I had to wait at the gate to be let in because, being on such a busy street, there are gates and a code to enter. The director, Michelle Bertollini, came and let me in.

The school has a very family-oriented environment and accepts children between the ages of two to five. Each age group has their own classroom with two teachers per room. There is prayer time before snack and before lunch every day. The children go to Chapel, which is on campus, once a week or every other week depending on if they are full or part-time students. They do not have specific things to do at specific times and the children are free to learn about whatever they choose. In the four-year-olds classroom, one of the children was having a birthday party and his mother had hired a company to bring in reptiles, to teach all the students about them. They were all very well-behaved as they watched a huge lizard wander around the classroom. As I entered, a young girl informed me in a very serious voice that "today is reptile day," which was very sweet. In the next classroom I visited, the children were in music class, so I was able to look around the classroom a little more. They have sections of the room dedicated to specific things. One corner was science, another was drawing, and another was play. Each classroom that I visited had a pet. In most classrooms, it was a bunny.

The school had a very happy feeling to it. All the children were very talkative and interested in what I was doing there. They all seemed to be very intrigued by everything and they wanted to learn as much as they could. The music room was another reflection of this, the children had instruments that they learned how to play, and listened to while others played. The chapel is next to the music room. It is set up like a normal church. It has stained glass windows and wooden pews, and is where the children are taught age-appropriately about their religion and the bible. The children are taught how to sit in church, and how to behave. Usually they are in the Chapel for no longer than twenty minutes, once a week. At the beginning of the year, the students have their picture and their name on their cubby (locker), and by the end of the year, they can recognize their name, so they only put their names on the cubby. This is a great example of how the school works. They let the children develop on their own. Some children can spell when they first come to class, while others can not. It is the teacher's job to guide them in the right learning direction, without forcing them.

BACKGROUND

The school was established in 1986 by the First Lutheran Church of Manhattan Beach. The pastor at the time was Reverend Leslie Beale.

BIRD'S EYE VIEW

	Non-existent	Poor	Fair	Good	Excellent
Learning to Read Children learn to explore the world of books					🦉
Dress-Up Children experiment with different roles and imagination					🦉
Hand-Eye Children develop fine motor skills by using fingers and hands					🦉
Building Blocks Children practice symbolic representation. They are developing an understanding of the relationships between size and shape, and the basic math concepts of geometry and numbers					🦉
Arts and Crafts Children are developing small muscle control as well as creativity					🦉
Body Coordination Children crawl through tunnels, climb and balance					🦉
Meeting Time Gathering place to listen to the teacher and to stories					🦉
Weights and Measures Water and Sand tables					🦉
Beakers and Bunnies Classroom pets, aquariums....planting...					🦉
Counting 1-2-3 A good preschool will stock basic early-learner software such as phonics or counting games				🦉	
Outdoor Play Encourage large muscle control and coordination					🦉

Q & A

HOW THEY LEARN

What is your school's teaching philosophy? We believe that children, wonderful gifts of God, learn most effectively through play in an environment that purposefully encourages exploration and offers age-appropriate activities.

How do you implement the philosophy? All of our teachers are trained in the developmental philosophy. Learning activities are planned that offer a wide array of opportunities to explore and investigate this world.

What specialty teachers are brought into the school? We bring in specialty teachers for music, Spanish, and physical education.

What is the teaching method? Developmental.

At what age do the children start? To what age is the school licensed? The children may start at two-and-a-half. We are licensed for children to six years of age.

HOW TO GET IN

Are there open house dates? When are tours given? We do tours/open houses throughout the school year by appointment. Group tours take place in January, February and March.

Is there an interview? With the child or without? With the child.

Is preference given to applicants whose siblings are alumni? Yes.

Are letters of recommendation encouraged? From what types of people? No.

How many applications do you receive each year? About 300.

How many open spots are there each year? 75.

What are some of the schools that children go on to after finishing their education at your preschool? Manhattan Beach Public Schools, Hermosa Beach Public Schools, American Martyrs School, Journey of Faith School.

PIGGY BANK

Apart from tuition, what other fees do you charge? A registration fee of $125.

How is tuition broken down? It varies according to the number of days the child attends per week. Preschool only: for two mornings per week: $310; three mornings per week: $455 four mornings per week: $550; and five mornings per week: $780 monthly.

What are the different payment plans available? None. Payment is due on or before the tenth of each month.

What is the fee schedule? No feedback received.

Is there a contract? There is a contract.

Do you have a tuition insurance program? No tuition insurance.

HELPING HANDS

What accreditation is necessary for the teachers to work at your school? All teachers must have completed a minimum of 12 early childhood education units at the college level. All of our teachers have completed at least 18 units. Three have a B.A. and one has an M.A. in education.

How many teachers are there? There are ten teachers.

How many aides? One aide.

Do they come from other preschools? They have all taught at other preschools except one.

IN THE 'ROOM

What's the adult-to-child ratio? 10:1.

What are the policies for initial separation between parent and child? Parents are encouraged to bring their child to our school for a visit a week or two prior to the beginning of their adventure with us. The first week, the parent may stay for an hour or two if necessary each day. They are encouraged to let go fairly rapidly to facilitate the child's trust of the teachers.

Can you visit any time unannounced? Yes.

What are the hours? Open from 7 a.m.-6 p.m. for child care. Preschool is from 9 a.m.-12 p.m.

Do you offer early bird or after-hours pickup? If so, is there an extra fee? Extended care is $5 per hour.

Please describe a typical day for a child at your school. Drop-off is from 9-9:15 a.m., 9:15-9:30 a.m. is bible story read (or told to children through praise song and prayer), free time on the playground until 10:15 a.m., clean-up and potty time until 10:30 a.m., snack time until 10:45 a.m., and center time and indoor free play is from 10:45-11:40 a.m. Various centers are set up to explore the Theme of the Week (insects, trees, etc.). Circle time is from 11:40 a.m. until noon, where books related to the weekly theme are read to the children, and they sing.

What kinds of academic activities are offered? Pre-math, pre-science and pre-reading.

What kinds of art activities are offered? The easels are always set up for painting. Drawing, cutting, pasting, and using a wide array of media to express their ideas.

Is the child's time structured or unstructured, or a mixture of both? It's a mixture. We provide an overall plan for activities but as the day unfolds, we adapt to what happens.

If a child is not interested in a particular activity, does he/she have other choices or is he/she encouraged to try it anyway? We subscribe to a gentle "try it, you'll like it" approach but never force the issue.

How are disputes handled when they occur between the children? They learn to apologize when they're out of line and accept an apology from another child.

When and for how long is nap time? Nap time is between 12:30 p.m. to about 2:30 p.m.

What kinds of beds do you use? We use washable cots that have four inch legs. Each child provides his/her own bedding and we store it in plastic boxes.

What do you do when a child is dropped off in the morning and is obviously not well? What do you do when a child becomes sick during the day? When a child is dropped off who is obviously not well, we send the child home with the parent. When a child gets sick during school hours, we isolate that child from the other students and call the parent to pick him/her up. While waiting, we keep the child warm and comfortable.

Can you accommodate children with special needs? Our campus is on a slope with many stairs. We have accommodated children with Asberger's Syndrome.

KEEPING IT SAFE

Please describe your security measures for arriving and leaving the school. Our campus is protected by a six foot tall wrought Iron fence. The gates are equipped with coded locks. There is a call box at the front gate for strangers to use to request entrance. Our policy is to go to the gate and visually inspect visitors prior to opening the gate.

What medical supplies do you have on hand, and what medical experience does your staff have? Is your staff trained in CPR? All teaching staff are child/infant/adult CPR certified. Several have completed the Red Cross 15-hour first aide course. We keep the standard first aid supplies on hand plus mouthpieces for CPR.

Please describe your earthquake-preparedness plan, and what special equipment do you have on hand in the event of a disaster? Special equipment: 150 bins that contain three days of food and water, a mylar blanket and a light stick. Children supply their own bag of personal supplies (a change of clothes, sweatshirt, pictures of mom and dad, and a special toy). We also have hatchets, crowbars and a special wrench to shut off the gas line. Children are regularly drilled on fire/earthquake and disaster procedures.

SWINGS 'N THINGS

Please describe your playground. Does it have plenty of shade? Our playground was completely remodeled during the summer of 2002. It is spacious and the play equipment is embedded in the most forgiving surface: sand. We have four swings in addition to our large play structure. There is a separate area where the children may ride tricycles. There is a shade structure overhead.

Do you put sunscreen on the children? We do help the children apply sunscreen.

What kind of toilet training is available? None. Children must be potty-trained before they are admitted.

HELPING OUT

What kinds of fundraising events are at your school each year? We have a Trike-A-Thon each year in the spring. Everyone has a great time and we also raise money. The children are delighted to participate and receive a special certificate for their contribution to the event.

How much participation is required by each parent? Parent participation is not required.

KEEPING IN TOUCH

How do you communicate with parents? Is there a newsletter or phone tree? We have a newsletter and we also distribute letters to parents. The teachers as well as the office staff are happy to answer questions.

Does the school publish an address book with all the parents' information in it? Yes, with permission.

preschool

FIRST PRESBYTERIAN NURSERY SCHOOL

1248 Second St.
Santa Monica, CA 90401
Phone: (310) 451-9259
www.first-pres.net
See Map D on page 286

Contact: Mary Hartzell, Director

- ACCREDITATION: NAEYC
- NOT-FOR-PROFIT
- FINANCIAL AID IS AVAILABLE
- NUMBER OF KIDS: 110
- TUITION: CALL SCHOOL
- WE HAVE KIDS WITH SPECIAL NEEDS

WHEN TO APPLY: APPLICATIONS ACCEPTED JANUARY-DECEMBER FOR THE FOLLOWING SEPTEMBER. CUT OFF DATE IS IN DECEMBER.

First Presbyterian Nursery School began in 1959, among rolling hills and an ocean view. Although skyscrapers now surround them, the school has maintained its sense of community. Their curriculum emerges from the children's interests and investigations. The children decide their day in a morning meeting. Adults may consider it playing, but it is the children's work, investigation and ways of figuring things out. Spanning the walls, windows, and almost every available surface are very creative and innovative art projects. The most prominent are variations on the Taffy Tower. This started with a field trip to the tower, then the children drew (created "blue prints") of what their own tower would look like. In the classrooms, there are additional sculptures and creations. Each classroom has individual rooms within the classroom for art, imaginative play etc.

First Presbyterian Nursery School also documents daily progress, thoughts, discoveries and inquiries, and these are recorded in writing, in photographs and in artwork. There is a wall of compelling self-portraits, and a photo wall in each classroom, with photographs that capture the essence of each child. "It is amazing what you understand about how and what a child is thinking, if you listen to them," says Mary Hartzell. Hartzell has been the school director for twenty years, but she has also been here for forty years.

Children are divided into "school groupings" and stay together for two to three years. "We are committed to quality early education, and what supports that. The child, the teacher and the family are all protagonists in the learning process. We are not a school to do more, better, faster. When you do things faster, there is a depth and strength that is missed. We actually slow things down, not speed them up! Children only have a short attention span for things we want them to do. On their own, sometimes their attention span lasts for days, even weeks," explains Hartzell. The school believes in a strong sense of collaboration between teachers, parents, and children.

BACKGROUND

First Presbyterian Nursery School was established in 1959. Eleanor Dilworth was the first director, followed by Ida Bucher, and now Mary Hartzell.

Bird's Eye View

	Non-existent	Poor	Fair	Good	Excellent
Learning to Read Children learn to explore the world of books					✓
Dress-Up Children experiment with different roles and imagination					✓
Hand-Eye Children develop fine motor skills by using fingers and hands					✓
Building Blocks Children practice symbolic representation. They are developing an understanding of the relationships between size and shape, and the basic math concepts of geometry and numbers					✓
Arts and Crafts Children are developing small muscle control as well as creativity					✓
Body Coordination Children crawl through tunnels, climb and balance					✓
Meeting Time Gathering place to listen to the teacher and to stories					✓
Weights and Measures Water and Sand tables					✓
Beakers and Bunnies Classroom pets, aquariums....planting...					✓
Counting 1-2-3 A good preschool will stock basic early-learner software such as phonics or counting games					✓
Outdoor Play Encourage large muscle control and coordination					✓

Q & A

HOW THEY LEARN

What is your school's teaching philosophy? The teaching method is the Reggio Emilia approach to early childhood education.

How do you implement the philosophy? Through teacher mentoring, curriculum and environment.

What specialty teachers are brought into the school? No feedback received.

What is the teaching method? Developmental.

At what age do the children start? To what age is the school licensed? Two-and-a-half to five years old.

HOW TO GET IN

Are there open house dates? When are tours given? There are once-a-month tours on Tuesdays at 9:30 a.m.

Is there an interview? With the child or without? No.

Is preference given to applicants whose siblings are alumni? Yes.

Are letters of recommendation encouraged? From what types of people? No.

How many applications do you receive each year? Up to 200.

How many open spots are there each year? 40-50.

What are some of the schools that children go on to after finishing their education at your preschool? Franklin, Roosevelt, Canyon, Crossroads, P.S. #1, Wildwood.

PIGGY BANK

Apart from tuition, what other fees do you charge? There is a registration fee of $100 and an application fee of $50.

What are the different payment plans available? One annual payment, four payments, or ten payments.

What is the fee schedule? Payments are due the first of the month.

Is there a contract? Yes.

Do you have a tuition insurance program? No.

HELPING HANDS

What accreditation is necessary for the teachers to work at your school? Minimum of 12 ECE credits.

How many teachers are there? Twenty teachers.

How many aides? No feedback received.

Do they come from other preschools? Most have experience at other schools.

IN THE 'ROOM

What's the adult-to-child ratio? Varies from 1:8 to 1:2, depending on the groups.

What are the policies for initial separation between parent and child? Parents stay until the child is comfortable.

Can you visit any time unannounced? Yes.

What are the hours? 9 a.m.-12:30 p.m.

Do you offer early bird or after-hours pick-up? If so, is there an extra fee? An extra fee for early care (8:30-9 a.m.) and extended care (12:30-5:30 p.m.).

Please describe a typical day for a child at your school. Morning meetings, small group activities, snack, inside/outside experiences, stories, songs, lunch, closing circle.

What kinds of academic activities are offered? Science investigations, beginning experiences in literacy, reading, writing and drawing.

What kinds of art activities are offered? Watercolors, paint, charcoal, clay, wire, wood, tile, fabric and many other materials.

Is the child's time structured or unstructured, or a mixture of both? Both.

If a child is not interested in a particular activity, does he/she have other choices or is he/she encouraged to try it anyway? Both techniques are used, depending on the activities or situations.

How are disputes handled when they occur between the children? Teacher intervention, encouraging problem-solving, and discussion between children.

When and for how long is nap time? One hour.

What kinds of beds do you use? Cots or mats.

What do you do when a child is dropped off in the morning and is obviously not well? What do you do when a child becomes sick during the day? Call the parents to pick up the child.

Can you accommodate children with special needs? Sometimes.

KEEPING IT SAFE

Please describe your security measures for arriving and leaving the school. The entrance has two separate gates. The second gate is accessible only by keypad and code.

What medical supplies do you have on hand, and what medical experience does your staff have? Is your staff trained in CPR? Basic medical supplies. All teachers are trained in First Aid and CPR.

Please describe your earthquake-preparedness plan, and what special equipment do you have on hand in the event of a disaster? We have First Aid kits, food and emergency supplies to last three days.

SWINGS 'N THINGS

Please describe your playground. Does it have plenty of shade? Two playgrounds, two sandboxes, several climbing structures, woodworking area, outdoor studio area, outdoor stage, hard surface for balls, wooden bike path, chicken coop.

Do you put sunscreen on the children? No feedback received.

What kind of toilet training is available? Children have the option to wear diapers or use the toilet, whichever they are most comfortable doing.

HELPING OUT

What kinds of fundraising events are at your school each year? Annual giving, family festival, silent auction, bake sales, holiday sales.

How much participation is required by each parent? No requirement—as much or as little as you like.

KEEPING IN TOUCH

How do you communicate with parents? Is there a newsletter or phone tree? Daily journals, class notes, newsletters, email, phone tree.

Does the school publish an address book with all the parents' information in it? Yes.

preschool to kindergarten

FLINTRIDGE MONTESSORI

739 Foothill Blvd.
La Cañada Flintridge, CA 91011
Phone: (818) 790-8844
www.flintridge-montessori.com
See Map B on page 286

Contact: Rohini David

- ACCREDITATION: NONE
- FOR-PROFIT
- FINANCIAL AID IS NOT AVAILABLE
- NUMBER OF KIDS: 95
- TUITION: $420-$760 MONTH
- WE HAVE KIDS WITH SPECIAL NEEDS

WHEN TO APPLY: ONGOING, BASED ON AVAILABILITY

The Montessori-based teaching philosophy is known throughout the world, and this Montessori school appears much more stringent in comparison with others, based on its sense of structure, academics and admission. Founded in June of 2000, the Flintridge Montessori School currently has 95 children enrolled between its preschool and kindergarten programs. The teacher-to-student ratio is 10:1 and the look and feel of the school is affable and cheery with a playground set in the middle of the courtyard. Amongst the ten fully qualified teachers, the attrition rate is high, as seven out of ten of them have been on board since the inception of the school.

Rohini David shares director responsibilities with three other women. During our conversation, I get the sense that this school means business and it wants to foster these students with academics starting as young as preschool. Of course, there's still running and playing and the plethora of "preschool" activities, but academic excellence and socialization skills are underscored as the leitmotif of the school. Rohini states that our children "become very socially advanced, well adjusted and confident young people."

Through various areas of study (language, math, sensorial and practical life exercises) there are different materials and concepts introduced that not only bestow knowledge but "make the child independent of the adult." Additionally, karate, gym, ballet, modern dance, art and hands-on computer through an instructor are introduced at this early age. Altogether, the school presents quite an array of challenging activities for its preschoolers.

BACKGROUND

The school was established in June 2000.

BIRD'S EYE VIEW

	Non-existent	Poor	Fair	Good	Excellent
Learning to Read Children learn to explore the world of books					✓
Dress-Up Children experiment with different roles and imagination					✓
Hand-Eye Children develop fine motor skills by using fingers and hands					✓
Building Blocks Children practice symbolic representation. They are developing an understanding of the relationships between size and shape, and the basic math concepts of geometry and numbers					✓
Arts and Crafts Children are developing small muscle control as well as creativity					✓
Body Coordination Children crawl through tunnels, climb and balance					✓
Meeting Time Gathering place to listen to the teacher and to stories					✓
Weights and Measures Water and Sand tables				✓	
Beakers and Bunnies Classroom pets, aquariums....planting...					✓
Counting 1-2-3 A good preschool will stock basic early-learner software such as phonics or counting games					✓
Outdoor Play Encourage large muscle control and coordination				✓	

Q & A

HOW THEY LEARN

What is your school's teaching philosophy? Montessori-based.

How do you implement the philosophy? What specialty teachers are brought into the school? We bring in people from the community—firemen, policemen, etc.

What is the teaching method? Montessori method.

At what age do the children start? To what age is the school licensed? 2 years to 6.

HOW TO GET IN

Are there open house dates? When are tours given? Ongoing, contact school for details.

Is there an interview? With the child or without? Yes, with the child.

Is preference given to applicants whose siblings are alumni? Yes.

Are letters of recommendation encouraged? From what types of people? Letters are encouraged from alumni.

How many applications do you receive each year? From 50-60.

How many open spots are there each year? Approximately 30, but it varies from year to year.

What are some of the schools that children go on to after finishing their education at your preschool? No feedback received.

PIGGY BANK

Apart from tuition, what other fees do you charge? There is a $100 application fee and a $125 registration fee, $200-250 for materials, $30/month diaper fee.

What are the different payment plans available? There are varied plans; contact the school for details.

How is the tuition broken down? $420-760 per month.

Is there a contract? No feedback received.

Do you have a tuition insurance program? Yes, half a month's tuition deposit.

HELPING HANDS

What accreditation is necessary for the teachers to work at your school? A minimum of 12 ECE units and two years' work experience is required.

How many teachers are there? Ten teachers.

How many aides? One aide.

Do they come from other preschools? No feedback received.

IN THE 'ROOM

What's the adult-to-child ratio? 10:1.

What are the policies for initial separation between parent and child? Allowed, but not encouraged to drop in during the day. Can stay with the child at the beginning of the school year.

Can you visit any time unannounced? Yes, of course.

What are the hours? 7 a.m.-6 p.m.

Please describe a typical day for a child at your school. Free play, circle time, working with Montessori materials, lunch, nap time, circle time again. Outdoor play and extracurricular activities begin after 3 p.m.

What kinds of academic activities are offered? Language, math, sensorial and practical life exercises.

What kinds of art activities are offered? Piano, dance, varied arts, and hands-on computer.

Is the child's time structured or unstructured, or a mixture of both? Both.

If a child is not interested in a particular activity, does he/she have other choices or is he/she encouraged to try it anyway? Yes.

How are disputes handled when they occur between the children? We appeal to their senses—make eye contact and speak to the child, drawing out the reason for bad behavior.

When and for how long is nap time? 12:30 p.m.-2:30 p.m.

What kinds of beds do you use? We use cots.

What do you do when a child is dropped off in the morning and is obviously not well? What do you do when a child becomes sick during the day? We have the parent take the child home until he/she feels better. We call the parents immediately, isolate the child from others and wait for the parent to arrive.

Can you accommodate children with special needs? Only a few.

KEEPING IT SAFE

Please describe your security measures for arriving and leaving the school. The full signature of parents is recorded. Non-family members must have written authorization.

What medical supplies do you have on hand, and what medical experience does your staff have? Is your staff trained in CPR? All teachers are trained in first aid and CPR.

Please describe your earthquake-preparedness plan, and what special equipment do you have on hand in the event of a disaster? Each child has an earthquake kit in their cubby, and earthquake drills are run once a month.

SWINGS 'N THINGS

Please describe your playground. Does it have plenty of shade? There is plenty of shade.

Do you put sunscreen on the children? We put sunscreen on the children.

What kind of toilet training is available? Between the age 2 to 3 1/2 toilet training.

HELPING OUT

What kinds of fundraising events are at your school each year? There is a silent auction in December and a spring fundraiser.

How much participation is required by each parent? Participation is required, but we only get about 80% participation.

KEEPING IN TOUCH

How do you communicate with parents? Is there a newsletter or phone tree? We meet parents in the morning. There is a newsletter every three months.

Does the school publish an address book with all the parents' information in it? No, information is kept confidential.

school to kindergarten

FOUNTAIN DAY SCHOOL

1128 N. Orange Grove Ave.
West Hollywood, CA 90046
Phone: (323) 654-8958
See Map C on page 286
www.fountaindayschool.com

Contact: Ms. Jane Dwinell, Principal

- ACCREDITATION: NONE
- FOR-PROFIT
- FINANCIAL AID IS AVAILABLE TO ONGOING FAMILIES ONLY
- NUMBER OF KIDS: 118
- TUITION: $1,250 MONTH
- WE HAVE KIDS WITH SPECIAL NEEDS

WHEN TO APPLY: YEAR-ROUND. REGISTRATION IS IN APRIL.

As you enter the Foutain Day School, you walk past a "peace pole." There are three thousand of these around the world, and Fountain Day has number one. There is a definite kindred spirit to the environment. "Mr. Andrew," my utterly charming tour guide (and the school's general manager), teachers and administrators (and me!) are addressed as Miss or Mister, and your first name to continue the family type feel and relationship. This gem of a school was inspiring. That is how I knew I had stumbled upon something truly special, and by the time I completed the tour, I was excited and energized, and wanted to attend the school myself!

The campus itself is impressive. They are constantly improving and evolving as a campus and community. There is a pool for swimming lessons with year-round swimming at least twice a week, a science yard, a completely revamped playground, and a brand new parking lot, with a turn-around for parents to drop-off/pick-up their children. This is not a traditional drop-off, the school doesn't really encourage just dropping your child at school, but creating the transition into the school day with them when you are 'leaving' them at school. "We guide them into the things that make the family stronger and united", says Mr. Andrew. Fountain Day school really services the working parent, and understands that need for flexibility and support.

The curriculum includes yoga on Wednesdays, dance on Thursdays and exotic animals that come to visit! They also have the latest media technology, including computers and projectors. There are also two full time cleaning staff, two full service kitchens, and Whole Foods provides the all organic food and snacks! Though the school is non-denominational, they pray at lunchtime. Children eagerly greeted me and proudly showed me what they were working on. There is a definite confidence and full-self expression in this huge extended "family." As I completed my tour, I was given a "Kitchen Keepsakes" from the Fountain Day Family cookbook, which parents receive on their tour! Family recipes, I'm sure!

As of fall 2008, Fountain Day only goes through Kindergarten. There was an increasing demand for preschool by parents and Fountain Day wanted to meet that need.

If you're looking for a fabulous preschool, this is it!

Background

Fountain Day School was founded in 1957 by Ms. Evangeline Brooks. It began as a pre-school for working families and single mothers who found themselves in need of childcare. Ms. Brooks was a big-hearted woman who cared for children as if they were her own. The original building included her personal apartments upstairs. Often in those days, Ms. Brooks would end up babysitting children late into the night. Forty-eight years later, the school has a student population of 175-200 students and incorporates an elementary school as well. Fountain Day School is now operated by her daughters, Ms. Mary and Ms. Jane. Ms. Mary's two daughters work in the pre-school and a great-grandchild is a student here, representing four generations of family love and service to the community.

Bird's Eye View

	Non-existent	Poor	Fair	Good	Excellent
Learning to Read Children learn to explore the world of books					✓
Dress-Up Children experiment with different roles and imagination					✓
Hand-Eye Children develop fine motor skills by using fingers and hands					✓
Building Blocks Children practice symbolic representation. They are developing an understanding of the relationships between size and shape, and the basic math concepts of geometry and numbers					✓
Arts and Crafts Children are developing small muscle control as well as creativity					✓
Body Coordination Children crawl through tunnels, climb and balance					✓
Meeting Time Gathering place to listen to the teacher and to stories					✓
Weights and Measures Water and Sand tables					✓
Beakers and Bunnies Classroom pets, aquariums....planting...					✓
Counting 1-2-3 A good preschool will stock basic early-learner software such as phonics or counting games					✓
Outdoor Play Encourage large muscle control and coordination					✓

Q & A

HOW THEY LEARN

What is your school's teaching philosophy? Our teaching method consists of the carefully integrated "Open Court, Hot Teaching" System. In this philosophy, each subject material plays an important, well-thought-out role in the school program as a whole. Teachers are active and engaged moving around the class getting full participation from all their students. Class sizes are kept small with a teacher and assistant per class to provide the maximum attention and supervision. Students and parents address our teachers and administrators by using a salutation such as Mr. or Ms. and then their first names. This helps foster the family-like image/relationship we provide at our school: caring with respect and discipline.

How do you implement the philosophy? Most of the teachers have been with Fountain Day School between six and twenty-seven years. We have 48 years of experience working with families making education a fun and exciting experience. Our results speak for themselves with CTBS scores among the best in the nation. We have regular staff meetings to incorporate new opportunities.

What specialty teachers are brought into the school? We have specialty teachers to teach yoga, dance, and physical education. We bring in various artists and performers and educators during the year to share their specialized knowledge with our students.

What is the teaching method? Traditional structure to try new things that work in our changing environment.

At what age do the children start? Our preschool starts with 2-year-olds (very limited and competitive enrollment). Our facility is licensed by the Department of Social Services.

HOW TO GET IN

Are there open house dates? When are tours given? Starting in mid-September through May, Tuesdays at 11am.

Is there an interview? Our tours are part of the interview process.

Is preference given to applicants whose siblings are alumni? Siblings, yes, alumni, no.

Are letters of recommendation encouraged? From what types of people? Absolutely. From community members, especially from charities the family is involved in.

How many applications do you receive each year? 50-200 per year.

How many open spots are there each year? 25-50.

What are some of the schools that children go on to after finishing their education at your preschool? After preschool, most children stay with us through Kindergarten, or continue their education at local private schools including Campbell Hall, Buckley, Pacific Hills, L.A. Magnet Schools.

PIGGY BANK

Apart from tuition, what other fees do you charge? There is a $650 new family fee and a $65 application fee.

How is tuition broken down? Preschool is $1,250 per month with a 12-month contract.

What are the different payment plans available? Pre-pay with discount. Post-dated checks or credit card (no discount).

What is the fee schedule? Tuition payment arrangements must be made with administration prior to the academic school year.

Is there a contract? Yes, our contracts are twelve months and renewable yearly. Families or school may cancel the contract at any time with a 30-day notice.

Do you have a tuition insurance program? No feedback received.

HELPING HANDS

What accreditation is necessary for the teachers to work at your school? Preschool requires valid ECE units. Elementary school, a minimum B.A. or B.S. and passing the CBEST, plus one to five years of experience.

How many teachers are there? Twenty teachers.

How many aides? No feedback received.

Do they come from other preschools? Most have been with us for over two years.

IN THE 'ROOM

What's the adult-to-child ratio? 1:7 in preschool.

What are the policies for initial separation between parent and child? Each family is supported as individuals through this difficult process. We have a two-way mirror in our office for parents' viewing needs.

Can you visit any time unannounced? Yes, but we encourage families not to disturb the children while they are eating or, as in the case of preschoolers, napping.

What are the hours? Hours of operation are 8 a.m.-5 p.m., and are inclusive in the tuition.

Do you offer early bird or after-hours pick-up? If so, is there an extra fee? There is a late fee charge for pick-ups after 6 p.m.

Please describe a typical day for a child at your school. 8:30 a.m. flag salute in the yard, academics, fun, academics, fun, lunch, fun, academics and more fun.

What kinds of academic activities are offered? We specialize in the basic fundamentals of reading, writing and arithmetic.

What kinds of art activities are offered? Art is a favorite activity in our school, incorporated into school projects as well as school-wide, competition-organized shows.

Is the child's time structured or unstructured, or a mixture of both? Both. Structure is encouraged to help children with focus and social discipline. We believe it helps them establish boundaries and preferred behavior. Unstructured activities are provided to help children discover personal attributes and allow their imagination to self-express.

If a child is not interested in a particular activity, does he/she have other choices or is he/she encouraged to try it anyway? Children are encouraged to try new activities and participate with the teacher and their fellow students.

How are disputes handled when they occur between the children? We allow children to experience the "real world." We encourage children to explore conflict resolution amongst themselves. When necessary a teacher or administrator gets involved. When Preschool children fight over a toy, it's the toy that gets the "time out."

When and for how long is nap time? Naps are 1-3 p.m.

What kinds of beds do you use? We use cots.

What do you do when a child is dropped off in the morning and is obviously not well? What do you do when a child becomes sick during the day? If a child is obviously not well, the parent/guardian will be called to pick up the child. If a child is sick or injured we call the parent and let the child communicate with the parents, then we decide with the parent what action is necessary for the welfare of the child.

Can you accommodate children with special needs? We can accommodate some children with special needs, i.e., speech impediments.

KEEPING IT SAFE

Please describe your security measures for arriving and leaving the school. One family entrance only, with doorknobs high up at parent eye level.

What medical supplies do you have on hand, and what medical experience does your staff have? Is your staff trained in CPR? All staff are Red-Cross trained and have updated certificates. Medicine is provided and administered with parental written consent.

Please describe your earthquake-preparedness plan, and what special equipment do you have on hand in the event of a disaster? We have a complete and detailed earthquake-preparedness plan. Each class is equipped with earthquake kits that are updated regularly.

SWINGS 'N THINGS

Please describe your playground. Does it have plenty of shade? The playground has plenty of shade. The outdoor pool is securely enclosed and locked and also has a canopy for sunny summer months.

Do you put sunscreen on the children? We will put sunscreen on the children if requested and the correct product is supplied.

What kind of toilet training is available? We do potty train.

HELPING OUT

What kinds of fundraising events are at your school each year? The Friends of Fountain Day School is our parent committee that has one or two opportunities a year for fundraising events.

How much participation is required by each parent? No feedback received.

KEEPING IN TOUCH

How do you communicate with parents? Is there a newsletter or phone tree? Face-to-face, FOFDS meetings and mail, or a message in their child's backpack.

Does the school publish an address book with all the parents' information in it? No! Parent information is strictly confidential.

preschool to 2nd grade

GLENDALE MONTESSORI

413 W. Doran St.
Glendale, Ca 91203
Phone: (818) 240-9415
www.glendalemontessorielementaryschool.com
See Map B on page 286

Contact: Arnolda C. Utrecht

- ACCREDITATION: NCME/AMS/AMI
- FOR-PROFIT
- FINANCIAL AID IS NOT AVAILABLE
- NUMBER OF KIDS: 75
- TUITION: $850-$900 MONTH
- WE HAVE KIDS WITH SPECIAL NEEDS

WHEN TO APPLY: ANY TIME DURING THE YEAR. NO CUTOFF DATE UNLESS FULL.

Glendale Montessori is the sort of school that you almost don't want to tell anyone about. It's such a gem that I was tempted to keep its whereabouts a secret. When you first look at the school, it appears to have an urban setting, with a paved front yard and three classrooms grouped around a common courtyard. Don't let looks deceive you. If you look behind the caretaker's bungalow in the adjoining lot, you'll discover that the entire space has been converted into a shaded playground with a variety of climbing structures and masses of (dust-free) clean sand to play in, giving it the feel of being in a very rural setting. Mrs. Utrecht, the school's director, proudly tells me that when they took over the property, they planted all the trees that we can see today.

I arrived one morning to watch a friend's daughter graduate from the preschool. It was a very sweet affair—the ceremony was not too long and all the kids seemed so happy. Mercifully absent is the non-stop plea for funds over and above tuition. Glendale Montessori does not do fundraising, however, they are open to parent participation for special events. I saw a few helping out that morning. Most of the kids will stay for first and second grade. Mrs. Utrecht, when asked why she won't add more grades, simply says, "I feel the school is just fine the way it is." She runs the school with an understated grace, in a reserved but always approachable manner.

The Montessori program allows children to work at their own pace and developmental level. There's no need to rush a child who is not grasping certain concepts, or to hold back a gifted child who is ready for more. Here at GM, the method of teaching is sensorial as well as concrete. An example of this would be when a child begins writing numbers with a pencil, it is because he/she started out by writing the number in sand or tracing a sandpaper number with his/her finger. All the teachers have completed special Montessori training in addition to their regular credentials and many of them have been here for over ten years. This says alot about the school. The classrooms are clean and well-stocked with materials that are state-of-the-art. At GMS, one thing is very clear: the children are the focus. All the of the school's resources go back to the students with the goal of providing them with the best education possible. Definitely worth a visit.

BACKGROUND

Glendale Montessori was opened by Arnolda C. Utrecht in 1971. It was expanded in 1986 school by adding a huge playground on the property next door.

BIRD'S EYE VIEW

	Non-existent	Poor	Fair	Good	Excellent
Learning to Read Children learn to explore the world of books					✓
Dress-Up Children experiment with different roles and imagination					✓
Hand-Eye Children develop fine motor skills by using fingers and hands					✓
Building Blocks Children practice symbolic representation. They are developing an understanding of the relationships between size and shape, and the basic math concepts of geometry and numbers					✓
Arts and Crafts Children are developing small muscle control as well as creativity					✓
Body Coordination Children crawl through tunnels, climb and balance					✓
Meeting Time Gathering place to listen to the teacher and to stories					✓
Weights and Measures Water and Sand tables					✓
Beakers and Bunnies Classroom pets, aquariums....planting...					✓
Counting 1-2-3 A good preschool will stock basic early-learner software such as phonics or counting games					✓
Outdoor Play Encourage large muscle control and coordination					✓

Q & A

HOW THEY LEARN

What is your school's teaching philosophy? We use the Montessori method of teaching.

How do you implement the philosophy? According to Maria Montessori's philosophy.

What specialty teachers are brought into the school? We have a music specialist and a Spanish teacher.

What is the teaching method? Montessori.

At what age do the children start? To what age is the school licensed? Ages 2 (if toilet trained) up to 6 years old.

HOW TO GET IN

Are there open house dates? When are tours

given? No open houses. Tours are 9.30 a.m.-11 a.m. daily by appointment, and from 1-2 p.m., also by appointment.

Is there an interview? With the child or without? There is an interview and we do need to see the child before enrollment.

Is preference given to applicants whose siblings are alumni? Yes.

Are letters of recommendation encouraged? From what types of people? No.

How many applications do you receive each year? About 100.

How many open spots are there each year? 25.

What are some of the schools that children go on to after finishing their education at your preschool? Glendale Montessori Elementary School, Campbell Hall, Polytechnic and Crestview.

PIGGY BANK

Apart from tuition, what other fees do you charge? There is a $250 application fee.

How is tuition broken down? Tuition is $850 for 8.30 a.m.-1 p.m. and $900 for 8.30 a.m.-3 p.m.

What are the different payment plans available? Parents pay monthly.

What is the fee schedule? See above.

Is there a contract? Yes.

Do you have a tuition insurance program? No insurance. If parents leave before the end of the year, we do not hold them to pay the remainder.

HELPING HANDS

What accreditation is necessary for the teachers to work at your school? A four-year college degree plus a Montessori teaching credential.

How many teachers are there? Eight (including 1st and 2nd grade)

How many aides are there? None.

IN THE 'ROOM

What's the child-to-adult ratio? 12:1.

What are the policies for initial separation between parent and child? Several visits before enrollment. On the first day the child stays for one hours and gradually builds up to the full half-day or full day.

Can you visit any time unannounced? Yes.

What are the hours? 8 a.m.-3 p.m.

Do you offer early bird or after-hours pick-up? If so, is there an extra fee? Yes, and yes.

Please describe a typical day for a child at your school. Children arrive between 8 and 8:30 a.m. and is encouraged to choose their "favorite work." After their work is checked, they move on to the next work. There is 10am Spanish or music class, followed by 10:30 am Outside Play, 11:45 am lunchtime, 12:30 group. At 1, some of the children go home. Work time from 1-2:30 p.m., 3 p.m. school closes.

What kinds of academic activities are offered? All our work is geared towards developing concentration skills. We have an individual program for each child. In our multi-age classroom, children learn on different levels.

What kinds of art activities are offered? Art is an area of free choice as every is every area of our classrooms. This includes painting at the easel, cutting, drawing and coloring. Special art projects are done for each unit of study and for special occasions.

Is the child's time structured or unstructured, or a mixture of both? A mixture of both.

If a child is not interested in a particular activity, does he/she have other choices or is he/she encouraged to try it anyway? Yes, they have other choices; they sometimes they are encouraged to try it anyway.

How are disputes handled when they occur between the children? The child needs to find solutions but it is teacher guided.

When and for how long is nap time? No naptime. Children who need a nap leave at 1 p.m.

What kinds of beds do you use? No beds.

What do you do when a child is dropped off in the morning and is obviously not well? What do you do when a child becomes sick during the day? The child is brought to the office and the parent is called. If the child becomes sick during the day, then the child stays in the office until the parent arrives.

Can you accommodate children with special needs? We can accommodate some special needs, but it is limited. Inquire at school.

KEEPING IT SAFE

Please describe your security measures for arriving and leaving the school. Supervision at the gate. There are sign-in and sign-out sheets.

What medical supplies do you have on hand, and what medical experience does your staff have? Is your staff trained in CPR? Staff is CPR and First Aid certified, and there is a First Aid kit on the premises.

Please describe your earthquake-preparedness plan, and what special equipment do you have on hand in the event of a disaster? There are monthly earthquake and fire drills.

There is an earthquake kit available for each child.

SWINGS 'N THINGS

Please describe your playground. Does it have plenty of shade? Big, beautiful shady playground with ten huge trees and one small apricot fruit tree.

Do you put sunscreen on the children? Sunscreen is applied in the morning by the parents, and some give us their sunscreen cream to put on the children ourselves.

What kind of toilet training is available? Children arrive toilet trained, although we do expect accidents and are there to help the child if it happens.

HELPING OUT

What kinds of fundraising events are at your school each year? There is no fundraising.

How much participation is required by each parent? None. We ask for help at special events. Parents quite often offer to come in and teach the kids about something they do.

KEEPING IN TOUCH

How do you communicate with parents? Is there a newsletter or phone tree? The school publishes a newsletter that goes to parents.

Does the school publish an address book with all the parents' information in it? Yes.

preschool to 12th grade

HIGHLAND HALL WALDORF SCHOOL

17100 Superior St. Northridge, CA 91325
Phone: (818) 349-1394
www.highlandhall.org
See Map A on page 286

Contact: Edward J. Eadon

- ACCREDITATION: WASC, AWSNA
- NOT-FOR-PROFIT
- FINANCIAL AID IS AVAILABLE
- NUMBER OF KIDS: 92
- TUITION: $11,500-$12,500 YEAR
- WE HAVE KIDS WITH SPECIAL NEEDS

WHEN TO APPLY: OPEN ENROLLMENT POLICY; APPLICATIONS ACCEPTED ANY TIME WE HAVE OPENINGS.

The landscape alone makes this preschool an appetizing place to drop a child off every day for them to begin the first leg of their education. Set high on a hill in Northridge, the 11-acre campus that houses preschool through twelfth grade is a secure and secluded setting. The first Waldorf School was founded in 1919 in Stuttgart, Germany by Rudolf Steiner, an Austrian educator, scientist and philosopher. Waldorf education is a worldwide independent educational movement, with over 800 schools on six continents. In-the-box thinking and the test dogma are clearly not endorsed by this school. Highland Hall focuses on the arts, the environment, the individual and developmental learning, which lend to a very different overall feel.

The classrooms themselves are gorgeous and orderly, while at the same time, obviously filled to the brim with books, arts and crafts, dramatic play area, blocks and the usual accoutrements that go along with this age group in a learning environment. Seventy children are enrolled in the preschool with a teacher-to-student ratio of 1:15 (plus an assistant teacher), and while the importance placed on teaching children, beginning at an early age, that "society is not disposable," and the students have to learn to work things out.

Many of the students that start in the preschool will stay on at Highland Hall Waldorf to become "lifers." In other words, they stay enrolled through high school graduation. Approximately half of the students that start in the preschool or kindergarten graduate from the twelfth grade. Children here cook soup with their teacher, learn to help to clean up and are encouraged to become critical and independent thinkers. Art and the integration of art into academic learning is a staple in the Waldorf way of learning that does begin at this level. All in all, this is an amazing place for any child to begin the lifelong journey of education.

BACKGROUND

Established in 1955 by a group of individuals interested in starting a Waldorf school.

BIRD'S EYE VIEW

	Non-existent	Poor	Fair	Good	Excellent
Learning to Read Children learn to explore the world of books					✓
Dress-Up Children experiment with different roles and imagination					✓
Hand-Eye Children develop fine motor skills by using fingers and hands					✓
Building Blocks Children practice symbolic representation. They are developing an understanding of the relationships between size and shape, and the basic math concepts of geometry and numbers					✓
Arts and Crafts Children are developing small muscle control as well as creativity					✓
Body Coordination Children crawl through tunnels, climb and balance					✓
Meeting Time Gathering place to listen to the teacher and to stories					✓
Weights and Measures Water and Sand tables					✓
Beakers and Bunnies Classroom pets, aquariums....planting...					✓
Counting 1-2-3 A good preschool will stock basic early-learner software such as phonics or counting games				✓	
Outdoor Play Encourage large muscle control and coordination					✓

Q & A

HOW THEY LEARN

What is your school's teaching philosophy? Our curriculum and philosophy are based on Rudolf Steiner's view of human development. We strive to nurture the child's head, heart and hands through imaginative play, storytelling and circle games.

How do you implement the philosophy? The teachers consciously create a nurturing, home-like environment where the children's spiritual natures are recognized and their instinct for play realized.

What specialty teachers are brought into the school? No feedback received.

What is the teaching method? No feedback received.

At what age do the children start? 2 1/2.

To what age is the school licensed? No feedback received.

HOW TO GET IN

Are there open house dates? When are tours given? Call for a schedule.

Is there an interview? With the child or without? The interview consists of the teacher speaking with the parents while the child plays.

Is preference given to applicants whose siblings are alumni? Yes.

Are letters of recommendation encouraged? From what types of people? No.

How many applications do you receive each year? 45.

How many open spots are there each year? 18.

What are some of the schools that children go on to after finishing their education at your preschool? Our school goes through high school, and most students continue into kindergarten and then first grade.

PIGGY BANK

Apart from tuition, what other fees do you charge? There is a $1,000 entrance fee and a $100 application fee.

How is tuition broken down? $11,500-$12,500 per month.

What are the different payment plans available? Annual, semi-annual, quarterly and monthly payment plans.

What is the fee schedule? No feedback received.

Is there a contract? There is a contract.

Do you have a tuition insurance program? There is a tuition insurance program.

HELPING HANDS

What accreditation is necessary for the teachers to work at your school? Teachers must have Waldorf teacher training and early childhood education units.

How many teachers are there? Two teachers.

How many aides? Two assistants.

Do they come from other preschools? They do not usually come from other preschools.

IN THE 'ROOM

What's the adult-to-child ratio? Varies, from 2:10 to 2:15.

What are the policies for initial separation between parent and child? We consider the needs of each family on an individual basis, and the teachers guide and support the parents through this delicate process. For some children, success is on the first day. For others, the parent might stay for a few days to a week.

Can you visit any time unannounced? Yes.

What are the hours? 8 a.m.-3:15 p.m.

Do you offer early bird or after-hours pick-up? If so, is there an extra fee? Aftercare is from 3:15-6 p.m. for an extra fee.

Please describe a typical day for a child at your school. Our day class consists of a healthy balance between indoor free play, outdoor free play, circle time, story time, snack/lunch, nature walks, gardening and painting.

What kinds of academic activities are offered? We are a developmental, play-oriented preschool and do not offer academic activities.

What kinds of art activities are offered? Painting, drawing, candle making, baking and cooking.

Is the child's time structured or unstructured, or a mixture of both? A mixture of both.

If a child is not interested in a particular activity, does he/she have other choices or is he/she encouraged to try it anyway? During free play, either indoor or outdoor, the children can choose what they want to do. At circle time and story time, all children participate.

How are disputes handled when they occur between the children? With patience and understanding, we work to support the children as they master the necessary social skills to navigate throughout their day.

When and for how long is nap time? Nap time is from 12:30-2 p.m.

What kinds of beds do you use? We use covered cots with soft bedding.

What do you do when a child is dropped off in the morning and is obviously not well? What do you do when a child becomes sick during the day? We call the parents and send the child home.

Can you accommodate children with special needs? Sometimes, depending on the need.

KEEPING IT SAFE

Please describe your security measures for arriving and leaving the school. Parents sign children in and out. Our front gate is secured and coded. Any persons other than the child's parents who pick the child up must be on an emergency contact list and show identification.

What medical supplies do you have on hand, and what medical experience does your staff have? Is your staff trained in CPR? We have standard First Aid kits and all lead teachers are trained in CPR and First Aid.

Please describe your earthquake-preparedness plan, and what special equipment do you have on hand in the event of a disaster? We have an Earthquake Preparedness Committee, a plan and fully stocked supplies and equipment. We have regularly scheduled earthquake drills.

SWINGS 'N THINGS

Please describe your playground. Does it have plenty of shade? We have a large shaded playground with plenty of trees, grass, plants and a garden area. We have swings, a sandbox, wooden playhouse, slides, and a climbing structure. We also have a chicken coop.

Do you put sunscreen on the children? No feedback received.

What kind of toilet training is available? We do accept children who are not toilet trained and we work closely with the parents on this issue.

HELPING OUT

What kinds of fundraising events are at your school each year? There is an annual giving campaign, silent auctions, dinners, Jog-a-thons, etc.

How much participation is required by each parent? Parents are asked to volunteer 50 hours a year in such areas as working at fairs, attending parent/teacher conferences, working on a committee, etc.

KEEPING IN TOUCH

How do you communicate with parents? Is there a newsletter or phone tree? With a weekly news bulletin, a bi-monthly newsletter, class phone trees, monthly mailings, as well as letters and emails from teachers. We have parent evenings about every six weeks and regularly-scheduled parent conferences.

Does the school publish an address book with all the parents' information in it? Yes, unless a parent does not want their information published.

preschool to 6th grade

HOGG'S HOLLOW

4490 Cornishon Ave.
La Cañada, CA 91011
Phone: (818) 790-1700
www.hoggshollowschool.com
See Map B on page 286

Contact: Rose Hogg

- ACCREDITATION: NONE
- FOR-PROFIT
- FINANCIAL AID IS NOT AVAILABLE
- NUMBER OF KIDS: 27
- TUITION: $500-$895 MONTH
- WE HAVE KIDS WITH SPECIAL NEEDS

WHEN TO APPLY: THE APPLICATIONS FOR SEPTEMBER ARE DUE BY THE END OF FEBRUARY.

For a while, I was playing tennis every Friday up in La Cañada at the wonderful free tennis courts they have up there. One day while waiting for the other players, I noticed a sign that read "Hogg's Hollow." The name intrigued me and since the school was right across the street and I had some time, I decided to take a look. I let myself in through a gate and said hello to one of the teachers outside, and asked if I could go in. She told me that would be fine and that the owner was inside. I walked into the classroom and introduced myself to Rose Hogg (hence the name). She has been running this preschool for almost thirty years now. She opened the school in 1975 to provide a safe and happy place for her son and his friends in which to learn in.

The school shares its campus with an elementary school. In fact, this street has several schools on it and a large playing field and tennis courts where the children are frequently taken for fun and games. Field trips are another interesting thing about this preschool. As Rose Hogg says, "There is very little a teacher can compare to the enthusiasm children exhibit as a direct result of going on a field trip, be it a snail hunt, a trip to a construction site combined with a ride on a tractor, or a camping trip to a brand new spot where water-play is in abundance and the new signs are waiting to be explored." For these reasons and all the other obvious advantages of being outdoors, Hogg's Hollow students go on field trips three or four days out of every month. The school believes that lots of outdoor physical activities and their field trips during the year reflect a well-balanced curriculum, and make for happy and healthy children.

I saw a classroom full of children engaged in all sorts of activities. Some were writing, others painting and still more engaged in free play. Everyone was very busy indeed! I walked through the classroom and out into the yard which was small but well stocked with climbing equipment and tables on which to do art projects. A mother arrived with her child who was crying and I wondered how she was going to be able to leave, but as soon as she opened the gate, Rose welcomed the little chap into her arms and the crying stopped almost immediately. A very grateful mum said goodbye and left quietly leaving her son in what looked to me to be a very good pair of hands!

BACKGROUND

Rose Hogg opened the school in 1975 to provide a safe and happy place for her son and his friends to learn in, and has been running the preschool since then.

BIRD'S EYE VIEW

	Non-existent	Poor	Fair	Good	Excellent
Learning to Read Children learn to explore the world of books				✓	
Dress-Up Children experiment with different roles and imagination				✓	
Hand-Eye Children develop fine motor skills by using fingers and hands				✓	
Building Blocks Children practice symbolic representation. They are developing an understanding of the relationships between size and shape, and the basic math concepts of geometry and numbers			✓		
Arts and Crafts Children are developing small muscle control as well as creativity					✓
Body Coordination Children crawl through tunnels, climb and balance				✓	
Meeting Time Gathering place to listen to the teacher and to stories					✓
Weights and Measures Water and Sand tables					✓
Beakers and Bunnies Classroom pets, aquariums....planting...					✓
Counting 1-2-3 A good preschool will stock basic early-learner software such as phonics or counting games			✓		
Outdoor Play Encourage large muscle control and coordination					✓

Q & A

HOW THEY LEARN

What is your school's teaching philosophy? We view each child as a spiritual being with infinite potential.

How do you implement the philosophy? Our environment is tailored to the individual needs of our students. We provide activities that are involving by nature and challenge 3-5 year olds to excel.

What is the teaching method? As each student shows a readiness for learning, our instructor provides private lessons which enable the student to move forward at their own pace.

At what age do the children start? To what age is the school licensed? No feedback received.

HOW TO GET IN

Are there open house dates? When are tours given? No feedback received.

Is there an interview? With the child or without? No feedback received.

Is preference given to applicants whose siblings are alumni? Siblings given priority.

Are letters of recommendation encouraged? From what types of people? No feedback received.

How many applications do you receive each year? No feedback received.

How many open spots are there each year? No feedback received.

What are some of the schools that children go on to after finishing their education at your preschool? No feedback received.

PIGGY BANK

Apart from tuition, what other fees do you charge? $25 application fee.

What are the different payment plans available? No feedback received.

How is the tuition broken down? $500-$895 per month.

Is there a contract? No feedback received.

Do you have a tuition insurance program? No feedback received.

HELPING HANDS

What accreditation is necessary for the teachers to work at your school? No feedback received.

How many teachers are there? No feedback received.

How many aides? No feedback received.

Do they come from other preschools? No feedback received.

IN THE 'ROOM

What's the adult-to-child ratio? 6:1.

What are the policies for initial separation between parent and child? Varies.

Can you visit any time unannounced? Yes.

What are the hours? No feedback received.

Do you offer early bird or after-hours pick-up? If so, is there an extra fee? No feedback received.

Please describe a typical day for a child at your school. Alternates between inside and outside activities.

What kinds of academic activities are offered? No feedback received.

What kinds of art activities are offered? No feedback received.

Is the child's time structured or unstructured, or a mixture of both? There is some structured time, and we have centers.

If a child is not interested in a particular activity, does he/she have other choices or is he/she encouraged to try it anyway? Children can make choices in each activity, outside or inside. There are child-directed and teacher-directed activities. Teachers listen to each child's needs. Guidance helps.

How are disputes handled when they occur between the children? With tons of communication—no benching.

When and for how long is nap time? No naps.

What kinds of beds do you use? No naps.

What do you do when a child is dropped off in the morning and is obviously not well? What do you do when a child becomes sick during the day? No feedback received.

Can you accommodate children with special needs? No feedback received.

KEEPING IT SAFE

Please describe your security measures for arriving and leaving the school. No feedback received.

What medical supplies do you have on hand, and what medical experience does your staff have? Is your staff trained in CPR? No feedback received.

Please describe your earthquake-preparedness plan, and what special equipment do you have on hand in the event of a disaster? No feedback received.

SWINGS 'N THINGS

Please describe your playground. Does it have plenty of shade? Lots of shade and water.

Do you put sunscreen on the children? Yes.

What kind of toilet training is available? No toilet training is available; children must be potty trained.

HELPING OUT

What kinds of fundraising events are at your school each year? No feedback received.

How much participation is required by each parent? No feedback received.

KEEPING IN TOUCH

How do you communicate with parents? Is there a newsletter or phone tree? No feedback received.

Does the school publish an address book with all the parents' information in it? No feedback received.

preschool to 8th grade

HOLLYWOOD SCHOOL HOUSE

1233 N. McCadden Pl.
Los Angeles, CA 90038
Phone: (323) 465-1320
www.hollywoodschoolhouse.org
See Map C on page 286

Contact: Lisa Beiras

- ACCREDITATION: NAEYC
- NOT-FOR-PROFIT
- FINANCIAL AID IS AVAILABLE
- NUMBER OF KIDS: 230
- TUITION: $11,930 YEAR (Pre-K)
- WE HAVE KIDS WITH SPECIAL NEEDS

WHEN TO APPLY: APPLICATIONS ARE AVAILABLE YEAR-ROUND. TOURS ARE GIVEN SEPTEMBER THROUGH JANUARY.

Set on busy Highland Avenue in Hollywood, the sign on the front of the building used to read "Hollywood Little Red School House," and it still looks like one. But before your mind starts creating "Little House on the Prairie" fantasies, remember that appearances can be deceiving. The minute that you walk into the reception area, you see why they took the "Little" out of the original name—according to Early Childhood Director Ilise Faye, "What used to be a mom and pop establishment built in 1945 has turned into a very successful non-profit, independent organization," with a campus and a 35-foot swimming pool to match.

The unique thing about the Hollywood School House is that it still has that little-school feel. Although the tuition is steep, there's no trace of that antiseptic feel that often permeates other well-off schools. The rooms buzz with energy and the approach to learning is incredibly (and successfully) creative. The teacher turnover rate at the school is incredibly low—almost every one has been therefore over a decade. There's a real sense of community between them, serving as a wonderful example for the kids. As you observe them, you're transported back to the closeness that must have existed in those one-room schoolhouses.

Any successful organization starts with a great leader, and Ilise obviously falls in that category. The kids LOVE her, as soon as they get a glimpse of her, they run up for hugs, and she knows and loves every one of them in return. Getting in isn't easy. The school receives a few hundred applications a year for 20 to 25 open spots, and the school is licensed through eigth grade. Most kids exit out between sixth going into seventh grade and go on to secondary independent private schools such as Harvard Westlake, Buckley, Pacific Hills, Campbell Hall, and Viewpoint.

Children must be two before July of the year they begin at Hollywood School House.

BACKGROUND

The school was established in 1945 by Ruth Pease with one simple philosophy: to provide a nurturing environment where children are supported to develop their individual abilities. Our elementary and middle school programs were founded as an outgrowth of the success of our early program. In 2001, the school was transferred to a non-profit entity. Our Early Childhood Director is Ilise Faye, and our Interim Head of School is Susan Walker. We have governed by a board of trustees and we have an active Parents Association.

BIRD'S EYE VIEW

	Non-existent	Poor	Fair	Good	Excellent
Learning to Read Children learn to explore the world of books					✓
Dress-Up Children experiment with different roles and imagination					✓
Hand-Eye Children develop fine motor skills by using fingers and hands					✓
Building Blocks Children practice symbolic representation. They are developing an understanding of the relationships between size and shape, and the basic math concepts of geometry and numbers					✓
Arts and Crafts Children are developing small muscle control as well as creativity					✓
Body Coordination Children crawl through tunnels, climb and balance					✓
Meeting Time Gathering place to listen to the teacher and to stories					✓
Weights and Measures Water and Sand tables					✓
Beakers and Bunnies Classroom pets, aquariums....planting...				✓	
Counting 1-2-3 A good preschool will stock basic early-learner software such as phonics or counting games					✓
Outdoor Play Encourage large muscle control and coordination					✓

Q & A

HOW THEY LEARN

What is your school's teaching philosophy? The Hollywood Schoolhouse recognizes that just as each individual is unique, so is each style of learning. From early childhood classes in the preschool through all of the grade levels, our staff seeks to recognize each child's abilities and challenges in order to nurture confidence, foster creativity and to best prepare our students for their future. We believe the school environment should provide a warm and caring atmosphere where children feel comfortable to express themselves and take the risks necessary for their intellectual and emotional development. Our well-balanced approach nurtures the child's self-esteem while promoting awareness of the world around them.

How do you implement the philosophy? Children come to experience the world in a nurturing, community setting, offering children a variety of multi-sensory activities to cultivate their enthusiasm for learning. Types of activities include story-time, puppets, science projects, language development, hands-on art, cooking and plenty of physical activities.

What specialty teachers are brought into the school? We have specialty teachers for music, dance and Spanish once a week as well a weekly visit to our library. We also have a big cultural element in which each family provides a profile for us. We include all holidays that are celebrated within our community and incorporate them in our curriculum. Our families' diverse backgrounds provide wonderful learning experiences for us all.

What is the teaching method? Our preschool curriculum is center based.

HOW TO GET IN

Are there open house dates? When are tours given? We typically have two open houses in the fall. Tours are given weekly, by appointment only.

Is there an interview? With the child or without? Preschool families may be asked to interview without their child. They are also encouraged to attend an open house with the child.

Is preference given to applicants whose siblings are alumni? Preference is only given to current siblings and staff children, but not alumni.

Are letters of recommendation encouraged? From what types of people? Yes, from current families, volunteer organizations or educators.

How many applications do you receive each year? No feedback received.

How many open spots are there each year? No feedback received.

What are some of the schools that children go on to after finishing their education at your preschool? No feedback received.

PIGGY BANK

Apart from tuition, what other fees do you charge? There is a $1,000 new family fee.

What are the different payment plans available? Up-front payment gets a 5% discount. There is also a ten-month payment plan. Credit cards are also accepted.

How is the tuition broken down? $11,930 annually.

What is the fee schedule? March-February. The first payment is due upon signing the contract.

Is there a contract? Yes.

Do you have a tuition insurance program? We offer tuition insurance.

HELPING HANDS

What accreditation is necessary for the teachers to work at your school? No feedback received.

How many teachers are there? No feedback provided.

How many aides? No feedback provided.

Do they come from other preschools? No feedback received.

IN THE 'ROOM

What's the adult-to-child ratio? No feedback received.

What are the policies for initial separation between parent and child? Two-week transition period for families; this is not mandatory and the transition is more individualized depending on the child and family needs.

Can you visit any time unannounced? Yes, the campus is always open to current families. However, it is usually easier on the children and the teacher if you schedule your participation in class.

What are the hours? Complementary child care from 7:30 a.m.-9 a.m. The ECE day is from 9 a.m.-3 p.m., with complementary child care for pick-up time from 3-4 p.m.

Do you offer early bird or after-hours pick-up? If so, is there an extra fee? There is a separate fee and contract for 4-6 p.m.

Please describe a typical day for a child at your school. Approximately from 9-11:30 a.m. there is morning circle, snack, curriculum (centers and either music, dance, Spanish or library time), outside time, lunch from 11:30 a.m.-12:30 p.m., nap time from 12:30-2:30 p.m., snack time and closing circle from 2:30 p.m., 3-4 p.m. pick-up, 4-6 p.m. after-school program.

What kinds of academic activities are offered? We expose the children to all concepts, but do not look at it as academics.

What kinds of art activities are offered? Our entire art program (through elementary/middle school) is completely process-oriented, and children are absolutely encouraged to express themselves through art activities.

Is the child's time structured or unstructured, or a mixture of both? We have a set routine each day, as we believe that children thrive with routine. We are a center-based preschool, and the children are free to experience the centers at their will.

If a child is not interested in a particular activity, does he/she have other choices or is he/she encouraged to try it anyway? Absolutely not.

How are disputes handled when they occur between the children? We teach children conflict resolution. We narrate for the children, use positive reinforcement. No time outs.

When and for how long is nap time? Nap time is approximately 12:30-2:30 p.m.

What kinds of beds do you use? Each child has a cot.

What do you do when a child is dropped off in the morning and is obviously not well? What do you do when a child becomes sick during the day? We have a strict illness policy. If a child comes to school ill, they are sent to the infirmary and must be picked up as soon as possible. They must be fever free for 24 hours before returning to school.

Can you accommodate children with special needs? We can accommodate some needs but we do not have a one-to-one ration to assist will all special needs.

KEEPING IT SAFE

Please describe your security measures for arriving and leaving the school. We have a double buzzer system. No one can enter the facility unaccompanied.

What medical supplies do you have on hand, and what medical experience does your staff have? Is your staff trained in CPR? The entire straff is trained in CPR and First Aid.

Please describe your earthquake-preparedness plan, and what special equipment do you have on hand in the event of a disaster? A full disaster plan is in the staff and parent handbook.

SWINGS 'N THINGS

Please describe your playground. Does it have plenty of shade? We have two playgrounds that are used in the ECE division. Both have padded surfacing and new play equipment. There are riding toys in the younger playground and trees provide shade for the little ones.

Do you put sunscreen on the children? The teachers ask that you put sunscreen on your child before coming to school, and they will reapply as needed.

What kind of toilet training is available? We assist with toilet training for our youngest. If they are over three, we prefer that they are already trained.

HELPING OUT

What kinds of fundraising events are at your school each year? Fall Carnival, Holiday Party, Silent Auction, Spring Picnic.

How much participation is required by each parent? Nothing is required, but we are a non-profit and encourage our families to support the school to gain full participation. We hope that each family will contribute to the best of their ability.

KEEPING IN TOUCH

How do you communicate with parents? Is there a newsletter or phone tree? E-newsletters, Friday folders, class representatives may set up phone trees, email, voicemail.

Does the school publish an address book with all the parents' information in it? No feedback received.

preschool

La Cañada – Flintridge Community Center Preschool

4469 Chevy Chase Drive
La Cañada, CA 91011
Phone: (818) 790-8687
www.lcfccpreschool.com
See Map B on page 286

Contact: Danielle Caputo, Director

- ACCREDITATION: NONE
- NOT-FOR-PROFIT
- FINANCIAL AID IS AVAILABLE
- NUMBER OF KIDS: 75 PER DAY
- TUITION: $230-$445 MONTH
- WE HAVE KIDS WITH SPECIAL NEEDS

WHEN TO APPLY: APPLICATIONS FOR OUR RANDOM SELECTION PROCESS ARE AVAILABLE THE BEGINNING OF FEBRUARY AND ARE ACCEPTED UNTIL MID TO LATE FEBRUARY.

When you hear the words "community center" and "preschool," you immediately think of a rather tatty building with outdated facilities. but this school looks smarter than most of the private preschools I visited. It's gorgeous! The rooms are bright and airy, they have been recently whitewashed and are full of fun toys and things to play with. There is plenty of space to work outside and create wonderful paintings, not to mention the kid-size stores that one parent built and donated to the school.

I arrived unannounced and the school's director, Danielle Caputo could not have been more welcoming. She is an attractive, petite woman with a big personality and lots of heart. This is a developmental non-academic school that concentrates on skill development by using lots of hands-on experiences. Every classroom has its own messy outside area, and you could see how creative her children were being. "We have lots of dramatic play here at the mini village," she said as she took me past those kid-sized stores and through the expansive play area. Later we went out in the back and around to the front, where some parents were waiting to pick up their children. Everyone seemed very relaxed and happy.

School is every day for the five-year-olds in pre-kindergarten. The three-year-olds come Tuesdays and Thursdays from 9 a.m.-12 p.m., and the four-year-olds on Mondays, Tuesdays and Wednesdays. "It works out really well," Danielle tells me as she points out two newer classrooms which have recently been added to the already sprawling campus. When asked how she resolves conflict between the children, she tells me, "I don't make them say sorry, here we respect their feelings and then redirect them and move on." Well it was time for me to move on, so I said my good-byes and left with the feeling that kids going to this preschool were having the times of their lives!

BACKGROUND

The Roger Barkley Community Center (formerly known as the Youth House) opened in 1951 after several years of planning. The Community Center has served the needs of thousands of children and adults alike, offering a variety of enriching, recreational and educational opportunities for members of our community and surrounding areas. The preschool is an extension of the Community Center, offering a half-day program for children aged three through five.

BIRD'S EYE VIEW

	Non-existent	Poor	Fair	Good	Excellent
Learning to Read Children learn to explore the world of books					✓
Dress-Up Children experiment with different roles and imagination					✓
Hand-Eye Children develop fine motor skills by using fingers and hands					✓
Building Blocks Children practice symbolic representation. They are developing an understanding of the relationships between size and shape, and the basic math concepts of geometry and numbers					✓
Arts and Crafts Children are developing small muscle control as well as creativity					✓
Body Coordination Children crawl through tunnels, climb and balance					✓
Meeting Time Gathering place to listen to the teacher and to stories					✓
Weights and Measures Water and Sand tables					✓
Beakers and Bunnies Classroom pets, aquariums....planting...					✓
Counting 1-2-3 A good preschool will stock basic early-learner software such as phonics or counting games				✓	
Outdoor Play Encourage large muscle control and coordination					✓

Q & A

HOW THEY LEARN

What is your school's teaching philosophy? The preschool strives to provide a warm, safe and nurturing atmosphere with a wide variety of age appropriate activities designed to promote the social, intellectual, physical and emotional aspects of learning. Our teachers work to create an environment for the children to learn through active exploration and discovery. We stretch their imaginations and extend their learning by stimulating their thinking.

How do you implement the philosophy? Manipulative toys, creative experiences, group time, floor toys, blocks, paints, Play-Doh, sand and water are offered on a daily basis. Particular emphasis is placed on helping to develop social skills such as talking, helping, listening, sharing and negotiating.

What specialty teachers are brought into the school? A professional music teacher is brought in once a week for each child to learn music appreciation.

What is the teaching method? Developmental.

At what age do the children start? To what age is the school licensed? We have a three-year-old through five-year-old program. We are licensed only through six years of age.

HOW TO GET IN

Are there open house dates? When are tours given? We conduct tours for inquiring families on Tuesdays and Thursdays at 9:30 a.m., by appointment only.

Is there an interview? With the child or without? There is no interview process.

Is preference given to applicants whose siblings are alumni? Yes. Preference is given to siblings who attended the school within three years.

Are letters of recommendation encouraged? From what types of people? Not necessarily.

How many applications do you receive each year? Varies from year to year.

How many open spots are there each year? It depends on how many available spots there are after priority registration takes place. It varies from year to year.

What are some of the schools that children go on to after finishing their education at your preschool? Mostly La Cañada or Glendale Unified. Some go to local private schools such as Crestview, St. Bede's or Chandler.

PIGGY BANK

Apart from tuition, what other fees do you charge? There is a non-refundable registration fee of $50 due only upon acceptance.

How is tuition broken down? Pre-kindergarten is $445 per month (five days a week), the three-year-old class is $230 per month (two days a week), and the four-year-old class is $310 per month (three days a week).

What are the different payment plans available? Cash, check or credit card.

What is the fee schedule? The last month's tuition is due June 1st of the previous year. Tuition is due at the first of every month.

Is there a contract? The parents sign an admission agreement.

Do you have a tuition insurance program? No.

HELPING HANDS

What accreditation is necessary for the teachers to work at your school? The lead teachers must have a minimum of 12 early childhood education units.

How many teachers are there? We have five lead teachers.

How many aides are there? There are six assistants/aides.

IN THE 'ROOM

What's the child-to-adult ratio? 8:1.

What are the policies for initial separation between parent and child? Parents drop children off in the classroom with their teachers and say a quick goodbye. We try not to allow the parents to linger for too long and we engage the children in activities immediately.

Can you visit any time unannounced? We allow the parents to visit any time, unless it is a child who may have a hard time seeing a parent during school hours.

What are the hours? We have an optional lunch time from 12-12:30 p.m. for a fee of $5.00.

Do you offer early bird or after-hours pick-up? If so, is there an extra fee? There is and an optional extended day program from 12-3:30 p.m. for a fee of $16.

Please describe a typical day for a child at your school. They are welcomed into a warm environment. The children will start with a rug time in which they will greet each other and learn about the activities the teacher has planned for the day. They will move throughout the classroom and explore many available centers. They will be encouraged to take risks and be challenged during art, craft and cooking activities. They will be expected to listen to several stories and share ideas during rug times. They will sing songs each day. They will play in the playground for an hour each day in order to develop their large motor skills. They will be loved, nurtured and respected on a daily basis.

What kinds of academic activities are offered? Each classroom has a math, science and writing center where the children are free to explore at any time.

What kinds of art activities are offered? Each day, an easel is put out for the children to use at will. Also each day, there is a different type of art project for the children, to challenge their fine motor skills as well as their imagination.

Is the child's time structured or unstructured, or a mixture of both? A mixture of both. Very balanced.

If a child is not interested in a particular activity, does he/she have other choices or is he/she encouraged to try it anyway? At first they are encouraged, and if completely apprehensive, they may have other choices throughout the classroom.

How are disputes handled when they occur between the children? We try to encourage children to problem solve on their own, with an adult nearby to mediate.

When and for how long is nap time? Nap time is from 12:30-2 p.m. and only for those who stay for the optional extended day program.

What kinds of beds do you use? Floor mats.

What do you do when a child is dropped off in the morning and is obviously not well? What do you do when a child becomes sick during the day? If a child is dropped off ill, we will contact the parents to pick them up from school. The same applies when a child becomes ill during class time.

Can you accommodate children with special needs? Yes.

KEEPING IT SAFE

Please describe your security measures for arriving and leaving the school. All children have an emergency form filled out by parents that are kept in the classrooms as well as in their files. Parents or approved adult must sign in and out each day. All gates in the facility are locked during school hours except for the main gate which faces the entrance to the school.

What medical supplies do you have on hand, and what medical experience does your staff have? Is your staff trained in CPR? Each class has First Aid supplies for minor injuries. All staff members are certified in pediatric and adult First Aid and CPR every year.

Please describe your earthquake-preparedness plan, and what special equipment do you have on hand in the event of a disaster? We have enough food, water and first aid supplies to keep us for three days in case of a major disaster. All the teachers and aides have specific duties they must provide which is posted in the office.

SWINGS 'N THINGS

Please describe your playground. Does it have plenty of shade? We have a beautiful tree which provides plenty of shade. We have a very large sand area, play houses, climbing structure and a tricycle path.

Do you put sunscreen on the children? We do not put sunscreen on children because of skin allergies.

What kind of toilet training is available? Students must be potty trained upon admission.

HELPING OUT

What kinds of fundraising events are at your school each year? We have two main fundraisers: a gift wrap sale in which we receive fifty percent of the total sold, and our annual Western Roundup Carnival/Silent Auction.

How much participation is required by each parent? There are many opportunities for the parents to get involved, but only one mandatory hour—to staff a booth at our annual fundraiser.

KEEPING IN TOUCH

How do you communicate with parents? Is there a newsletter or phone tree? We have a newsletter printed three times a year, and our room parents contact the class about important events as well. We also have parent/teacher conferences.

Does the school publish an address book with all the parents' information in it? Each class has a class roster printed up at the beginning of the school year with parents and student names, addresses and phone numbers.

preschool to pre-k

LA CAÑADA PRESCHOOL

4460 Oakwood Ave.
La Cañada, CA 91011
Phone: (818) 790-2764
www.lacañadapreschool.com
See Map B on page 286

Contact: Debbie Bacino, Head of School

- ACCREDITATION: NONE
- FOR-PROFIT
- FINANCIAL AID IS AVAILABLE
- NUMBER OF FAMILIES: 60
- TUITION: $300-$600 MONTH
- WE HAVE KIDS WITH SPECIAL NEEDS

WHEN TO APPLY: APPLICATIONS ARE ACCEPTED ON AN ONGOING BASIS THROUGHOUT THE SCHOOL YEAR.

I arrived outside the school–a very pleasant-looking converted house on a residential street at lunchtime and was directed through the playground, into the kitchen and back into the office of the school's director, Debbie, who was having a quick bite with another member of the staff. I was invited to join them, which I did happily, having been on my feet all morning. If I had to give out an award for the cheeriest of directors, it would have to go to Debbie. She is the third owner of a school that has been around since 1949. Now in her second year as director of this very prestigious preschool in one of Los Angeles' most affluent neighborhoods, Debbie is upbeat, down-to-earth and incredibly warm. What makes her rather unique is that she is also one of the teachers there. She's a graduate from U.C. Berkeley and the Harvard School of Education in Boston.

Debbie believes in mixed-age grouping of her children. Groups of eleven three-to-five-years-old spend the morning rotating through different rooms every thirty minutes, sharing four teachers and doing the same in the afternoon with three. Never a dull moment here, folks! Oh, yes, and there's a male teacher here affectionately known as Mr. Tony who obviously adores his precious charges; he was bringing a group of them in after playtime outside in their very spacious and well-equipped yard. When I asked Debbie what her teaching philosophy is, she doesn't miss a beat. "Structure with freedom and lots of creativity, based on the teachings of Reggio Emilia."

The school offers a pre-kindergarten class in the afternoons where they teach the four-to-five-year-olds Zoophonics. It's a world-wide recognized phonics program that all her teachers have been trained in, and as I walked around the classrooms, I could see that by the time her kids left the school they would be quite ready for kindergarten. When I asked what sort of discipline she uses if one kid hurts another or gets into an argument, she answered, "Do you know what the word discipline means?" I look down at my feet. "It means to teach, and I like to teach conflict resolution—in any situation there is a perpetrator and a victim. We always comfort the victim, then empower the child to confront the perpetrator." The school has a peace table where the kids can go any time to resolve problems that they are having with a friend. I wish I could use it myself sometimes!

BACKGROUND

Kathleen Yager established the school in 1949.

BIRD'S EYE VIEW

	Non-existent	Poor	Fair	Good	Excellent
Learning to Read Children learn to explore the world of books				✓	
Dress-Up Children experiment with different roles and imagination					✓
Hand-Eye Children develop fine motor skills by using fingers and hands					✓
Building Blocks Children practice symbolic representation. They are developing an understanding of the relationships between size and shape, and the basic math concepts of geometry and numbers					✓
Arts and Crafts Children are developing small muscle control as well as creativity					✓
Body Coordination Children crawl through tunnels, climb and balance					✓
Meeting Time Gathering place to listen to the teacher and to stories					✓
Weights and Measures Water and Sand tables					✓
Beakers and Bunnies Classroom pets, aquariums....planting...					✓
Counting 1-2-3 A good preschool will stock basic early-learner software such as phonics or counting games					✓
Outdoor Play Encourage large muscle control and coordination					✓

Q & A

HOW THEY LEARN

What is your school's teaching philosophy? The school is grounded by a developmental philosophy where we value a strong positive self-concept, which will allow the each child to enjoy an ever-expanding competence in dealing fairly, confidently and enthusiastically with her/him and the surrounding world.

How do you implement the philosophy? The core of our curriculum is art, music and literature. This is implemented by the children's exposure every day to three different teachers with three different lesson plans.

What specialty teachers are brought into the school? We bring in music professionals once a month for music, and we have an artista who enhances our art lessons.

What is the teaching method? The children have a mixed-age classroom with three different teachers. Teaching is child-centered and child-directed.

At what age do the children start? To what age is the school licensed? Two years, nine months old to five years old is our range.

HOW TO GET IN

Are there open house dates? When are tours given? Tours are available year round by appointment.

Is there an interview? With the child or without? No interview.

Is preference given to applicants whose siblings are alumni? Siblings are guaranteed a spot in our school.

Are letters of recommendation encouraged? From what types of people? No letters are needed.

How many applications do you receive each year? Between thirty and forty.

How many open spots are there each year? Between thirty and forty.

What are some of the schools that children go on to after finishing their education at your preschool? Primarily public, with about 20% private in La Cañada, Pasadena and Glendale.

PIGGY BANK

Apart from tuition, what other fees do you charge? There is a yearly registration fee of $100. No application fee.

How is tuition broken down? Tuition is $190 per month for two mornings, $280 for three mornings, $415 for five mornings, and $440 for pre-kindergarten which runs five afternoons from 12:30-3:30 p.m.

What are the different payment plans available? Monthly.

What is the fee schedule? No feedback received.

Is there a contract? There is a simple contract.

Do you have a tuition insurance program? No tuition insurance.

HELPING HANDS

What accreditation is necessary for the teachers to work at your school? Teachers must have 24 units in early childhood education.

How many teachers are there? Three teachers per morning, two teachers in the afternoon.

How many aides are there? One aide in the morning, one aide in the afternoon.

IN THE 'ROOM

What's the child-to-adult ratio? 8:1.

What are the policies for initial separation between parent and child? We encourage parents to separate from the first day by reassuring the child and leaving them with us. We do allow parents to stay if needed.

Can you visit any time unannounced? Yes.

What are the hours? 9 a.m.-12 p.m. for the morning, with a lunch option from 12-1 p.m. The pre-kindergarten hours are form 12:30-3:30 p.m.

Do you offer early bird or after-hours pickup? If so, is there an extra fee? No feedback received.

Please describe a typical day for a child at your school. Free play, art and sensory activities from 9-10 a.m., meal time from 10-10:30 a.m., group learning time from 10:30 a.m.-12 p.m. The children rotate during the group learning time between three different teachers in groups of 10.

What kinds of academic activities are offered? We work with children in their last year on kindergarten readiness skills such as cooperative play, staying on task, follow-through, all through and concrete materials.

What kinds of art activities are offered? Process art, painting, collage making, clay, dimensional art, open-ended projects.

Is the child's time structured or unstructured, or a mixture of both? A mixture of both.

If a child is not interested in a particular activity, does he/she have other choices or is he/she encouraged to try it anyway? There are always other choices.

How are disputes handled when they occur between the children? There is developmental discipline. We teach this through conflict resolution skills.

When and for how long is nap time? No naps.

What kinds of beds do you use? No naps.

What do you do when a child is dropped off in the morning and is obviously not well? What do you do when a child becomes sick during the day? We check each child in upon arrival. We will call parents or the caretaker to pick up a sick child.

Can you accommodate children with special needs? On a case-by-case basis.

KEEPING IT SAFE

Please describe your security measures for arriving and leaving the school. Children are only dismissed to parents or authorized caretakers.

What medical supplies do you have on hand, and what medical experience does your staff have? Is your staff trained in CPR? A complete First Aid kit. Each teacher is re-trained in First Aid every two years.

Please describe your earthquake-preparedness plan, and what special equipment do you have on hand in the event of a disaster? Supplies are on campus for 34 children to be contained for three days.

Please describe your playground. Does it have plenty of shade? Shade mixed with sunny areas encompass a cozy yard with a playhouse, swings, a rabbit habitat and tables for activities.

Do you put sunscreen on the children? No feedback received.

What kind of toilet training is available? Children are required to be toilet independent.

HELPING OUT

What kinds of fundraising events are at your school each year? One per year for school improvement. For a $100 donation, you will receive a photo CD of your child at preschool set to music.

How much participation is required by each parent? None.

KEEPING IN TOUCH

How do you communicate with parents? Is there a newsletter or phone tree? Monthly newsletter, email and daily communication in person.

Does the school publish an address book with all the parents' information in it? No.

preschool

L.A. FAMILY SCHOOL

2646 Griffith Park Blvd.
Los Angeles, CA 90039
Phone: (323) 663-8049
www.lafamilyschool.org
See Map C on page 286

Contact: Sarpi Idolor, Director
Angel Lopez, Board of Trustees

- ACCREDITATION: NONE
- FOR-PROFIT
- FINANCIAL AID IS AVAILABLE
- NUMBER OF KIDS: 60
- TUITION: $850-$975 MONTH
- WE HAVE KIDS WITH SPECIAL NEEDS

WHEN TO APPLY: APPLICATIONS ARE AVAILABLE AT EACH ORIENTATION AND ORIENTATIONS ARE HELD MONTHLY. THERE IS NO CUTOFF DATE FOR APPLICATIONS.

The Los Angeles Family School is located on three-and-a-half acres of property. The only concrete in this natural environment is the bike/trike path. The open, bi-level yard houses one of the best playgrounds that I have seen, and it is also home to a variety of animals. I may have missed one or two, but animals in residence include cockatiels, hummingbirds fish, turtles and a chicken (whose eggs are used during snack time). There is a garden that the children all tend, and snacks are also cooked from the garden. There is also a turtle bog, a compost (great for gardening!), and The L.A. Family School is wheelchair accessible.

This is a parent participation school, which means that the teachers are professional, and parents help run the school. One of the mothers present shared with me why she loves the school. "Well, you get parental guidance and help as a parent. There is huge community and support. I felt like 'Wow! I get an education too.' Issues are dealt with holistically—the home, parent, teacher and child all together… there is just an organic flow that isn't stopped or hindered. There is this ability of the kids to get into their modality, what they're going for, they are allowed to go for… my first thought when I saw the school was, 'I want to go here.'" I second that thought! It is very tempting to play on the playground, feed the chicken and play with the water, sand, mud and paints. Here, children are encouraged to get messy! Having to worry about getting dirty cramps their style and prevents them from learning the kinds of concepts that messy play affords; color, texture, weight, mass, volume, gravity. They don't wear aprons or smocks because young children tend to be very spontaneous, and many will forgo an activity if they have to suit up first.

L.A. Family School uses a child-centered curriculum because they know that children learn best about things that interest them most. For this reason, they do not impose a set curriculum. Instead, they expand upon the topics and materials and interests the children bring into the program. The school philosophy is built on the idea that every person possesses a unique set of abilities, challenges, and character traits. Each child comes to school with a special set of plans and preferences. School is not something we do to kids, but something that creates a partnership with them. We tell children what we are going to do and why. School rules have reasons. Though we like to see kids participate in all activities offered, we honor a child's choice to be an observer or to focus on those activities that interest him/her. We support kids as they join in, get messy, take risks, and try something new.*

* from the Los Angeles Family School tour hand-out

Background

Kenneth Reiner started the school in the 1960s for his own children and other children in his neighborhood, and it was called Midtown School. It was located at 4155 Russell Avenue, which is the current Lycee International de Los Angeles location. The school closed in 1972 at that location, and a group of parents didn't want to lose the school, so parents used various locations including houses and rented locations throughout the Los Angeles area. Eventually they purchased the current site on Griffith Park Boulevard approximately 28 years ago, and the name became Los Angeles Family School. This is also when the school became a non-profit school owned by the current members, which includes current staff and parents.

Bird's Eye View

	Non-existent	Poor	Fair	Good	Excellent
Learning to Read — Children learn to explore the world of books					✓
Dress-Up — Children experiment with different roles and imagination					✓
Hand-Eye — Children develop fine motor skills by using fingers and hands					✓
Building Blocks — Children practice symbolic representation. They are developing an understanding of the relationships between size and shape, and the basic math concepts of geometry and numbers					✓
Arts and Crafts — Children are developing small muscle control as well as creativity					✓
Body Coordination — Children crawl through tunnels, climb and balance					✓
Meeting Time — Gathering place to listen to the teacher and to stories					✓
Weights and Measures — Water and Sand tables					✓
Beakers and Bunnies — Classroom pets, aquariums....planting...					✓
Counting 1-2-3 — A good preschool will stock basic early-learner software such as phonics or counting games					✓
Outdoor Play — Encourage large muscle control and coordination					✓

Q & A

HOW THEY LEARN

What is your school's teaching philosophy? The philosophy is based on the concept that children are important, valid persons who have the capacity to make good decisions for themselves. We believe that it is essential to create an atmosphere of trust and safety in order to allow children to become autonomous. By establishing common sense limits for children and allowing freedom within those limits, we enable them to make the choices that affect their school play. Selecting activities and playmates, deciding how to use materials and spend time, and in fact choosing whether to participate—these are respected by the staff as options belonging to the child. We find that children of all ages can and will make good choices about their time at school if they are given realistic limits and caring support from the staff. The second major tenet of our philosophy is that feelings, for both children and adults, are an important part of life requiring attention and expression. We as a staff strive to be direct and open with our own feelings and we encourage the children to do the same. We believe that both pleasant and uncomfortable feelings are real and that school should be a safe place to explore them. We try to support children in recognizing, expressing verbally and non-verbally, and working through their feelings. It is clear to us that children who can experience, identify, accept and act on their own feelings in appropriate ways will develop an inner strength that will allow them to cope with whatever situation life throws their way. By valuing children's autonomous decisions and expressions of feelings, we are fostering their ability to live in the world as competent, caring individuals.

How do you implement the philosophy? The developmental philosophy is present within the school climate. Teachers encourage children to express their needs in words and they are there to facilitate issues that come up among children. Also, the school uses the land as an indoor-outdoor program that includes both environments.

What specialty teachers are brought into the school? No specialty teachers are brought in to implement the school's philosophy.

What is the teaching method? The teaching method is developmental. Teachers assist children with discussions that are children-based upon students' ideas, interests and thoughts.

At what age do the children start? To what age is the school licensed? Children may start at two, and the school is licensed through the age of five.

HOW TO GET IN

Are there open house dates? When are tours given? Orientations are held monthly. Currently, they are on the second Tuesday of the month starting at 4:15 p.m. without children. Families call the office to reserve a spot according to availability.

Is there an interview? With the child or without? There isn't a formal interview, but children and their parents are invited for a visit. At this visit, the child has an opportunity to be a visitor with the current children and an informal interview is done with the parents as well.

Is preference given to applicants whose siblings are alumni? Siblings of alumni are taken into consideration, but family involvement and participation is also factored into the decision and there are no guarantees.

Are letters of recommendation encouraged? From what types of people? Letters of recommendation are not encouraged, but from time to time families include them.

How many applications do you receive each year? Many more applications than we can enroll, unfortunately.

How many open spots are there each year? Most of the openings are in Group 1 and Group 3. There are also a few openings in Groups 2 and 4, depending on vacancies that become available.

What are some of the schools that children go on to after finishing their education at your preschool? L.A.F.S. children go on to various schools. Ivanhoe and Franklin are two of the public schools that students attend after L.A.F.S. Independent schools include Children's Community School, The Sequoyah School, Oakwood School, The Country School, The Oaks and The Waverly School (not limited to just these, as students apply to many schools in the greater Los Angeles area). Some students go on to Charter and Magnet schools as well.

PIGGY BANK

Apart from tuition, what other fees do you charge? There is an application fee of $35, and a one-time non-refundable fee of $80 per child (required prior to enrollment).

How is tuition broken down? Current tuition ranges from $850-$975 and is determined by group and full-day/half-day programs.

What are the different payment plans available? Tuition is paid on a monthly basis. Payment is due by the 10th day of each month. Students in Group 3 and 4 pay on a ten-month basis.

What is the fee schedule? There are monthly tuition payments.

Is there a contract? There is a tuition agreement that is renewed annually.

Do you have a tuition insurance program? No tuition insurance program.

HELPING HANDS

What accreditation is necessary for the teachers to work at your school? Teachers must be licensed and qualified.

How many teachers are there? There are ten teachers currently staffed at L.A.F.S.

How many aides are there? There are no aides, but each classroom has a head teacher and an assistant teacher.

IN THE 'ROOM

What's the child-to-adult ratio? The child-to-adult ratio follows licensing requirements. In the lower groups, it's 5:1, and in the upper groups it is no more than 10:1.

What are the policies for initial separation between parent and child? Always done on an individual basis based on each child's needs. Group 1 staggers the start date for their students so added attention is available for each child when they begin the program. Teachers work well with each parent to meet each child's needs and sensitivity is given to each unique situation. By the older groups, children are used to saying goodbye to their parents and do so in their own special way.

Can you visit any time unannounced? Yes.

What are the hours? L.A.F.S. is open from 7:45 a.m.-6 p.m., Monday through Friday. Within these hours, two programs are available—a half-day program from 8:30 a.m.-12:30 p.m., and a full-day program from 8:30 a.m.-4 p.m., along with early and late care.

Do you offer early bird or after-hours pickup? If so, is there an extra fee? We also offer extended day care for early morning from 7:45-8:30 a.m., and late afternoons from 4-6 p.m. There is an extra fee for both the early care and late care.

Please describe a typical day for a child at your school. The school uses all of the indoor and outdoor space for numerous activities that children get to choose from. The environment is nature-friendly and sand, dirt and mud are part of typical L.A.F.S. day. Each day, the teachers put together a variety of activities that are developmentally age-appropriate that are put out for the children to use. Some of these activities include a reading corner, dramatic play area, blocks, sand, water and mud activities, and art stations which include paint, markers and Play-doh. Most of the school day, kids can move freely from activity to activity. Snack and lunch are family style in nature as children visit while eating as a group. This and a developmentally-appropriate circle time are the two structured activities in the day. The younger groups have rest/nap time after lunch, which is 30 minutes long for children who rest, and it can be up to two hours for those who nap. The activities and classes are developmental from 9 a.m.-3 p.m., and the early and extended programs are multi-age programs. Each day, a different group prepares the school-wide afternoon snack. Group 4 has a garden and uses ingredients that they grow in preparing their snack.

What kinds of academic activities are offered? Students are encouraged to question and learn more about areas of specific interest. For example, the cycles of the seasons are learned about through an informal learning experience that includes experiencing the lesson. Throughout the day children have access to every type of building block and book. Through their play children learn and through play there are many teachable moments. Students are encouraged to explore and experience with the idea that there is not one right answer.

What kinds of art activities are offered? Ninety-nine percent of art activities are exploratory in nature. Paint, Play-doh and glue are a few of the variety of materials students can use. Activities range from body painting to dying spaghetti and putting it into a waiting pool for the children to play in. Sand, mud, volcanic rivers and dirt activities are also a part of the students' art experiences; an open-ended experience valuing the process, not the end result, are a part of every art activity. Panting on paper or painting on their bodies is part of the art experience at L.A.F.S. No cover-ups are used by the children or teachers, as a free and total experience is valued. Students make houses and fortresses for bugs and insects they find using grass, leaves and other materials around them.

Is the child's time structured or unstructured, or a mixture of both? There is skeletal structure throughout the school day, but children choose their activities for most of the day. The few structured activities are incorporated around many opportunities for individual choices among students.

If a child is not interested in a particular activity, does he/she have other choices or is he/she encouraged to try it anyway?

Children are always allowed to make their own choices, but children are naturally curious to try things and this is done through socialization. A child is not required to participate in circle time, but are asked to be present during this time as they also are not required to eat snack, but are asked to sit at the table to socialize during snack.

How are disputes handled when they occur between the children? Disputes are handled through conflict resolution that students of all ages are familiar with, and teachers are there to help facilitate these resolutions among children.

When and for how long is nap time? After lunch, the younger classroom children are required to rest for 30 minutes. Students who do not nap are allowed to participate in a classroom or outdoor activity after 30 minutes. Students who nap can sleep for two hours depending on how long it takes them to fall asleep.

What kinds of beds do you use? No feedback received.

What do you do when a child is dropped off in the morning and is obviously not well? What do you do when a child becomes sick during the day? If a student is dropped off in the morning and is obviously not feeling well a teacher will check their temperature and other possible symptoms. Parents are called if a child is not feeling well and needs to be picked up. This is what occurs throughout the school day. Each class has an area for a child waiting to be picked up. The school has a strict policy for children's return after illness or injury based on all children's health and safety.

Can you accommodate children with special needs? It depends, as each individual situation is different and needs to be considered.

KEEPING IT SAFE

Please describe your security measures for arriving and leaving the school. The school is surrounded by a chain link fence and all gates have a lock on them. The entry to the school has two gates that are latched, so children cannot leave or enter the school without an adult.

What medical supplies do you have on hand, and what medical experience does your staff have? Is your staff trained in CPR? Every teacher is trained annually in infant, child and adult CPR and First Aid. Medical supplies that are suggested by CPR and First Aid trainer are kept at the school. The school has an earthquake plan in place and supplies are kept on hand in case of an earthquake, or other disaster. The school keeps various supplies in an earthquake shed and each student has their own individual earthquake backpack as well.

Please describe your earthquake-preparedness plan, and what special equipment do you have on hand in the event of a disaster? There are earthquake supplies that are provided by both the school and each individual student's emergency backpack.

SWINGS 'N THINGS

Please describe your playground. Does it have plenty of shade? The various play areas of L.A.F.S. are well-shaded, and most of those areas are made up of sand, mud and dirt.

Do you put sunscreen on the children? Sunscreen is put on by parents before school. On a private basis, some students may need sunscreen to be re-applied, but that's on an individual need.

What kind of toilet training is available? L.A.F.S. is developmental in nature, so children do not need to be potty trained. Students come with whatever diapers they need and toilet training takes place when a child shows interest.

HELPING OUT

What kinds of fundraising events are at your school each year? There are various fundraisers throughout the school year. The Spring Faire is the largest fundraising event and is held sometime in April. Other fundraising activities include rummage sales, sample sales and annual giving.

How much participation is required by each parent? L.A.F.S. is a parent-participation school and each family is expected to work a minimum of eight hours per school quarter. During the third quarter, each family is expected to work a minimum of 20 hours due to the Spring Faire, which is the biggest fundraiser of the school year.

KEEPING IN TOUCH

How do you communicate with parents? Is there a newsletter or phone tree? Each group has a room parent that coordinates class specific activities. There is a school newsletter and each family has a mailbox for information to be distributed as well. Bulk email to all members is also available for those with email addresses. A school website is also being put together as an information source as well.

Does the school publish an address book with all the parents' information in it? There is a school roster for L.A.F.S. use only.

preschool

LA PLAYA COOPERATIVE PRESCHOOL

5041 Rhoda Way
Culver City, CA 90230
www.laplayacooperative.com
Phone: (310) 839-1579
See Map D on page 286

Contact: Marni Parsons, Director of Admissions
Ruth Hollensteiner, Head of School

- ACCREDITATION: NONE
- NOT FOR-PROFIT
- FINANCIAL AID IS AVAILABLE
- NUMBER OF FAMILIES: 40
- TUITION: $200-$561 MONTH
- WE HAVE KIDS WITH SPECIAL NEEDS

WHEN TO APPLY: APPLICATIONS ARE AVAILABLE AT MONTHLY TOURS. THERE ARE NO CUT-OFF DATES.

Located in the community center of Lindberg Park in Culver City, La Playa Co-op Nursery School is unusual in many ways. The school offers half-days, which end at 12:30 p.m., because other organizations use the center later in the day. I am amazed that, as a result of this shared space, the parents and teachers that run La Playa must set up and break down their environment every day. Director Ruth Hollensteiner is on the local board of the NAEYC, but because they do not have control of their physical space, they are not accredited. For some people, it is not have a structured enough program. However, La Playa offers plenty of other things. One parent volunteer shared with me, "In some schools, you don't know what is going on. Here, they are all 'our kids,' and everyone is committed to being here. I was 19-years-old when I started here with my first child, and I learned so much about being a parent." La Playa has a parent education program, with training primarily in conflict resolution, to provide techniques of working with children, and insight into human relationships.

La Playa's primary goal is to provide an environment in which all children can succeed—one that fosters children's curiosity about their physical, social and emotional selves and about others. They provide a rich, accurate, non-stereotypical base of experience about gender, race and physical abilities. There is "Circle Time" at 10 a.m. each day, which introduces new concepts. It is a time to discover through songs, games, finger play, and discussion. The inside and outside circle times are geared towards the different age groups (and attention span/sit still ability!).

La Playa really is a family experience. Co-director Marni Parsons states, "It is exciting that the parents will be the teachers in their child's first school experience. Being at La Playa is as much about growing as a parent as it is about the growth of the children." There is no real screening process for prospective families. The family as a whole is considered, if the parents are interested and willing to do the work, and if there is room available. Parents are required to serve on a committee as well as be involved with fundraising activities. There is a strong sense of community at La Playa, a home spun and natural feel that goes beyond simply being a school. Co-presidents Rebecca Crocker and Emily Glick agree. "We are the village it takes to raise a child."

BACKGROUND

The school started in 1948 as a playgroup by a group of parents in the neighborhood.

Bird's Eye View

	Non-existent	Poor	Fair	Good	Excellent
Learning to Read Children learn to explore the world of books				🦉	
Dress-Up Children experiment with different roles and imagination					🦉
Hand-Eye Children develop fine motor skills by using fingers and hands					🦉
Building Blocks Children practice symbolic representation. They are developing an understanding of the relationships between size and shape, and the basic math concepts of geometry and numbers				🦉	
Arts and Crafts Children are developing small muscle control as well as creativity					🦉
Body Coordination Children crawl through tunnels, climb and balance				🦉	
Meeting Time Gathering place to listen to the teacher and to stories				🦉	
Weights and Measures Water and Sand tables					🦉
Beakers and Bunnies Classroom pets, aquariums....planting...			🦉		
Counting 1-2-3 A good preschool will stock basic early-learner software such as phonics or counting games				🦉	
Outdoor Play Encourage large muscle control and coordination			🦉		

• • • • • • • **Q & A** • • • • • • •

HOW THEY LEARN

What is your school's teaching philosophy? Developmentally-appropriate practices.

How do you implement the philosophy? Hands-on activities, child-directed play, and age-appropriate materials.

What specialty teachers are brought into the school? We hire a music teacher and a movement teacher.

What is the teaching method? Process-oriented. Teachers set up a learning environment where the children are free to explore. There is also a group time each day.

At what age do the children start? To what age is the school licensed? Two-and-a-half to five.

HOW TO GET IN

Are there open house dates? When are tours given? Tours are held monthly from November through May. Call for the next scheduled tour date, no RSVP is required.

Is there an interview? With the child or without? There is no interview.

Is preference given to applicants whose siblings are alumni? Yes, there is preference given to siblings of alumni, assuming the family is in good standing.

Are letters of recommendation encouraged? From what types of people? No.

How many applications do you receive each year? 50.

How many open spots are there each year? 15-25.

What are some of the schools that children go on to after finishing their education at your preschool? We serve mostly the Culver City area and surrounding neighborhoods, therefore most children go to the local public schools.

PIGGY BANK

Apart from tuition, what other fees do you charge? There is a $50 non-refundable application fee. No entrance fee.

How is tuition broken down? Tuition ranges from $200 to $561 per month, and this changes annually.

What are the different payment plans available? Tuition is paid monthly.

What is the fee schedule? No feedback received.

Is there a contract? Yes.

Do you have a tuition insurance program? No.

HELPING HANDS

What accreditation is necessary for the teachers to work at your school? Meet state requirements.

How many teachers are there? There are two teachers.

How many aides are there? There are six to eight parent volunteers each day.

IN THE 'ROOM

What's the child-to-adult ratio? 4:1.

What are the policies for initial separation between parent and child? Individual, based on the need of the child and parent.

Can you visit any time unannounced? Yes.

What are the hours? 9:30 a.m.-12:30 p.m.

Do you offer early bird or after-hours pickup? If so, is there an extra fee? No.

Please describe a typical day for a child at your school. Children arrive at 9:30 a.m., there is free play, a 10 a.m. circle time, 10:30 a.m. snack time, free play at 11 a.m., 11:45 a.m. is story time, followed by lunch at noon and school ends at 12:30 p.m.

What kinds of academic activities are offered? All academic activities are choices (puzzles, games, etc.).

What kinds of art activities are offered? Finger painting, collage, easel paint, Play-doh.

Is the child's time structured or unstructured, or a mixture of both? Mixture of both.

If a child is not interested in a particular activity, does he/she have other choices or is he/she encouraged to try it anyway? Children are encouraged to participate in group times. All other activities are choices.

How are disputes handled when they occur between the children? Teachers and parents are trained in a conflict resolution model aimed at problem solving, not punishment.

When and for how long is nap time? There are no naps.

What kinds of beds do you use? No naps.

What do you do when a child is dropped off in the morning and is obviously not well? What do you do when a child becomes sick during the day? Children are sent home.

Can you accommodate children with special needs? Limited.

KEEPING IT SAFE

Please describe your security measures for arriving and leaving the school. Each visitor must check in with the director and each child must be signed in and out each day, according to licensing requirements.

What medical supplies do you have on hand, and what medical experience does your staff have? Is your staff trained in CPR? Teachers are CPR-trained and can administer First Aid.

Please describe your earthquake-preparedness plan, and what special equipment do you have on hand in the event of a disaster? We have a standard equipment disaster package that will suffice in the event of any emergency. This equipment is updated annually, and includes such things as water, food and blankets.

SWINGS 'N THINGS

Please describe your playground. Does it have plenty of shade? There is a large open space, some shade, sand box and climbing structure.

Do you put sunscreen on the children? No feedback received.

What kind of toilet training is available? Children are not required to be toilet trained.

HELPING OUT

What kinds of fundraising events are at your school each year? Fundraising varies depending upon need and desire of parent community. The events typically consist of such things as silent auctions, garage sales, raffles and benefit concerts.

How much participation is required by each parent? Due to the nature of La Playa being a parent cooperative, we require 100% parent participation to run our program. Members who are not willing to participate are asked to leave.

KEEPING IN TOUCH

How do you communicate with parents? Is there a newsletter or phone tree? We have monthly membership meetings, a monthly newsletter and a bulletin board, as well as day-to-day communication.

Does the school publish an address book with all the parents' information in it? We do publish a roster that is available only to current members.

preschool

LITTLE VILLAGE NURSERY SCHOOL CO-OP

11827 W. Pico Blvd.
Los Angeles, CA 90066
Phone: (310) 479-8468
www.lvns.org
See Map D on page 286

Contact: Sylvia Rath, Director

- ACCREDITATION: NONE
- NOT-FOR-PROFIT
- FINANCIAL AID IS AVAILABLE
- NUMBER OF KIDS: 40
- TUITION: $540 MONTH
- WE HAVE KIDS WITH SPECIAL NEEDS

WHEN TO APPLY: APPLICATIONS ARE ONLY AVAILABLE ON THE TOURS. WE'LL STOP TAKING APPLICATIONS FOR MORNING SCHOOL IN DECEMBER. AFTERNOON PROGRAMS, YEAR-ROUND.

Little Village Nursery School Co-op has been around since 1937. The colorful front gate is the only sign that indicates that this "store front" is different from the others on the street. One walks through the gate to a bright world of laughter and play. Director Sylvia Rath (who has a very Diane Weist quality about her, with her explosive smile and twinkle in her eyes) welcomed me along with other parents and one blonde, curious little girl who accompanied her father on the tour.

Along with Rath, there are also two teachers who have been here for twenty years; on any given day, there are many parents who assist and fill in the blanks. Since it is a cooperative, the parents are the owners and help keep the school afloat. Once a month there is a parent workday, and parents have committees and duties they are responsible for. Uniquely, 50-60% of the school's once-a-year fundraiser is used to financially assist families who need monetary scholarship. "In L.A., there is no sense of community. In a co-op, there is a community. You are joining a community," says the young mother who has the job of giving school tours.

Little Village is great for fostering conflict resolution skills. "We don't use punishment," says Rath. "We set limits, and there are consequences. We teach them appropriate behavior. We don't say 'no,' we teach them what things are used for." Little Village believes that a positive pre-school experience influences a child's social, physical and emotional development for years to come. Their goal is to help each child develop positive feelings about himself/herself in a way that encourages and stimulates learning. There is a carpool lane for drop-off and pick-up, and an after school program for parents who may need a later pick-up time. The separation process for children new to the school is very gradual. Four children at a time start the week-long transition (four new children start each week), so the separation is natural once the school year actually begins. Sylvia Rath also gave realistic advice that I hadn't heard at any other school: "Preschools are very competitive. We encourage people to put in applications at several schools."

BACKGROUND

A group of parents founded this developmental cooperative preschool back in 1947.

BIRD'S EYE VIEW

	Non-existent	Poor	Fair	Good	Excellent
Learning to Read Children learn to explore the world of books				●	
Dress-Up Children experiment with different roles and imagination					●
Hand-Eye Children develop fine motor skills by using fingers and hands					●
Building Blocks Children practice symbolic representation. They are developing an understanding of the relationships between size and shape, and the basic math concepts of geometry and numbers					●
Arts and Crafts Children are developing small muscle control as well as creativity					●
Body Coordination Children crawl through tunnels, climb and balance					●
Meeting Time Gathering place to listen to the teacher and to stories				●	
Weights and Measures Water and Sand tables					●
Beakers and Bunnies Classroom pets, aquariums....planting...				●	
Counting 1-2-3 A good preschool will stock basic early-learner software such as phonics or counting games				●	
Outdoor Play Encourage large muscle control and coordination					●

Q & A

HOW THEY LEARN

What is your school's teaching philosophy? At Little Village, our goal is simple: to help each child develop positive feelings of self in a way that encourages and stimulates learning and socialization skills.

How do you implement the philosophy? We believe that children learn through play and we provide opportunities for learning in different areas around the play yard and classrooms. We have large blocks of free play time to encourage imaginative play and socialization with other children. The teachers act as facilitators to encourage expanding learning and teach conflict resolution skills to the children.

What specialty teachers are brought into the school? We have an outside music specialist come to the school once a week, in addition to the music program at circle times.

What is the teaching method? We believe that mistakes are opportunities for learning and encourage personal growth from experiences. Our teachers act as facilitators to help the children become problem solvers. We encourage independent thoughts and value children's ideas through documentation and emergent curriculum.

At what age do the children start? To what age is the school licensed? Children can start at 2 1/2.

HOW TO GET IN

Are there open house dates? When are tours given? Morning tours: just show up at 9:30 a.m. Afternoons, RSVP.

Is there an interview? With the child or without? No interview process.

Is preference given to applicants whose siblings are alumni? Yes, siblings have priority.

Are letters of recommendation encouraged? From what types of people? Letters are wonderful, but we really choose from many criteria.

How many applications do you receive each year? No feedback received.

How many open spots are there each year? About 15 in the 2-3 class.

What are some of the schools that children go on to after finishing their education at your preschool? Cross Roads, PS1, Willows, All local public schools, Westwood Charter.

PIGGY BANK

Apart from tuition, what other fees do you charge? There is a $75 non-refundable application fee. Check the website for additional fees and information.

How is tuition broken down? $540 per month.

What are the different payment plans available? Annual or monthly payment options.

What is the fee schedule? Check the website for information.

Is there a contract? Yes, there is a contract.

Do you have a tuition insurance program? No.

HELPING HANDS

What accreditation is necessary for the teachers to work at your school? Lead teachers must have at least an associate's degree in early childhood education (many have B.A. degrees).

How many teachers are there? There are seven team teachers.

How many aides are there? No feedback received.

IN THE 'ROOM

What's the child-to-adult ratio? It is 5:1 in our two- to-three-year-old class. The oldest class is 8:1.

What are the policies for initial separation between parent and child? Each family is worked with on an individual basis. We encourage one parent to plan on staying at least the first week. They start by sitting in the classroom and when they feel comfortable they may move to the office and when they feel more comfortable they are encouraged to leave and come back early. We understand that the first separation can be hard on both children and parents and we want to work together to help make it smooth and painless for the whole family.

Can you visit any time unannounced? Of course! We love having parents visit, play and help in the classrooms.

What are the hours? Our morning program is 8:45 a.m.-12:30 p.m.

Do you offer early bird or after-hours pick-up? If so, is there an extra fee? Extended care is from 12:30-3:30 p.m.

Please describe a typical day for a child at your school. Check the website for information.

What kinds of academic activities are offered? We offer a process-oriented art program. The children are encouraged to use materials, and to explore and expand their own ideas.

What kinds of art activities are offered? No feedback received.

Is the child's time structured or unstructured, or a mixture of both? Most of our time is free choice with one structured story time, 15-20 minutes of rug time and snack time.

If a child is not interested in a particular activity, does he/she have other choices or is he/she encouraged to try it anyway? Sometimes we invite but we never push a child. They are always offered choices.

How are disputes handled when they occur between the children? We have a step-by-step conflict resolution process which is first facilitated by the teachers and often the children help, too.

When and for how long is nap time? We have a nap for our extended care program.

What kinds of beds do you use? Mats.

What do you do when a child is dropped off in the morning and is obviously not well? What do you do when a child becomes sick during the day? We call the parents to pick the child up in the office, where they are kept comfortable and cared for. All staff are CPR and First Aid certified.

Can you accommodate children with special needs? Yes.

KEEPING IT SAFE

Please describe your security measures for arriving and leaving the school. Each child must be signed out by a parent or approved pick-up arrangement which we would have on file.

What medical supplies do you have on hand, and what medical experience does your staff have? Is your staff trained in CPR? We have medical supplies in each room and in the office.

Please describe your earthquake-preparedness plan, and what special equipment do you have on hand in the event of a disaster? We have water and food to last a week, and a full evacuation plan in published in each parent's handbook.

SWINGS 'N THINGS

Please describe your playground. Does it have plenty of shade? Little Village has a lovely secret garden type of setting, with huge trees providing both beauty and shade. The playground cannot be seen from the street.

Do you put sunscreen on the children? No feedback received.

What kind of toilet training is available? Wonderful small toilets and an open bathroom policy provide many opportunities for practice. We work with each family and child as they become ready.

HELPING OUT

What kinds of fundraising events are at your school each year? Silent auction, scrap, photo fundraiser, t-shirt sales and wrapping paper sales.

How much participation is required by each parent? There is one school work day per month and half a credit of committee work each year; that is our minimum requirement.

KEEPING IN TOUCH

How do you communicate with parents? Is there a newsletter or phone tree? We use email and a weekly newsletter as well as a quarterly news letter that a parent volunteer publishes.

Does the school publish an address book with all the parents' information in it? Yes, included in our handbook.

3 months - 4 years

MALIBU METHODIST NURSERY SCHOOL AND INFANT TODDLER CENTER

30128 Morning View Drive
Malibu, CA 90265
Phone: (310) 457-5144
See Map D on page 286

Contact: Kay Gabbard, Director

- ACCREDITATION: NONE
- NOT-FOR-PROFIT
- FINANCIAL AID IS AVAILABLE
- NUMBER OF KIDS: 54
- TUITION: $375-$700 MONTH
- WE HAVE KIDS WITH SPECIAL NEEDS

WHEN TO APPLY: NEW CHILDREN ARE ACCEPTED WHEN SPACE IS AVAILABLE.

Malibu Presbytarian experienced massive fire damage in 2008. They have since moved to a temporary campus while they reconstruct.

Malibu United Methodist Nursery School is sort of in the middle of nowhere! But for the families in the area, M.M.N.S. tries to be as flexible as possible, because of the geographical location. Flexibility is key in their approach. We believe that a structured and formal learning introduced too early, does not prepare children for a creative and rapidly changing world. Neither does it provide a solid conceptual foundation for future academic experiences. Therefore, we provide a curriculum that flows from the children's needs and interests, rather than one imposed upon them by us," says school director Kay Gabbard.

Malibu Methodist Nursery School is a mixed-age school, and believes the children have the curriculum inside of them. The environment encourages them to use their interests and curiosity to create the day. "Nothing is based on a book or a syllabus. 'It's November, this is what we do in November' kind of thinking. There is no flexibility there. Here, every day is a surprise," says Kay Gabbard, who joined as the director in 1978. "The ratio is one teacher to every six children, and there is so much more you can do when you only have six children to be with during the day!"

The school has many animals (rabbits and chickens, from what was immediately visible), a trampoline, a great outdoor playground, with a little 'risk' built into it… and books available everywhere. There are four classrooms, and whenever a room is open, a child can go into it. The art studio space rivals some adult contemporary studios, which probably don't even have as much available to them! Malibu Methodist Nursery School's philosophy of education and caring for young children is well known throughout Malibu and beyond. The centerpiece of this philosophy is the principle that children learn in an environment that is rich in 'hands-on' explorations, with staff guidance that is supportive and that encourages risk taking, reflection, problem solving, and individuality.

BACKGROUND

The school was established by a former church member, Fern Johnson. She was Director for about ten years, and Kay Gabbard has been the Director for the last 30 years.

BIRD'S EYE VIEW

	Non-existent	Poor	Fair	Good	Excellent
Learning to Read Children learn to explore the world of books					✓
Dress-Up Children experiment with different roles and imagination					✓
Hand-Eye Children develop fine motor skills by using fingers and hands					✓
Building Blocks Children practice symbolic representation. They are developing an understanding of the relationships between size and shape, and the basic math concepts of geometry and numbers					✓
Arts and Crafts Children are developing small muscle control as well as creativity					✓
Body Coordination Children crawl through tunnels, climb and balance					✓
Meeting Time Gathering place to listen to the teacher and to stories					✓
Weights and Measures Water and Sand tables					✓
Beakers and Bunnies Classroom pets, aquariums....planting...					✓
Counting 1-2-3 A good preschool will stock basic early-learner software such as phonics or counting games					✓
Outdoor Play Encourage large muscle control and coordination					✓

Q & A

HOW THEY LEARN

What is your school's teaching philosophy? Malibu M.N.S. philosophy of education and caring for young children is well-known throughout Malibu and beyond. We believe that a structured and formal learning introduced too early does not prepare children for a creative and rapidly changing world. Nor does it provide a solid conceptual foundation for future academic experiences. Therefore, we provide a curriculum that flows from the children's needs and interests rather than one imposed upon them by us.

How do you implement the philosophy? The centerpiece of this philosophy is the principle that children learn in an environment that is rich in 'hands-on" explorations, with staff guidance that is supportive and that encourages risk taking, reflection, problem solving, cooperation and respect for the individual.

What specialty teachers are brought into the school? No feedback provided.

What is the teaching method? We as a teaching staff set up an environment rich in open-ended and natural materials. We listen and watch the children interact with this environment, reflect and debrief often as a staff and change the environment accordingly.

At what age do the children start? To what age is the school licensed? We start children at three months in the infant program and two years in the preschool.

HOW TO GET IN

Are there open house dates? When are tours given? Call and arrange a date.

Is there an interview? With the child or without? No!

Is preference given to applicants whose siblings are alumni? If we have space, we have space.

Are letters of recommendation encouraged? From what types of people? No.

How many applications do you receive each year? Unknown.

How many open spots are there each year? 25 or so.

What are some of the schools that children go on to after finishing their education at your preschool? Local public schools, Calmont, Our Lady of Malibu, View Point.

PIGGY BANK

Apart from tuition, what other fees do you charge? There is a $20 registration fee. No application fee.

How is tuition broken down? Tuition varies by program, length of days, or number of days per week.

What are the different payment plans available? No feedback received.

What is the fee schedule? No feedback received.

Is there a contract? There is a contract.

Do you have a tuition insurance program? No tuition insurance program.

HELPING HANDS

What accreditation is necessary for the teachers to work at your school? A.A. in early childhood education and two years of experience.

How many teachers are there? Six teachers.

How many aides are there? Six aides.

IN THE 'ROOM

What's the child-to-adult ratio? 4:1 for infant/toddler; 6:1 for preschoolers.

What are the policies for initial separation between parent and child? We encourage parents to visit with the child many times before the first day of school. We often ask for the first days to be shorter than regular. We ask parents to say goodbye—not just leave—and to let their child know how long they will be staying and then really leave when they say they are leaving. Don't drag on the goodbye.

Can you visit any time unannounced? Of course.

What are the hours? 8 a.m.-5:30 p.m.

Do you offer early bird or after-hours pick-up? If so, is there an extra fee? No feedback received.

Please describe a typical day for a child at your school. Children check in with their teachers in the morning when they arrive. They are then asked to decide in what classroom of the school they will begin their day. The rest of the day is spent moving from classroom to classroom, inside and outside, etc.

What kinds of academic activities are offered? Small muscle, large muscle, cooperative, individual, cooking, lots of science, lots of art/studio time, nature walks and much, much more.

What kinds of art activities are offered? Open-ended—very often initiated by something that is happening in the life of the child or in the life of the studio (a book the teacher has placed on a table, an arrangement the staff has put out of new materials, reflections from the day before).

Is the child's time structured or unstructured, or a mixture of both? Unstructured (by us) most of the time. They structure their days quite a bit, we find.

If a child is not interested in a particular activity, does he/she have other choices or is he/she encouraged to try it anyway? They will be invited to join. The decision is theirs.

How are disputes handled when they occur between the children? Staff serve as facilitators, model appropriate behavior, help children put their problems into words, help children finds solutions that work for all involved.

When and for how long is nap time? Nap time starts about 12:30 p.m. and lasts until children wake, but usually not past 3 p.m.

What kinds of beds do you use? Cots.

What do you do when a child is dropped off in the morning and is obviously not well? What do you do when a child becomes sick during the day? We call the parents in either case if they have already left, or we suggest parents take their child home if they appear sick on arrival.

Can you accommodate children with special needs? No feedback received.

KEEPING IT SAFE

Please describe your security measures for arriving and leaving the school. Parents walk their child into school through a latched gate. Doors have high knobs, there is a check in/check out with computer codes on our keypad. No one takes a child unless they are on the child's authorized list. We are very serious about this. We keep current, up-to-date notebooks of emergency phone numbers in various places in the school.

What medical supplies do you have on hand, and what medical experience does your staff have? Is your staff trained in CPR? There is annual infant/child CPR for the entire staff. Band-aids, soap, First Aid references and a local doctor is on call for phone conferences when necessary.

Please describe your earthquake-preparedness plan, and what special equipment do you have on hand in the event of a disaster? We have monthly drills, under tables, under doorways. We have cribs on wheels for babies. We have earthquake kits in each room which contain water, blankets, some food, flashlight, radio, First Aid supplies, etc. Fire readiness is more prominent for us. Parents know where our local shelter would be.

SWINGS 'N THINGS

Please describe your playground. Does it have plenty of shade? Our outdoor classroom is UNBELIEVABLE.

Do you put sunscreen on the children? We ask parents to put hats on their children and sunscreen daily all year long. We sunscreen at midday or after a water play activity.

What kind of toilet training is available? Whatever it takes. Our bathrooms are child-friendly (no closed stalls) and open all day long. The changing table is across from the toilets, so there is a lot of modeling going on.

HELPING OUT

What kinds of fundraising events are at your school each year? Cook's Tour, a home tour of four lovely Malibu homes.

How much participation is required by each parent? Every family must send at least one family member to help that day. Parents are encouraged to help with the planning of this event as well.

KEEPING IN TOUCH

How do you communicate with parents? Is there a newsletter or phone tree? E-mail, bulletin boards, letters from the director, articles of interest, meetings, open houses, parenting classes, woman's group, Dad's breakfast, Grandparents Day, Family Day at school, etc. We have phone trees for immediate dismissal in case of emergency.

Does the school publish an address book with all the parents' information in it? No.

preschool

MALIBU PRESBYTERIAN NURSERY SCHOOL

3324 Malibu Canyon Rd.
Malibu, CA 90265
Phone: (310) 456-6615
See Map D on page 286

Contact: Cindy Ludwig, Director

- ACCREDITATION: NONE
- NOT FOR-PROFIT
- FINANCIAL AID IS NOT AVAILABLE
- NUMBER OF KIDS: 40 A DAY
- TUITION: $300-$675 MONTH
- WE HAVE KIDS WITH SPECIAL NEEDS

WHEN TO APPLY: APPLICATIONS ARE AVAILABLE AT ANY TIME.

The Malibu Presbytarian Nursery School experienced massive damage from the 2008 wildfires, and is in a temporary campus on Malibu Knolls Road.

When I arrived at Malibu Presbyterian Nursery School, tucked away on Malibu Canyon Road, I was greeted by a diverse group of children all dressed in their p.j.'s. "It's pajama day!" grinned one little boy in Spiderman pajamas. There is a lot to grin about here at Malibu Presbyterian Nursery School. Most immediate is the amazing view of the ocean, which juxtaposes the playground and outside lunch and play area and, exciting news…the outdoor playground area is expanding and is being completely renovated

"At Malibu Presbyterian Nursery School, we believe that parents are the primary caretakers of their children. Our purpose is to form a partnership with parents and together provide opportunity for the developmentally appropriate social, physical, emotional, spiritual, and cognitive growth of each child. We strive to be a place where children and their families are treated with love and respect. We believe that each child is a unique and gifted creation of God, to be affirmed and encouraged in his or her individuality. We will provide an atmosphere that encourages and empowers each child to develop a positive self-concept and the ability to independently resolve situations within the peer group. Our hope is that each child will leave the school knowing that "I am special" and "I can make a difference in this world."*

Everything at M.P.N.S. is unstructured within a structure. They operate on a 'flow system"(explained to me by Director Cindy Ludwig). There are five classrooms, and children can play wherever there is a teacher. The schedule is always the same, however, the teachers rotate, or flow, from room to room. Each teacher stays in one particular room for two weeks, then on to the next room. It enables them to completely focus on the 'task at hand' (depending on the room). Rooms can have art, dramatic play, blocks, story time/reading, and there is a skills room, which is academic pre-kindergarten. Cindy Ludwig explains the strength of the 'flow system.' "Under this structure, children come to know and trust several different teachers, so the temporary absence of one does not become a devastating experience of loss. Our pre-schoolers are also able to interact with children both older and younger than themselves, while still maintaining a close relationship with a smaller group of peers at the same developmental stage. The daily program includes creative arts, music, nature and science experiences, stories, outdoor play, and pre-kindergarten readiness. Children 'flow' through different areas in age-related groups, making new friends and developing essential life skills along the way."

*Philosophy Statement of M.P.N.S

BACKGROUND

Malibu Presbyterian Nursery School was established in 1965 as an outreach ministry of Malibu Presbyterian Church to the children of the community. Mrs. Verle Riggle was the founding director, and Director until her retirement in 1991. Cindy Ludwig became the Director after Mrs. Riggle's retirement.

BIRD'S EYE VIEW

	Non-existent	Poor	Fair	Good	Excellent
Learning to Read Children learn to explore the world of books					✓
Dress-Up Children experiment with different roles and imagination					✓
Hand-Eye Children develop fine motor skills by using fingers and hands					✓
Building Blocks Children practice symbolic representation. They are developing an understanding of the relationships between size and shape, and the basic math concepts of geometry and numbers				✓	
Arts and Crafts Children are developing small muscle control as well as creativity					✓
Body Coordination Children crawl through tunnels, climb and balance					✓
Meeting Time Gathering place to listen to the teacher and to stories					✓
Weights and Measures Water and Sand tables					✓
Beakers and Bunnies Classroom pets, aquariums....planting...				✓	
Counting 1-2-3 A good preschool will stock basic early-learner software such as phonics or counting games				✓	
Outdoor Play Encourage large muscle control and coordination				✓	

Q & A

HOW THEY LEARN

What is your school's teaching philosophy? We are primarily a developmental school, with a structure. Our statement of philosophy: "At Malibu Presbyterian Nursery School, we believe that parents are the primary caretakers of their children. Our purpose is to form a partnership with parents and together provide opportunity for the developmentally appropriate social, physical, emotional, spiritual, and cognitive growth of each child. We strive to be a place where children and their families are treated with love and respect. We believe that each child is a unique and gifted creation of God, to be affirmed and encouraged in his or her individuality. We will provide an atmosphere that encourages and empowers each child to develop a positive self-concept and the ability to independently resolve situations within the peer group. Our hope is that each child will leave the school knowing that "I am special", and "I can make a difference in this world."

How do you implement the philosophy? Our "flow" system is, we believe, one of the strengths of our school. Under this structure, children come to know and trust several different teachers, so the temporary absence of one does not become a devastating experience of loss. The daily program includes creative arts, music, nature and science experiences, stories, outdoor play, and pre-kindergarten readiness. Children "flow" through different areas in age-related groups, making new friends and developing essential life skills along the way.

What specialty teachers are brought into the school? No feedback provided.

What is the teaching method? Children are encouraged to explore and experiment, with a teacher standing by to facilitate if necessary. Teachers are trained in developmental practice, and employ the philosophies of Piaget and Vygotsky. Kindness and Christian values are also emphasized here.

At what age do the children start? To what age is the school licensed? Children must be at least 2 years, 9 months to start. They may stay here until they are ready for kindergarten.

HOW TO GET IN

Are there open house dates? When are tours given? Tours may be arranged by appointment with the director.

Is there an interview? With the child or without? No, but parents are encouraged to see the school and speak with the director before applying.

Is preference given to applicants whose siblings are alumni? Yes. Some preference is also given to children of Malibu Presbyterian Church members, those who attend the "Mommy and Me" or MOPS groups here, and children who have been on the waiting list in the previous year.

Are letters of recommendation encouraged? From what types of people? No.

How many applications do you receive each year? Each year, we receive more applications that we have space available, after re-enrolling current children and admitting younger siblings. The number varies from year to year.

How many open spots are there each year? The number varies. Usually there are from 25 to 40 spots available. New children usually enroll for two or possibly three days per week.

What are some of the schools that children go on to after finishing their education at your preschool? Most of our graduates attend local public or parochial schools, Viewpoint, Carl Thorpe, Crossroads, Brentwood, and Conejo Carden schools, among others.

PIGGY BANK

Apart from tuition, what other fees do you charge? There is a $50 application fee. No entry fee.

How is tuition broken down? Current tuition for two days a week is $275 per month; for three days a week, it is $400 per month; for four days a week, it is $550 per month.

What are the different payment plans available? Tuition can be paid monthly or for the entire year. We accept credit cards, cash or checks.

What is the fee schedule? Tuition is due on the first school day of every month. Exceptions can be arranged with the director.

Is there a contract? No.

Do you have a tuition insurance program? No.

HELPING HANDS

What accreditation is necessary for the teachers to work at your school? All teachers have completed at least 15 early childhood education units, and most have B.A.'s. The director has an M.A. in early childhood education. Teachers must be Christians, with previous teaching experience or some record of working with young children. Continuing education each year is required.

How many teachers are there? We currently have eight fully qualified teachers.

How many aides are there? Two teacher aides with B.A. who are working on completing their ECE units.

IN THE 'ROOM

What's the child-to-adult ratio? 5:1.

What are the policies for initial separation between parent and child? We believe that every child handles separation differently, and we try to help parents and children make this important adjustment on an individual basis. Parents are welcome to stay as long as they or their child need to. We will provide separation strategies when the time is right.

Can you visit any time unannounced? Yes, though family members not known to the teachers or director may be asked for identification.

What are the hours? The regular school day is 9 a.m.-1 p.m. Children may arrive as early as 8:45 a.m.

Do you offer early bird or after-hours pickup? If so, is there an extra fee? Extended hours (until 3 p.m.) are available on an as-needed basis, Monday through Thursday. The fee for an extended day is $15 per day.

Please describe a typical day for a child at your school. A typical day looks like this: 9-9:30 a.m. arrival, free play; 9:30-9:45 a.m. is welcome time (music, rhymes and announcements in a large group); 9:45 a.m.-12:15 p.m. Group Time; children are divided by age and development level into five groups (6-14 children each) for story, art, snack, yard and pre-kindergarten experiences; 12:15-12:40 p.m. is lunch and social time; 12:40-1 p.m. is free play and departure.

What kinds of academic activities are offered? A "skills" rotation is a part of each morning for all pre-kindergarten children. This rotation is facilitated by a credentialed kindergarten/early childhood specialist, and focuses on developing cognitive and listening skills in an age-appropriate way.

What kinds of art activities are offered? Art is an important part of each day at M.P.N.S. All children spend at least 30 minutes per day experiencing art in a developmentally-appropriate, process-oriented setting.

Is the child's time structured or unstructured, or a mixture of both? Both. Our program is "unstructured with a structure."

If a child is not interested in a particular activity, does he/she have other choices or is he/she encouraged to try it anyway? Children are encouraged (but not forced) to try all activities presented to them.

How are disputes handled when they occur between the children? Children are encouraged to resolve their own conflicts, with an adult standing by to facilitate. Our discipline policy follows: "All discipline at Malibu Presbyterian Nursery School will be of a positive, affirming nature. We have found that in an atmosphere of love and acceptance, with a good balance of structured and free time, very little formal discipline is necessary. Usually a simple change of scenery or re-directing of attention will diffuse any problems. Children are encouraged to solve relational problems among peers by using their words and their reasoning abilities, with a teacher standing by to provide encouragement and intervene if necessary. Our credo here at Malibu Presbyterian is "you may not hurt yourself, another person, or any equipment." Teachers are trained to help each child adhere to this philosophy. If we reach an impasse with a child, we will enlist the parent's help before taking further steps."

When and for how long is nap time? Since we adhere to a half-day schedule, no nap times are necessary or provided.

What kinds of beds do you use? No naps.

What do you do when a child is dropped off in the morning and is obviously not well? What do you do when a child becomes sick during the day? Obviously, unwell children are asked not to stay at school. If a child becomes ill during the morning, the parent or other caregiver is called and asked to pick the child up. Parents are called in the event of more serious injuries.

Can you accommodate children with special needs? Yes. If we are otherwise a good fit for the child, we are delighted to include him/her in our program.

KEEPING IT SAFE

Please describe your security measures for arriving and leaving the school. Parents or caregivers sign each child in upon arrival. At dismissal, children are released only to parents or others designated on their emergency forms. The director is present at arrival and departure each day, to monitor the process and ensure the safety of each child.

What medical supplies do you have on hand, and what medical experience does your staff have? Is your staff trained in CPR? All staff members are certified in CPR and Pediatric First Aid, but we choose not to administer medications (other than Band-Aids and soap and water) here.

Please describe your earthquake-preparedness plan, and what special equipment do you have on hand in the event of a disaster? We have earthquake kits here for each child, and teachers are trained in CPR and First Aid. In the event of an emergency, teachers will stay with the children until their parents arrive.

SWINGS 'N THINGS

Please describe your playground. Does it have plenty of shade? Our playground was newly installed in 2002. It is center-based, with a sand area, a grass area, a sliding, climbing, and swing area (on Tot Turf), and a bike riding/ball playing asphalt area. Three permanent shade structures will be installed in March 2005.

Do you put sunscreen on the children? Sunscreen is available for all children at the check-in counter.

What kind of toilet training is available? Children are expected to be at least "in process" toilet training when they enroll. Teachers will change children when necessary, but do not engage in formal toilet training.

HELPING OUT

What kinds of fundraising events are at your school each year? Typically, a small auction is part of the Parent-Teacher Get Acquainted Party in the fall, and parents later raise money for the Teacher Appreciation Luncheon in the spring.

How much participation is required by each parent? No participation is required. Parents who are interested may become part of the Parent Guild and participate in the fundraising efforts.

KEEPING IN TOUCH

How do you communicate with parents? Is there a newsletter or phone tree? A telephone list is sent home to the parents. Addresses are kept confidential, and released to parents on request through the Director.

Does the school publish an address book with all the parents' information in it? A telephone list is sent home to the parents. Addresses are kept confidential and released to parents, upon request, through the Director.

---

preschool to 8th grade

MANHATTAN ACADEMY

1740 Manhattan Beach Blvd.
Manhattan Beach, CA 90266
Phone: (310) 374-1804
www.manhattanacademy.com
Map E on page 286

Contact: Marcia K. Mar, Directress

- ACCREDITATION: NONE
- FOR-PROFIT
- FINANCIAL AID IS AVAILABLE
- NUMBER OF KIDS: 200
- TUITION: $8,950-$10,450 YEAR
- WE HAVE KIDS WITH SPECIAL NEEDS

WHEN TO APPLY: APPLICATIONS ARE AVAILABLE YEAR-ROUND. THE PROGRAM IS RUN SEPTEMBER THROUGH MID-JUNE, WITH A TEN-WEEK SUMMER PROGRAM AVAILABLE. RE-ENROLLMENT OF CURRENT STUDENTS ENDS IN JANUARY, APPLICATIONS ARE THEN HANDLED FOR PROSPECTIVE STUDENTS.

I pulled up to the front of the school, which was white with a blue sign, and was greeted by the assistant director, Mrs. Giovanni—a very friendly, warm woman who shook my hand with a firm handshake. We got started with the tour right away. The first classroom that I visited was a double classroom. It was essentially one large room, however it had two classes in it. A shelf of toys divided the room, and each class had its own rug, set of learning materials and teachers. This was the only class of this nature, yet it showed how confident the teachers are with their teaching method. If the children were loud and difficult to control, this set-up would never work. All of the other rooms were single classrooms.

Mrs. Giovanni then showed me around each room, where I was met by many bright-eyed children. They were very interested in the reason for my visit. They asked many questions about why I was there, and if I had any pets. One student was so persistent that she tried to follow me out of the room and into another class, at which point her teacher had to coax her back into the room with an exciting new game. Initially, I was very surprised at how well the children worked on their own. Each had his/her own project, and the to freedom choose what he/she wanted to work on; some children were working in pairs, but most worked alone. I asked Mrs. Giovanni what the children were instructed to do, and she said that it was their free play time. I was astonished that these children were playing, yet the classroom was very quiet. A child in one of the classrooms was sewing with three different colored yarns on a loom; she sat very patiently and I was impressed by how developed her fine motor skills were; she was very precise and rarely had to correct herself. Every toy in the classroom is educational, so no matter what activity is choosen, will expand their minds.

This school uses the Montessori ideas in their classrooms. Each room has educational toys based on five different ideas—Practical Life, Sensorial, Math, Language and Culture. The Practical Life area had things like flower arranging and sewing. The sensorial toys included beading to develop fine motor skills. The math toys were counting, with beans or marbles. Language toys were letters such as "A" and picture cards such an "apple," and the children had to match the two cards. The culture section was mainly map puzzles, and tracing maps. The children also had their own garden where they get to plant things and watch them grow. Every year on Earth Day parents come in and the children work with the parents and plant a whole new garden. Next to the garden was the playground; the playground was unimpressive. Because Manhattan Academy is on a main street, the lots for the buildings are very small, so they did not have very much room for a playground. It is located under a tree and covered in seedpods from the tree. It had a slide and some tunnels for the children to crawl through. When I was visiting there were no children playing in the playground. Next to the playground it what looks like an empty lot that the school has purchased and turned into a field for the children to play in. This was very nice, and although there were no children playing on it at the time, it looked like they could have a lot of fun with it.

Background

Established in 1975 and founded on the principals of Dr. Maria Montessori.

BIRD'S EYE VIEW

	Non-existent	Poor	Fair	Good	Excellent
Learning to Read Children learn to explore the world of books					✓
Dress-Up Children experiment with different roles and imagination					✓
Hand-Eye Children develop fine motor skills by using fingers and hands					✓
Building Blocks Children practice symbolic representation. They are developing an understanding of the relationships between size and shape, and the basic math concepts of geometry and numbers					✓
Arts and Crafts Children are developing small muscle control as well as creativity					✓
Body Coordination Children crawl through tunnels, climb and balance					✓
Meeting Time Gathering place to listen to the teacher and to stories					✓
Weights and Measures Water and Sand tables					✓
Beakers and Bunnies Classroom pets, aquariums....planting...					✓
Counting 1-2-3 A good preschool will stock basic early-learner software such as phonics or counting games				✓	
Outdoor Play Encourage large muscle control and coordination		✓			

Q & A

HOW THEY LEARN

What is your school's teaching philosophy? Toddler and preschool programs are Montessori—children work at their level, at their own pace.

How do you implement the philosophy? Toddler and preschool lead teachers are Montessori-trained, with a special postgraduate program beyond the B.A. education program.

What specialty teachers are brought into the school? No feedback received.

What is the teaching method? Montessori.

At what age do the children start? To what age is the school licensed? Our Montessori program is from 18 months through seven years of age; we also have a preparatory school that runs from second through eigth grades.

HOW TO GET IN

Are there open house dates? When are tours given? Community tours given October 10, January 20 and February 20, April 3, May 15.

Is there an interview? With the child or without? The child is observed by the directoress in an informal play setting. Parents are required to attend a meeting prior to starting. The directoress makes a point to individually meet and get to know prospective parents during the tours and application process. We work from a "you're in unless proven differently" standpoint—that is, rather than put undue stress on children to "perform," our assumption is they are all wonderful. We wean out the 1/100th later that don't fit. We look more closely to the parents—how they discipline when the family's visiting the campus, and how the children behave when visiting the campus.

Is preference given to applicants whose siblings are alumni? Yes, and there is a 5% sibling discount for siblings attending during the same term.

Are letters of recommendation encouraged? From what types of people? We look at any reports we receive from prior schools attended; we have many current families who recommend certain families to our school. With the knowledge of our current families' behavior, we place great weight on their remarks/recommendations of prospective families.

How many applications do you receive each year? No feedback received.

How many open spots are there each year? We do not have many open spaces available.

What are some of the schools that children go on to after finishing their education at your preschool? Obviously we prefer they stay with us through eigth grade. It depends on the parents' financial situation. Some who do leave prior to eigth grade go to public school, others go to private schools where they will be able to complete high school (such as Chadwick).

PIGGY BANK

Apart from tuition, what other fees do you charge? There is a $200 non-refundable application fee (due at the time of application), a $150 re-registration fee, an annual insurance fee of $85, an enhancement fee of $200, and an earthquake preparedness fee of $50.

How is tuition broken down? Tuition is $8,950 for half-day students, and $10,450 for full-day students.

What are the different payment plans available? Monthly, semi-annual, annual.

What is the fee schedule? The re-registration fee is due in February, and the annual insurance and enhancement fees are due in July. The earthquake preparedness fee is renewable every four years.

Is there a contract? There is a financial contract.

Do you have a tuition insurance program? There is an insurance fee for liability.

HELPING HANDS

What accreditation is necessary for the teachers to work at your school? Teachers must have a B.A. plus Montessori accreditation (post-graduate degree). Assistant teachers usually have their B.A. degrees but no Montessori training; some have A.A. degrees. Rarely do we hire anyone as an assistant with at least an A.A. degree—only if there's been many years of experience and they come highly recommended.

How many teachers are there? No feedback received.

How many aides are there? No feedback received.

IN THE 'ROOM

What's the child-to-adult ratio? It varies by the number of students, but usually 4:1 for infant/toddler; 9:1 for preschoolers.

What are the policies for initial separation between parent and child? We work a transition schedule with the parents, which varies depending on the child's age and their previous separation experience with the parents. It can be one to four, or more, days; we also encourage the child to visit during playtime for several days in advance of the start date.

Can you visit any time unannounced? No.

What are the hours? Open from 7 a.m.-6 p.m.

Do you offer early bird or after-hours pick-up? If so, is there an extra fee? There is no charge for morning child care from 7-9 a.m.

Please describe a typical day for a child at your school. For preschool, there is the typical "Montessori work period" (usually 9-11:30 a.m.) where the child works on appropriate lessons for himself/herself. Lessons are initially presented by a Montessori directress (our word for teacher, also our word for the headmistress of the school), where the child has the ability to work inside an assigned classroom or in the outdoor environment where a teacher is stationed. Gardening, science, hammering, art and other work is done outside. There are times where lessons are one-on-one; some are small group. There is a lunch period where close attention is paid to "Grace and Courtesy" (same academic level in a particular subject) or whole class lesson (such as the "Purpose" lessons). After lunch is outdoor playtime. For those staying beyond 2:30 p.m., there is a 90-minute nap if desired, then additional snacks and playtime—

no TV unless it's a rainy day, and no cartoon videos. Lots of art and cooking after school. Also, enrichment classes are available if someone wishes to sign up for tae kwon do, gymnastics, art, piano or dance.

What kinds of academic activities are offered? Montessori uses phonetics in language teaching. Montessori materials are used throughout the classroom, most especially in the area of math. Activities are determined by each child's individual needs and capacity.

What kinds of art activities are offered? Daily art projects, guided and free. A composer or artist is studied each month by the class.

Is the child's time structured or unstructured, or a mixture of both? A mixture of both.

If a child is not interested in a particular activity, does he/she have other choices or is he/she encouraged to try it anyway? Yes, the child is empowered. The teacher has specific lessons that are appropriate for each child, but the child is given choices as to which lesson to work on at a given time. We are great at "noodging"—getting a child to "think outside of the box, work outside of the box"—and trying something new!

How are disputes handled when they occur between the children? We teach children early on to "use their words." We do not like the children to become adult-dependent in settling differences. We let them know we will help if they are having difficulty in communicating with the other person involved. We have what we call a "peace table," where children can sit together to settle a dispute; whoever is holding the peace beads gets to speak and express his/her feelings, then the other one has a turn, and together they try to come to an agreement.

When and for how long is nap time? Nap time is 60-90 minutes, from 2:30-4 p.m.

What kinds of beds do you use? Cots. Children bring their favorite blankie for nap time.

What do you do when a child is dropped off in the morning and is obviously not well? What do you do when a child becomes sick during the day? The parent is immediately called. Parents learn quickly that we will not accept sick children, exposing the other children as well as the staff. Parents are required to sign a Sick Policy agreement that lists when children must be kept at home.

Can you accommodate children with special needs? We do have children with ADD and ADHD. Some are on medication, some are not.

We have diabetic students. Our experience indicates Montessori seems to be too sensorial-rich for children with autism and too overwhelming for them.

KEEPING IT SAFE

Please describe your security measures for arriving and leaving the school. The toddler building is secured/locked; visitors must be buzzed to be let in. The main building has someone stationed at the front desk at all times; that's the only entrance to the building. All three of our buildings have silent alarms connected directly to the Manhattan Beach Police Department. Toddler and preschool children must be signed in and out. Children are not allowed to leave with someone not listed on the child's forms; phone calls for such requests are not accepted, and must be in writing.

What medical supplies do you have on hand, and what medical experience does your staff have? Is your staff trained in CPR? Every staff member is required to complete CPR and First Aid training EVERY year for infant, toddler, child and adult level**s**.

Please describe your earthquake-preparedness plan, and what special equipment do you have on hand in the event of a disaster? We meet state regulations–too lengthy to write! We have training, materials, and plans for both on-campus and off-campus housing as needed in an emergency.

SWINGS 'N THINGS

Please describe your playground. Does it have plenty of shade? We have a beautiful full lot-sized playground for running, with lots of shade trees, and another play area with play equipment.

Do you put sunscreen on the children? We ask parents to apply sunscreen to the children BEFORE they dress each morning, for optimal benefit.

What kind of toilet training is available? Our toddler staff does handle toilet training.

HELPING OUT

What kinds of fundraising events are at your school each year? The PTA did fundraising through this year. Beginning with the 2005-06 school year, there will be a $200 enhancement fee per family instead of fundraising projects.

How much participation is required by each parent? We encourage parent participation and have a high rate of it, but there are no specific requirements.

KEEPING IN TOUCH

How do you communicate with parents? Is there a newsletter or phone tree? There's a Wednesday folder—each Wednesday, all information goes home including a school-wide newsletter, as well as specific classroom newsletters once a month. Room parents also act as a "phone tree" as needed.

Does the school publish an address book with all the parents' information in it? Yes.

preschool

MANN FAMILY EARLY CHILDHOOD CENTER

11661 West Olympic Boulevard
Los Angeles, CA 90064
Phone: (310) 445-1280
www.wbtla.org
See Map D on page 286

Carol Bovill, Director of Early Childhood Education

- ACCREDITATION: NAEYC
- NOT-FOR-PROFIT
- FINANCIAL AID IS AVAILABLE
- NUMBER OF KIDS: 250
- TUITION: $9,500-$16,500 YEAR
- WE HAVE KIDS WITH SPECIAL NEEDS

WHEN TO APPLY: BY EARLY DECEMBER, YEAR PRIOR TO ADMISSION.

The Mann Family Early Childhood Center shares the same building as Brawerman Elementary of the Wilshire Boulevard Temple. Director Carol Bovill gave me a tour of the campus (which was a little quiet during the summer months) but still bustling with activity during their summer program. One hallway was decorated with a beautiful rainforest display, and while walking through their classrooms the kids were working on the next art project, playing with clay or putting together puzzles while teachers attentively provided guidance. There were so many colorful toys and puzzles available, all designed to enhance phonics, measuring, counting and many other lessons.

MFECC is a reform Jewish day school that draws from various teaching methods, and incorporates these philosophies with reform Judaism. During my visit, Carol shared about her recent travels to Italy, where she had been continuing her studies in Montessori and Reggio teaching philosophies. She believes in challenging the children while meeting their needs. In my opinion, the school has achieved a nice balance. The curriculum very much reflects what she talks about, and Carol has a wonderful relationship with the children, and addressed each one by first name.

Carol emphasized one thing throughout my visit: respect for the child. As their number one priority, MFECC's kids are encouraged to make empowering choices in their day-to-day activities. They encourage kids to pour their own juice, and ask that they assist in forming the daily curriculum. This past spring, they happened to be studying planets during Passover. The next thing you know, they were off to the planetarium while integrating it in their study of the solar system! What a way to bring the holidays to outer space!

The children were so engaged with their activities, but at the same time very interested in my visit, and all very eager to chat with me. With so many wonderful activities and lessons planned throughout the school year, it's no wonder that the kids are happy to be here.

The family is very involved in their child's learning. Just before graduation, the children create their own torah and decorate it with the help of their parents and grandparents. Carol showed me an example, and I was touched by how much of a thoughtful keepsake and tradition this was.

MFECC accepts applications from everyone, but gives priority to the Wilshire Boulevard Temple members. There is a serious wait list, but consider applying to this preschool especially if you would like your children to attend Brawerman Elementary after they graduate from MFECC. You must take a tour of the campus to receive an application. Admission is highly competitive, so apply early!

I thoroughly enjoyed visiting the Mann Family Childhood Center and I hope you will too.

BACKGROUND

Wilshire Boulevard Temple, one of the country's most highly respected Reform Jewish congregations first opened its doors in 1929 on Wilshire Boulevard in the Wilshire Center neighborhood of Los Angeles. As the Jewish community in Los Angeles moved westward, the Temple developed a campus on the corner of Barrington and Olympic in West Los Angeles. Dedicated in 1998, this campus houses the Mann Family Early Childhood Center in addition to Brawerman Elementary School, a Religious School, a chapel and meeting, social service and educational facilities for children and adults. In the fall of 2008 Wilshire Boulevard Temple opened its second early childhood program to serve East LA.

BIRD'S EYE VIEW

	Non-existent	Poor	Fair	Good	Excellent
Learning to Read Children learn to explore the world of books					✓
Dress-Up Children experiment with different roles and imagination					✓
Hand-Eye Children develop fine motor skills by using fingers and hands					✓
Building Blocks: Children practice symbolic representation. They are developing an understanding of the relationships between size and shape, and the basic math concepts of geometry and numbers					✓
Arts and Crafts Children are developing small muscle control as well as creativity					✓
Body Coordination Children crawl through tunnels, climb and balance					✓
Meeting Time Gathering place to listen to the teacher and to stories					✓
Weights and Measures Water and Sand tables					✓
Beakers and Bunnies Classroom pets, aquariums....planting...					✓
Counting 1-2-3 A good preschool will stock basic early-learner software such as phonics or counting games					✓
Outdoor Play Encourage large muscle control and coordination					✓

Q & A

HOW THEY LEARN

What is your school's teaching philosophy? Our school offers a developmental program that draws from three educational early childhood philosophies: High Scope, Reggio Emilia, and Montessori.

How do you implement the philosophy? We incorporate the High Scope practice of self-directed centers during indoor play. We embrace the Reggio Emilia emphasis on respecting every child and the things they are interested in and create. We also draw from the Reggio practice of emergent curriculum, creating lessons and activities based on the interests of the children. And we use the Montessori emphasis on sensory experiences in the classroom.

What specialty teachers are brought into the school? Our program includes a music specialist, soccer specialist and art specialist every week.

What is the teaching method? We teach academics using developmental practices.

At what age do the children start? Children must be two-years-old by August 31 of the fall they enter school.

To what age is the school licensed? Kindergarten age.

HOW TO GET IN

Are there open house dates? When are tours given? Monthly open house tours are offered throughout the year. Parents meet with the Director, learn about our school's unique blend of philosophies, visit classrooms and then given an application. Parents should call the school office to reserve a space on a tour.

Is there an interview? With the child or without? The Director meets every family that applies to the program.

Is preference given to applicants whose siblings are alumni? Yes, preference is given to applicants whose siblings have gone through our program.

Are letters of recommendations encouraged? From what types of people? Letters of recommendation are not required for admissions.

How many applications do you receive each year? We receive more than two applications for each available spot.

How many open spots are there each year? Between 70-85.

What are some of the schools that children go on to after finishing their education at your preschool? Brawerman Elementary School, Brentwood, Buckley, Carlthorpe, Corrine Seeds/ UCLA Lab School (UES), Crossroads, Curtis, Echo Horizon, John Thomas Dye, Lawrence, Mirman, PS#1, Village School, Wildwood, Willows and local public schools.

PIGGY BANK

Apart from tuition, what other fees do you charge? Emergency preparedness fee is $100, Parent Association Fee is $150.

How is tuition broken down? Tuition varies depending on the age of the child and length of the program they attend.

What are the different payment plans available? Three options: 1. Pay all at once, two payments or four payments. Payment can be in the form of cash, check or credit card.

What is the fee schedule? See question three.

Is there a contract? Yes all families sign a tuition agreement.

Do you have a tuition insurance program? No.

HELPING HANDS

What accreditation is necessary for the teachers to work at your school? We prefer our teachers to hold Master's and Bachelor's degrees and at least two years of early childhood education classroom experience. Teachers must also have at least 12 early childhood education units.

How many teachers are there? We have a total of 42 teachers.

How many aides are there? We do not use teacher aides in the classroom; all of our teachers are equal as co-teachers.

IN THE ROOM

What's the child-to-adult ratio? The ratio depends on the age of the children. In our youngest class, the ratio is 4 children to one teacher. In our oldest class, the ratio is 8 children to one teacher.

What are the policies for initial separation between parent and child? Consistent with developmental practice, parents may stay in the classroom as long as their child needs.

Can you visit any time unannounced? Our classrooms are always open and parents are welcome to visit at anytime.

What are the hours? Depending on the age of the children, we offer programs from: 9-12, 9-2:30 p.m., 12:15-3:15 p.m., or 12:45-3:45 p.m.. Enrichment classes are offered Monday through Thursday from 1 to 2 p.m.

Do you offer early bird or after-hours pick-up? If so, is there an extra fee? For an additional fee, children may be dropped off at 7:45 a.m. for early morning care. We also offer after school care until 3:10 p.m.

Please describe a typical day for a child at your school? Indoor play time during which children may choose from any/all of the following: a math center offering Unifix blocks, geo boards, fine motor manipulatives, sequencing, sorting or stacking, and/or small unit blocks; a language arts center with puzzles, matching games, wipe-off boards, journals, letter games, and alphabet magnets; an art center with an array of creative materials; a sensory center where the children are exposed to a variety of textures and consistencies; a dramatic play center that includes such things as dress-up clothes, play kitchens, tools and a work bench for imaginative play; a science center with magnets, magnifiers, mirrors, plants, pets, and balance scales to explore with; and a library area for book exploration and quiet reflection. Children and teachers convene for a group meeting time which includes sharing of ideas, music and singing, flannel stories and books, and games and movement. A nutritious snack is provided by the school. Activities available on our yards include sand play, tricycles, running, climbing, sliding, art on our built-in easels, and water play at our water tables. All children eat lunch in school.

What kind of academic activities are offered? Academics are woven into all of the developmental activities we offer. For example, children may learn math, science, and listening skills through cooking, vocabulary and language arts through songs, rhymes and word play, etc.

What kinds of activities are offered? All kinds! We offer creative play, building, art, music, cooking, gross motor activities indoors and outdoors such as climbing, running, bicycle riding, etc.

Is the child's time structured or unstructured or a mixture of both? A child's time at school is usually a mixture of both.

If a child is not interested in a particular activity, does he/she have other choices or is he/she encouraged to try it anyway? Children are encouraged to try new things but are never forced to participate in an activity.

How are disputes handled when they occur between the children? Dialoguing and empathy are used in conflict resolution.

What and for how long is nap time? We have no nap time.

What kinds of beds do you use? n/a

What do you do when a child is dropped off in the morning and is obviously not well? What do you do when a child becomes sick during the day? Teachers greet every child each day and assess his/her health. If a child appears sick upon arrival, we ask the adult to please take him/her home. If a child becomes sick during the day, he/she is isolated in an administrator's office, and a parent is called to come pick the child up.

Can you accommodate children with special needs? Once it is determined that a child has special needs, we work with the families to establish if a child can benefit from our program with the assistance of a family provided, therapeutic companion. In this way, we are able to accommodate the special needs of many children.

KEEPING IT SAFE

Please describe your security measures for arriving and leaving the school? There is a security gate at the entrance to our campus, everyone must stop there and be checked. All families must display security stickers on their cars to enter the parking lot. The door into the school is kept locked at all times; people who wish to enter are viewed by security camera and must be buzzed in. Parents must sign children in and out of the classroom every day.

What medical supplies do you have on hand, and what medical experience does your staff have? Is your staff trained in CPR? We have first aid kits in every classroom and in all administrative offices. We have three days of earthquake supplies on site. All staff receives first aid and CPR training annually.

Please describe your earthquake-preparedness plan, and what special equipment do you have on hand in the event of a disaster? We conduct monthly earthquake drills. Our supplies include portable toilets, food, potable water, blankets and first aid supplies.

SWINGS 'N THINGS

Please describe your playground. Does it have plenty of shade? We have four state of the art playgrounds. Each one has safety surfaces, exciting climbing structures, multi-leveled sandboxes, a variety of riding toys including tricycles and cars, basketball hoops, built-in easels, water fountains, and shade canopies.

Do you put sunscreen on the children? Parents are asked to apply sunscreen at home before coming to school. What kind of toilet training is available?

Children do not need to be toilet trained to attend school. We work with families as their children begin to train. Our Director conducts a series of popular workshops, one of which is entitled "Toilet Learning," is very popular with our parents!

HELPING OUT

What kinds of fundraising events are at your school each year? We have four annual fundraisers: a holiday gift boutique, a book fair, a main adult fundraiser and silent auction, and a family fundraiser at the Santa Monica Pier.

How much participation is required by each parent? We ask that every parent participate in some way, whatever way works for them.

KEEP IN TOUCH

How do you communicate with parents? Is there a newsletter or phone tree? Before starting school, each child in our school receives a visit in their home from their teacher. This home visit enables the child to meet their teacher for the first time in an environment that is comfortable and familiar to them. At the beginning of the school year our teachers phone the parents each evening to answer any questions that the parents may have. The lines of communication between school and the family home are always open. Every teacher has a school email address that she/he uses to communicate with parents on an ongoing, as-needed basis. Teachers and administration call home when necessary. We have an emergency phone tree for the families, as well. In addition, a weekly newsletter from the Director is emailed to families. This newsletter includes articles from each of the classroom teachers about the activities in each class.

Does the school publish an address book with all parent's information in it? Yes. This directory is published and distributed for the exclusive personal use of the students, families and teachers of our schools.

preschool

MONTESSORI OF MANHATTAN BEACH

315 S. Peck Ave.
Manhattan Beach, CA 90266
Phone: (310) 379-9462
www.montessorimbrpv.com
See Map E on page 286

Contact: Traci Sell, Director of School

- ACCREDITATION: NONE
- FOR-PROFIT
- FINANCIAL AID IS NOT AVAILABLE
- NUMBER OF KIDS: 300
- TUITION: $780-$930 MONTH
- WE HAVE KIDS WITH SPECIAL NEEDS

WHEN TO APPLY: APPLICATIONS ARE AVAILABLE ANY TIME. WE HAVE A WAITING LIST.

Montessori on Peck sits on a hill, has a white picket fence around it, and looks picture-perfect from the outside. It is in a quiet, pleasant part of town, just down the street from a couple of other schools. As I walked through the gates and into the office, I was greeted by the school's director, Erna Moore. She seemed very proud of her school as she introduced herself and agreed to take me around. This wasn't the longest tour I'd ever been on, but it was long enough to give me a good look at how a school of this size operates—it's big! This Montessori school works like most other good Montessori schools. Each classroom has four categories of toys: Math, Sensorial, Language and Practical Life. Math toys have to do with counting and multiplying. Sensorial toys generally focus on perfecting fine motor skills. Language toys focus mainly on spelling, however they do also have a Spanish program. Practical Life toys are generally things that reflect upon everyday activities, such as pouring water into a funnel and seeing where it ends up.

They have over 300 students, and it was very apparent while walking around campus. There were children everywhere! Some were on the playground, others in the bathroom, and the rest were in the many classrooms. The children were all very bright and cheery, and they greeted Ms. Moore with big smiles. Some of the classrooms have pets; in one there was a bunny and in another, a frog. The children who were looking after the frog were very eager to tell me all about him and what he likes to do! Nearly all the classrooms have mixed ages of children. They range in age from 2-6. There is one classroom that has only two-year-olds, and another with only six-year-olds. Children are placed in these classrooms if they need a little extra help getting ready for either kindergarten (the six-year-olds) or being put into mixed age classrooms (the two-year-olds).

The playground area was huge and had many different toys that helped the children with coordination, large motor skills, and large muscle control. The whole thing was built on a very forgiving surface. It felt almost like silicone but looked like green asphalt very pleasing to the eye.

There were three separate playgrounds, one suited specially for the younger children with smaller objects. The largest playground had a big wooden truck in it that the children were pretending to drive. It was fun watching them. This school also has two sister schools—one is in Rancho Palos Verdes and there is another in Manhattan Beach, closer to the ocean. Ms. Moore tells me that the two other schools are academically identical to this one. The only thing that is different is the campus and playgrounds. If you are interested in the Montessori method of teaching, then please take a look at these schools.

BACKGROUND

Judy Ernst founded the Montessori School of Manhattan Beach in 1968. MSMB/MSRPV is the only Montessori school in the South Bay owned by a credentialed Montessori teacher with over 20 years of teaching experience. There are two locations—one in Manhattan Beach and one in Rancho Palos Verdes. We are a private school providing academic programs by qualified teachers.

BIRD'S EYE VIEW

	Non-existent	Poor	Fair	Good	Excellent
Learning to Read Children learn to explore the world of books					✓
Dress-Up Children experiment with different roles and imagination					✓
Hand-Eye Children develop fine motor skills by using fingers and hands					✓
Building Blocks Children practise symbolic representation. They are developing an understanding of the relationships between size and shape, and the basic math concepts of geometry and numbers					✓
Arts and Crafts Children are developing small muscle control as well as creativity					✓
Body Coordination Children crawl through tunnels, climb and balance					✓
Meeting Time Gathering place to listen to the teacher and to stories					✓
Weights and Measures Water and Sand tables					✓
Beakers and Bunnies Classroom pets, aquariums....planting...					✓
Counting 1-2-3 A good preschool will stock basic early-learner software such as phonics or counting games				✓	
Outdoor Play Encourage large muscle control and coordination					✓

Q & A

HOW THEY LEARN

What is your school's teaching philosophy? The school is dedicated to upholding the right of every child to progress at their own pace, in their own individual way, and to be provided with the tools they need for their physical, emotional, social and intellectual development.

How do you implement the philosophy? Not only is the Montessori classroom a place for individual learning, it offers a mixture of ages. The older child learns through teaching the younger child. The younger child, in turn, is inspired to do more advanced work by having the older child in the same environment. After showing an interest in an activity and receiving a lesson from the teacher, the child continues working with the materials and returns it to its proper place. Therefore, the Montessori classroom is a community of workers with freedom of movement and choice.

What specialty teachers are brought into the school? No feedback provided.

What is the teaching method? In Montessori, we begin with practical and social skills, not just academic. Keeping track of belongings, putting things away, dressing oneself, sharing materials and respecting the limits of the community, are some of the initial benefits of total development of the Montessori classroom. These form foundations for growing independence.

At what age do the children start? To what age is the school licensed? Children are 24 months old to six years old.

HOW TO GET IN

Are there open house dates? When are tours given? Tours are best without the child, and then we require three visits with the parent and the child. No.

Is preference given to applicants whose siblings are alumni? Yes. There is also a 20% discount off the tuition of a second child, when two children of the family are enrolled at the same time.

Are letters of recommendation encouraged? From what types of people? No.

How many applications do you receive each year? The waiting list has over 200 applicants.

How many open spots are there each year? Varies.

What are some of the schools that children go on to after finishing their education at your preschool? Mostly public, but some private. Chadwick, Rolling Hill, Country Day.

PIGGY BANK

Apart from tuition, what other fees do you charge? There is a one-time, non-refundable $200 application fee. If needed, $100 per month for toilet training.

How is tuition broken down? Tuition ranges between $780-930 per month. Extended daycare is between $20-800 month.

What are the different payment plans available? Yearly or monthly.

What is the fee schedule? Monthly payment is due on the 1st and no later than the tenth of the month.

Is there a contract? No.

Do you have a tuition insurance program? No.

HELPING HANDS

What accreditation is necessary for the teachers to work at your school? Montessori teaching credentials.

How many teachers are there? Nineteen teachers.

How many aides are there? Twelve assistants.

IN THE 'ROOM

What's the child-to-adult ratio? 12:1.

What are the policies for initial separation between parent and child? No feedback received.

Can you visit any time unannounced? No feedback received.

What are the hours? 9 a.m.-6 p.m.

Do you offer early bird or after-hours pick-up? If so, is there an extra fee? Child care is available before school beginning at 7 a.m. and after school until 6 p.m. The morning care is offered without charge; child care after 3 p.m. is $80 per month, $70 for occasional use (1-2 days per week), or $20 per day for daily use.

Please describe a typical day for a child at your school. Although most of the class time is spent in individual or small groups, some part of each day is spent in whole class activities, (circle time) such as singing, storytelling, movement exercises or large muscle activities.

What kinds of academic activities are offered? See website for more information.

What kinds of art activities are offered? See website for more information.

Is the child's time structured or unstructured, or a mixture of both? Each class has a schedule.

If a child is not interested in a particular activity, does he/she have other choices or is he/she encouraged to try it anyway? Many other choices.

How are disputes handled when they occur between the children? We teach problem-solving skills and conflict resolution.

When and for how long is nap time? Nap time is from 1-2:45 p.m.

What kinds of beds do you use? Vinyl mats and bedding from home.

What do you do when a child is dropped off in the morning and is obviously not well? What do you do when a child becomes sick during the day? We call to have them picked up.

Can you accommodate children with special needs? It depends.

KEEPING IT SAFE

Please describe your security measures for arriving and leaving the school. Sign in and out. Forms are on hand for authorized pick-up from school.

What medical supplies do you have on hand, and what medical experience does your staff have? Is your staff trained in CPR? All staff is CPR and First Aid trained and current.

Please describe your earthquake-preparedness plan, and what special equipment do you have on hand in the event of a disaster? We have earthquake kits for each child.

SWINGS 'N THINGS

Please describe your playground. Does it have plenty of shade? No feedback received.

Do you put sunscreen on the children? No feedback received.

What kind of toilet training is available? Potty training is an additional $100 per month. If your child needs to be potty trained, we will gently help in this process as your child begins to show an interest.

HELPING OUT

What kinds of fundraising events are at your school each year? The Parent/Teacher Organization has fundraisers.

How much participation is required by each parent? Volunteer.

KEEPING IN TOUCH

How do you communicate with parents? Is there a newsletter or phone tree? E-mail, a monthly newsletter and parent/teacher conferences.

Does the school publish an address book with all the parents' information in it? No.

preschool

MONTESSORI SHIR-HASHIRIM

6047 Carlton Way
Los Angeles, CA 90028
Phone: (323) 465-1638
www.montessorihollywood.org
See Map C on page 286

Contact: Elena Cielak, Director

- ACCREDITATION: NONE
- FOR-PROFIT
- FINANCIAL AID IS NOT AVAILABLE
- NUMBER OF KIDS: 43
- TUITION: $1,300-$1,500 MONTH
- WE HAVE KIDS WITH SPECIAL NEEDS

WHEN TO APPLY: OCTOBER THROUGH JANUARY.

Tucked off the street in busy Hollywood, Montessori Shir-Hashirim looks like a lush, well-cared-for private home! The bright blue house with red trim, complete with white picket fence, looks like something right out of, well, a Hollywood movie! The lime tree in front, with two of the largest palm trees I've seen, and the expansive front porch greet you as you walk to the front door. Only when you get closer do you see signs of children. Bulletin boards with school activities (including Karate for Kids), and festive children's artwork bid you welcome.

As I was admitted at the door, I walked into several adjoining rooms absolutely animated and bustling with children engaged in a multitude of activities. Yet, for all of the flurry, there was an incredible sense of order and controlled chaos. A bell rings, and each child stops in their tracks, puts down whatever they are working on and gathers on the large open rug area for "Shakespeare for Kids." Under the trellis covering the back deck, I was treated to a modern version of Shakespeare in the Park, starring actors and actresses from three to six years old. As with the music, dance and art that is part of the creative self-expression, children are encouraged to "tell a story" through the various mediums. The other visiting parents and myself couldn't help but chuckle in delight at these children painting a picture with Shakespeare's language.

"We don't water things down for them. We appeal to their sensibility and humor. They can handle Shakespeare. In their innocence, they integrate what they get here into all parts of their lives. When their parents are stressed, they tell them to relax and show them yoga positions and how to breathe!" Chuckles Director Elena Cielak. Her jovial demeanor reveals the extreme amusement and joy she gets from the surprising things the children say and do. It appears that humor and lightness are always a part of her, even when she is being straightforward, effective, and gets down to business. There are low, very accessible counters in the kitchen area where children can prepare their snacks as well as child size toilets, though they do not provide toilet training here.

BACKGROUND

The school was established in 1985 and is run by Director Elena Cielak. There is another Montessori Shir-Hashirim school at 1260 North Vermont in Los Angeles, run by Nelida Gawlick.

BIRD'S EYE VIEW

	Non-existent	Poor	Fair	Good	Excellent
Learning to Read Children learn to explore the world of books					✓
Dress-Up Children experiment with different roles and imagination					✓
Hand-Eye Children develop fine motor skills by using fingers and hands					✓
Building Blocks Children practice symbolic representation. They are developing an understanding of the relationships between size and shape, and the basic math concepts of geometry and numbers					✓
Arts and Crafts Children are developing small muscle control as well as creativity					✓
Body Coordination Children crawl through tunnels, climb and balance				✓	
Meeting Time Gathering place to listen to the teacher and to stories					✓
Weights and Measures Water and Sand tables					✓
Beakers and Bunnies Classroom pets, aquariums....planting...					✓
Counting 1-2-3 A good preschool will stock basic early-learner software such as phonics or counting games					✓
Outdoor Play Encourage large muscle control and coordination					✓

Q & A

HOW THEY LEARN

What is your school's teaching philosophy? Montessori with an individual approach.

How do you implement the philosophy? All the teachers are Montessori trained.

What specialty teachers are brought into the school? Mandarin, French, Spanish and dance.

What is the teaching method? Montessori.

At what age do the children start? To what age is the school licensed? From two years old through six years old.

HOW TO GET IN

Are there open house dates? When are tours given? Tours are Wednesdays from 9-10 a.m. by appointment only, beginning in October.

Is there an interview? With the child or without? With parents only.

Is preference given to applicants whose siblings are alumni? Yes.

Are letters of recommendation encouraged? From what types of people? No.

How many applications do you receive each year? No feedback received.

How many open spots are there each year? No feedback received.

What are some of the schools that children

go on to after finishing their education at your preschool? No feedback received.

PIGGY BANK

Apart from tuition, what other fees do you charge? The application fee is $100, and there is a $900 entrance fee.

How is tuition broken down? Tuition is $1,300 monthly (half-day) and $1,500 monthly (full day). New student enrollment is in March, current students are re-enrolled in February.

What are the different payment plans available? Once a year, two payments, or eleven monthly payments.

What is the fee schedule? No feedback received.

Is there a contract? Yes.

Do you have a tuition insurance program? No.

HELPING HANDS

What accreditation is necessary for the teachers to work at your school? A college degree and Montessori teacher training.

How many teachers are there? The Carlton Way location has six teachers, and the Vermont location has four teachers.

How many aides are there? No feedback received.

IN THE 'ROOM

What's the child-to-adult ratio? 8:1.

What are the policies for initial separation between parent and child? We have a transition program on Saturdays from 9:30-11 a.m.

Can you visit any time unannounced? Yes.

What are the hours? 8 a.m.-5:30 p.m.

Do you offer early bird or after-hours pick-up? If so, is there an extra fee? No.

Please describe a typical day for a child at your school. Yoga, Spanish, French, drama, gardening, music, dance.

What kinds of academic activities are offered? No feedback received.

What kinds of art activities are offered? An art appreciation class once a week.

Is the child's time structured or unstructured, or a mixture of both? A mixture of both.

If a child is not interested in a particular activity, does he/she have other choices or is he/she encouraged to try it anyway? No feedback received.

How are disputes handled when they occur between the children? We encourage talking. We have the kids talk about their conflict. We do not encourage physical abuse at all.

When and for how long is nap time? Nap time is 90 minutes.

What kinds of beds do you use? Mats, and the children bring their own sleeping bags.

What do you do when a child is dropped off in the morning and is obviously not well? What do you do when a child becomes sick during the day? Sick kids cannot attend.

Can you accommodate children with special needs? Yes.

KEEPING IT SAFE

Please describe your security measures for arriving and leaving the school. No feedback received.

What medical supplies do you have on hand, and what medical experience does your staff have? Is your staff trained in CPR? No feedback received.

Please describe your earthquake-preparedness plan, and what special equipment do you have on hand in the event of a disaster? Everyone has an earthquake kit.

SWINGS 'N THINGS

Please describe your playground. Does it have plenty of shade? Great.

Do you put sunscreen on the children? No feedback received.

What kind of toilet training is available? None.

HELPING OUT

What kinds of fundraising events are at your school each year? Concerts, plays, talks, adult education.

How much participation is required by each parent? None.

KEEPING IN TOUCH

How do you communicate with parents? Is there a newsletter or phone tree? Email, newsletter and phone tree.

Does the school publish an address book with all the parents' information in it? Yes.

OAKDALE SCHOOL

12140 Riverside Drive
Valley Village, CA 91607
Phone: (818) 506-4304
See Map A on page 286

Contact: Patti Cunha and Nancy Hutton, Co-Directors

- ACCREDITATION: NONE
- FOR-PROFIT
- FINANCIAL AID IS AVAILABLE
- NUMBER OF KIDS: 74
- TUITION: $400-$910 MONTH
- WE HAVE KIDS WITH SPECIAL NEEDS

WHEN TO APPLY: NO APPLICATION CUT-OFFS.

"Play is a child's work." Said Patti Cunha, one of Oakdale's directors, as I set down for a chat in her busy office overlooking the preschool's play yard. She explained that the preschool, where she shares director responsibilities with Nancy Hutton, is an environment where "all families are welcome," and one of their purposes is to serve the community. The school focuses on art, which is a large part of the child's day. "We believe in process, not product, exposing children to different mediums and seeing where they'll take it," states Cunha, elaborating on the learning process. Free expression is definitely encouraged here.

Oakdale is all but impossible to find, located on a busy street corner, neatly tucked behind large shrubs. The building has three classrooms with two teachers in each, along with a floating aide. A play-based, family-oriented and community-rooted environment is the crux of this preschool's methodology. The firm belief in the young child as an individual and the knowledge that this is a time in a life where one should be allowed to run free and play, is also the heart of the ideology.

After my tour and as I'm back briefly in the Director's office, I hear a bunch of excited voices, and look over my shoulder to see a single file of barefoot preschoolers, with big smiles on their faces.skipping and singing. The sight of these "free spirits" was a perfect testament to Cunha's vision!

BACKGROUND

The school was established 38 years ago and founded by Tony Eden.

BIRD'S EYE VIEW

	Non-existent	Poor	Fair	Good	Excellent
Learning to Read Children learn to explore the world of books					✓
Dress-Up Children experiment with different roles and imagination				✓	
Hand-Eye Children develop fine motor skills by using fingers and hands				✓	
Building Blocks Children practice symbolic representation. They are developing an understanding of the relationships between size and shape, and the basic math concepts of geometry and numbers				✓	
Arts and Crafts Children are developing small muscle control as well as creativity				✓	
Body Coordination Children crawl through tunnels, climb and balance				✓	
Meeting Time Gathering place to listen to the teacher and to stories				✓	
Weights and Measures Water and Sand tables			✓		
Beakers and Bunnies Classroom pets, aquariums....planting...			✓		
Counting 1-2-3 A good preschool will stock basic early-learner software such as phonics or counting games				✓	
Outdoor Play Encourage large muscle control and coordination				✓	

Q & A

HOW THEY LEARN

What is your school's teaching philosophy? Play-based, developmental, non-academic, experimental.

How do you implement the philosophy? Implement through experience. "Free expression."

What specialty teachers are brought into the school? No feedback provided.

What is the teaching method? Play-based experimental.

At what age do the children start? To what age is the school licensed? Ages two through six.

HOW TO GET IN

Are there open house dates? When are tours given? Year-round, Mondays and Wednesdays.

Is there an interview? With the child or without? No formal interview.

Is preference given to applicants whose siblings are alumni? First come, first served.

Are letters of recommendation encouraged? From what types of people? No feedback received.

How many applications do you receive each year? No feedback received.

How many open spots are there each year? It depends on the year. Some people register when they are pregnant.

What are some of the schools that children go on to after finishing their education at your preschool? No feedback received.

PIGGY BANK

Apart from tuition, what other fees do you charge? There is a $200 registration fee.

How is tuition broken down? Mornings: $555 three day week, $630 four day week, $690 five days. Afternoons: $625 for three days, $725 for four, $825 for five days.

What are the different payment plans available? Open to anything as long as they pay.

What is the fee schedule? Bill every four weeks, 13 payments per year.

Is there a contract? There is a yearly contract.

Do you have a tuition insurance program? No tuition insurance.

HELPING HANDS

What accreditation is necessary for the teachers to work at your school? Everything. Very highly-educated. None of the teachers work full-time.

How many teachers are there? Six teachers in the morning, eight teachers in the afternoon.

How many aides are there? Two aides in the morning, one aide in the afternoon.

IN THE 'ROOM

What's the child-to-adult ratio? 6:1, or 5:1 for students under the age of three.

What are the policies for initial separation between parent and child? Case-by-case basis.

Can you visit any time unannounced? Absolutely.

What are the hours? 1:15-5 p.m.

Do you offer early bird or after-hours pick-up? If so, is there an extra fee? No feedback received.

Please describe a typical day for a child at your school. Transition classes are Tuesday and Thursday, 1:15-3:15 p.m., first-year class is 3, 4 or 5 in the afternoon.

What kinds of academic activities are offered? Play-based, hands-on developmental.

What kinds of art activities are offered? Everything.

Is the child's time structured or unstructured, or a mixture of both? Teachers set up environment for play.

If a child is not interested in a particular activity, does he/she have other choices or is he/she encouraged to try it anyway? So many choices for the children each day.

How are disputes handled when they occur between the children? Discipline is part of the curriculum. Varies according to age. Teachers directed to teach critical thinking.

When and for how long is nap time? No nap time—half-day programs only.

What kinds of beds do you use? No feedback received.

What do you do when a child is dropped off in the morning and is obviously not well? What do you do when a child becomes sick during the day? Call the family ASAP to pick up.

Can you accommodate children with special needs? Yes.

KEEPING IT SAFE

Please describe your security measures for arriving and leaving the school. No feedback received.

What medical supplies do you have on hand, and what medical experience does your staff have? Is your staff trained in CPR? CPR and First Aid.

Please describe your earthquake-preparedness plan, and what special equipment do you have on hand in the event of a disaster? No feedback received.

SWINGS 'N THINGS

Please describe your playground. Does it have plenty of shade? Plenty of shade.

Do you put sunscreen on the children? Yes.

What kind of toilet training is available? None.

HELPING OUT

What kinds of fundraising events are at your school each year? None.

How much participation is required by each parent? No feedback received.

KEEPING IN TOUCH

How do you communicate with parents? Is there a newsletter or phone tree? **Newsletter, phone, verbal meeting.**

Does the school publish an address book with all the parents' information in it? Parent roster.

preschool

Pacific Oaks Children's School

714 W. California Blvd.
Pasadena, CA 91105
Phone: (626) 397-1363
See Map B on page 286

Contact: Jane Rosenberg

- ACCREDITATION: NONE
- NOT-FOR-PROFIT
- FINANCIAL AID IS AVAILABLE
- NUMBER OF KIDS: 220
- TUITION: $290-$1,400 MONTH
- WE HAVE KIDS WITH SPECIAL NEEDS

WHEN TO APPLY: APPLICATIONS ARE DUE BY FEBRUARY OF THE PRECEDING SCHOOL YEAR. PARENTS MUST ATTEND TOUR TO RECEIVE AN APPLICATION.

This school, which provides programs to children from six months through preschool, occupies what once was a small neighborhood of Craftsmen homes circa 1905. In a society where kids don't necessarily get to play on the block, these preschoolers come to a neighborhood each day they attend school. Pacific Oaks Children's School has been in existence for fifty years. Current Director Jane Rosenberg and I toured around the campus and I was shown each of the homes that has been converted into a classroom building. Down the middle of them runs Shady Lane, what was once the actual street these classroom homes presently reside on.

I noticed much activity amongst the children—busy children, loud children, free children, much teacher interaction and an entire playground per house. The different homes accommodate different age groups, ranging from infant/toddler/parent through four-and six-year-olds. Rosenberg explains that the children "do a lot of choice making" and experience "hands-on learning." They're constantly being read to, and there is a push to develop reading and pre-literacy. She boasts of the excellent teachers working at this school who are so well versed with their craft and nimbly allow the students to develop their ideas into rich and meaningful lessons in the classroom. Methodology here is based on the following—anti-bias education, emergent curriculum, peaceful conflict resolution and experiential learning. Pacific Oaks has an international reputation as a school with a progressive philosophy that has been in existence for fifty years.

The school prides itself on choosing from a pool of families from various backgrounds and in the admissions process the "goal is to create the most diverse environment in each classroom," according to Rosenberg. There is a deliberate focus on reading and art. The outdoor art studio is filled with amazing creations from this school's youngsters. The library has some 7,000 books and the different groups of students attend the library once a week. In addition, the parents and teachers are able to check out books. In this progressive, non-traditional environment, families from as far as the west side of Los Angeles make the journey to have their children enrolled here.

As of fall 2008, Pacific Oaks no longer has kindergarten. They are focusing their efforts on preschool.

BACKGROUND

Pacific Oaks Children's School was founded by seven Quaker families in 1945.

BIRD'S EYE VIEW

	Non-existent	Poor	Fair	Good	Excellent
Learning to Read Children learn to explore the world of books					✓
Dress-Up Children experiment with different roles and imagination					✓
Hand-Eye Children develop fine motor skills by using fingers and hands					✓
Building Blocks Children practice symbolic representation. They are developing an understanding of the relationships between size and shape, and the basic math concepts of geometry and numbers					✓
Arts and Crafts Children are developing small muscle control as well as creativity					✓
Body Coordination Children crawl through tunnels, climb and balance					✓
Meeting Time Gathering place to listen to the teacher and to stories					✓
Weights and Measures Water and Sand tables					✓
Beakers and Bunnies Classroom pets, aquariums....planting...					✓
Counting 1-2-3 A good preschool will stock basic early-learner software such as phonics or counting games				✓	
Outdoor Play Encourage large muscle control and coordination					✓

Q & A

HOW THEY LEARN

What is your school's teaching philosophy? The curriculum at Pacific Oaks is influenced by our Quaker heritage and dedication to the principles of social justice and peace education. Our teachers skillfully facilitate problem solving and peaceful conflict resolution, teach respect for each other, promote social responsibility and integrate an anti-bias perspective into every aspect of our early childhood education programs. Further enrichment is provided by our team of specialists including an artist and musician-in-residence, children's librarian and consultant to assist children, families and teachers with a variety of special needs.

How do you implement the philosophy? Our capable teachers ask insightful questions and help children expand upon their thinking as they build meaningful curriculum from the emerging interests of their students, who have abundant opportunities for experiential learning as they participate in hands-on activities with a variety of open-ended materials.

What specialty teachers are brought into the school? We have a full-time artist-in-residence on campus as well as an outdoor art studio.

What is the teaching method? Experimental.

At what age do the children start? To what age is the school licensed? Pacific Oaks

Children's School provides outstanding programs for children from six months through preschool.

HOW TO GET IN

Are there open house dates? When are tours given? Call for a schedule of upcoming tours.

Is there an interview? With the child or without? We do not interview children. We strive to create a diverse learning community.

Is preference given to applicants whose siblings are alumni? Yes.

Are letters of recommendation encouraged? From what types of people? Letters of recommendation are not necessary.

How many applications do you receive each year? Varies.

How many open spots are there each year? Varies.

What are some of the schools that children go on to after finishing their education at your preschool? Children enter both public and private schools after graduating from Pacific Oaks Children's School. Some private schools include Walden School, Sequoyah School, Polytechnic School, Chandler School and Waverly School.

PIGGY BANK

Apart from tuition, what other fees do you charge? There is a $50 application fee. No entrance fee.

How is tuition broken down? Tuition varies based on the part-time or full-time program selected.

What are the different payment plans available? Tuition is paid monthly.

What is the fee schedule? Call the school office for a current fee schedule.

Is there a contract? We require 30 days' notice prior to withdrawing.

Do you have a tuition insurance program? No feedback received.

HELPING HANDS

What accreditation is necessary for the teachers to work at your school? Our Head Teachers are required to have a minimum of a bachelor's degree, however most have completed their master's degree.

How many teachers are there? Thirty-seven teachers are employed.

How many aides are there? No feedback received.

IN THE 'ROOM

What's the child-to-adult ratio? Infants are 1:1, two-year-olds are 5:1, three-year-olds are 7:1, and four-year-olds are 8:1.

What are the policies for initial separation between parent and child? Adults remain with their children in the infant/toddler program. Parents may choose when they are comfortable separating in our other programs, typically at age 2 to 3. Parents are always welcome visitors at school.

Can you visit any time unannounced? Yes.

What are the hours? School hours vary, depending upon program selection.

Do you offer early bird or after-hours pickup? If so, is there an extra fee? No feedback received.

Please describe a typical day for a child at your school. Children work in small groups, one-on one, in large group activities and at their own individual pace. The day includes child initiated and teacher directed activities with abundant opportunities for choice making. Social development is a central focus of our programs.

What kinds of academic activities are offered? The curriculum includes language and literacy acquisition, phonemic awareness, dramatic play, block building, numeral development, art projects, children's personal stories and science and nature education.

What kinds of art activities are offered? Children work with paint, clay, collage, sculpture etc.

Is the child's time structured or unstructured, or a mixture of both? Both structured and unstructured times are available. For children under the age of three, most of the day is unstructured allowing for free choice.

If a child is not interested in a particular activity, does he/she have other choices or is he/she encouraged to try it anyway? We offer both child-initiated and teacher-directed activities throughout the day. Children are never forced to participate in classroom activities.

How are disputes handled when they occur between the children? We facilitate problem solving and conflict resolution between children.

When and for how long is nap time? Nap times vary depending upon the age and needs of each child.

What kinds of beds do you use? No feedback received.

What do you do when a child is dropped off in the morning and is obviously not well?

What do you do when a child becomes sick during the day? When a child becomes ill, we contact the parents to pick-up their child from school.

Can you accommodate children with special needs? Yes.

KEEPING IT SAFE

Please describe your security measures for arriving and leaving the school. Parents are required to sign their child in and out of school each day.

What medical supplies do you have on hand, and what medical experience does your staff have? Is your staff trained in CPR? All of our teacher have Red Cross certification in both infant/child first aid and CPR.

Please describe your earthquake-preparedness plan, and what special equipment do you have on hand in the event of a disaster? We have disaster supplies on hand for three days for each child and teacher, which includes food, water, first aid supplies, blankets, flashlight, battery-powered radios, etc.

SWINGS 'N THINGS

Please describe your playground. Does it have plenty of shade? Our expansive one-and-a-half acre campus provides an ideal environment for learning and exploration with tree shaded play areas, original Craftsman homes, state-of-the-art play yards, children's library, art studio and neighborhood-like atmosphere.

Do you put sunscreen on the children? No feedback received.

What kind of toilet training is available? Toilet training is not required. We will support parents efforts in a non-stressful and relaxed manner.

HELPING OUT

What kinds of fundraising events are at your school each year? Parents are required to support three events per year including our Annual Fund Drive, Fall Festival and Silent Auction each spring.

How much participation is required by each parent? A minimum of 10 hours of volunteer work per year is required for each family.

KEEPING IN TOUCH

How do you communicate with parents? Is there a newsletter or phone tree? We have a school newsletter, evening parent meetings, email messaging and parent/teacher conferences.

Does the school publish an address book with all the parents' information in it? Yes.

preschool

PARENTS AND CHILDREN'S NURSERY SCHOOL

4603 Indianola Way
La Cañada 91011
Phone: (818) 790-2103
See Map B on page 286

Contact: Marji Golden

- ACCREDITATION: NONE
- NOT-FOR-PROFIT
- FINANCIAL AID IS AVAILABLE
- NUMBER OF KIDS: 120
- TUITION: $210-$465 MONTH
- WE HAVE KIDS WITH SPECIAL NEEDS

WHEN TO APPLY: THEY START FROM THEIR WAITING LIST, BUT THERE IS NO APPLICATION CUT OFF DATE.

I arrived mid-morning, the sun shining as I pulled up into the cul-de-sac outside the school in La Cañada. The first thing that caught my eye was a large brightly painted cut out of a cake made out of wood with the words: Early Childhood Education, Filled with Lots of Fun, At Parents and Children. It was proudly displayed right outside the entrance to the school attached to a wooden stake, which had been hammered into the grass—perfect! I entered the school and was greeted by Marji, the director of Parents and Children, a charming woman whose calm manner definitely sets the tone at her preschool in one of Los Angeles most affluent areas. She couldn't wait to show me around.

The school is made up of two ranch style California bungalows that sit side by side. One houses the 2-to-3 years olds and the other the 4-to-5 years old. Both are very roomy with lots of space for the children to learn and play in. Each school house has its own yard where the children do their art projects, with lots of drawings everywhere hanging out to dry. But what really took my breath away was the huge park-like playground that the school had been given when the City of La Cañada decided to build a freeway close by. Yes it's a little noisy, but the children didn't seem to mind and I soon forgot as I watched a group of little ones being released into the park to play. What fun they were all having, I wanted to join in!

In the 2009 school year, PCNS added a new afterschool program, where they incorporate a new activity each day of the week. See the Q&A section for details.

When I asked the Director, Marjie what she thought the role of a teacher should be, she said simply "my teachers are gentle and the guidance is constant." She also believes that in 20 years her kids will be creatively solving problems using the tools that they learned from their time in her preschool. Most of the kids go into the wonderful public school system that La Cañada offers, but some do go off to private schools such as St. Bedes and Crestview. The staff of teachers at Parents and Children were all wonderfully welcoming to me. They did not seem at all fussed by my unexpected visit and carried on as if I wasn't there. No airs or graces here. If the kids get into a fight, they are encouraged to problem solve. The teachers will bring them together in an effort to help them do this. If that doesn't work then the kids might be asked to take a break and spend a little time alone thinking about what's happened.

BACKGROUND

Our school was founded in 1942 by a group of parents who wanted their children to have positive group play experiences before starting kindergarten. Our providing an age-appropriate developmental program, which encourages creativity and exploration, stimulates cognitive growth while fostering social and emotional maturity in preparedness not only for kindergarten, but for life.

BIRD'S EYE VIEW

	Non-existent	Poor	Fair	Good	Excellent
Learning to Read Children learn to explore the world of books					✓
Dress-Up Children experiment with different roles and imagination				✓	
Hand-Eye Children develop fine motor skills by using fingers and hands					✓
Building Blocks Children practice symbolic representation. They are developing an understanding of the relationships between size and shape, and the basic math concepts of geometry and numbers					✓
Arts and Crafts Children are developing small muscle control as well as creativity					✓
Body Coordination Children crawl through tunnels, climb and balance					✓
Meeting Time Gathering place to listen to the teacher and to stories					✓
Weights and Measures Water and Sand tables					✓
Beakers and Bunnies Classroom pets, aquariums....planting...					✓
Counting 1-2-3 A good preschool will stock basic early-learner software such as phonics or counting games					✓
Outdoor Play Encourage large muscle control and coordination					✓

Q & A

HOW THEY LEARN

What is your school's teaching philosophy? We are a developmental program where the children learn through art, literature, music, exploration and communication.

How do you implement the philosophy? When hiring, we let the new teachers observe first, talk to them about our approach, and make sure that they share the same ideas.

What specialty teachers are brought into the school? No feedback received.

What is the teaching method? Developmental. We are very creative with our curriculum and specialize in a very loving, gentle approach with a lot of emphasis on communication.

At what age do the children start? To what age is the school licensed? We accept children who are 2 years, 9 months and toilet independent through kindergarten entrance age.

HOW TO GET IN

Are there open house dates? When are tours given? We run tours year round.

Is there an interview? With the child or without? No interviews, but we like it when the parents bring their children with them for the tour so that parents can see the child's reaction to our school.

Is preference given to applicants whose siblings are alumni? Yes.

Are letters of recommendation encouraged? From what types of people? No.

How many applications do you receive each year? 25-30.

How many open spots are there each year? Around 80.

What are some of the schools that children go on to after finishing their education at your preschool? La Cañada Public, Crestview, St. Bede's, Village Christian.

PIGGY BANK

Apart from tuition, what other fees do you charge? There is a $100 registration fee. No application fee.

How is tuition broken down? Tuition is $210 monthly (two days a week), $288 monthly (three days a week), and $465 monthly (five days a week).

What are the different payment plans available? Billed monthly.

What is the fee schedule? No feedback received.

Is there a contract? There is an admissions contract stating what fees are non-refundable.

Do you have a tuition insurance program? No feedback received.

HELPING HANDS

What accreditation is necessary for the teachers to work at your school? Teachers are required to have 12 early childhood development credits.

How many teachers are there? This year, we have 10 teachers.

How many aides are there? Six aides.

IN THE 'ROOM

What's the child-to-adult ratio? Three-year-olds are 10:1, four-year-olds are 12:1.

What are the policies for initial separation between parent and child? Whatever makes the parent and child comfortable.

Can you visit any time unannounced? Yes.

What are the hours? Preschool hours are from 9 a.m.-12:30 p.m.

Do you offer early bird or after-hours pick-up? If so, is there an extra fee? We open at 8 a.m. for early arrivals and close at 4 p.m. for late departures; the fee is $7 per hour.

Please describe a typical day for a child at your school. Alternates between inside and outside play. We have music, story, sharing times. A variety of activities are always available as well as inside art projects and outside art time, which is usually more free and creative. We offer a lot of tactile experiences.

What kinds of academic activities are offered? There is constant learning through our creative program. The four-year-olds also discuss calendar and alphabet.

What kinds of art activities are offered? Free art using a variety of paints, shaving cream glue, etc., as well as more craft-oriented art involving cutting, gluing, constructing with wood objects. The new afterschool program includes different activities everyday of the week. Mondays includes art class, Tuesdays is kid's art, sports are on Wednesdays, drama and imagination on Thursdays, and kid's music in motion on Fridays.

Is the child's time structured or unstructured, or a mixture of both? No feedback received.

If a child is not interested in a particular activity, does he/she have other choices or is he/she encouraged to try it anyway? No feedback received.

How are disputes handled when they occur between the children? Lots of communication, conflict resolution.

When and for how long is nap time? We call it rest time, because most children will not sleep here. It is 45 minutes with the lights down low, only for children who will stay after our regular program has ended.

What kinds of beds do you use? No feedback received.

What do you do when a child is dropped off in the morning and is obviously not well? What do you do when a child becomes sick during the day? We have emergency cards that have all the appropriate phone numbers on them so we can call home or whenever and have the child picked up. The children stay in the office until they are picked up. We are not allowed to do much with injuries except to wash the wound with water and place a bandage on it.

Can you accommodate children with special needs? It depends how severe.

KEEPING IT SAFE

Please describe your security measures for arriving and leaving the school. Parents need to sign their children in and out. If someone we don't know is picking up, we require to be notified by the parent and then ask for their I.D.

What medical supplies do you have on hand, and what medical experience does your staff have? Is your staff trained in CPR? We take CPR and First Aid classes as a group every other year from the Red Cross.

Please describe your earthquake-preparedness plan, and what special equipment do you have on hand in the event of a disaster? We have emergency water, blankets and food in a shed in a big open area. That area is where we would gather in the case of an emergency.

SWINGS 'N THINGS

Please describe your playground. Does it have plenty of shade? We have a lot of outdoor area. It is mostly sand, some grass, a fair amount of trees and two covered patio areas.

Do you put sunscreen on the children? No feedback received.

What kind of toilet training is available? None.

HELPING OUT

What kinds of fundraising events are at your school each year? Our biggest fundraiser is a silent auction in March. We have a small one at our open house in October and in May.

How much participation is required by each parent? Three hours per year is required, but we count on the generous support of parents for more time than that.

KEEPING IN TOUCH

How do you communicate with parents? Is there a newsletter or phone tree? We have a monthly newsletter as well as notes from teachers, and constant communication from the director and assistant director by phone.

Does the school publish an address book with all the parents' information in it? Yes.

preschool to 12th grade

PILGRIM PRESCHOOL

540 S. Commonwealth Ave.
Los Angeles, CA 90020
Phone: (213) 385-7351
www.pilgrim-school.org
See Map C on page 286

Contact: Susan Swan

- ACCREDITATION: NONE
- NOT-FOR-PROFIT
- FINANCIAL AID IS NOT AVAILABLE
- NUMBER OF KIDS: 60
- TUITION: $1,250 MONTH
- WE HAVE KIDS WITH SPECIAL NEEDS

WHEN TO APPLY: APPLICATIONS ARE ALWAYS AVAILABLE.

Established in 1958 and located in the Wilshire Center close to downtown Los Angeles, Pilgrim School looks like some sort of granite European cathedral, minus the crosses. There is something sweetly out of place about it, both in its setting and feel. This is not a sparkling, state-of-the-art facility with a parking lot full of luxury SUVs; and while the four pre-school classrooms are colorful, everything seems well-worn--not with neglect but with use. The day that I visited was Kristine Vardanyan's second day as the acting preschool director, having been the assistant admissions director before that. The kids in all four of the classrooms were very orderly and well-behaved—in fact, they were amongst the quietest of all that I'd seen. Two classes were eating snacks, one was doing an art project, and one was listening to a story. With two teachers per classroom, there's a 1:6 ratio between teacher and student, perhaps explaining the rather calm atmosphere.

Perhaps because of its location, there is a great deal of diversity. This was clearly demonstrated by the cultural presentations given by the various parents of a particular country's dress, food, music and holidays that could be seen throughout the classrooms, culminating in the school-wide International Folk Festival. Pilgrim may not be the fanciest school in the town, but as evidenced by the fact that seventy five to eighty percent of the preschoolers continue their education there, it obviously works.

BACKGROUND

The school was established in 1958 as an independent college preparatory school, and Pilgrim enrolls students from preschool to twelfth grade. Located in the Wilshire Center, ten minutes from Downtown Los Angeles, we are convenient for families who work downtown—from nearby Hancock Park, Larchmont and Los Feliz, and from throughout greater Los Angeles. We feature small classrooms that allow for personal attention. We are at once relaxed and demanding, traditional and forward-looking, warm and challenging, serious and fun-loving, practical and idealistic. With its unusually diverse student community and its pursuit of academic excellence, Pilgrim is a model for independent schools.

BIRD'S EYE VIEW

	Non-existent	Poor	Fair	Good	Excellent
Learning to Read Children learn to explore the world of books					✓
Dress-Up Children experiment with different roles and imagination				✓	
Hand-Eye Children develop fine motor skills by using fingers and hands					✓
Building Blocks Children practice symbolic representation. They are developing an understanding of the relationships between size and shape, and the basic math concepts of geometry and numbers					✓
Arts and Crafts Children are developing small muscle control as well as creativity					✓
Body Coordination Children crawl through tunnels, climb and balance					✓
Meeting Time Gathering place to listen to the teacher and to stories					✓
Weights and Measures Water and Sand tables					✓
Beakers and Bunnies Classroom pets, aquariums....planting...				✓	
Counting 1-2-3 A good preschool will stock basic early-learner software such as phonics or counting games					✓
Outdoor Play Encourage large muscle control and coordination					✓

Q & A

HOW THEY LEARN

What is your school's teaching philosophy? Our preschool adheres to a developmentally appropriate method of teaching. The program is applied through an age appropriate manna. We believe that all children are special and important. Children are competent learner capable of engaging with ideas and the world around them. Play is their work. Our curriculum emphasizes on solid skill, building friendship, respect for the other and conflict resolution and advocacy for on own ideas and feeling.

How do you implement the philosophy? Our teachers attend education classes frequently.

What is the teaching method? Developmental.

At what age do the children start? To what age is the school licensed? We accept children who are 2 years, 9 months and toilet independent through kindergarten entrance age.

HOW TO GET IN

Are there open house dates? When are tours given? Tours are given on a regular basis, call to confirm.

Is there an interview? With the child or without? Informal interview, just to get to know the family and child.

Is preference given to applicants whose siblings are alumni? Yes.

Are letters of recommendation encouraged? From what types of people? Yes, from previous preschool teacher.

How many applications do you receive each year? No feedback received.

How many open spots are there each year? No feedback received.

What are some of the schools that children go on to after finishing their education at your preschool? No feedback received.

PIGGY BANK

Apart from tuition, what other fees do you charge? There is a $125 application fee, and a $300 registration fee.

How is tuition broken down? Tuition is $1,250 a month.

What are the different payment plans available? Once a month.

What is the fee schedule? $1,135 a month.

Is there a contract? Yes we do have a contract; it is on a monthly basis (subject to change yearly).

Do you have a tuition insurance program? No feedback received.

HELPING HANDS

What accreditation is necessary for the teachers to work at your school? Teachers need A.A. degrees and experience.

How many teachers are there? Ten teachers only.

How many aides are there? No aides.

IN THE 'ROOM

What's the child-to-adult ratio? 6:1.

What are the policies for initial separation between parent and child? Different for each family, each child is different, too.

Can you visit any time unannounced? Yes.

What are the hours? 7 a.m.-6 p.m.

Do you offer early bird or after-hours pick-up? If so, is there an extra fee? No extra fees.

Please describe a typical day for a child at your school. Our preschool curriculum involves reading readiness, arithmetic concepts, science, writing and social lessons.

What kinds of academic activities are offered? Manipulations are used to develop mathematical thinking, including counting, number and numeral recognition, and one-to-one correspondence. They engage in a rich array of language experiences that develop the essential prerequisites for reading and writing.

What kinds of art activities are offered? We use a wide variety of media such as clay, paint and collage to allow children to explore and develop an appreciation and love of artistic expression. Emphasis is placed on exploration and creativity rather than the end product.

Is the child's time structured or unstructured, or a mixture of both? We have both structured and unstructured activities.

If a child is not interested in a particular activity, does he/she have other choices or is he/she encouraged to try it anyway? No.

How are disputes handled when they occur between the children? Children participate in conflict resolution skills, problem solving, and embrace an appreciation for themselves and others.

When and for how long is nap time? No feedback received.

What kinds of beds do you use? No feedback received.

What do you do when a child is dropped off in the morning and is obviously not well? What do you do when a child becomes sick during the day? Sick kids go to the nurse's office.

Can you accommodate children with special needs? Yes.

KEEPING IT SAFE

Please describe your security measures for arriving and leaving the school. Security and cameras all over the campus. We need I.D. for all pick-up and the person who picks up children has to be on the emergency list.

What medical supplies do you have on hand, and what medical experience does your staff have? Is your staff trained in CPR? No feedback received.

Please describe your earthquake-preparedness plan, and what special equipment do you have on hand in the event of a disaster? Assigned staff, teachers and administrators do search team, comforting and contacting parents. We have a fire alarm and drill every two months.

SWINGS 'N THINGS

Please describe your playground. Does it have plenty of shade? Plenty of shade and water.

Do you put sunscreen on the children? Sunscreen is provided by parents.

What kind of toilet training is available? Toilet training is based differently for each child.

HELPING OUT

What kinds of fundraising events are at your school each year? No feedback received.

**How much participation is required by each

parent? Thirty hours a year or more.

KEEPING IN TOUCH

How do you communicate with parents? Is there a newsletter or phone tree? Newsletter, phone, in person.

Does the school publish an address book with all the parents' information in it? Yes.

preschool to 6th grade

PLAY MOUNTAIN PLACE

6063 Hargis St.
Los Angeles, Ca 90034
Phone: (323) 870-4381
www.playmountain.org
See Map C on page 286

Contact: Judy Accardi, Director

- ACCREDITATION: NONE
- NOT-FOR-PROFIT
- FINANCIAL AID IS AVAILABLE
- NUMBER OF KIDS: 50 (pre) 50 (K-6)
- TUITION: $5,950-$11,550 YEAR
- WE HAVE KIDS WITH SPECIAL NEEDS

WHEN TO APPLY: APPLICATIONS ARE AVAILABLE YEAR-ROUND. DEADLINE IS MARCH OF THE SAME YEAR THAT THE CHILD WILL BEGIN.

Founded in 1949, Play Mountain Place is located on a shady residential side street on the eastern edge of Culver City. An unassuming, hand-painted sign tells you that you have found the right place. I opened the wooden gate and stepped into a world like nothing I have ever seen! The school property is sheltered by a multitude of old trees, creating a living roof for this model school of alternative humanistic education in action. The day begins officially at 10 a.m. with the "morning meeting." This is the one time of day when children are assembled in their separate groups: Little Nursery, Big Nursery, House Group, Primary and Mountain Yard. Written on a chalkboard are the words "Problems, Plans, and Shares." Problems are emotional housecleaning. Children may talk about whatever is bothering them, so that they can clean their slate and release whatever negative thing might be in their space. A three-year-old girl piped up, while munching on a grape, "I have a problem. I miss Mommy and Daddy." It was immediately written on the board.

Shares is a loosely defined conversation time including show and tell, personal stories, jokes...you name it! It is the opportunity for a child to have the floor, and talk about themselves or their interests while the group listens. For the "Plans" portion of this meeting, children plan their day's activities. Many choose whom they wish to play with during the day, and not just what they want to do. A plan gives the children a self-chosen direction, and a very intentional way to start the day. Director Judy Accardi states, "Play Mountain is all about choice and freedom for children; communication, respect and how we are all related to each other. The children are constantly being challenged to rely on their own critical thinking." The whole program. is very integrated and organic, emphasizing creative expression, intellectual expression, and emotional relationship. As a result, there is a very apparent sense of self-definition among the student body. Non-verbal shouts of "This is who I am!" Mixed with a cacophony of boundless self-expression. Outlets for this expression include (but is by no means limited to) one full day a week in the outdoor ceramic studio, and another once a week percussion session under another of the domed gazebo type structures. I must add here, that it was amazing to see a two-year-old banging on small drums with mallets, while several other students contributed their own rhythm, including a five-year old girl keeping beat on bongos not much smaller than herself.

If it seems like there is not much order to this chaos, don't be fooled. "Things have to be very defined and structured in order to offer all that choice and freedom." (Accardi). There is a very, very high adult-to-child ratio, and parents are extremely interactive and supported here. There is a mandatory communication workshop for parents, as well as many different optional parent meetings. In addition, I was thoroughly impressed by the area in each yard, referred to as the "Moosh Area." Peppered with mini punching bags, plastic jugs to bang together, newspapers for tearing and cardboard boxes to stomp on, the moosh area is a place for children to constructively and safely express intense emotions like anger or fear. They have things available and everywhere handy for expressing hostility safely. I must admit that I found this brilliant! Children here have an outlet so they don't get caught up in their heads about what they are going to do with this hostility, or take it out on their peers, siblings, or parents! The Play Mountain Place philosophy, however, is not for everyone. Enrollment meetings are scheduled to explore whether this is a right fit for the child, parent, and school.

Background

Play Mountain Place, founded in 1949, is the one of the oldest humanistic alternative schools in the U.S. Its founder, child development specialist Phyllis Fleishman, created a preschool that was respectful of each child's individuality. She encouraged self-motivation, expression of feelings, strong bonds of friendship, cooperation, and development of self-confidence. Ten years later, in the post-Sputnik era of academic rigidity, parents requested that Play Mountain Place extend its revolutionary child development methods to kindergarten and elementary school. In expanding the school for older children, Play Mountain was influenced by the humanistic psychology of Carl Rogers. The school also adopted some of the methods of A.S. Neill, founder of Great Britain's famous Summerhill school. Although Play Mountain's approach differs somewhat from the British school, Play Mountain is widely known as "the Summerhill of the West."

BIRD'S EYE VIEW

	Non-existent	Poor	Fair	Good	Excellent
Learning to Read Children learn to explore the world of books					🦉
Dress-Up Children experiment with different roles and imagination					🦉
Hand-Eye Children develop fine motor skills by using fingers and hands					🦉
Building Blocks Children practice symbolic representation. They are developing an understanding of the relationships between size and shape, and the basic math concepts of geometry and numbers					🦉
Arts and Crafts Children are developing small muscle control as well as creativity					🦉
Body Coordination Children crawl through tunnels, climb and balance					🦉
Meeting Time Gathering place to listen to the teacher and to stories					🦉
Weights and Measures Water and Sand tables					🦉
Beakers and Bunnies Classroom pets, aquariums....planting...					🦉
Counting 1-2-3 A good preschool will stock basic early-learner software such as phonics or counting games				🦉	
Outdoor Play Encourage large muscle control and coordination					🦉

Q & A

HOW THEY LEARN

What is your school's teaching philosophy? Children play, explore and learn at their own pace, supported by a curriculum that fosters self-motivation, critical thinking, social responsibility, and compassion for others. The program deeply and profoundly actualizes the school's philosophy of respect and empowerment of children.

How do you implement the philosophy? Our program follows the child's personal growth path in each of these areas. Learning, growth and development are natural and exciting arts and don't need external incentives, so we do not use rewards, punishments, coercion or grades. Children can choose from student-offered or teacher-offered curriculum activities, but are not required to participate. We allow a very wide range of choices and behaviors, but are very active as adult role models in setting limits of respect and limits for safety.

What is the teaching method? On a daily basis, our teachers cultivate and model what humanistic psychologist Carl Rogers called "unconditional positive regard." All children are encouraged to express their feelings while teachers help them find safe outlets for anger, fear, jealousy and sadness. A "problem" between children presents a teachable moment where tolerance and conflict resolution skills are learned, and limits are set without blame or judgment. We honor a child's own inner pace of development, and trust his or her choices. That means children are not pressured here, whether it be about transitioning out of diapers, sharing a toy or learning to read.

At what age do the children start? To what age is the school licensed? Children do their best in the group environment when they are two-and-a-half years old and older. Legally, we are licensed to start children at two years of age. Play Mountain enrolls children from ages 2 to 13. The school is divided into several small groups; a Little Nursery which serves children from ages 2 to 3. Big Nursery/House Group serves children from ages 3 to 6. Elementary/Mountain Yard serves ages 5 to 13. These groups are intentionally balanced by sex, ethnicity and economically. Children frequently visit other yards, making friends and participating in activities with teachers and children from other age groups

HOW TO GET IN

Are there open house dates? When are tours given? Open house dates are every Wednesday morning or every other Wednesday morning from 9:30 am until 11:30am. Reservations must be made in advance for these adults only visits.

Is there an interview? With the child or without? Once both parents have visited, they can request an enrollment meeting with the Director (adults only). Once the meeting has happened and the parents and the Director feel this is the right match, the child is on a waiting list for the first possible enrollment space. When the child is definitely enrolled, the Director will often set up a visit day (usually a few hours) for the child to be in the program with the support of at least one parent.

Is preference given to applicants whose siblings are alumni? We do give preference to siblings of Alumni, because the family is already invested in the school and the philosophy, and the parents are usually putting their children on the waiting list early.

Are letters of recommendation encouraged? From what types of people? We generally do not get letters of recommendations.

How many applications do you receive each year? We receive approximately 20 to 25 new families who are interested in enrollment each year.

How many open spots are there each year? We can accommodate approximately 14 to 16 new spaces each year.

What are some of the schools that children go on to after finishing their education at your preschool? Many children who leave Play Mountain attend New Roads, Pacifica Charter, or other private schools known for their progressive program. Some children just go to public school.

PIGGY BANK

Apart from tuition, what other fees do you charge? We charge an application fee of $100, a Peaceful Parenting Fee of $400 which includes a four part workshop entitled 'Communication Skills and Conflict Resolution Workshop' and monthly parenting seminars led by the Director, as well as constant availability from the Director for parents who have questions or problems regarding parenting and communication issues. We also charge a $200 registration fee.

How is tuition broken down? The tuition can be paid in ten monthly installments of ten percent of the annual tuition, or can be pre-paid with a discount.

What are the different payment plans available? See above.

Is there a contract? The parents sign an Enrollment Agreement.

Do you have a tuition insurance program? We do not have a tuition insurance program.

HELPING HANDS

What accreditation is necessary for the teachers to work at your school? Teachers must have between 12 to 18 units in ECE. Most of our head teachers hold higher degrees in education.

How many teachers are there? We have eight teachers.

How many aides are there? Four aides and six to eight parent participants who volunteer one day per week.

IN THE 'ROOM

What's the child-to-adult ratio? At least 6:1 (two- and three-year-olds); 8:1 (four- and five-year-olds).

What are the policies for initial separation between parent and child? We support an individualized and gradual separation where a child's attachments are respected. A close relationship between teachers and parents is needed to understand and support the parents'

needs as well.

Can you visit any time unannounced? Parents are listed in the child's registration card and can visit any time unannounced.

What are the hours? The school day begins at 9 a.m. until 3 p.m.

Do you offer early bird or after-hours pick-up? If so, is there an extra fee? We offer before school care from 8 a.m. until 9 a.m., and After school care from 3 p.m. until 6 p.m. There are extra costs for these extended hours.

Please describe a typical day for a child at your school. The day consists of supporting the child-initiated curriculum, and teachers offer developmentally appropriate activities integrated into a program that is safe and allows children to have emotional expression and learn conflict resolution skills.

What kinds of academic activities are offered? Academic activities are offered to children. There is socialization, peer relationship tasks and play.

What kinds of art activities are offered? Children are fully engaged to express themselves and most art plans allow for exploration and use of materials in many creative ways.

Is the child's time structured or unstructured, or a mixture of both? The child's time is largely unstructured rather than them being dependent on the adults to provide structure. Teachers offer a variety of centers for choices.

If a child is not interested in a particular activity, does he/she have other choices or is he/she encouraged to try it anyway? Teachers support, encourage and respect children's decisions about which activities they choose to participate in.

How are disputes handled when they occur between the children? Teachers facilitate non-authorization problem solving.

When and for how long is nap time? Nap/quiet time is provided for tired children, however we do not have a formula or required naptime for children.

What kinds of beds do you use? Nap mats are used.

What do you do when a child is dropped off in the morning and is obviously not well? What do you do when a child becomes sick during the day? When a child is sick, we call a parent to pick them up. If they come sick, we ask the parent to take the child home.

Can you accommodate children with special needs? We have in the past accommodated some children with mild special needs, such as low degrees of autism, however, we really are not set-up or staffed for more serious special needs.

KEEPING IT SAFE

Please describe your security measures for arriving and leaving the school. Our front gate is open from 8 a.m. until 9:30 a.m., then is locked until 2:30 pm. Visitors must enter through the office. Adults who are not the child's parents are not allowed to leave the school with a child unless their name appears on an authorization form filled out by the parents.

What medical supplies do you have on hand, and what medical experience does your staff have? Is your staff trained in CPR? We have First Aid kits in each yard with the standard day care requirements. Our staff takes child first aid and CPR yearly.

Please describe your earthquake-preparedness plan, and what special equipment do you have on hand in the event of a disaster? We hold fire drills and earthquake drills monthly. We store three days of emergency supplies including water, snacks, etc.

SWINGS 'N THINGS

Please describe your playground. Does it have plenty of shade? Our playground is a very natural setting with sand, trees, climbing structures, plenty of shade and plenty of water, and space to run.

Do you put sunscreen on the children? Parents provide sunscreen but we are always prepared to do so.

What kind of toilet training is available? We believe that children toilet train themselves when they are physically and emotionally ready to do it. Adults do not pressure children to be toilet trained. Clean bathrooms and potties are available.

HELPING OUT

What kinds of fundraising events are at your school each year? We hold four major fundraising events each year. An Art Show, an Annual Giving Campaign, a Bazaar, and **our Silent Auction Party.**

How much participation is required by each parent? Each family must sign-up for a Work Commitment each year. Various fun jobs are offered in all different areas. The Work Commitment is usually 35 to 50 hours per year.

KEEPING IN TOUCH

How do you communicate with parents? Is

there a newsletter or phone tree?
Parent meetings.

Does the school publish an address book with all the parents' information in it? We offer a complete roster to all parents, which includes all parents' and children's names, phone and addresses, including the staff, board members and other affiliated parties.

preschool

THE PLYMOUTH SCHOOL

315 S. Oxford Ave.
Los Angeles, CA 90020
Phone: (213) 387-7381
See Map C on page 286

Contact: Penny Cox

- ACCREDITATION: NONE
- FOR-PROFIT
- FINANCIAL AID IS NOT AVAILABLE
- NUMBER OF KIDS: 55
- TUITION: $400-$900 MONTH
- WE HAVE KIDS WITH SPECIAL NEEDS

WHEN TO APPLY: WAITING LIST WITH AVAILABILITY.

Located on Oxford Avenue, on the border of Hancock Park and Koreatown, Plymouth School is in a sweet little clapboard house that looks more like your grandmother's house in New England than one of the longest-running, well-loved Hancock Park institutions. Director Penny Cox was one of the five founders of the school back in 1972 and although it's probably time for her to retire, she said. "They'll probably end up carrying me out!"

No one seems to leave Plymouth—not the teachers and not the families. They currently have the grandchildren of the original families enrolled, and this year there's only nine non-siblings enrolled. It's one of the few schools in town were kids can come as often or little as they want—two to five days a week, half day or full day. It's also one of the few schools I came across where teachers do a home visit before each child starts so that when the child comes to school, they will feel more comfortable and remember the teacher has been to their house. Inside the main house, painted a cheery yellow, various groups of the older children held tea parties, built a city and did puzzles. In the kitchen, a mother dressed for work protected her suit with an apron while she supervised the painting of shapes. Behind the house and through the play yard, the church houses two classrooms where the younger kids learn.

If you're looking for diversity, Plymouth isn't the place. Despite its (relatively) new Koreatown location, almost all the kids are still from Hancock Park and there's not a lot of color. However, like Hancock Park itself, there's a great deal of history and tradition that gives you a sense of a small town feel that's very charming. Once they leave for kindergarten, most of the kids end up going on to St. Brendan's, St. James, Third Street School, Willows Community School, Turning Point, or The Oaks School.

BACKGROUND

Founded in 1972.

Bird's Eye View

	Non-existent	Poor	Fair	Good	Excellent
Learning to Read Children learn to explore the world of books					✓
Dress-Up Children experiment with different roles and imagination					✓
Hand-Eye Children develop fine motor skills by using fingers and hands					✓
Building Blocks Children practice symbolic representation. They are developing an understanding of the relationships between size and shape, and the basic math concepts of geometry and numbers				✓	
Arts and Crafts Children are developing small muscle control as well as creativity					✓
Body Coordination Children crawl through tunnels, climb and balance				✓	
Meeting Time Gathering place to listen to the teacher and to stories					✓
Weights and Measures Water and Sand tables				✓	
Beakers and Bunnies Classroom pets, aquariums....planting...				✓	
Counting 1-2-3 A good preschool will stock basic early-learner software such as phonics or counting games					✓
Outdoor Play Encourage large muscle control and coordination					✓

Q & A

HOW THEY LEARN

What is your school's teaching philosophy? The birthright of every child is a learning environment that simulates and develops his or her own intellectual capacity. The wide variety of experiences and activities at Plymouth help children build self-confidence. They experience the joy of discovery as they explore their world through play.

How do you implement the philosophy? Our objective is to see the children grow in self-knowledge and self-direction, enjoy broadened relationships with their peers and adults, and increase their understanding of the world around them.

What specialty teachers are brought into the school? No specialty teachers. Our teachers are qualified to do art, music, library.

What is the teaching method? Non-academic, developmental. We teach through our normal daily activities, at the child's pace.

At what age do the children start? To what age is the school licensed? From two-and-a-half years old up to five-and-a-half years old.

HOW TO GET IN

Are there open house dates? When are tours

given? Personal tours are given from November through April.

Is there an interview? With the child or without? Casual conversation is held during the tour; preferably with child.

Is preference given to applicants whose siblings are alumni? Absolutely.

Are letters of recommendation encouraged? From what types of people? No.

How many applications do you receive each year? Over fifty.

How many open spots are there each year? No feedback received.

What are some of the schools that children go on to after finishing their education at your preschool? No feedback received.

PIGGY BANK

Apart from tuition, what other fees do you charge? Per-year registration fee is $100.

How is tuition broken down? See the school's brochure for details.

What are the different payment plans available? Monthly payments due.

What is the fee schedule? Tuition is paid in advance and is due on or before the fifteenth of each month.

Is there a contract? No.

Do you have a tuition insurance program? No.

HELPING HANDS

What accreditation is necessary for the teachers to work at your school? Early childhood education credentials.

How many teachers are there? Five teachers.

How many aides are there? One aide.

IN THE 'ROOM

What's the child-to-adult ratio? No feedback received.

What are the policies for initial separation between parent and child? We prefer that parents stay until not needed by the child (or parent).

Can you visit any time unannounced? Yes.

What are the hours? 8:45 a.m.-3:45 p.m.

Do you offer early bird or after-hours pick-up? If so, is there an extra fee? Early/late hours available.

Please describe a typical day for a child at your school. Inside play, art, music, group play, outside play, story time.

What kinds of academic activities are offered? Various activities.

What kinds of art activities are offered? Painting, other creative activities.

Is the child's time structured or unstructured, or a mixture of both? Unstructured.

If a child is not interested in a particular activity, does he/she have other choices or is he/she encouraged to try it anyway? We encourage them but don't demand that they do.

How are disputes handled when they occur between the children? We stay close by to see if they can work it out by themselves. If they can't, we step in and help.

When and for how long is nap time? 1-2 p.m.

What kinds of beds do you use? Cots are used.

What do you do when a child is dropped off in the morning and is obviously not well? What do you do when a child becomes sick during the day? No medicine except bandages.

Can you accommodate children with special needs? Mild problems.

KEEPING IT SAFE

Please describe your security measures for arriving and leaving the school. No feedback received.

What medical supplies do you have on hand, and what medical experience does your staff have? Is your staff trained in CPR? CPR and child First Aid.

Please describe your earthquake-preparedness plan, and what special equipment do you have on hand in the event of a disaster? No feedback received.

SWINGS 'N THINGS

Please describe your playground. Does it have plenty of shade? A large sand area, swings, large and small slides, climbing, huge tunnel, sand toys, play houses. Small and huge tree.

Do you put sunscreen on the children? Parents provide the sunscreen.

What kind of toilet training is available? We encourage children to use the toilet.

HELPING OUT

What kinds of fundraising events are at your school each year? None.

How much participation is required by each parent? None, it's all voluntary.

KEEPING IN TOUCH

How do you communicate with parents? Is there a newsletter or phone tree? A daily contact newsletter.

Does the school publish an address book with all the parents' information in it? No.

preschool to 6th grade

RABBI JACOB PRESSMAN ACADEMY OF TEMPLE BETH AM EARLY CHILDHOOD CENTER

1055 S. La Cienega Blvd.
Los Angeles, CA 90035
Phone: (310) 652-7354
www.pressmanacademy.org
See Map C on page 286

Contact: Angie Bass

- ACCREDITATION: NONE
- NOT-FOR-PROFIT
- FINANCIAL AID IS NOT AVAILABLE
- NUMBER OF KIDS: 135
- TUITION: $5,895-$10,575 YEAR
- WE HAVE KIDS WITH SPECIAL NEEDS

WHEN TO APPLY: APPLICATIONS ARE AVAILABLE IN MID-OCTOBER. THEY FILL UP QUICKLY, APPLY BY DECEMBER.

Pressman Academy is located on La Cienega Boulevard just south of Olympic, in a very formidable (and very secure) building. However, once inside, what's so striking is its rather homey feel—partly due to the fact that they incorporate Reggio techniques into their developmental program. Although teachers must submit lesson plans, they're allowed to determine the direction of where the learning goes, resulting in a very creative environment within the structure of a Jewish school.

In fact, according to Mina Rush, "Our Judaic curriculum is seamlessly incorporated into the regular curriculum, which is vibrant and full of life." Not only is there celebration of Shabbat and the Jewish holidays, but four-year-olds spend one full day a week in Hebrew immersion class.

There are about 22 two-year-old spots open every year and about 80-85% of the kids end up going on to the day school. Those who don't, end up going to school in the Beverly Hills district.

BACKGROUND

The school was established in 1986.

BIRD'S EYE VIEW

	Non-existent	Poor	Fair	Good	Excellent
Learning to Read Children learn to explore the world of books					🦉
Dress-Up Children experiment with different roles and imagination					🦉
Hand-Eye Children develop fine motor skills by using fingers and hands					🦉
Building Blocks Children practice symbolic representation. They are developing an understanding of the relationships between size and shape, and the basic math concepts of geometry and numbers					🦉
Arts and Crafts Children are developing small muscle control as well as creativity					🦉
Body Coordination Children crawl through tunnels, climb and balance					🦉
Meeting Time Gathering place to listen to the teacher and to stories					🦉
Weights and Measures Water and Sand tables					🦉
Beakers and Bunnies Classroom pets, aquariums....planting...					🦉
Counting 1-2-3 A good preschool will stock basic early-learner software such as phonics or counting games					🦉
Outdoor Play Encourage large muscle control and coordination					🦉

Q & A

HOW THEY LEARN

What is your school's teaching philosophy? A mixture of various philosophies (i.e. Developmental, Reggio, etc.).

How do you implement the philosophy? We teach each child the way they should be taught.

What specialty teachers are brought into the school? There is a music specialist, a fitness specialist and a Hebrew specialist.

What is the teaching method? A mixture of various philosophies (i.e. Developmental, Reggio, etc.).

At what age do the children start? To what age is the school licensed? No feedback received.

HOW TO GET IN

Are there open house dates? When are tours given? Throughout the fall.

Is there an interview? With the child or without? There is no official interview but more of a play date. We invite children and parents. Very informal setting.

Is preference given to applicants whose siblings are alumni? Siblings and temple members have preference.

Are letters of recommendation encouraged? From what types of people? No.

How many applications do you receive each

year? 50.

How many open spots are there each year? It varies. About 22 spots for two-year-olds are available each year.

What are some of the schools that children go on to after finishing their education at your preschool? About 80-85 % of the kids go on to the day school. Others attend school in the Beverly Hills District.

PIGGY BANK

Apart from tuition, what other fees do you charge? There is a non-refundable $300 application fee, but no entrance fee.

How is tuition broken down? Tuition is $10,575 for full-day classes (9 a.m.-3 p.m.), $5,895 for three days per week (9 a.m.-1 p.m.)

What are the different payment plans available? Please inquire at school.

What is the fee schedule? Payments start in May and are received over a ten-month period.

Is there a contract? Yes.

Do you have a tuition insurance program? No.

HELPING HANDS

What accreditation is necessary for the teachers to work at your school? Teachers must have required units in early childhood education.

How many teachers are there? Eight.

How many aides are there? 11.

IN THE 'ROOM

What's the child-to-adult ratio? 2:1.

What are the policies for initial separation between parent and child? There is a gradual transition.

Can you visit any time unannounced? Yes.

What are the hours? 9 a.m.-3 p.m.

Do you offer early bird or after-hours pick-up? If so, is there an extra fee? There is an early drop-off from 8-9 a.m. for $500 per year (Monday-Thursday) and a late pick-up from 3-5:30 p.m. (Fridays, 3-4 p.m.) for $260 per year.

Please describe a typical day for a child at your school. Morning lineup for the entire school, Pledge of Allegiance, National Anthem (American and Israeli), circle time, morning prayers, open centers, art, outside play, snack, soft playroom, music and sports. On Friday, there is a Shabbat.

What kinds of academic activities are offered? Kids are allowed to work on what they want.

What kinds of art activities are offered? Various art projects.

Is the child's time structured or unstructured, or a mixture of both? A mixture of both.

If a child is not interested in a particular activity, does he/she have other choices or is he/she encouraged to try it anyway? Yes.

How are disputes handled when they occur between the children? Each child describes what happened and comes up with a better way to handle the situation.

When and for how long is nap time? There is a nap time but it is not enforced.

What kinds of beds do you use? Cots.

What do you do when a child is dropped off in the morning and is obviously not well? What do you do when a child becomes sick during the day? We call parents ASAP. The child remains in the office.

Can you accommodate children with special needs? Yes, but it depends on what their needs are.

KEEPING IT SAFE

Please describe your security measures for arriving and leaving the school. There is extensive security. The temple underground garage has a security guard.

What medical supplies do you have on hand, and what medical experience does your staff have? Is your staff trained in CPR? Staff has CPR training and there are First Aid kits in the classrooms.

Please describe your earthquake-preparedness plan, and what special equipment do you have on hand in the event of a disaster? Students have an earthquake kit, there are evacuation routes that are practised every month, and we keep an emergency book with phone numbers.

SWINGS 'N THINGS

Please describe your playground. Does it have plenty of shade? There is a sandbox side with a covered tent, slide, climbing equipment, bike path with trikes. On the other side is more climbing equipment.

Do you put sunscreen on the children? We ask that parents put sunscreen on their children.

What kind of toilet training is available? We will work with parents but do not offer toilet training.

HELPING OUT

What kinds of fundraising events are at your

school each year? The PTA holds gift wrap sales and the day school does a lot of fundraising.

How much participation is required by each parent? None, but we strongly encourage parent participation.

KEEPING IN TOUCH

How do you communicate with parents? Is there a newsletter or phone tree? Weekly newsletter, email, lots of events for entire family (pajama party, pizza and ice cream social).

Does the school publish an address book with all the parents' information in it? The temple and the school put out rosters.

preschool

RUSTIC CANYON COOPERATIVE PRESCHOOL

601 Latimer Rd.
Santa Monica, CA 90402
Phone: (310) 459-1049
www.rusticcanyonns.org
See Map D on page 286

Contact: Eve Pontius, Director

- ACCREDITATION: NONE
- NOT FOR-PROFIT
- FINANCIAL AID IS AVAILABLE
- NUMBER OF KIDS: 17
- TUITION: $4,350-$7,350 YEAR
- WE HAVE KIDS WITH SPECIAL NEEDS

WHEN TO APPLY: APPLICATIONS ACCEPTED THE YEAR BEFORE A CHILD IS EXPECTED TO ENTER THE SCHOOL. APPLICATIONS ARE AVAILABLE ON THE WEBSITE FROM AUGUST TO JANUARY.

The Rustic Canyon Co-Op Preschool is literally the "one-room schoolhouse" built in 1923, located inside the Rustic Canyon Recreation Park. I walked into a bustling room with two young children playing dress-up as a groom and bride, children reading, playing with blocks, at the sand tables, at the art table, and at the IBM Little Tykes young explorer computer center. Even though this is all happening in one room, there is plenty of space for everyone.

As a Co-op, parents are completely involved in this wonderful time of their children's lives. Parents learn how to speak to children, watch their child interact with other children in a school setting. There is as much growth in the parent as in the child. Parent involvement includes parent meetings once a month, in addition to workshops, guest speakers, fundraisers, and a once a year workday. Director Eve Pontius, who has been at Rustic Canyon for 19 years, also schedules home visits once a year, right before the parent-teacher conference. This is an opportunity for the child to share their home life, toys, pets, or whatever activity they want to do with Eve, on their turf!

The little schoolhouse holds 17 children per day, with 22 families overall. Children come here five days per week. Rustic Canyon is a multi-age classroom with the three-to five-year-olds learning and playing together. Children here tend to write earlier, because they see other children do it! Pontius adds, "They watch the older children and think, 'I can do that!'" One of the most charming attributes to Rustic Canyon is the open, grassy playground area. It gives you a sense of being safe, has a backyard feel, and without (literally) being fenced in. The main drawback to this lovely little school, as far as I can tell, is that because of its size, there are many more applications than there is space for new students!

BACKGROUND

Established by local community parents in 1950, incorporated in 1956.

BIRD'S EYE VIEW

	Non-existent	Poor	Fair	Good	Excellent
Learning to Read Children learn to explore the world of books					✓
Dress-Up Children experiment with different roles and imagination					✓
Hand-Eye Children develop fine motor skills by using fingers and hands					✓
Building Blocks Children practice symbolic representation. They are developing an understanding of the relationships between size and shape, and the basic math concepts of geometry and numbers				✓	
Arts and Crafts Children are developing small muscle control as well as creativity					✓
Body Coordination Children crawl through tunnels, climb and balance					✓
Meeting Time Gathering place to listen to the teacher and to stories					✓
Weights and Measures Water and Sand tables				✓	
Beakers and Bunnies Classroom pets, aquariums....planting...					✓
Counting 1-2-3 A good preschool will stock basic early-learner software such as phonics or counting games				✓	
Outdoor Play Encourage large muscle control and coordination					✓

Q & A

HOW THEY LEARN

What is your school's teaching philosophy? Children learn through play and through socialization skills, and also through discovery. Process, not product.

How do you implement the philosophy? We have multi-age classrooms and go with the flow of discovery. We have music and gymnastics once a week. We go on ten field trips a year.

What is the teaching method? Developmental, cooperative school.

At what age do the children start? To what age is the school licensed? Children have to be three years old by September 1 to enter, and as they leave and go off to kindergarten, they are around five years old.

HOW TO GET IN

Are there open house dates? When are tours given? We have tours every Monday from the end of September until the end of February, then on Mondays in May through August.

Is there an interview? With the child or without? Parent interview without the child, because we are a co-op.

Is preference given to applicants whose siblings are alumni? Yes, but not complete priority.

Are letters of recommendation encouraged? From what types of people? No.

How many applications do you receive each year? Between 30 and 40.

How many open spots are there each year? About 10-20 each year.

What are some of the schools that children go on to after finishing their education at your preschool? Local public schools, Marquez, Canyon Elementary, Brentwood Elementary, John Thomas Dye.

PIGGY BANK

Apart from tuition, what other fees do you charge? There is a $60 entrance fee. Field trip fee is $100 per year; the supply fee is $100 for five days.

How is tuition broken down? Anually, tuition is $4,350 for three days a week, $5,280 for four days a week, and $7,350 for five days a week.

What are the different payment plans available? In full in August, two half-payments (one in August, one in January), or in ten increments (starting in August and ending in May).

What is the fee schedule? Fees for field trips are pro-rated, proportionate for three-day and four-day students.

Is there a contract? Yes.

Do you have a tuition insurance program? No.

HELPING HANDS

What accreditation is necessary for the teachers to work at your school? Units in early childhood education as required by the state, and CPR training.

How many teachers are there? Two full-fledged teachers.

How many aides are there? One working parent.

IN THE 'ROOM

What's the child-to-adult ratio? 17:3.

What are the policies for initial separation between parent and child? Parents can stay as long as necessary, within reason. We will intervene if it seems like it is the parent having difficulty separating!

Can you visit any time unannounced? Yes.

What are the hours? 9 a.m.-2 p.m.

Do you offer early bird or after-hours pick-up? If so, is there an extra fee? There is a $10 fee before 8:30 a.m. or after 2:30 p.m.

Please describe a typical day for a child at your school. Morning choosing time from 9-10:20 a.m., clean-up from 10:20-10:30 a.m., snack time, music and movement and rug time from 10:45 a.m.-11:20 a.m., outside time until 12:10 p.m., inside story time until 12:20 p.m., lunch from 12:20-12:45 p.m., outside choosing time from 12:45-1:30 p.m., story time from 1:45-2 p.m.. There is also a summer session available.

What kinds of academic activities are offered? Work on alphabet letter recognition, pre-math, name writing, numbers, sequencing, lots of reading.

What kinds of art activities are offered? Painting, drawing, gluing, collage. There are art projects every day. It's open-ended.

Is the child's time structured or unstructured, or a mixture of both? A mixture of both.

If a child is not interested in a particular activity, does he/she have other choices or is he/she encouraged to try it anyway? Encouraged, but we don't force them if they are not interested.

How are disputes handled when they occur between the children? No time outs. We work through every situation. Encourage children to use their words, help them communicate in their own words with their own guidance.

When and for how long is nap time? No nap time.

What kinds of beds do you use? No nap time.

What do you do when a child is dropped off in the morning and is obviously not well? What do you do when a child becomes sick during the day? Call the parents and the child must be picked up.

Can you accommodate children with special needs? Yes, but limited. Depends on the need.

KEEPING IT SAFE

**Please describe your security measures for

arriving and leaving the school. Walk the child in and pick up inside class. Children must be signed in and out. Alternate persons need to be listed, and I.D. is required.

What medical supplies do you have on hand, and what medical experience does your staff have? Is your staff trained in CPR? CPR training, standard First Aid kit. We do not administer medicine.

Please describe your earthquake-preparedness plan, and what special equipment do you have on hand in the event of a disaster? Each child is given a list of earthquake supplies, enough for two days' worth of emergency equipment including water, candles, matches, flashlights. Required.

SWINGS 'N THINGS

Please describe your playground. Does it have plenty of shade? Plenty of shade, lots of grass, sand box, beautiful open play area.

Do you put sunscreen on the children? No sunscreen, and can put hat in child's cubby.

What kind of toilet training is available? Must already be toilet trained.

HELPING OUT

What kinds of fundraising events are at your school each year? A variety. In December, there is a holiday boutique created by kids. In February, there's an annual parent fundraiser. There is a pajama party in March for kids only. We call them FUNraisers.

How much participation is required by each parent? Parents have to work one time per month. Every parent either holds a board position or a committee position. Once a month parent meetings, not on school grounds.

KEEPING IN TOUCH

How do you communicate with parents? Is there a newsletter or phone tree? They are in the classroom. Posted signs outside for drop-off and pick-up.

Does the school publish an address book with all the parents' information in it? No.

preschool

SAND TOTS PARENT PARTICIPATION NURSERY SCHOOL

2227 Artesia Blvd.
Redondo Beach, CA 90278
Phone: (310) 370-4300
www.sandtots.com
See Map E on page 286

Contact: Sandra Rojas, Director

- ACCREDITATION: NONE
- NOT-FOR-PROFIT
- FINANCIAL AID IS AVAILABLE
- NUMBER OF KIDS: 105
- TUITION: $200-$415 MONTH
- WE HAVE KIDS WITH SPECIAL NEEDS

WHEN TO APPLY: WAIT LIST APPLICATIONS ARE AVAILABLE ONLINE OR BY MAIL. CHILDREN ARE WAITLISTED FROM BIRTH UP.

The front of Sand Tots Preschool looks like a regular office building, with muted yellow and white, and is accessed by the keypad-controlled security entrance around the back. The playground contains brightly-colored climbing equipment and a bike area. Director Sandra Rojas, a warm and very personable woman, came out to greet me. She smiled and shook my hand. The first thing I noticed was a large mural of the Manhattan Beach pier, it was painted with bright colors and had the words "Sand Tots" written in the sand. The second thing that I noticed was how she greeted every child on the way by their first name. I felt very comforted knowing that she knew every child and could see that she was very hands-on. Every classroom had stations set up including a science table, writing/drawing table and a dramatic play area. The dramatic play area was filled with exciting costumes for the children to wear. The design of the building is very creative. Every inch of the classroom is used, even under the stairs was painted like a castle with a small door to enter.

This school is non-curriculum-based and the children are free most of the day to choose what they want to learn more about. Every toy in the room is educational, so the children are learning no matter what they do. If a child feels like they want to do whatever the day's science project is, they can; if another child wants to pretend that they are a princess in dramatic play, then that is okay as well. Their philosophy is really geared towards children learning what they want to learn, and only having guidance when needed. Every child develops at a different rate , so it is important that children are not forced to develop a certain skill before they are ready. Sand Tots is also a parent participation school, meaning that at the beginning of the year, the parents are given a schedule which tells them when they will help out. On the assigned day, the parent comes into their child's classroom and helps the teacher. This is not because they are understaffed, but because they think it is important for the parent to know what their child is doing at school. The parent can use some of the same ideas that the children are taught in school at home. The school believes this is important so that the child has a consistent school and home learning environment. The two-year olds have their own separate area within the school.

The entrance door is still in the main hallway, but it has a lock on it, and a little gate so that the children cannot wander out. Since these children are a little small to be playing with all the older children in the playground, they have their own playground with age-appropriate toys. When I visited the room on my way out, the children were having snack time, and they were all sitting nicely around the child-sized table. They looked much like a family having dinner, all sitting in their chairs and talking to each other—it was really very sweet to watch.

BACKGROUND

Sand Tots was founded in 1973 by a group of ten moms who wanted to actively participate in their child's preschool experience.

Bird's Eye View

	Non-existent	Poor	Fair	Good	Excellent
Learning to Read Children learn to explore the world of books					✓
Dress-Up Children experiment with different roles and imagination					✓
Hand-Eye Children develop fine motor skills by using fingers and hands					✓
Building Blocks Children practice symbolic representation. They are developing an understanding of the relationships between size and shape, and the basic math concepts of geometry and numbers					✓
Arts and Crafts Children are developing small muscle control as well as creativity					✓
Body Coordination Children crawl through tunnels, climb and balance					✓
Meeting Time Gathering place to listen to the teacher and to stories					✓
Weights and Measures Water and Sand tables					✓
Beakers and Bunnies Classroom pets, aquariums....planting...					✓
Counting 1-2-3 A good preschool will stock basic early-learner software such as phonics or counting games					✓
Outdoor Play Encourage large muscle control and coordination					✓

Q & A

HOW THEY LEARN

What is your school's teaching philosophy? Children learn best through play, where academics are provided in an open-ended, hands-on, rich environment. We focus on problem solving, communication and cooperation.

How do you implement the philosophy? Our staff is well trained and educated in the field of early childhood education. We also provide ongoing staff enrichment opportunities.

What is the teaching method? We consider our practice "developmentally appropriate," which respects the developmental level of each child.

At what age do the children start? To what age is the school licensed? We are licensed for children ages 2-6. Children must be two years old by September 30th of that school year.

HOW TO GET IN

Are there open house dates? When are tours given? We conduct tours roughly twice a month during the school year.

Is there an interview? With the child or without? We provide literature prior to the enrollment commitment.

Is preference given to applicants whose siblings are alumni? Yes.

Are letters of recommendation encouraged? From what types of people? No, we look at wait list status.

How many applications do you receive each year? About 50-75.

How many open spots are there each year? It fluctuates based on siblings and alumni, about 20-25.

What are some of the schools that children go on to after finishing their education at your preschool? Manhattan Beach Unified, Hermosa Beach, Redondo Beach, American Martyrs Catholic School, Chadwick.

PIGGY BANK

Apart from tuition, what other fees do you charge? There is a $40 application fee and a security deposit of $300 per child. Liability insurance is $50 per child.

How is tuition broken down? Two days a week is $200 per month for two-year-olds, three days is $300 per month for 2 to 3 1/2-year-olds. The cost for three-year-olds attending three days a week is $315 per month, $315 for four-year-olds attending three days a week, and $415 for four-year-olds attending four days a week.

What are the different payment plans available? Monthly check, annual check, auto-debit.

What is the fee schedule? Monthly, based on a ten-month school year.

Is there a contract? There is a contract.

Do you have a tuition insurance program? We use the security deposit for the tuition insurance.

HELPING HANDS

What accreditation is necessary for the teachers to work at your school? A.A., B.A., M.A.

How many teachers are there? Seven lead teachers.

How many aides are there? Three teacher aides.

IN THE 'ROOM

What's the child-to-adult ratio? 4:1 or 3:1.

What are the policies for initial separation between parent and child? No feedback received.

Can you visit any time unannounced? Gradual if necessary. Teachers provide guidance with the process.

What are the hours? 9 a.m.-12 p.m.

Do you offer early bird or after-hours pick-up? If so, is there an extra fee? We offer extended day lunch bunch, from 12-1:45 p.m.

Please describe a typical day for a child at your school. Creative art activities, free play, snack time, rug time, outdoor activities, music time.

What kinds of academic activities are offered? Science, writing and math activities.

What kinds of art activities are offered? Wide variety, mostly open-ended projects.

Is the child's time structured or unstructured, or a mixture of both? Fairly unstructured, with some structured events (rug time, snack, science activities).

If a child is not interested in a particular activity, does he/she have other choices or is he/she encouraged to try it anyway? We would offer choices.

How are disputes handled when they occur between the children? Conflict resolution is done by assisting children in articulating their feelings and taking responsibilities for their actions.

When and for how long is nap time? No naps–half-day schedule.

What kinds of beds do you use? No naps.

What do you do when a child is dropped off in the morning and is obviously not well? What do you do when a child becomes sick during the day? We assess with our morning greeting. If a child is sick, we call parents or nanny to pick up child.

Can you accommodate children with special needs? We have parent assistance, so we have limited professionals in the classroom. Some children need more consistency.

KEEPING IT SAFE

Please describe your security measures for arriving and leaving the school. Locked gate around the perimeter of the school.

What medical supplies do you have on hand, and what medical experience does your staff have? Is your staff trained in CPR? Emergency backpacks, and individual students have medication.

Please describe your earthquake-preparedness plan, and what special equipment do you have on hand in the event of a disaster? Evacuation plan, food and water storage, and earthquake kits for each child.

SWINGS 'N THINGS

Please describe your playground. Does it have plenty of shade? A combination of surfaces—sand, rubber, cement—and plenty of shade.

Do you put sunscreen on the children? No feedback received.

What kind of toilet training is available? We support the children's desire to use the potty. We do not require toilet training; it always happens naturally in twos or threes, in our experience.

HELPING OUT

What kinds of fundraising events are at your school each year? Fall event (progressive dinner or bowling/auction), Spring event (main auction in a variety of settings).

How much participation is required by each parent? Two to three hours per month is required for all parents.

KEEPING IN TOUCH

How do you communicate with parents? Is there a newsletter or phone tree? Communication is via newsletters, email and child folders.

Does the school publish an address book with all the parents' information in it? Yes.

THE SHERMAN OAKS NURSERY SCHOOL

5520 Van Nuys Blvd.
Sherman Oaks, CA 91401
Phone: (818) 787-6481
See Map A on page 286

Contact: Kathy Hilton, Director

- ACCREDITATION: NONE
- NOT FOR-PROFIT
- FINANCIAL AID IS AVAILABLE
- NUMBER OF KIDS: 151
- TUITION: $320-795 MONTH
- WE HAVE KIDS WITH SPECIAL NEEDS

WHEN TO APPLY: YEAR-ROUND. NO REAL CUT OFF.

The Sherman Oaks Nursery School is very well protected. It took me three tries before I finally found the gated entrance on Killion Street. The school is located in a residential neighborhood, and the entrance is discreetly situated for maximum privacy and security. The mission of TSONS is to provide an environment that is both stimulating and supportive, where children can discover that they are important and where learning can be fun. The school's philosophy is to recognize and accept the uniqueness of each child, to create an initial school experience where children can comfortably and freely explore themselves and their environment, to permit development in ways which are natural for every child. The goals of TSONS are two-fold: 1) to educate the "total child" (cognitively, socially, emotionally and physically), and 2) to provide a partnership for parents as they raise and educate their children.

There is a small community available for parents, and TSONS is a total partner with the parent at school and at home. Their goal is to offer guidance as parents make important decisions regarding developmental and educational issues, as well as providing a community that will be enjoyable and satisfying for the whole family. There is a full working garden that the children tend and maintain (and it rivals something a landscaper would create!). There is also a pool that is used during summer session, and a brand-new outdoor "stage" built and donated by parents. One of the most appealing qualities of TSONS is their transition class. This class is a bridge between toddler (parent and me) classes and the regular Nursery School program for children who just miss the cut-off age for nursery school in September. Children who are 2 years, 3 months to 2 years, 8 months in September are eligible for these classes.

"We have a balanced approach to the total child's development. We are creating children who have self-esteem, respect for others, who have a voice, who are capable and confident with themselves and in a school environment," says Janice Lang, the assistant director for TSONS. Now, for the not so good news: getting in. There is a lengthy waiting list, and priority goes to the Parent and Me and transition classes. Then it goes in chronological order of applications on the waiting list. The school consistently maintains full enrollment. It is not surprising that Los Angeles magazine recognized TSONS as one of the top 20 nursery schools in the Los Angeles area. If you are interested in this school, go visit and apply immediately!

BACKGROUND

Founding Director Wendy Cummings and a group of dedicated parents started the school in 1988.

BIRD'S EYE VIEW

	Non-existent	Poor	Fair	Good	Excellent
Learning to Read Children learn to explore the world of books					✓
Dress-Up Children experiment with different roles and imagination					✓
Hand-Eye Children develop fine motor skills by using fingers and hands					✓
Building Blocks Children practice symbolic representation. They are developing an understanding of the relationships between size and shape, and the basic math concepts of geometry and numbers					✓
Arts and Crafts Children are developing small muscle control as well as creativity					✓
Body Coordination Children crawl through tunnels, climb and balance					✓
Meeting Time Gathering place to listen to the teacher and to stories					✓
Weights and Measures Water and Sand tables					✓
Beakers and Bunnies Classroom pets, aquariums....planting...					✓
Counting 1-2-3 A good preschool will stock basic early-learner software such as phonics or counting games				✓	
Outdoor Play Encourage large muscle control and coordination					✓

Q & A

HOW THEY LEARN

What is your school's teaching philosophy? We are your full partner in this phase of your child's development. This is total development—you can't rush or force it.

How do you implement the philosophy? Designed for skill and success. Pre-kindergarten are writing and cutting every day. Social and emotional. They are part of a group of peers (that they are aware of), a lot of modeling and talking in the first few years.

What is the teaching method? No feedback received.

At what age do the children start? To what age is the school licensed? Parent and Me classes are from 12 months to 2.8 years. Nursery school is from 2.9 months to five years.

HOW TO GET IN

Are there open house dates? When are tours given? We conduct tours on Tuesdays and Thursdays at 9:30 a.m., and Thursday at 1:30 p.m.

Is there an interview? With the child or without? No.

Is preference given to applicants whose siblings are alumni? Yes.

Are letters of recommendation encouraged? From what types of people? No.

How many applications do you receive each year? We have nursery school applications through 2007.

How many open spots are there each year? Varies.

What are some of the schools that children go on to after finishing their education at your preschool? Berkley Hall, Campbell Hall, Laurence and Laurel Hall.

PIGGY BANK

Apart from tuition, what other fees do you charge? There is a $50 application fee and a $100 registration fee with one month's deposit required.

How is tuition broken down? Two days is $320 per month, three days is $480 per month, four days is $635 per month, and five days is $795 per month. Parent and Me classes are $45 per day.

What are the different payment plans available? Tuition payment options are either monthly or one full year payment, and are offered only at the beginning of the school year.

What is the fee schedule? No feedback received.

Is there a contract? No.

Do you have a tuition insurance program? Yes. September or first month. There is a one-time yearly insurance fee of $100.

HELPING HANDS

What accreditation is necessary for the teachers to work at your school? Twelve units of early childhood education.

How many teachers are there? Two lead teachers plus one floater, 15 to 16 total.

How many aides are there? No feedback received.

IN THE 'ROOM

What's the child-to-adult ratio? Cottage is 7:1 or 8:1. Pre-2 is 8:1 or 9:1. Pre-kindergarten is 10:1.

What are the policies for initial separation between parent and child? Separation lasts as long as the parent or child requires. Parents into nursery school must stay at least two days in the classroom, then when the child primarily stays engaged, the parent will spend most of the time "out of sight" in our family room. When the child successfully separates, you may leave after giving us your cell phone number.

Can you visit any time unannounced? Yes. We are an open school. No parent aides in the classroom, but there are opportunities to participate.

What are the hours? 9 a.m.-12 p.m., or 1-4 p.m., with extended enrichment on Tuesdays from 4-5 p.m.

Do you offer early bird or after-hours pick-up? If so, is there an extra fee? No feedback received.

Please describe a typical day for a child at your school. Half-day from mid-September through mid-June. Optional supervised lunchtime as well as enrichment classes. Daily schedule is planned to provide a balance of activities such as indoor/outdoor, quiet/active, individual/group, large muscle/small muscle and child-initiated and staff-initiated tasks.

What kinds of academic activities are offered? Letter of the Week, pre-reading, pre-science, pre-math. No workbooks, no lectures. We are proud of that! That shouldn't be at this stage of development.

What kinds of art activities are offered? Seasonal art, free art, easel painting, water colors, pudding painting, everything!

Is the child's time structured or unstructured, or a mixture of both? Basic structure to the day, but within each time period there is freedom of choice.

If a child is not interested in a particular activity, does he/she have other choices or is he/she encouraged to try it anyway? Encouraged to try it anyway, if it is a teacher-directed activity or art activity of the day.

How are disputes handled when they occur between the children? By hands-on modeling, giving pre-kindergarten a longer leash to verbally work that out on their own.

When and for how long is nap time? No naps.

What kinds of beds do you use? No naps.

What do you do when a child is dropped off in the morning and is obviously not well? What do you do when a child becomes sick during the day? Call parents to come and pick up child. Sick children cannot stay at school.

Can you accommodate children with special needs? Not too many in the classroom, on a limited individual basis.

KEEPING IT SAFE

Please describe your security measures for arriving and leaving the school. Sign in and out. Anyone not a parent must be on a parent-approved list.

What medical supplies do you have on hand, and what medical experience does your staff have? Is your staff trained in CPR? CPR-trained and First Aid. Not licensed to administer medication other than band-aids. Need written permission from doctors for allergies.

Please describe your earthquake-preparedness plan, and what special equipment do you have on hand in the event of a disaster? Earthquake kit, individual bags. Can house kids for two to three days, and we have supplies in three to four locations.

SWINGS 'N THINGS

Please describe your playground. Does it have plenty of shade? Divided into two yards, plus a third yard for Parent and Me. Yards are shaded.

Do you put sunscreen on the children? Advised to come with sunscreen.

What kind of toilet training is available? We work with the parents in the process.

HELPING OUT

What kinds of fundraising events are at your school each year? Wrapping paper, cookbooks, several minor fundraisers throughout the year, one major spring event.

How much participation is required by each parent? No set expectation.

KEEPING IN TOUCH

How do you communicate with parents? Is there a newsletter or phone tree? Online communication is coming! Papers are put in parents' files in classroom, bulletin boards.

Does the school publish an address book with all the parents' information in it? Parent roster.

preschool-kindergarten

SILVERLAKE INDEPENDENT JEWISH COMMUNITY CENTER PRESCHOOL

1110 Bates Ave.
Los Angeles, CA 90029
Phone: (323) 663-9155
www.silverlakejcc.org
See Map C on page 286

Contact: Ruth Shavit, Director

- ACCREDITATION: NONE
- NOT-FOR-PROFIT
- FINANCIAL AID IS NOT AVAILABLE
- NUMBER OF KIDS: 95
- TUITION: $665-$961 MONTH
- WE HAVE KIDS WITH SPECIAL NEEDS

WHEN TO APPLY: APPLICATIONS ARE AVAILABLE ALL YEAR AND THERE IS NO CUT OFF DATE TO APPLY.

Located on a side street off Sunset Boulevard in Silverlake, the Silverlake JCC Preschool is somewhat of a drab building, but don't let that fool you. Inside its gates reside some very happy children who, according to director Ruth Shavit—an elegant and incredibly warm woman—are "teaching themselves" with the help of some very caring teachers who "create a lot of experiences for them, filled with many teachable moments." It was lunchtime when I visited, and although the kids were eating, the energetic teachers still managed to manufacture a bunch of "teachable moments" as the kids discussed the various healthy elements of their respective lunches.

Part of the JCC of Greater Los Angeles for almost forty years, the Silverlake JCC became independent three years ago. Although Jewish, it's open to everyone and while they celebrate the Jewish holidays, the look at the human elements of the celebration rather than the religious ones. While the staff of the school is very diverse (African-American, Latino, even a Muslim!), the kids are not. Most of the families are from the Silverlake/Los Feliz area, which, as Ruth explained, has become quite upscale and the kids (and parents) I saw seemed to be hip and artsy.

If you are looking for aesthetically pleasing surroundings for your child, this isn't the place—although clean, you can tell that the building's been around for a while and the six classrooms are rather unremarkable. But if you're looking for a real sense of community both for your child and yourself, it's terrific.

BACKGROUND

The school was founded in 1953 by a group of local Jewish families. In 1963, they joined the J.C.C. of Greater Los Angeles. In 2001, the school became independent again. Ruth Shavit has been the director for the last 19 years.

BIRD'S EYE VIEW

	Non-existent	Poor	Fair	Good	Excellent
Learning to Read — Children learn to explore the world of books			🦉		
Dress-Up — Children experiment with different roles and imagination				🦉	
Hand-Eye — Children develop fine motor skills by using fingers and hands				🦉	
Building Blocks — Children practice symbolic representation. They are developing an understanding of the relationships between size and shape, and the basic math concepts of geometry and numbers				🦉	
Arts and Crafts — Children are developing small muscle control as well as creativity					🦉
Body Coordination — Children crawl through tunnels, climb and balance				🦉	
Meeting Time — Gathering place to listen to the teacher and to stories				🦉	
Weights and Measures — Water and Sand tables			🦉		
Beakers and Bunnies — Classroom pets, aquariums....planting...				🦉	
Counting 1-2-3 — A good preschool will stock basic early-learner software such as phonics or counting games				🦉	
Outdoor Play — Encourage large muscle control and coordination				🦉	

Q & A

HOW THEY LEARN

What is your school's teaching philosophy? The school's philosophy is developmentally-appropriate, with emphasis on working with each child as an individual.

How do you implement the philosophy? We use the teachable moment to help them learn by creating different experiences for them, but ultimately they teach themselves.

What is the teaching method? The school's philosophy is developmentally-appropriate, with emphasis on working with each child as an individual.

At what age do the children start? To what age is the school licensed? From age two through kindergarten.

HOW TO GET IN

Are there open house dates? When are tours given? Tours are twice a month—the second and last Wednesdays. There is no need to RSVP, just show up. October through May, open houses are held the last Thursday of the month at 10:30 a.m.

Is there an interview? With the child or without? There's no interview.

Is preference given to applicants whose siblings are alumni? Yes. Preference is also given to families who are enrolled in the Parent and

Me class. They provide a special time for parent and child to be together in an enriching environment. It is a guided social environment for children and a place for parents to learn early childhood education practices and spend time with other families.

Are letters of recommendation encouraged? From what types of people? No.

How many applications do you receive each year? About 100.

How many open spots are there each year? No feedback received.

What are some of the schools that children go on to after finishing their education at your preschool? No feedback received.

PIGGY BANK

Apart from tuition, what other fees do you charge? There is a membership fee of $750 for membership and building fees. For new children, there is also a $25 earthquake kit fee. The application fee is $15.

How is tuition broken down? Classes held five days a week, from 9 a.m.-12:15 p.m., are $665 per month). Five days a week from 9 a.m.-3 p.m. are $878. Classes held five days a week from 9 a.m.-6 p.m. are $961.

What are the different payment plans available? Payment is due every month.

What is the fee schedule? A check for membership, building and first month is due in September. Ten postdated checks must be turned in then as well.

Is there a contract? There is a contract.

Do you have a tuition insurance program? No.

HELPING HANDS

What accreditation is necessary for the teachers to work at your school? All teachers must meet the state requirements for teaching.

How many teachers are there? Eight teachers.

How many aides are there? Seven aides.

Do they come from other preschools? Yes. There is a very low turn-over rate; our teachers never leave for another school.

IN THE 'ROOM

What's the child-to-adult ratio? 5:1.

What are the policies for initial separation between parent and child? Parents can stay as long as they need to. They must stay on the first day.

Can you visit any time unannounced? Yes.

What are the hours? 9 a.m.-3 p.m.

Do you offer early bird or after-hours pick-up? If so, is there an extra fee? There is early drop-off starting at 8 a.m. for an additional $50 per month; this is free for children attending from 9 a.m.-6 p.m. There is aftercare until 6 p.m. for an additional $165 per month.

Please describe a typical day for a child at your school. The day is broken into three program units, from 9 a.m.-12 p.m., 12-3 p.m. and 3-6 p.m. Half of the time is spent inside, and half the time outdoors. Each program unit includes story time and circle time.

What kinds of academic activities are offered? Since we are a developmentally-appropriate school, we believe that in order for them to become abstract thinkers they must learn three things—comparing/contrasting, grouping and superlatives. Throughout the day, those activities will be presented to them (i.e. "put all the blue blocks together.")

What kinds of art activities are offered? Everything—markers, paint, clay.

Is the child's time structured or unstructured, or a mixture of both? A mixture of both.

If a child is not interested in a particular activity, does he/she have other choices or is he/she encouraged to try it anyway? Yes, they are encouraged to try it anyway. The teacher's awareness of where the child's interests lie determines what they will encourage.

How are disputes handled when they occur between the children? Conflict resolution—what happened, what do you want and what should we do about it.

When and for how long is nap time? Nap time is only for two-year-olds and young three-year-olds. It is from 12:30-2:30 p.m.

What kinds of beds do you use? There are cots and children bring their own blanket.

What do you do when a child is dropped off in the morning and is obviously not well? What do you do when a child becomes sick during the day? We call parents right away and they pick them up.

Can you accommodate children with special needs? Yes.

KEEPING IT SAFE

Please describe your security measures for arriving and leaving the school. No feedback received.

What medical supplies do you have on hand, and what medical experience does your staff have? Is your staff trained in CPR?

No feedback received.

Please describe your earthquake-preparedness plan, and what special equipment do you have on hand in the event of a disaster? No feedback received.

SWINGS 'N THINGS

Please describe your playground. Does it have plenty of shade? There are three playgrounds—one with a big field, one with climbing equipment, and one with swings and riding equipment. It's well shaded.

Do you put sunscreen on the children? We do not provide sunscreen.

What kind of toilet training is available? Children can come in diapers, and the school will work with the kids when ready.

HELPING OUT

What kinds of fundraising events are at your school each year? Many fundraising events include a silent auction, sample sales, and a winter fair.

How much participation is required by each parent? Twenty hours a year.

KEEPING IN TOUCH

How do you communicate with parents? Is there a newsletter or phone tree? Parents' cubbies, email. There is a newsletter, but it's less frequent.

Does the school publish an address book with all the parents' information in it? Yes.

preschool

ST. GEORGE'S PRESCHOOL

808 Foothill Blvd.
La Cañada, CA 91011
Tel: (818) 790 3842
See Map B on page 286

Contact: Cherie McSweeney

- ACCREDITATION: NAES
- NOT-FOR-PROFIT
- FINANCIAL AID IS AVAILABLE
- NUMBER OF KIDS: 126
- TUITION: $245-$290 MONTH
- WE HAVE KIDS WITH SPECIAL NEEDS

WHEN TO APPLY: PRIORITY IS GIVEN TO CHILDREN CURRENTLY ENROLLED IN THE SCHOOL, SIBLINGS AND PARISHIONERS OF THE CHURCH, ALL OTHER SPACES ARE FILLED BY A LOTTERY.

The preschool is housed within St. George's Church. It's a beautiful place with large airy classrooms, two playgrounds with plenty of shade and a large grass common directly outside the school where the parents can meet before and after school. I arrived at the end of the morning session and met Cherie McSweeney, the Director. She was bubbling with pride and with eight years under her belt at the helm, she had every right to be! The first thing that caught my eye was an outside library cart that was set up each day for the children to borrow books from. After that it was classroom after classroom filled with toys and artwork, each with its own loft area for the children to retreat up into. Cherie had wished for one herself when she was young, so she made sure that her kids could have the loft that she never had.

This is a developmental preschool with an emphasis on the social/emotional development of each child. "You know, we sit before we crawl and crawl before we stand. We stand before we walk, and walk before we run—here, we attend to the developmental skills of the child step-by-step. If a child isn't ready for kindergarten, they are welcome to spend an extra year here." Cherie took me outside and through two large wonderfully equipped playgrounds and down into a wonderful dining area for the kids to eat lunch and take a rest, and another huge room that's used as an outside playground, inside in bad weather. When I asked her how she resolved conflict between her kids she told me.

"Here at St. George's we teach verbal skills. When two kids are having a problem, we will hear both sides by getting down beside each child and really letting them know that we are hearing what they have to say. We will then give them choices of how to resolve their differences." The school brings in people to teach the children movement education, which includes balancing and working with balls. On Tuesday afternoons, one of the parents is beginning ballet classes. They have a parent board which organizes a fall family dinner. a fund-raising event, known as the Dragon Fair in April. The children attend chapel once a week.

BACKGROUND

Began in 1969 as an outreach from the Episcopal Church.

BIRD'S EYE VIEW

	Non-existent	Poor	Fair	Good	Excellent
Learning to Read Children learn to explore the world of books					✓
Dress-Up Children experiment with different roles and imagination					✓
Hand-Eye Children develop fine motor skills by using fingers and hands					✓
Building Blocks Children practice symbolic representation. They are developing an understanding of the relationships between size and shape, and the basic math concepts of geometry and numbers				✓	
Arts and Crafts Children are developing small muscle control as well as creativity					✓
Body Coordination Children crawl through tunnels, climb and balance					✓
Meeting Time Gathering place to listen to the teacher and to stories					✓
Weights and Measures Water and Sand tables					✓
Beakers and Bunnies Classroom pets, aquariums....planting...				✓	
Counting 1-2-3 A good preschool will stock basic early-learner software such as phonics or counting games					✓
Outdoor Play Encourage large muscle control and coordination					✓

Q & A

HOW THEY LEARN

What is your school's teaching philosophy? St. George's Preschool provides a warm and nurturing atmosphere in which emotional, social, physical and intellectual growth take place. Within appropriate boundaries, individual choice is encouraged to allow all children to participate and learn about the world around them.

How do you implement the philosophy? The staff creates a positive environment that encourages each child to develop a healthy self-concept.

What is the teaching method? We are a developmentally-based school.

At what age do the children start? To what age is the school licensed? Children must be three by December 2nd of the year enrolled, and we go through the fifth year.

HOW TO GET IN

Are there open house dates? When are tours given? Tours are given by appointment.

Is there an interview? With the child or without? Tours only.

Is preference given to applicants whose siblings are alumni? Yes.

Are letters of recommendation encouraged? From what types of people? No.

How many applications do you receive each year? Varies from year to year.

How many open spots are there each year? Varies from year to year.

What are some of the schools that children go on to after finishing their education at your preschool? Public and private schools in the surrounding area.

PIGGY BANK

Apart from tuition, what other fees do you charge? An enrollment fee is collected each year. There is no application fee.

How is tuition broken down? $245-$290 per month.

What are the different payment plans available? Tuition is due the first of each month, based on a ten-month pay scale.

What is the fee schedule? No feedback received.

Is there a contract? An admission and policy agreement is signed each year.

Do you have a tuition insurance program? No.

HELPING HANDS

What accreditation is necessary for the teachers to work at your school? All teachers are certified in early childhood development.

How many teachers are there? Twelve teachers.

How many aides are there? No aides.

Do they come from other preschools? No feedback received.

IN THE 'ROOM

What's the child-to-adult ratio? 9:1.

What are the policies for initial separation between parent and child? Child and parent attend a one-hour play time in their classroom prior to the beginning of regular classes. Teachers work with children and parents if separation issues occur.

Can you visit any time unannounced? Parents of enrolled students may visit at any time. Prospective parents of students must schedule a tour.

What are the hours? The three-year-old program is Tuesday-Thursday, 9 a.m.-11:30 a.m. The four-year-old program is Monday, Wednesday and Friday from 9 a.m.-12 p.m. Pre-kindergarten is Monday-Friday, 9 a.m.-12 p.m.

Do you offer early bird or after-hours pick-up? If so, is there an extra fee? There is an optional extended day program available until 2:30 p.m.

Please describe a typical day for a child at your school. Children engage in outdoor and indoor activities. Snack, story time and a wide variety of activities are offered.

What kinds of academic activities are offered? All cognitive skills are enhanced through a developmentally-appropriate environment.

What kinds of art activities are offered? A wide variety of activities are provided daily.

Is the child's time structured or unstructured, or a mixture of both? A daily routine with flexibility.

If a child is not interested in a particular activity, does he/she have other choices or is he/she encouraged to try it anyway? Children are encouraged but not forced.

How are disputes handled when they occur between the children? The teacher helps each child express their feelings and opinions, and helps them to problem-solve.

When and for how long is nap time? Sleep is not required. A quiet time with books, stuffed animals and music follows lunch for 45 minutes.

What kinds of beds do you use? Mats.

What do you do when a child is dropped off in the morning and is obviously not well? What do you do when a child becomes sick during the day? Ill children are sent home. First Aid supplies are on hand and the entire staff re-certifies in First Aid and CPR each year.

Can you accommodate children with special needs? Limited.

KEEPING IT SAFE

Please describe your security measures for arriving and leaving the school. Parent or caregiver walks the child to and from the classroom.

What medical supplies do you have on hand, and what medical experience does your staff have? Is your staff trained in CPR? No feedback received.

Please describe your earthquake-preparedness plan, and what special equipment do you have on hand in the event of a disaster? No feedback received.

SWINGS 'N THINGS

Please describe your playground. Does it have plenty of shade? Two different yards provide for large motor activity and socialization with the use of swings, a climbing structure, large tires, a tire swing, bikes, sand and water play, and a playhouse.

Do you put sunscreen on the children? No feedback received.

What kind of toilet training is available? Children must be toilet trained.

HELPING OUT

What kinds of fundraising events are at your school each year? A yearly "Dragon Faire" with game booths, food and a silent auction.

How much participation is required by each parent? At least one hour on the day of the faire, and other opportunities are also available.

KEEPING IN TOUCH

How do you communicate with parents? Is there a newsletter or phone tree? Daily connection at drop-off and pick-up, scheduled conferences, notices and a newsletter.

Does the school publish an address book with all the parents' information in it? Class rosters are given to all class members.

preschool to 6th grade

St. Mark's Preschool

1050 E. Altadena Drive
Altadena, CA 91001
Phone: (626) 798-8858
www.saint-marks.org
See Map B on page 286

*Contact: Annella Lewis, Preschool Director
Dr. Doreen Oleson, Head of School*

- ACCREDITATION: NAEYC
- NOT-FOR-PROFIT
- FINANCIAL AID IS AVAILABLE
- NUMBER OF KIDS: 70
- TUITION: $3,270-$7,410 YEAR
- WE HAVE KIDS WITH SPECIAL NEEDS

WHEN TO APPLY: APPLICATIONS ARE ONLY AVAILABLE AFTER VISITING THE SCHOOL. WE BEGIN TAKING APPOINTMENTS FOR ADMISSION ORIENTATION VISITS IN OCTOBER FOR THE FOLLOWING FALL ADMITTANCE. THE DEADLINE FOR TURNING IN AN APPLICATION VARIES SLIGHTLY EACH YEAR BUT IS GENERALLY LATE JANUARY OR EARLY FEBRUARY.

St. Mark's Episcopal School is a neighborhood school- long on heart and spirit. It is located on a tree-lined, residential street in Altadena. St Mark's was founded in 1960 by a group of parents interested in creating a neighborhood school teaching Christian values with a warm, home-like atmosphere and inspirational, nurturing teachers. St. Mark's School is sponsored by St. Mark's Church, which shares the six-acre property. The preschool is bright and cheerful, and the pitched ceiling gives it a wonderful, open-space feeling. The walls are covered with the children's artwork, and the whole atmosphere is nurturing and loving. St. Mark's preschool program is designed to provide a friendly, nurturing atmosphere of acceptance, to inspire confidence and a positive self-image.

The staff interacts with the children from a developmental perspective with an emphasis on learning through play. Each child is encouraged to develop at his/her own pace enabling the child to have a successful school experience. The goal is to provide a loving atmosphere of acceptance, inspiration, and confidence. Daily children's activities and programs offer numerous opportunities to develop positive relationships with peers and adults. Lots of hands-on experiences with creative/manipulative materials and indoor and outdoor play complement the strong pre-kindergarten experiences. All aspects of the child's development, social, emotional, creative, physical and cognitive are considered to be equally important in terms of program planning as well as eventual consideration for entrance into kindergarten. Subject areas are not dealt with independently but rather are integrated into all phases of the child's day. St. Mark's seeks to offer a comprehensive and well-rounded education.

This preschool definitely tries to make learning a joy rather than an assignment and encourages self-discipline, self-motivation and responsibility in its students. The school works closely with the family and community to support each child's efforts. This relationship can best be described as one of cooperation and partnership. In keeping with its desire to educate the whole child, the school believes that the moral, social and spiritual development of its students is of equal importance to their intellectual growth. The staff strives, by example and action, to instill in its students not only a respect for learning but for moral and ethical responsibility.

Here at this school they encourage their young students to become self-confident, direct in purpose, self-reliant in personality and aware of responsibilities to self, home, school and the world community. The St. Mark's Episcopal School is an undiscovered gem for those looking for a preschool at a (comparatively) low price!

BACKGROUND

Saint Mark's School was established in 1960 as a co-educational Episcopal parish day school. The founders were active members of St. Mark's Church who sought to create a preschool and elementary program where children could learn and prosper in an environment of acceptance and respect for differences in ethnic, racial, religious and cultural backgrounds. The diversified student body reflects the community served.

BIRD'S EYE VIEW

	Non-existent	Poor	Fair	Good	Excellent
Learning to Read Children learn to explore the world of books					✓
Dress-Up Children experiment with different roles and imagination					✓
Hand-Eye Children develop fine motor skills by using fingers and hands					✓
Building Blocks Children practice symbolic representation. They are developing an understanding of the relationships between size and shape, and the basic math concepts of geometry and numbers					✓
Arts and Crafts Children are developing small muscle control as well as creativity					✓
Body Coordination Children crawl through tunnels, climb and balance					✓
Meeting Time Gathering place to listen to the teacher and to stories					✓
Weights and Measures Water and Sand tables					✓
Beakers and Bunnies Classroom pets, aquariums....planting...					✓
Counting 1-2-3 A good preschool will stock basic early-learner software such as phonics or counting games				✓	
Outdoor Play Encourage large muscle control and coordination					✓

Q & A

HOW THEY LEARN

What is your school's teaching philosophy? Our program is based on the belief and educational philosophy that children learn best through play, and the environment in the classrooms and outdoor areas are carefully constructed and planned for learning to occur. All aspects of the child's development are considered to be equally important in terms of program planning. The preschool program is designed to inspire confidence and develop a positive self-image.

How do you implement the philosophy? The staff interacts with the children from a developmental perspective with an emphasis on learning through play. Themes that are relevant to children are used to teach age-appropriate facts and information. Subject areas are not dealt with independently, they are integrated into all phases of the child's day. Each child is encouraged to develop at his or her own pace, enabling them to become self-directed learners and to have a positive and successful school experience. Children are allowed to make choices daily from a variety of materials and planned activities. There is also a preschool chapel service twice a month.

What specialty teachers are brought into the school? We provide a music resource teacher, a motor development teacher and story time with our librarian.

What is the teaching method? The preschool and elementary programs are traditional in scope. The preschool program is designed to provide a friendly, nurturing atmosphere of acceptance, to inspire confidence and develop a positive self-image.

At what age do the children start? To what age is the school licensed? Children must be three years old and potty trained as of October 1st to be considered for entrance. The preschool is licensed for ages three to five.

HOW TO GET IN

Are there open house dates? When are tours given? Small group tours for admission are conducted from October through January, they are by appointment only.

Is there an interview? With the child or without? There is no formal interview with or without the child. The admission orientations are done in small groups from four to six families.

Is preference given to applicants whose siblings are alumni? Preference in admission is given to siblings of current students, alumni families, and active members of St. Mark's parish.

Are letters of recommendation encouraged? From what types of people? Letters of recommendation are not requested.

How many applications do you receive each year? About 250.

How many open spots are there each year? Approximately 35 in our three-year-old program, and 6-8 in our four-year-old program. The number varies each year because we offer the option of two, three or five days in our three-year-old program. Our four-year-old program is a five-day program.

What are some of the schools that children go on to after finishing their education at your preschool? Approximately 85-90% of our students transition into our kindergarten program. Others go to independent schools in the area including Chandler, High Point, etc. Other students enter into the Catholic parochial school system. And some go to our local public schools for kindergarten.

PIGGY BANK

Apart from tuition, what other fees do you charge? The application fee is $65, and a one-time, non-refundable New Family Fee of $1,500.

How is tuition broken down? Tuition fees for the morning (8:45 a.m.-12 p.m.) preschool program are: $3,055 per year for two days, $4,590 per year for three days, and $7,410 per year for five days.

What are the different payment plans available? Tuition is for the entire academic year. However, arrangements may be made to prorate payments over the school year. Tuition can be paid in one payment, two payments or ten payments. There is a per-family carrying fee assessed.

What is the fee schedule? There is a registration fee that is non-refundable and payable with the registration contract. This covers materials, emergency supplies, textbooks, field trips, assemblies, technology surcharge, school calendar, yearbook and parent financial commitment to the Educational Field Study Trips. The fee is $350 for two days, $400 for three days and $500 for five days.

Is there a contract? There is a contract for the entire academic school year.

Do you have a tuition insurance program? We do not have a tuition insurance program.

HELPING HANDS

What accreditation is necessary for the teachers to work at your school? All teachers exceed the state requirements for an early childhood teacher. Continuing education is encouraged and supported financially by the school. Although we are not accredited by NAEYC, all of the teachers are members. We attend their workshops and conferences and use their guidelines for developmentally age-appropriate practices in implementing our program.

How many teachers are there? There are six preschool teachers, plus the music resource teacher and motor development teacher.

How many aides are there? Six assistants.

Do they come from other preschools? No feedback received.

IN THE 'ROOM

What's the child-to-adult ratio? The ratio in our three-year-old program is 6:1 and in our four-year-old program is 7:1.

What are the policies for initial separation between parent and child? We have a visit day just prior to the start of the school year for parents and children to come and meet the teacher, find their cubbie and meet other families in the class. We expect for most children that they will be brought to the classroom and after a brief transition time, the parent will leave. If this does not work for a particular child, then we work out a specific plan to help that child and parents with the separation.

Can you visit any time unannounced? Parents are allowed to visit unannounced; they are required to enter through the office and get a visitor badge before coming to the classroom. Parents are encouraged to participate in classroom activities.

What are the hours? Our morning preschool is from 8:45 a.m.-12 p.m.

Do you offer early bird or after-hours pickup? If so, is there an extra fee? We offer care from 7 a.m.-6 p.m. There is a variety of plans for use of our extended care as well as on an hourly on-call basis. Fees vary with plans.

Please describe a typical day for a child at your school. Each morning there is a large block of time for free choice. Most of our materials and equipment are on open shelves at the child's level. In addition, interest/discovery centers are set up through out the classroom. During this time, there will also be a planned activity with the teacher. These activities are done in small groups to allow the teacher to interact with the children and for them to converse with each other about what they are doing. This time is balanced with an appropriate amount of time outdoors because what we do outdoors is just as important to young children's development. The play yards provide a wide range of activities from which the children can make choices. There is a snack time that provides for social conversation amongst the children. There is also a group or circle time each day. Activities during circle time include: stories, finger plays, songs, activity records, etc.

What kinds of academic activities are offered? Skills and cognitive learning are woven into the child's day. Children are provided with many opportunities to see how language, reading and writing are useful. Relationships are drawn between the written and spoken word. Language activities are provided throughout the day to develop language and literacy through meaningful experiences. Children learn math, science, social studies, health and other content areas through the use of learning centers and integrated activities.

What kinds of art activities are offered? Creativity is encouraged in a variety of ways. The children are given enough time to enjoy, create, manipulate and experiment with a variety of media. Play-doh, clay and other molding materials are offered on a regular basis. A distinction is made between projects that are used to teach content information and creative activities. Creative activities stress the process, not the finished product.

Is the child's time structured or unstructured, or a mixture of both? Our day is a mixture of structured and unstructured time. There are many opportunities within the time structure of the day for children to make their own choices about what they want to do.

If a child is not interested in a particular activity, does he/she have other choices or is he/she encouraged to try it anyway? Children are encouraged to participate in all activities, but not forced to do so. During circle time and in resource classes, children are expected to be part of the group.

How are disputes handled when they occur between the children? Our goal is to always help children to internalize problem solving. We model and help children to express in words their feelings and needs.

When and for how long is nap time? Children who stay for our extended care in the afternoon have an hour and a half nap.

What kinds of beds do you use? We have cots and sheets for the children. They provide their own blankets.

What do you do when a child is dropped off in the morning and is obviously not well? What do you do when a child becomes sick during the day? Teachers make a visual inspection of each child at drop-off and will ask parents to take their child home if they are not well. If the child becomes ill during the day, the child is isolated in the office and the parent is called to pick him or her up.

Can you accommodate children with special needs? No.

KEEPING IT SAFE

Please describe your security measures for arriving and leaving the school. All visitors must enter through the school office and get a visitor badge. Children coming to school are walked to the classroom and signed in. Children going home are picked up from the classroom and signed out. No child is allowed to leave unless the person is listed on the child's authorization to pick-up form.

What medical supplies do you have on hand, and what medical experience does your staff have? Is your staff trained in CPR? We have standard First Aid medical supplies. All of our staff has CPR/First Aid training each year. All have also had the additional hours for the health and safety component.

Please describe your earthquake-preparedness plan, and what special equipment do you have on hand in the event of a disaster? We have a thorough earthquake-preparedness plan. We have food, housing, medical supplies and emergency equipment stored on campus. We can support our students for three days.

SWINGS 'N THINGS

Please describe your playground. Does it have plenty of shade? We have three play yards. One contains our ride toys, paint easel, sensory table, a large sand area and a variety of large and small motor skill activities. It has shade trees and large umbrellas over the tables. Our other play yard is one year old and contains our swings, a slide and climbing equipment; two-thirds of this yard is covered with a shade cover. We also have a small yard for the three-year-old classroom that contains many of the same elements as our ride toy play yard.

Do you put sunscreen on the children? We do not provide sunscreen.

What kind of toilet training is available? Children must be potty trained to enter.

HELPING OUT

What kinds of fundraising events are at your school each year? We have a fair/carnival in the fall and an auction in the spring. We also have a Jog-A-Thon and some other optional smaller fundraisers.

How much participation is required by each parent? Each parent is expected to give 25 hours of parent volunteer time each year.

KEEPING IN TOUCH

How do you communicate with parents? Is there a newsletter or phone tree? There is a school-wide publication four times a year. Individual preschool teachers send home a monthly letter describing what will be going on in the classroom. Teachers also write messages each day that can be viewed when picking up children. There are scheduled parent conferences during the year.

Does the school publish an address book with all the parents' information in it? A family roster is printed and distributed to families each year.

preschool to 8th grade

St. Matthew's Preschool

1031 Bienveneda Ave.
Pacific Palisades, CA 90272
(310) 454-1359
www.stmatthewsschool.com
See Map D on page 286

Contact: Linda Parson

- ACCREDITATION: NAES
- NOT-FOR-PROFIT
- FINANCIAL AID IS AVAILABLE
- NUMBER OF KIDS: 54
- TUITION: $12,600-$25,500 YEAR
- WE HAVE KIDS WITH SPECIAL NEEDS

WHEN TO APPLY: APPLICATIONS AVAILABLE OCTOBER, AND APPLICATION DEADLINE IS JANUARY.

St. Matthew's Preschool is located in Pacific Palisades one mile from the Pacific Ocean. The thirty-acre campus, founded in 1949, has rolling lawns and athletic fields, a swimming pool, tennis court, fruit trees line the walkways, and grand old trees throughout. A wooden sign at the office entrance, instructing, "Enter with a Happy Heart" is seemingly taken to… well, heart by the students and faculty of this charming school. As I toured the school with Les Frost, the Head of St. Matthew's, children in every room, ran up and hugged him and incredulously, he knew each child by name. There is a total of 325 students, and many stay the whole eleven years through the eigth grade. As a result, there is a small community on this gorgeous piece of property.

The preschool uses a developmental approach for its three- and four year-olds and occupies five classrooms, a library and four spacious playgrounds (designed for this age level) at the heart of the school's rustic setting. Children improve their skills through exploration of their environment and through hands-on problem solving. St. Matthew's is able to meet children where they are, and challenge them, without stress! The classrooms are carefully prepared to accommodate individual learning styles and levels of development. It was very interesting to look into each classroom and see life-sized paper cut outs of each child lining the walls. The curriculum integrates literature, art, music, movement, cooking, science, gardening (there is even a greenhouse), and field trips in activities that promote reading and mathematical literacy. The challenge, according to Les Frost, is how to weave all of these areas together and maintain a balance.

Each child, when they enter the school, 'signs' a Character Covenant. The covenant is an agreement that, "This is how we treat each other. Kindness. Honesty. Respect. This is who we are." So, when the agreement is broken, in some form of conflict the resolution is an obvious teachable moment.* "Our purpose is to create an awareness that we are all children of God and to awaken in each student a sense of self as significant, creative, and responsible member of society." The only drawback to this school is that so many parents want to have their children attend here. If you are seriously interested in enrolling your child the time to apply is NOW!

*Portions taken from the St. Matthew's mission statement.

BACKGROUND

The story of St. Matthew's Parish began on May 2, 1949 when the preschool opened its doors to 24 children on The Garland Ranch, a beautiful piece of land hidden behind a locked gate on a street called Bienveneda. Early on, the upper grades were added and the day school had more than 200 students in attendance. Already, applications for enrollment far exceeded capacity. During the years since, the school has grown and flourished. Today there are approximately 320 boys and girls enrolled in preschool through eighth grade. The facility houses 26 classrooms that include art and music rooms, two science labs, and five computer labs. In addition to the seven classroom buildings, there is an administrative building, a 10,000-volume library, a sports and performing arts center, a swimming pool, and the church which serves as the chapel.

BIRD'S EYE VIEW

	Non-existent	Poor	Fair	Good	Excellent
Learning to Read Children learn to explore the world of books					✓
Dress-Up Children experiment with different roles and imagination					✓
Hand-Eye Children develop fine motor skills by using fingers and hands					✓
Building Blocks Children practice symbolic representation. They are developing an understanding of the relationships between size and shape, and the basic math concepts of geometry and numbers					✓
Arts and Crafts Children are developing small muscle control as well as creativity					✓
Body Coordination Children crawl through tunnels, climb and balance					✓
Meeting Time Gathering place to listen to the teacher and to stories					✓
Weights and Measures Water and Sand tables					✓
Beakers and Bunnies Classroom pets, aquariums....planting...					✓
Counting 1-2-3 A good preschool will stock basic early-learner software such as phonics or counting games				✓	
Outdoor Play Encourage large muscle control and coordination					✓

Q & A

HOW THEY LEARN

What is your school's teaching philosophy? St. Matthew's Parish School, an Episcopal day school, is an integral part of the Parish of St. Matthew, serving the children and families of the parish and larger community. The school provides quality education through a challenging, caring and supportive program, developing intellectual, spiritual and physical growth. Our purpose is to create an awareness that we are all children of God and to awaken in each student a sense of self as a significant, creative, and responsible member of society. Throughout over fifty years of existence, the school has consistently sought to develop and challenge the best that is in its students. To accomplish this, the school provides a challenging and traditional academic program supported by a nurturing environment. Teachers are dedicated to a view of the whole child and are thus responsive to children as people. We believe, therefore, that education works best through a program which stresses intellectual, aesthetic, and physical and spiritual development; social involvement and responsibility; and moral understanding and maturity. Our vitality as a school and our success with each student depends upon our ability to help each child recognize, appreciate, and develop to the fullest of his or her potential.

How do you implement the philosophy? The staff interacts with the children from a developmental perspective with an emphasis on learning through play. Themes that are relevant to children are used to teach age-appropriate facts and information. Subject areas are not dealt with independently, they are integrated into all phases of the child's day. Each child is encouraged to develop at his or her own pace, enabling them to become self-directed learners and to have a positive and successful school experience. Children are allowed to make choices daily from a variety of materials and planned activities. There is also a preschool chapel service twice a month.

What specialty teachers are brought into the school? We provide a music resource teacher, a motor development teacher and story time with our librarian.

What is the teaching method? The preschool and elementary programs are traditional in scope. The preschool program is designed to provide a friendly, nurturing atmosphere of acceptance, to inspire confidence and develop a positive self-image.

At what age do the children start? To what age is the school licensed? Children must be three years old and potty trained as of October 1st to be considered for entrance. The preschool is licensed for ages three to five.

HOW TO GET IN

Are there open house dates? When are tours given? October.

Is there an interview? With the child or without? No interview.

Is preference given to applicants whose siblings are alumni? There is no legacy policy.

Are letters of recommendation encouraged? From what types of people? They are accepted but not encouraged. Anyone who knows the child and family very well.

How many applications do you receive each year? About 80.

How many open spots are there each year? About 27.

What are some of the schools that children go on to after finishing their education at your preschool? Most, if not all, move from kindergarten into our elementary school.

PIGGY BANK

Apart from tuition, what other fees do you charge? The application fee is $100, and the entrance fee is $1,500. There are no extra fees for preschool.

How is tuition broken down? $12,600 for preschool.

What are the different payment plans available? Ten payments, two payments, or paid in full.

What is the fee schedule? No feedback received.

Is there a contract? Yes.

Do you have a tuition insurance program? Yes.

HELPING HANDS

What accreditation is necessary for the teachers to work at your school? Teachers need to have a degree and a background in early childhood training.

How many teachers are there? Eight teachers.

How many aides are there? No aides.

Do they come from other preschools? Most have taught in other schools before coming to St. Matthew's.

IN THE 'ROOM

What's the child-to-adult ratio? 9:1.

What are the policies for initial separation between parent and child? We don't have a policy, we have a flexible attitude.

Can you visit any time unannounced? Yes, parents are welcomed.

What are the hours? 8:30-11:45 a.m.

Do you offer early bird or after-hours pick-up? If so, is there an extra fee? Optional until 3 p.m.

Please describe a typical day for a child at your school. Instructional time mixed with free play.

What kinds of academic activities are offered? Number and letter recognition, colors, shapes.

What kinds of art activities are offered? Age-appropriate coloring, drawing, paper mache, string painting, etc.

Is the child's time structured or unstructured, or a mixture of both? A mixture of both.

If a child is not interested in a particular activity, does he/she have other choices or is he/she encouraged to try it anyway? There is some group time where a child is expected to participate.

How are disputes handled when they occur between the children? Our goal is to always help children to internalize problem solving. We model and help children to express in words their feelings and needs.

When and for how long is nap time? Fifteen minutes in the afternoon.

What kinds of beds do you use? No feedback received.

What do you do when a child is dropped off in the morning and is obviously not well? What do you do when a child becomes sick during the day? Call the parents to come and pick up their child.

Can you accommodate children with special needs? Each case would have to be examined individually.

KEEPING IT SAFE

Please describe your security measures for arriving and leaving the school. Students need to be signed in and out.

What medical supplies do you have on hand, and what medical experience does your staff have? Is your staff trained in CPR? Yearly first aid and CPR.

Please describe your earthquake-preparedness plan, and what special equipment do you have on hand in the event of a disaster? We have earthquake supplies for three days after an earthquake.

SWINGS 'N THINGS

Please describe your playground. Does it have plenty of shade? Playground has shade.

Do you put sunscreen on the children? Sunscreen is optional.

What kind of toilet training is available? The school does not do toilet training.

HELPING OUT

What kinds of fundraising events are at your school each year? We have annual giving, an auction dinner, and a Town Faire.

How much participation is required by each parent? Parents are expected to volunteer in a myriad of ways according to their availability and capability.

KEEPING IN TOUCH

How do you communicate with parents? Is there a newsletter or phone tree? There is a weekly online newsletter and a phone tree.

Does the school publish an address book with all the parents' information in it? Yes.

preschool to 6th grade

St. James' Preschool

4270 w. 6th Street
Los Angeles, CA 90020
Phone: (213) 738-7871
www.saintjamespreschool.com
See Map C on page 286

Contact: Katarina Matolek

- ACCREDITATION: NAEYC
- NOT-FOR-PROFIT
- FINANCIAL AID IS NOT AVAILABLE
- NUMBER OF KIDS: 44
- TUITION: $1,000 MONTH
- WE HAVE KIDS WITH SPECIAL NEEDS

WHEN TO APPLY: APPLICATIONS ARE BEING ACCETED THROUGH DECEMBER, AND WILL BE NOTIFIED ABOUT THEIR ENROLLMENT BY MARCH.

I arrived on a very wet and windy morning and pulled into a small church parking lot. If you're looking for preschool that boasts all the bells and whistles on the outside, then you'll be disappointed with the physical appearance of this school. But if you look beyond this, then you will see a preschool that is being run by one of the most dynamic and forward-thinking preschool principals in town—Katarina Matolek. She is also a NAEYC accreditor, and advises evaluates teachers or schools throughout the accreditation process. The school has been given a small piece of the grounds within a Korean church on the outskirts of Hancock Park. There's not much to boast about in the way of fancy equipment or gardens, but there is a well-stocked playground and a large sandbox, and a bunny that the kids learn to look after. The great thing about this school is that it has only 44 kids. That means two classrooms of 22 kids each, with three teachers. You do the math—that's a ratio of about 7:1, which works out really well for both the teachers and the children. Beginning in fall 2008, the preschool will merge with the elementary school.

I was taken into the first classroom where a little girl piped up "I'm going to get a baby brother!" She was beaming from ear to ear. When I asked Katrina what made her school stand out, she replied, "I would say I'm different in the way we empower and respect the child. We are constantly working on ways to implement this method into our practice." She arrived from Croatia in 1995 and spent several years working at the Ocean Park Community Center with kids up to 17 years old. She's seen it all and loves working with small children. "Be the kid's advocate. Sometimes the parents are so busy providing for their children that they react to the child from a place of fear."

The tour of the school is over very quickly, but I've seen two large classrooms filled with things for the children to do as well as the ever more popular loft space that the kids use for a variety of pastimes. The school has a strong pre-kindergarten program. Over the past few years, they have made massive improvements to the school. they have new computers for both students and teachers. Everything is labeled so that when the child is asked to find something, they learn the word for it and how to spell it too. There's lots of writing and painting being produced by this happy group of kids and many of them will continue on to such schools as St. James, or attend Campbell Hall, Oakwood, The Oaks and The Willows to name a few. If you live in the neighborhood, I would strongly suggest a visit.

BACKGROUND

St. James' Preschool is the outreach of the St. James' Episcopal Church. It was establish in September of 1998. They are a non-profit institution and do not discriminate on the basis of race, religion or creed. They are committed to seeking a diverse student population including children from a variety of racial, ethnic, religious and socio-economic backgrounds. In the fall of 2008, the preschool merged with St. James School.

BIRD'S EYE VIEW

	Non-existent	Poor	Fair	Good	Excellent
Learning to Read — Children learn to explore the world of books					✓
Dress-Up — Children experiment with different roles and imagination					✓
Hand-Eye — Children develop fine motor skills by using fingers and hands					✓
Building Blocks — Children practice symbolic representation. They are developing an understanding of the relationships between size and shape, and the basic math concepts of geometry and numbers					✓
Arts and Crafts — Children are developing small muscle control as well as creativity					✓
Body Coordination — Children crawl through tunnels, climb and balance				✓	
Meeting Time — Gathering place to listen to the teacher and to stories					✓
Weights and Measures — Water and Sand tables				✓	
Beakers and Bunnies — Classroom pets, aquariums....planting...					✓
Counting 1-2-3 — A good preschool will stock basic early-learner software such as phonics or counting games					✓
Outdoor Play — Encourage large muscle control and coordination				✓	

Q & A

HOW THEY LEARN

What is your school's teaching philosophy?
St. James' Preschool, an outreach program of St. James' Episcopal Church, seeks to provide for the needs of two- to five-year-old students and their families by providing them with a loving and caring environment in which they learn the values and skills they need for a joyful transition into kindergarten. At St. James' Preschool, we keep abreast of educational advances and incorporate them into our philosophy whenever needed, creating a lively and continually evolving environment for both the staff and children. This is a child's first independent environment for both the staff and the children. This is a child's first independent learning experience outside of the home, and we

believe in making the transition into preschool a positive one. We consider the child as the focus and the teacher as the facilitator. At St. James,' our aim is to create both a nurturing and stimulating environment. We believe that this earliest educational experience is where children form their first impressions of the world around them. For it is here in our playgrounds and classrooms that our attitudes toward conflict resolution, community and a sense of our place in society is primarily developed. We believe these first impressions are lasting, and therefore it is vital to the moral and social integrity of each child that we honor each moment and transaction for its potential for human growth and development.

How do you implement the philosophy? Play is the essential for children to develop physically, intellectually, socially and emotionally. We have lots of hands-on activities, as well as using the five senses, where children are empowered to feel good about themselves, to think for themselves, and to have the integrity and sense of their own power. In today's world there is too much drilling of children at the expense of play, so at St. James' Preschool we are looking to see the world from the child's perspective. Honoring children in their uniqueness and the diversity of their families, we believe that "emotional intelligence" is the strongest predictor of happiness and success. Also, we support H. Gardener's Theory of Multiple Intelligences, T. Gordon's teaching, Piaget, Erikson, Vigotsky, Kohlberg by developing each child's self-esteem and to teach children in the context of the family, culture and individuality. Learning becomes fun through science projects, rhymes, books, songs, animal action stories, dance, yoga, puppetry, art and many more meaningful experiences. Newest brain research indicates that children who are learning through play are better readers, have better phonic awareness, and gain cognitive skills faster.

What specialty teachers are brought into the school? We have special extra-curricular classes: yoga, music and empathy and moral education thought by Rev. Cathy Grey from the St. James' Episcopal Church.

What is the teaching method? We focus on developmentally appropriate practice, with the high respect and empowerment of children. Our teachers are trained in active listening, encouragement, messages, promoting peaceful responses to conflict resolution, teaching healthy boundaries, facilitating multicultural growth, and working side by side with parents.

At what age do the children start? To what age is the school licensed? Children start at the age of two-and-a-half, until their entrance to kindergarten.

HOW TO GET IN

Are there open house dates? When are tours given? Open House is in the early fall, and tours are available on a monthly basis.

Is there an interview? With the child or without? Parents are asked to bring their child for the interview so we can see how we can accommodate the needs of their family, and at the same time, the family can learn all about our preschool.

Is preference given to applicants whose siblings are alumni? Parishioners and members of St. James' Church, as well as siblings of the current and past students have first priority of placement. Second priority is given to the residents of our community.

Are letters of recommendation encouraged? From what types of people?
No feedback received.

How many applications do you receive each year? 30 to 40.

How many open spots are there each year? Open spots become available when children graduate from our preschool, or when a family moves out of the neighborhood. Usually, we have between 18 to 20 spots open in September.

What are some of the schools that children go on to after finishing their education at your preschool? Children go to many different private and public schools like St. James' Elementary School, Campbell-Hall, The Oaks, Oakwood, Willows, Third Street and many others.

PIGGY BANK

Apart from tuition, what other fees do you charge? The application fee is $75, and there is a $1000 one-time enrollment fee.

How is tuition broken down? Tuition is $1,000 per month.

What are the different payment plans available? The family may pay monthly or in one lump sum.

What is the fee schedule? No feedback received.

Is there a contract? We ask parents to sign the contract.

Do you have a tuition insurance program? If parents give us six weeks' notice in advance of when their child is going to leave, their deposit will be used as the last month's tuition.

HELPING HANDS

What accreditation is necessary for the teachers to work at your school? Most of our teachers have B.A. or A.A. degrees in early childhood education. We encourage our teachers to be updated on the newest research in ECE and every year we all go together to the National Conference of the National Association of Education of Young Children.

How many teachers are there? Four qualified teachers.

How many aides are there? Two teacher assistants.

Do they come from other preschools? No feedback received.

IN THE 'ROOM

What's the child-to-adult ratio? The ratio is 7:1 or 8:1.

What are the policies for initial separation between parent and child? We honor the individual child's and parent's separation process. With each family there is a special plan developed on how to work together to ease the anxiety around separation, and to provide the most nurturing environment where the child can form a secure attachment. Most of the children respond well, and very soon we see a successful good-bye ritual with the parents at the door and a feeling of belonging to their classroom.

Can you visit any time unannounced? Our parents have a key to the gate and they are welcome to come at any time. We have an open door policy to our parents to come and join in a classroom project, planting flowers, field trips, birthdays, reading books, etc. They can also call their child and talk to them over the phone.

What are the hours? Opens at 8 a.m. and close at 5:30 p.m. Tuition covers these hours.

Do you offer early bird or after-hours pick-up? If so, is there an extra fee? No feedback received.

Please describe a typical day for a child at your school. Each classroom has their monthly curriculum and daily schedule posted for the parents. Every day, the schedule is followed to provide the child with a sense of security as well as a learning of time and what comes next. We are very flexible and are always centered on what is happening to the child in the moment by allowing the child to express their needs and desires. Day starts with free activities, followed by circle time, snack, outside time, and back inside again with group activities, then lunch time, outside time, inside nap time and afternoon activities.

What kinds of academic activities are offered? All of our activities are thoughtfully planned to put the child in situations where they feel successful and challenged at the same time. They all learn academics through developmentally appropriate curriculum like early literacy, math, computer, science, music, block building, cooking, empathy and moral education, social studies and anti-bias curriculum, dramatic play and art. There is a belief in the society that academics exclude play, and that play is excluded by academics. We believe that children are sensory learners and need to move, use their imaginations, use large and small muscle groups, and engage themselves mentally and emotionally through play. Today we know so much more about brain development, attachment, child psychology and development there is no need to follow old teaching styles where coloring books and work sheets are used. Instead we are promoting creativity and individuality, a sense of self and others, working together cooperatively, preparing foundations where young children can grow toward their optimum to matriculate to kindergarten.

What kinds of art activities are offered? We will follow recommendations of art education as being a way for children to express their own inner lives. We strongly recommend against the imposition of adult standards, i.e. "forced" competition, and grading of children's art, as these are harmful squelches of creativity and individuality. Art plays the important role of encouraging individualistic expression helping children become more themselves instead of more like everyone else. It contributes to learning in many areas. Children need time to experiment with materials, to push, and prod, to examine and to recognize the unique properties of each art material that is provided. We have drawings, painting, modeling with pay-dough and clay, charcoal, collage, cutting, gluing, and woodworking.

Is the child's time structured or unstructured, or a mixture of both? There is a daily schedule, but inside that schedule, there is always the opportunity for a child to choose something else to do.

If a child is not interested in a particular activity, does he/she have other choices or is he/she encouraged to try it anyway? We believe that children should be able to make their own choices. We acknowledge and honor their learning process and know how and when to intervene. In a case when a choice is not available (e.g., a child wants to stay outside and it is time to go inside), we will continue to listen and have a dialogue with the child so he/she feels that he/she has being heard.

How are disputes handled when they occur

between the children? Teachers will encourage children to communicate with each other; to brainstorm ideas how to solve the problem; to give a voice to voiceless ones; and to empower shy ones. They will teach children when you hurt somebody it is not enough sometimes to tell them how sorry you are, but instead to hold the ice pack, to draw an "I am sorry" card, to bring a cup of water, or to do something nice for a person you had a conflict with. It is important to underline here how we will not make a child say or do anything at all. Empathy learning is a long process, it comes from inside not from some imposed adult power and only, I am saying ONLY if people around you are nice to you will learn how to be nice to others when you are a child.

When and for how long is nap time? Nap time is part of our daily schedule and by following our respectful and empowering philosophy toward children everything we do is incorporated in that way of teaching. They know they can read a book or listen to a story and they also know to be quiet for the ones who are sleeping. Teachers will provide a relaxing atmosphere by playing soft music and rubbing backs. Children who are not asleep will be provided with a special quiet activity.

What kinds of beds do you use? Children have their own beddings on the mats and maybe their favorite stuffed animal.

What do you do when a child is dropped off in the morning and is obviously not well? What do you do when a child becomes sick during the day? We have all of our policies and procedures in the Parent and Teacher Handbooks. One of them is not to bring sick children to the preschool. We reserve the right not to accept a child who is sick or to call a parent to come and pick up their sick child. Everybody agrees with this policy.

Can you accommodate children with special needs? It depends on what kind of special needs we are talking about. We have to make sure we can accommodate the child and the family and that we can work together to have an open dialog about it.

KEEPING IT SAFE

Please describe your security measures for arriving and leaving the school. Our main gate is locked at all times. We do ask parents when they come in not to let strangers or anybody else in that they do not know.

What medical supplies do you have on hand, and what medical experience does your staff have? Is your staff trained in CPR? All of the teaching staff is trained in CPR and First Aid and there are First Aid kits in every classroom.

Please describe your earthquake-preparedness plan, and what special equipment do you have on hand in the event of a disaster? Each child also has their personal emergency kit and every month we practise emergency procedures for the evacuation of the school. In case of an emergency, we follow procedures outlined by the Fire Department and Red Cross. Each child has an earthquake kit which is required by the time of enrollment.

SWINGS 'N THINGS

Please describe your playground. Does it have plenty of shade? Our playground has a couple of shade tents, climbing structure with sponge safety surface underneath, sand box, area for riding bicycles, and also includes an area for water activities and art activities. There are also blocks and books. During nice weather, we do yoga outside.

Do you put sunscreen on the children? Each parent brings sunscreen, a towel and bathing suit for their child. We will apply the sunscreen when necessary.

What kind of toilet training is available? We call it "toilet learning," and we do not require a child to be out of diapers or pull-ups prior to admission. We believe that each child has their own timing for everything including toilet learning. We will support parents in that process and use books, puppetry, and dramatic play only when child is ready to learn.

HELPING OUT

What kinds of fundraising events are at your school each year? We have two major fundraising events: Fall Annual Giving and the Spring Event.

How much participation is required by each parent? Parents play an integral role in every aspect of our Pre-school community. Parental participation in the education process is central to the St. James' philosophy of early childhood education, and accordingly, is both expected and required. Active participation in at least one committee is expected of every family.

KEEPING IN TOUCH

How do you communicate with parents? Is there a newsletter or phone tree? We have a newsletter, parents mail folders, boards with information, and parent-teacher conferences.

Does the school publish an address book with all the parents' information in it? We have a family directory for parents so they can call each other or set up a play date for their child. Parents working on committees need to be able to reach each other for special preschool projects.

preschool-kindergarten

SUNSET MONTESSORI

1432 n. Sycamore Ave.
Los Angeles, CA 90028
Phone: (323) 465-8133
www.sunsetmontessori.com
See Map on D page 286

Contact: Liliya or Ilona Kordonskaya

- ACCREDITATION: NONE
- TUITION: $1,200-$1,300 MONTH
- NUMBER OF KIDS: 35-40
- FINANCIAL AID IS NOT AVAILABLE

WHEN TO APPLY: APPLICATIONS ARE ACCEPTED YEAR-ROUND.

A wooden fence separates Sunset Montessori from the corner of Sunset and La Brea. It's a two-story converted home right in the middle of Hollywood, and oh so comfortable, homey, clean and well organized. I felt welcome immediately. I was given a tour of the school by one of the teachers/co-founder, Ilona Kordonskaya, who is the daughter of Director, Liliya Kordonskaya.

While I observed in one of the classrooms, the children clearly looked happy. It seemed like they were free to do what they wanted, but with guided supervision. With an extraordinary child-adult ratio: 6/1, many adults were present, subtly engaging and working with the children. When I asked a young girl what she was drawing, she replied firmly, "I am drawing a large intestine!" And went right back to work. Ilona explained that the in the morning, the kids work individually or in small groups by choosing their own Montessori activities or "jobs," which are suited to each child's unique needs and interest. These include language, practical life, sensory, math, art, science and geography.

Once the morning portion is complete, the kids are offered many activities in the Enrichment Program, which includes drama, music, art, French, Spanish, dance and gymnastics. The outdoor area is almost entirely covered with a shade structure for ample sun protection. It was approaching 100 degrees that day, so the children were comfortably cool indoors. But on a cooler day, the children play outside on the playground with lots of toys. At an additional fee, karate, hip-hop dance and yoga are offered to all the children.

BACKGROUND

Owner Liliya Kordonskaya worked with kids in gymnastics for years before moving to America from the Ukraine. Kordonskaya became passionate about the Montessori philosophy while continuing as a gymnastics coach before opening Sunset Montessori School in 2002.

Bird's Eye View

	Non-existent	Poor	Fair	Good	Excellent
Learning to Read — Children learn to explore the world of books					✓
Dress-Up — Children experiment with different roles and imagination				✓	
Hand-Eye — Children develop fine motor skills by using fingers and hands					✓
Building Blocks: Children practice symbolic representation. They are developing an understanding of the relationships between size and shape, and the basic math concepts of geometry and numbers					✓
Arts and Crafts — Children are developing small muscle control as well as creativity					✓
Body Coordination — Children crawl through tunnels, climb and balance				✓	
Meeting Time — Gathering place to listen to the teacher and to stories					✓
Weights and Measures — Water and Sand tables				✓	
Beakers and Bunnies — Classroom pets, aquariums....planting...				✓	
Counting 1-2-3 — A good preschool will stock basic early-learner software such as phonics or counting games					✓
Outdoor Play — Encourage large muscle control and coordination					✓

• • • • • • Q & A • • • • • • •

HOW THEY LEARN

What is your school's teaching philosophy? Montessori philosophy.

How do you implement the philosophy? We have all Montessori materials and update them often.

What specialty teachers are brought into the school? Montessori certified.

What is the teaching method? No feedback received.

At what age do the children start? 2 years of age.

To what age is the school licensed? Until 6 years of age.

HOW TO GET IN

Are there open house dates? When are tours given? After a phone call we can set up a tour but usually on Tuesday's at 9:30.

Is there an interview? With the child or without? Parents first come to see the school and then if they like it they are welcome to come with the child.

Is preference given to applicants whose siblings are alumni? Yes.

Are letters of recommendations encouraged? From what types of people? No.

How many applications do you receive each year? Varies.

How many open spots are there each year? Varies, depends how many kids graduate.

What are some of the schools that children go on to after finishing their education at your preschool? Some go to Los Feliz or Larchmont Charter and most of them go to private schools: Center of Early Education, Willows, Campbell Hall, St. Brendon, St James.

PIGGY BANK

Apart from tuition, what other fees do you charge? Application and one time enrollment fee.

How is tuition broken down? Monthly.

What are the different payment plans available? Monthly, quarterly or yearly.

What is the fee schedule? No feedback received.

Is there a contract? Yes.

Do you have a tuition insurance program? No feedback received.

HELPING HANDS

What accreditation is necessary for the teachers to work at your school? Montessori certified.

How many teachers are there? Four teachers.

How many aides are there? Two aides.

IN THE ROOM

What's the child-to-adult ratio? 6/1.

What are the policies for initial separation between parent and child? It varies with each family. We are willing to meet every parent wishes.

Can you visit any time unannounced? Yes.

What are the hours? We are open from 8 to 5pm.

Do you offer early bird or after-hours pick-up? If so, is there an extra fee? No.

Please describe a typical day for a child at your school? The schedule is available online at www.sunsetmontessori.com.

What kind of academic activities are offered? No feedback received.

What kinds of activities are offered? We have a full enrichment program: dance, ballet, music, gymnastics, French, Spanish, drama, art and karate.

Is the child's time structured or unstructured or a mixture of both? No feedback received.

If a child is not interested in a particular activity, does he/she have other choices or is he/she encouraged to try it anyway? They have other choices but are encouraged to participate with the group.

How are disputes handled when they occur between the children? We talk and discuss each situation with children. We also read books and discuss scenarios at group time.

Is there nap time? If so for how long? 90 minutes.

What kinds of beds do you use? Parents provide sleeping beds. Children will need a small-sized sleeping back inside a labeled plastic bag.

What do you do when a child is dropped off in the morning and is obviously not well? What do you do when a child becomes sick during the day? We call the parent right away.

Can you accommodate children with special needs? No feedback received.

KEEPING IT SAFE

Please describe your security measures for arriving and leaving the school? We have a coded gate in front of the school.

What medical supplies do you have on hand, and what medical experience does your staff have? Is your staff trained in CPR? Yes and we do have a First Aid kit.

Please describe your earthquake-preparedness plan, and what special equipment do you have on hand in the event of a disaster? We have stored food and water and practice with children once a month the safety procedure.

SWINGS 'N THINGS

Please describe your playground. Does it have plenty of shade? Yes, lots of shade.

Do you put sunscreen on the children? No. Parents are encouraged to do that at home.

What kind of toilet training is available? We do toilet training.

HELPING OUT

What kinds of fundraising events are at your school each year? None.

How much participation is required by each parent? No feedback received.

KEEP IN TOUCH

How do you communicate with parents? Is there a newsletter or phone tree? Monthly newsletters and bulletin board.

Does the school. Publish an address book with all parent's information in it? Yes, but if you wish to keep your info private that can be accommodated.

preschool

SUNSHINE PRESCHOOL

11942 Sunset Blvd.
Los Angeles, CA 90049
Phone: (310) 472-2212
See Map D on page 286

Contact: Rita Cornyn, Directoress

- ACCREDITATION: NONE
- FOR-PROFIT
- FINANCIAL AID IS AVAILABLE
- NUMBER OF KIDS: 50 ON AVERAGE
- TUITION: $700-$1,400 MONTH
- WE HAVE KIDS WITH SPECIAL NEEDS

WHEN TO APPLY: COME FOR TOUR AND TODDLER PROGRAM. THERE IS A HEAVY WAIT LIST. CALL WHEN YOUR CHILD IS BETWEEN 10 AND 12 MONTHS.

Located on Sunset Boulevard in Brentwood, and set in a gorgeous house built in the late 1920s, you feel as if you're on vacation in the Hamptons or Martha's Vineyard when you walk into Sunshine Preschool. It may be the most exclusive preschool in town, with parents who are no strangers to the pages of newspapers and magazines, but you'd never know it—it's as warm and charming as could be, without a drop of attitude. Directress Rita Cornyn says, "I've been in school all my life and my goal is for the kids to love learning like I do." She also chooses teachers who love learning—and from the enthusiasm I saw while I was there, she's made terrific choices. It doesn't hurt that they're also all gorgeous and look like they've walked out of a Marc Jacobs ad!

While I was there, one group of children listened to a story, another group had a Spanish lesson, some did phonics, other kids painted, and the youngest ones were having circle time. All the kids were completely engaged in their activities, as were the teachers. The outside play area in the back yard is a huge grassy area, exquisitely landscaped with trees and flowers. I almost expected polo ponies to come galloping out. The yard also contains a bike path, a sandbox, climbing equipment and a playhouse with dolls and a dress-up area. The kids also eat their lunch out there under a covered area. Participation in fundraising isn't mandatory, but "parents fight to be involved." Many of the parents at Sunshine say that they feel like a part of a family, and there's many opportunities for them to meet their fellow family "members" at events such as Class Coffees and the school picnic.

The tuition may be steep, but it's immediately obvious that Sunshine is a very organized, well-oiled machine. It's not easy to get in—they receive about 150 applications for 46 openings, but once a child is there, they're destined to have a great experience with loving teachers. Many of the kids end up going on to schools in the area such as John Thomas Dye, Brentwood, Seeds University Elementary School, St. Martin's, Curtis, Village and Mirman.

BACKGROUND

Established in 1941 by Mrs. Knox. Bought by Rita Cornyn in 1976, who has been the Directoress ever since.

Bird's Eye View

	Non-existent	Poor	Fair	Good	Excellent
Learning to Read Children learn to explore the world of books					✓
Dress-Up Children experiment with different roles and imagination					✓
Hand-Eye Children develop fine motor skills by using fingers and hands					✓
Building Blocks Children practice symbolic representation. They are developing an understanding of the relationships between size and shape, and the basic math concepts of geometry and numbers					✓
Arts and Crafts Children are developing small muscle control as well as creativity					✓
Body Coordination Children crawl through tunnels, climb and balance					✓
Meeting Time Gathering place to listen to the teacher and to stories					✓
Weights and Measures Water and Sand tables				✓	
Beakers and Bunnies Classroom pets, aquariums....planting...					✓
Counting 1-2-3 A good preschool will stock basic early-learner software such as phonics or counting games					✓
Outdoor Play Encourage large muscle control and coordination					✓

Q & A

HOW THEY LEARN

What is your school's teaching philosophy? Learning through a hands-on experience.

How do you implement the philosophy? No feedback received.

What specialty teachers are brought into the school? There is a full-time Spanish teacher and a phonetics teacher.

What is the teaching method? It is a wide mix of developmental, academic, Montessori and others.

At what age do the children start? Youngest needs to be 2 years and 9 months.

To what age is the school licensed? Preschool through kindergarten.

HOW TO GET IN

Are there open house dates? When are tours given? Two open houses a year—one in January and one in February.

Is there an interview? With the child or without? We interview parents after open house meetings, but do not meet the child.

Is preference given to applicants whose siblings are alumni? Yes.

Are letters of recommendation encouraged? From what types of people? Not encouraged, but accepted and put into the file for consideration.

How many applications do you receive each year? Call school for details.

How many open spots are there each year? Call school for details.

What are some of the schools that children go on to after finishing their education at your preschool? Josh Thomas Dye, Brentwood. U.E.S., St. Martin's, Curtis Village, Mirman and Calthorpe.

PIGGY BANK

Apart from tuition, what other fees do you charge? $300 registration fee.

How is tuition broken down? Between $700 and $1,400 per month.

What are the different payment plans available? Usually monthly, but we can do it half-year or full-year.

What is the fee schedule? See above.

Is there a contract? Yes.

Do you have a tuition insurance program? No.

HELPING HANDS

What accreditation is necessary for the teachers to work at your school? Teachers have all met ECE requirements. Almost all have bachelor's degrees, and some are working on their master's.

How many teachers are there? Thirteen.

How many aides are there? None.

Do they come from other preschools? No feedback received.

IN THE 'ROOM

What's the child-to-adult ratio? The ratio is 15:2 and 12:1.

What are the policies for initial separation between parent and child? There is a sheet given to parents with extensive suggestions. It is on a case-by-case basis.

Can you visit any time unannounced? Yes.

What are the hours? 8:30 a.m.-3:15 p.m.

Do you offer early bird or after-hours pick-up? If so, is there an extra fee? No.

Please describe a typical day for a child at your school. Circle time, free play, outside time, snack, music and movement, art, centers, Spanish.

What kinds of academic activities are offered? Number readiness, Spanish, phonics, science, social studies, yoga, phonics for older kids.

What kinds of art activities are offered? Everything, all media.

Is the child's time structured or unstructured, or a mixture of both? Both.

If a child is not interested in a particular activity, does he/she have other choices or is he/she encouraged to try it anyway? All must participate in circle time. There are other choices but children are encouraged to participate.

How are disputes handled when they occur between the children? Teachers directed conflict resolution.

When and for how long is nap time? A half an hour, starting at 12:30 p.m.

What kinds of beds do you use? Mats.

What do you do when a child is dropped off in the morning and is obviously not well? What do you do when a child becomes sick during the day? Kids go into the office and sit with a teacher while waiting for the parent to arrive.

Can you accommodate children with special needs? Yes.

KEEPING IT SAFE

Please describe your security measures for arriving and leaving the school. The front door is always locked. The side entrance has a special code to open it. There are monitors in both the upstairs and downstairs offices.

What medical supplies do you have on hand, and what medical experience does your staff have? Is your staff trained in CPR? We have First Aid and CPR sessions once a year, and a room of medical supplies.

Please describe your earthquake-preparedness plan, and what special equipment do you have on hand in the event of a disaster? The earthquake shed has enough supplies for three days. The building has been retrofitted twice and all the windows are coated.

SWINGS 'N THINGS

Please describe your playground. Does it have plenty of shade? Sand, climbing equipment, play house, bike path.

Do you put sunscreen on the children? No feedback received.

What kind of toilet training is available? Kids must be toilet trained.

HELPING OUT

What kinds of fundraising events are at your school each year? Wine tasting, frozen food sale, Sunshine Preschool Cookbook, silent auction, gala. Half the money goes to the teacher bonuses, and the other half towards improvements in the yard and curriculum materials.

How much participation is required by each parent? Not required, but they love to do it.

KEEPING IN TOUCH

How do you communicate with parents? Is there a newsletter or phone tree? A newsletter, class coffees, back-to-school night, parent education speakers, school picnic, fall and spring fundraisers, subscribe to phone service which gets messages to all parents in one hour.

Does the school publish an address book with all the parents' information in it? Class list.

preschool

Temple Isaiah Preschool

10345 W. Pico Blvd.
Los Angeles, CA 90064
Phone: (310) 553-3552
www.templeisaiah.com
See Map C on page 286

Contact: Tamar Andrews, Director

- ACCREDITATION: NAEYC
- NOT-FOR-PROFIT
- FINANCIAL AID IS AVAILABLE
- NUMBER OF KIDS: 360
- TUITION: $1,325-$10,400 YEAR
- WE HAVE KIDS WITH SPECIAL NEEDS

WHEN TO APPLY: APPLICATIONS ARE AVAILABLE IN THE FIRST WEEK OF NOVEMBER. THE CUT OFF DATE IS JANUARY FOR TEMPLE MEMBERS AND FEBRUARY FOR THE COMMUNITY.

With 360 children in attendance, Temple Isaiah is the largest preschool in town. But despite its large size, it doesn't feel like a factory. It has clean and colorful hallways covered with artwork, which lead into large classrooms where energetic kids interact with caring teachers.

Some of the children engage in art projects while others play outside in the various huge playground areas—which, in addition to the requisite climbing equipment and sand areas, includes a basketball court. Temple membership is mandatory, and Shabbat is celebrated every Friday.

What makes Temple Isaiah unique, aside from the very qualified staff, is that it's also a lab school for Cal State Los Angeles and Santa Monica College. According to Director Tamar Andrews, "the staff really loves each other and there's very little staff turnover." Even though there's no advertising and everything is word-of-mouth, they still receive a few thousand applications a year for about 100 open spots. After leaving Temple Isaiah, a number of the kids go on to public schools (Warner, Canfield, Castle Heights, Westwood Charter, Beverly Hills), some to private (Echo Horizons, Willows) and some to Jewish day schools.

Background

The temple was founded in the 1960s.

BIRD'S EYE VIEW

	Non-existent	Poor	Fair	Good	Excellent
Learning to Read Children learn to explore the world of books					✓
Dress-Up Children experiment with different roles and imagination					✓
Hand-Eye Children develop fine motor skills by using fingers and hands					✓
Building Blocks Children practice symbolic representation. They are developing an understanding of the relationships between size and shape, and the basic math concepts of geometry and numbers					✓
Arts and Crafts Children are developing small muscle control as well as creativity					✓
Body Coordination Children crawl through tunnels, climb and balance					✓
Meeting Time Gathering place to listen to the teacher and to stories					✓
Weights and Measures Water and Sand tables					✓
Beakers and Bunnies Classroom pets, aquariums....planting...					✓
Counting 1-2-3 A good preschool will stock basic early-learner software such as phonics or counting games				✓	
Outdoor Play Encourage large muscle control and coordination					✓

Q & A

HOW THEY LEARN

What is your school's teaching philosophy? Our children are provided with a rich Judaic environment in which they can experience and learn about Jewish rituals, customs, celebrations and joys.

How do you implement the philosophy? We use active learning to promote cognitive, social, emotional, physical and creative development. Curriculum materials are designed to facilitate the construction of knowledge by encouraging them to explore, experiment, problem-solve and share ideas.

What specialty teachers are brought into the school? We have a sports specialist and a music specialist.

What is the teaching method? It is based on the work of Piaget and Vygotsky, current research into best practices in early childhood education and NAEYC Developmentally Appropriate Practice Guidelines.

At what age do the children start? To what age is the school licensed? No feedback received.

HOW TO GET IN

Are there open house dates? When are tours given? Tours are twice a month, from September to November.

Is there an interview? With the child or without? No.

Is preference given to applicants whose siblings are alumni? Yes.

Are letters of recommendation encouraged? From what types of people? No.

How many applications do you receive each year? A few thousand.

How many open spots are there each year? At least 100.

What are some of the schools that children go on to after finishing their education at your preschool? Public schools include Warner, Canfield, Castle Heights, Westwood Charter, Beverly Hills. Private schools include Echo Horizons, Willows, and Jewish day schools.

PIGGY BANK

Apart from tuition, what other fees do you charge? There is an application fee of $50, and a $500 fee upon acceptance.

How is tuition broken down? Annually, the Toddler Program (two years or older) is 1 day per week, 9-11 a.m. for $1,325. The Transition program from 9:30-11:45am is: $4,400 for 2 days, and $6,275 for 3 days. The Older Transition Program (three-year-olds between July and December) is 3-5 days per week, 9 a.m.-12 p.m.; $6,250 for three days, four days is $6,850, and $7,460 for five days per week. Preschool (three years old by 9/1) is 3-5 days per week from 9 a.m.-12 p.m.; the three-days is $6,250 and the four-day program is $6,850, and the five-day program is $7,460. Optional enrichment classes are from $800-$3,260.

What are the different payment plans available? Total payment must be received by July 1st. Half-payment is due on July 1st, with the other half on August 1st. There is a ten-month tuition plan.

What is the fee schedule? See above.

Is there a contract? Yes.

Do you have a tuition insurance program? No.

HELPING HANDS

What accreditation is necessary for the teachers to work at your school? The average lead teacher has a B.A.

How many teachers are there? There are 52 or 53 teachers.

How many aides are there? No aides.

IN THE 'ROOM

What's the child-to-adult ratio? The ratio for two-year-olds is 4:1. The ratio for three-year-olds is 5:1. The ratio for four-year-olds and five-year-olds is 6:1.

What are the policies for initial separation between parent and child? We suggest that the parent spend some time in the classroom while the child adjusts.

Can you visit any time unannounced? Yes, we encourage that.

What are the hours? Hours are from 8:30 a.m-12:30 p.m. Optional extended days are from 12-2:30 p.m.

Do you offer early bird or after-hours pick-up? If so, is there an extra fee? No feedback received.

Please describe a typical day for a child at your school. Circle time, outside and inside time, phonics, art, Hebrew.

What kinds of academic activities are offered? Developmentally appropriate.

What kinds of art activities are offered? Everything.

Is the child's time structured or unstructured, or a mixture of both? Child-initiated and teacher-directed.

If a child is not interested in a particular activity, does he/she have other choices or is he/she encouraged to try it anyway? Yes.

How are disputes handled when they occur between the children? Conflict resolution and redirection.

When and for how long is nap time? No naps.

What kinds of beds do you use? No naps.

What do you do when a child is dropped off in the morning and is obviously not well? What do you do when a child becomes sick during the day? We call parents as soon as possible.

Can you accommodate children with special needs? Yes. We have a full-time MFCC, speech therapist and occupational therapist on staff.

KEEPING IT SAFE

Please describe your security measures for arriving and leaving the school. The garage has a security guard, as does the front entrance.

What medical supplies do you have on hand, and what medical experience does your staff have? Is your staff trained in CPR? All staff has CPR, First Aid and pediatric health training.

**Please describe your earthquake-preparedness plan, and what special equipment do you have on hand in the event of a disaster? Each child has an earthquake personal kit. Each classroom has First Aid kits. In case of an emergency, kids would be evacuated to Chenot Recreation.

SWINGS 'N THINGS

Please describe your playground. Does it have plenty of shade? We have various playgrounds, all with UV covering, sand, climbing structures, basketball court.

Do you put sunscreen on the children? No feedback received.

What kind of toilet training is available? We will work with parents.

HELPING OUT

What kinds of fundraising events are at your school each year? Wrapping paper sales.

How much participation is required by each parent? Not required but strongly encouraged.

KEEPING IN TOUCH

How do you communicate with parents? Is there a newsletter or phone tree? Newsletters, phone, email.

Does the school publish an address book with all the parents' information in it? Yes.

preschool to 6th grade

TEMPLE ISRAEL NURSERY SCHOOL

7300 Hollywood Blvd.
Los Angeles, CA 90046
Phone: (323) 876-8330
www.tioh.org
See Map C on page 286

Contact: Sherry Fredman, Principal

- ACCREDITATION: NONE
- NOT-FOR-PROFIT
- FINANCIAL AID IS AVAILABLE
- NUMBER OF KIDS: 110
- TUITION: $7,125-$10,750 YEAR
- WE HAVE KIDS WITH SPECIAL NEEDS

WHEN TO APPLY: ALL YEAR. APPLICATIONS MUST BE IN BY OCTOBER.

Located on Hollywood Boulevard just west of La Brea, Temple Israel Nursery School provides a warm and loving environment."We teach children how to be *mensches*," says the school's Director Sherry Fredman, who herself is a complete and total *mensch*. As are the teachers, the rabbi, the security guard and everyone else within the buiding. And a *mensch* (for those who are not proficient in Yiddish) is a decent, responsible person with admirable characteristics.

Temple Israel provides a great balance of Jewish and secular learning in vibrante classrooms that contain fantastic artwork. the teachers have been there for quite some time, and the kids clearly love them like second mothers. Temple Israel teaches its children that part of being a good Jew is to give back to everyone–not just those in the Jewish community. To that end, the school adopted the Aliso Pico Preschool in Boyle Heights, where they donate time and funds to help those less fortunate.

The preschool celebrates Shabbat by lighting candles, followed by a story from the rabbi, and dancing and singing. In addition to Shabbat, all of the Jewish holidays become the "temple of the week," and are celebrated as such. Temple membership is mandatory and the temple fully embraces interfaith famailies, going sofar as to offer parents an online "celebrations guide" for all major Jewish families. The school offers twelve wonderful after-school enrichment programs, including an art appreciation program. The reditions of Van Gogh's "Vase With Irises" by a group of four-year-olds was stunning. The obvious talent of the students comes in handy when it's time for the school's one big fundraiser of the year, Art To Touch Your Heart, where children's art work can be ordered in various ways, including framing, on t-shirts, or note cards.

Temple Israel receives at least 100 applications for about 40 open spots a year. About eighty five to ninety percent of the students end up going on to their day school, and those who don't will go on to schools like Oakwood, the Center For Early Education, and Echo Horizons. If you are looking for a real sense of community where your child will not only learn how to be a good Jew, but a good person, definitely check out Temple Israel.

BACKGROUND

Temple Israel was founded in 1926. In the 1980s, a group of young temple members requested the Temple provide a preschool.

BIRD'S EYE VIEW

	Non-existent	Poor	Fair	Good	Excellent
Learning to Read Children learn to explore the world of books					✓
Dress-Up Children experiment with different roles and imagination					✓
Hand-Eye Children develop fine motor skills by using fingers and hands					✓
Building Blocks Children practice symbolic representation. They are developing an understanding of the relationships between size and shape, and the basic math concepts of geometry and numbers					✓
Arts and Crafts Children are developing small muscle control as well as creativity					✓
Body Coordination Children crawl through tunnels, climb and balance					✓
Meeting Time Gathering place to listen to the teacher and to stories					✓
Weights and Measures Water and Sand tables				✓	
Beakers and Bunnies Classroom pets, aquariums....planting...				✓	
Counting 1-2-3 A good preschool will stock basic early-learner software such as phonics or counting games					✓
Outdoor Play Encourage large muscle control and coordination					✓

Q & A

HOW THEY LEARN

What is your school's teaching philosophy? We offer a warm, creative environment in a Jewish atmosphere where each child is own unique style of living and learning is valued and nurtured. We teach the total child—emotional, social, intellectual, physical and spiritual. Our program addresses the four most important tasks of early childhood education which continue through life: separation and the achievement of autonomy, language acquisition, communication skills and socialization.

How do you implement the philosophy? Children are taught in small classroom groups to insure a sense of belonging. Classrooms are filled with abundant hands-on material, encouraging exploration creativity, building, fantasy and communication. We follow the yearly cycle of Jewish holidays. Each week is highlighted by the Friday Shabbat celebration. The Jewish values of kindness, consideration, compassion and fairness are an important part of the daily experience. Gymnastics is twice a week, and library is once a week.

What specialty teachers are brought into the school? We have a music specialist.

What is the teaching method? The teaching method is developmental.

At what age do the children start? To what age is the school licensed? From 2.6-5 years of age, we're licensed for 146 kids.

HOW TO GET IN

Are there open house dates? When are tours given? Tours are offered twice a week by personal appointment.

Is there an interview? With the child or without? Parents schedule a tour and international session with our direction. We recommend this is done without child so the parents can focus on the information they receive.

Is preference given to applicants whose siblings are alumni? Preference is given to families with a demonstration of commitment to our community (alumni siblings, temple members, families already involved in our toddler classes).

Are letters of recommendation encouraged? From what types of people? No.

How many applications do you receive each year? At least 100.

How many open spots are there each year? 40.

What are some of the schools that children go on to after finishing their education at your preschool? Oakwood, Center for Early Education and Echo Horizons, but 85-90% go on to Temple Israel Day School.

PIGGY BANK

Apart from tuition, what other fees do you charge? There is no entrance fee, just join the temple. Call for membership rates.

How is tuition broken down? $7,125 for three mornings, $8,475 for five mornings, and $10,750 for five days per week. There is extended care Monday through Thursday for $2,000 for the first year. Early drop off for an additional $1,600.

What are the different payment plans available? Can pay in two installments.

What is the fee schedule? See tuition (above).

Is there a contract? Yes.

Do you have a tuition insurance program? No.

HELPING HANDS

What accreditation is necessary for the teachers to work at your school? Lead teachers need a minimum of 12 hours/unit, and assistant teachers need a minimum of 6 hours/unit.

How many teachers are there? On our nursery school program, we presently have eight lead teachers.

How many aides are there? There are 17 assistant teachers.

IN THE 'ROOM

What's the child-to-adult ratio? Average ratio is 1:1. In the two youngest classes, it is 5:1.

What are the policies for initial separation between parent and child? During the initial separation, we expect an adult available to stay at school. Each child separates at his/her own pace; the adult spends less and less time until the separation is complete.

Can you visit any time unannounced? Parents can visit at any time unannounced, but since surprise visits are disruptive to the children, we ask that parents please let teachers know when they are coming.

What are the hours? Our basic hours are 9 a.m.-12 p.m. for the morning session and 1-4 p.m. for the afternoon. We also offer enrichment classes (such as karate) in the afternoons, also for additional fees.

Do you offer early bird or after-hours pick-up? If so, is there an extra fee? Students can stay until 12:30 p.m., 2:45 p.m. or 5:30 p.m., or can be dropped off early at 8 a.m. for additional fees.

Please describe a typical day for a child at your school. Our daily program is based on a developmental model that encounters age-appropriate social, cognitive, emotional and physical skills. Our students have indoor play-time, which consists of structured and unstructured activities at a variety of learning centers, circle time, outdoor play, story time, snack and lunch. Each class has weekly specialization, music, gymnastics and library visits as well.

What kinds of academic activities are offered? Developmental.

What kinds of art activities are offered? We strongly encourage process-oriented art projects appropriate to each age and to express him/herself in a variety of both structured and unstructured ways.

Is the child's time structured or unstructured, or a mixture of both? Structured and unstructured times are provided. We encourage self-initiative with our students and make sure they have opportunities for independent as well as structured activity. As explained above, we have centers available every day for a choice.

If a child is not interested in a particular activity, does he/she have other choices or is he/she encouraged to try it anyway? Usually not. However, a child must respect his/her peers' decision to participate and cannot disrupt or prevent others from participating. Children may make another choice in some cases or may watch peers participate in other cases such as during circle time.

How are disputes handled when they occur between the children? We strive to teach children to use their words to express their feelings, and to create a dialogue with peers and teachers. A teacher mediates and helps the children see how each other feels and hear each others' words. Teachers facilitate students in resolving conflicts themselves whenever is possible.

When and for how long is nap time? 12:30-1 p.m.

What kinds of beds do you use? Cots.

What do you do when a child is dropped off in the morning and is obviously not well? What do you do when a child becomes sick during the day? Teachers meet every child each morning and if the child is brought to school sick, the adult must turn around and take him/her home. If the child becomes sick during school hours, they are kept with a teacher until a parent can pick them up. Children must be free of fever, vomiting and diarrhea for a full 24 hours before returning to school.

Can you accommodate children with special needs? Yes, definitely.

KEEPING IT SAFE

Please describe your security measures for arriving and leaving the school. We have a guard posted at the entrance on the building who screens any unfamiliar visitors. All families must have a school sticker on their car to enter our parking lot. All children must be signed in and out by a parent daily. Children can only be picked up by people designated on a written consent form. We also have security cameras monitored by a different school office.

What medical supplies do you have on hand, and what medical experience does your staff have? Is your staff trained in CPR? All staff have CPR and basic First Aid certification annually.

Please describe your earthquake-preparedness plan, and what special equipment do you have on hand in the event of a disaster? We have an extensive disaster-preparedness plan in place. Staff and children have monthly fire and earthquake drills. Every student has a bag of emergency clothes and supplies stored off-site and every student and every student has an out of date contact at another school. The school stores three days of water and supplies off-site.

SWINGS 'N THINGS

Please describe your playground. Does it have plenty of shade? We have three playgrounds for three different age groups. Each has a sandbox, climbing structure and riding equipment. Each has an approved safety surface. One yard has natural partial shade and the others share canopies. Each yard has its own water fountain.

Do you put sunscreen on the children? No feedback received.

What kind of toilet training is available? We have one bathroom for two classrooms. Each bathroom has child-sized and regular-sized toilets. Bathrooms for our younger classes have changing toilets. Teachers work with parents to encourage toilets training once a child expresses interest.

HELPING OUT

What kinds of fundraising events are at your school each year? Art to Touch Your Heart (children do all the artwork), that can be ordered framed, on T-shirts, and note cards. There is also a silent auction with teachers donating time.

How much participation is required by each parent? Not required, but strongly suggested.

KEEPING IN TOUCH

How do you communicate with parents? Is there a newsletter or phone tree? We communicate with parents in a variety of ways. Our school has a weekly newsletter, a phone tree for emergencies, PACE calls (automated message sent to all parents) e-mail with the director, assistant director and most teachers, mailboxes for each student in each class for daily correspondence and monthly class newsletters. Teachers are available during all school hours.

Does the school publish an address book with all the parents' information in it? Each fall, we publish a parent handbook that contains all school policies and procedures as well as addresses of families and phone numbers.

preschool to 6th grade

THE CENTER FOR EARLY EDUCATION

563 N. Alfred Street
West Hollywood, CA 90048
Phone: (323) 651-0707
www.centerforearlyeducation.org
See Map C on page 286

Contact: Donna Degaetani, Director

- ACCREDITATION: NONE
- NOT-FOR-PROFIT
- FINANCIAL AID IS AVAILABLE
- NUMBER OF KIDS: 122
- TUITION: $14,370-$20,215 YEAR
- WE HAVE KIDS WITH SPECIAL NEEDS

WHEN TO APPLY: APPLICATIONS AVAILABLE FROM JULY -DECEMBER.

The Center for Early Education offers developmental education with all the extras. The school is located in West Hollywood not far from the Beverly Center, and is a glorious architectural achievement with clean, simple lines and well-planned exterior spaces. The classrooms are large, bright and full of all the modern educational tools money can buy. As taken from the school's literature, "In the middle of a thriving, culturally diverse, metropolitan city is an urban oasis where young minds are being nurtured, challenged, and readied to take on the leadership challenges of the 21st century. Located on over an acre with rooftop playgrounds, state-of-the-art computer and science labs, and the most up to date facilities, is a dynamic environment for early childhood and elementary age children."

Part of what is unique about the Center is… well, the learning centers. As integral components of each of the programs, learning centers are areas in the classroom that define a special focus or afford a specific opportunity for children to experience. Centers available in the classroom include block building, dramatic play, science, literature, cooking, music, and language. The idea of the centers is that children make choices, learn through direct engagement and by using a variety of materials, and ultimately build self-confidence as a result of learning skills. The early childhood education classes (it's not preschool, it is school) is a showcase for nursery schools. The campus is really nice and the playground just rocks! There is a fireman-type pole that is spiraled so you slide down the corkscrew.

The Center for Early Education strives to create an environment in which children receive a balance of experiences, affording them opportunities for exploration, growth, and success. "Our challenging programs are designed to encourage students to become lifelong learners and to instill in them a joy of learning, resilience, self-esteem, respect for others, and commitment to the community beyond the school."

BACKGROUND

The Center for Early Education was founded in 1939 as The School for Nursery Years, a nursery school in the Hancock Park area of Los Angeles. It moved to West Hollywood in the 1940s. In 1971, CEE was expanded to include an elementary school.

BIRD'S EYE VIEW

	Non-existent	Poor	Fair	Good	Excellent
Learning to Read Children learn to explore the world of books					✓
Dress-Up Children experiment with different roles and imagination					✓
Hand-Eye Children develop fine motor skills by using fingers and hands					✓
Building Blocks Children practice symbolic representation. They are developing an understanding of the relationships between size and shape, and the basic math concepts of geometry and numbers					✓
Arts and Crafts Children are developing small muscle control as well as creativity					✓
Body Coordination Children crawl through tunnels, climb and balance					✓
Meeting Time Gathering place to listen to the teacher and to stories					✓
Weights and Measures Water and Sand tables					✓
Beakers and Bunnies Classroom pets, aquariums....planting...					✓
Counting 1-2-3 A good preschool will stock basic early-learner software such as phonics or counting games					✓
Outdoor Play Encourage large muscle control and coordination					✓

Q & A

HOW THEY LEARN

What is your school's teaching philosophy? We are an independent co-ed day school committed to the education of preschool and elementary students of different ethnic and socio-economic backgrounds in a challenging, supportive setting. Programs are designed to encourage students to become lifelong learners and to instill in them a sense of self-esteem, joy of learning, resilience, respect for each other and commitment to the community beyond the school.

How do you implement the philosophy? Observing the behavior of children in a school situation, which considers each child's endowment and environment. Setting goals for both individual children and groups. Creating an environment in which children receive a balance of experiences.

What is the teaching method? We combine different kinds of methods.

At what age do the children start? To what age is the school licensed? Students must be two years old by August 1, and we are licensed to sixth grade.

HOW TO GET IN

Are there open house dates? When are tours given? Once you apply, you receive an invitation to an open house orientation and a tour of the school. These take place from October through January. Due to the large number of applicants and limited space, we are not able to interview all the applicant families.

Is there an interview? With the child or without? Parent interview process takes place from November to March. For toddler and nursery school applicants, only a parent interview. The children are not assessed.

Is preference given to applicants whose siblings are alumni? Siblings are not automatically accepted. Sibling families are expected to have demonstrated a level of support, commitment, involvement and participation within our community.

Are letters of recommendation encouraged? From what types of people? No.

How many applications do you receive each year? About 600.

How many open spots are there each year? 44.

What are some of the schools that children go on to after finishing their education at your preschool? About 99% go on here to our elementary. We don't really encourage coming here just for preschool.

PIGGY BANK

Apart from tuition, what other fees do you charge? The application fee is $85 and the entrance fee is $1,500.

How is tuition broken down? The toddler program is $14,370. The nursery school has four plans: Plan A, 9 a.m.-12 p.m. daily ($14,370); Plan B, 9 a.m.-3 p.m. on Mon., Wed. and Fri., and from 9 a.m.-12 p.m. on Tues. and Thurs. ($15,380); Plan C, 9 a.m.-3 p.m. daily ($16,495); and Plan D, 9 a.m.-3 p.m. on Tues. and Thurs., and 9 a.m.-12 p.m. on Mon., Wed. and Fri. ($14,870).

What are the different payment plans available? There is a one and two payment plan.

What is the fee schedule? One payment plan includes full balance of tuition and fees due by July. Two payment plan requires first payment (half the balance of tuition and fees plus required participation in the Tuition Refund Reserve Plan) due by July, second payment no later than December 1.

Is there a contract? No feedback received.

Do you have a tuition insurance program? No feedback received.

HELPING HANDS

What accreditation is necessary for the teachers to work at your school? No feedback received.

How many teachers are there? There is one master teacher.

How many aides are there? There are two assistant/co-teachers per classroom.

IN THE 'ROOM

What's the adult-to-child ratio? 22:3.

What are the policies for initial separation between parent and child? The Toddler Program is for children between two and three years of age. The initial goal is to transition children to a school setting. Each half-day program of 10-14 children requires the initial participation of a parent and leads to separation through a gradual, individualized process.

Can you visit any time unannounced? Yes.

What are the hours? Do you offer early bird or after-hours pick-up? If so, is there an extra fee? 9 a.m.-12 p.m. for Plan A; 9 a.m.-3 p.m. for Plans B, C and D; 3-6 p.m. for Day Care.

Please describe a typical day for a child at

your school. Thematic teaching, a theme for the week or the day, and all activities revolve around that theme.

What kinds of academic activities are offered? No formal academics, but exposure to letters and numbers, manipulatives and science.

What kinds of art activities are offered? Everything! Art is a big part of the daily curriculum.

Is the child's time structured or unstructured? Or a mixture of both? Mixed.

If a child is not interested in a particular activity, does he/she have other choices or is he/she encouraged to try it anyway? There are other choices, but they are encouraged to do it if they have never done a particular activity.

How are disputes handled when they occur between the children? Children are encouraged to use their own words.

When and for how long is nap time? One hour rest time for afternoon students.

What kinds of beds do you use? No feedback received.

What do you do when a child is dropped off in the morning and is obviously not well? What do you do when a child becomes sick during the day? The parent is called to pick up the sick child.

Can you accommodate children with special needs? Yes, depending on the need.

KEEPING IT SAFE

Please describe your security measures for arriving and leaving the school. Visitors and parents must come through the front gate and office, and sign in and out.

What medical supplies do you have on hand, and what medical experience does your staff have? Is your staff trained in CPR? First Aid kits.

Please describe your earthquake-preparedness plan, and what special equipment do you have on hand in the event of a disaster? Earthquake bags for each child.

SWINGS 'N THINGS

Please describe your playground. Does it have plenty of shade? We have an amazing state-of-the-art playground.

What kind of toilet training is available? Don't have to be toilet-trained to be a student.

HELPING OUT

What kinds of fundraising events are at your school each year? Auction gala and an annual fund drive.

How much participation is required by each parent? No feedback received.

KEEPING IN TOUCH

How do you communicate with parents? Is there a newsletter or phone tree? Once a week newsletter and a phone tree, two face-to-face conferences per year.

Does the school publish an address book with all the parents' information in it? Roster.

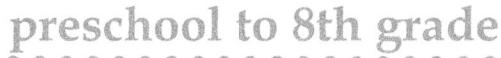

THE COUNTRY SCHOOL

5243 Laurel Canyon Blvd.
North Hollywood, CA 91607
Phone: (818) 769-2473
www.country-school.org
See Map A on page 286

Contact: Alaina Smith, Preschool Director

- ACCREDITATION: CAIS
- NOT-FOR-PROFIT
- FINANCIAL AID IS AVAILABLE
- NUMBER OF KIDS: 85
- TUITION: $3,050-$21,550 YEAR
- WE HAVE KIDS WITH SPECIAL NEEDS

WHEN TO APPLY: THERE IS NO CUT OFF DATE, BUT INTERESTED APPLICANTS SHOULD GET THEIR APPLICATIONS AT LEAST A YEAR BEFORE TO AVOID BEING PUT ON A WAITING LIST.

The gated and secure exterior of the Country School, a quaint and quiet façade, belies little of what is seen when walking into the courtyard, where the ring of children's laughter and the bustle of students in and out of classrooms brings the quiet buildings to life. The Country School was founded in 1948 as a preschool and was expanded in the 1970's to include elementary classes as well. Alaina Smith, the Preschool Director, is a 21-year veteran who boasts of the schools socio-economic diversity amongst its student body. Singer goes on to add, "We're not trying to create cookie cutter kids." There is a "diverse student body," of which 40 percent are receiving some kind of financial aid.

Alaina explains that the emphasis of the school's teaching is "problem solving, language and social/emotional development" and that 60-70% of these young children will stay on for the Country School's kindergarten through 8th grade program. The idyllic setting had me smiling along as I watched teachers and aides doing their jobs, with happy faces and friendly hellos. Alaina guided me through the parent tour which showcases the airy, high-ceilinged, bright classrooms. The preschool building is adjacent to the school's K-6 classrooms, divided by a playground and a long row of tables with umbrellas for lunchtime or outdoor schoolwork. There are airy, high-ceilinged and bright classrooms. Campus expansion includes organic garden beds, a butterfly garden, and a pollywog pond. The student-to-teacher ratio varies slightly among the 85 children currently enrolled in the preschool. In the two-year-old program, the ratio is 1:4; in the three-year-old program, it is 1:6/7, and 1:8/9 in the pre-kindergarten. This low ratio is possible as there are two teachers per classroom as well as one aide.

Admission is based on a first come first served basis while emphasis is placed on creating a diverse student body and in keeping with the Country School's philosophy of being a family-oriented school, priority consideration to sibling applications is granted. To sum it up best, one alumnae mother "picked the school because of the balance between academic, socialization and creative development."

BACKGROUND

The school was founded in 1948 by Rafe and Laura Ellis. Pioneers in the field of early childhood in their day. The preschool was based on the findings of John Dewey, Jean Piaget and Vigotsky. The school began as "Rafe's Rangers" and grew and expanded to include and elementary campus in 1972.

BIRD'S EYE VIEW

	Non-existent	Poor	Fair	Good	Excellent
Learning to Read Children learn to explore the world of books					✓
Dress-Up Children experiment with different roles and imagination					✓
Hand-Eye Children develop fine motor skills by using fingers and hands					✓
Building Blocks Children practice symbolic representation. They are developing an understanding of the relationships between size and shape, and the basic math concepts of geometry and numbers					✓
Arts and Crafts Children are developing small muscle control as well as creativity					✓
Body Coordination Children crawl through tunnels, climb and balance					✓
Meeting Time Gathering place to listen to the teacher and to stories				✓	
Weights and Measures Water and Sand tables				✓	
Beakers and Bunnies Classroom pets, aquariums....planting...					✓
Counting 1-2-3 A good preschool will stock basic early-learner software such as phonics or counting games					✓
Outdoor Play Encourage large muscle control and coordination					✓

Q & A

HOW THEY LEARN

What is your school's teaching philosophy?
All children should be given the opportunity to grow socially, emotionally and cognitively in a supportive, nurturing environment at their own pace. Our teachers use an emergent curriculum approach to teaching. The themes and activities are based around the interests of the children and the children are given opportunities to expand their knowledge on a topic of interest through exploration of a variety of hands on developmentally-appropriate materials.

How do you implement the philosophy? Our main goal for our pre-school is helping to nurture each child's social-emotional development, to help them become problem-solvers and to help them become self-confident individuals. Curiosity about pre-academic activities is also nurtured in a hands-on, age-appropriate manner.

What specialty teachers are brought into the school? The children have music with a music teacher visit twice a week, and the children visit the school library and are read to by the librarian once a week.

What is the teaching method? Our curriculum includes many open-ended activities and the teachers are free to take time with children and read a special story, engage in an activity or just take some time to really talk with an individual child about their day or what's on their mind. Because of our low ratios, teachers have time to be responsive to children's questions and can engage in real conversations with the children, as well as take care of each child's individual needs. The teachers spend a great deal of time carefully observing, interacting with and communicating with each child. They understand the individual needs and interests of each child and gain their trust and affection.

At what age do the children start? To what age is the school licensed? Our children start the Transition Program if they are 2 years old in September of their entry year, or if they are 2.9 years of age in September, they enter our Beginner Program. In the preschool, we are licensed from 2 to 5.

HOW TO GET IN

Are there open house dates? When are tours given? Tours are highly recommended and are given twice a week to interested applicants.

Is there an interview? With the child or without? We don't have an interview process because the children are so young when they begin school.

Is preference given to applicants whose siblings are alumni? Current and alumni siblings are given preference.

Are letters of recommendation encouraged? From what types of people? Letters of recommendation are not required.

How many applications do you receive each year? We average about 45 to 50 applicants each year with the majority for the youngest classes.

How many open spots are there each year? The majority of open spots are for the youngest classes—16 total for both Transition classes, and 12 for the Beginner Program. We might average four or five in the older classes, due to the slightly larger ratios.

What are some of the schools that children go on to after finishing their education at your preschool? A large amount of our graduates continue on into our elementary school program, others enroll in a number of independent schools in the area or in public school.

PIGGY BANK

Apart from tuition, what other fees do you charge? There is a $125 non-refundable application fee.

How is tuition broken down? For the current year, our preschool tuition is as follows: Transition: $3,050, 3x week: $9,335, 5x week: $11,645, Junior: $13,745, K-5: $16,720. 6-8: $20,980-$21,550.

What are the different payment plans available? Parents can choose to pay in full, in two installments, or break it up into six payments.

What is the fee schedule? Deposits are due with enrollment and are refundable until April. First payments are due July.

Is there a contract? Each parent signs a contract.

Do you have a tuition insurance program? Parents are required to enroll in the tuition insurance if they choose the two-or six-payment plan. It is optional for parents paying in full but highly encouraged in case of an unforeseen change.

HELPING HANDS

What accreditation is necessary for the teachers to work at your school? We require our teachers to have at least 12 units in Early Childhood regardless of their level of education. Most of our teachers have an Associate of Arts or a Bachelors Degree in Early Childhood. We encourage our teachers to go to conferences and workshops even after they have received a degree.

How many teachers are there? Nine teachers.

How many aides are there? Four aides.

Do they come from other preschools? Most of our teachers began their careers here as assistants or aides and then acquired the education and experience to become teachers. Many of our teachers remain with us long term and although many started their careers here at The Country School, we encourage all our staff members to visit other schools to investigate what other schools are doing.

IN THE 'ROOM

What's the adult-to-child ratio? Our ratios are based on the particular ages of the children and range from 4:1 for the two-year-olds to 8:1 for the pre-kindergarten.

What are the policies for initial separation between parent and child? Each parent stays until their child is comfortable with the teachers and environment. Some children separate in two days, some children take two weeks or longer. We feel the best way to accomplish this goal is gradual separation. We also feel that the child needs to know that the parent is leaving and for how long, and the parent may NEVER just sneak out without saying good-bye (even though sometimes this may seem easier).

Can you visit any time unannounced? The preschool has an open door policy. A parent can drop by unannounced at any time.

What are the hours? Do you offer early bird or after-hours pick-up? If so, is there an extra fee? The transition program is Monday/Wednesday (2-4 p.m.) or Tuesday/Thursday (2-4 p.m.). The beginner program is three or five days (1:15-4:15 p.m.), juniors are 8:45-1 p.m., and pre-kindergarten is 8:45 a.m.-2 p.m. Extended hours are available for the Junior and Pre-K students from 8-8:45 (no extra charge) and until 4:00 after class at an additional cost.

Please describe a typical day for a child at your school. A typical day would have the child beginning outside on the playground for about a half-hour when they first arrive. Then the students would go inside their rooms to have a short group time followed by snack. The children would then participate in free choice centers for about and hour or longer (depending on the age of the children). During free choice there are many different activities to participate including art, manipulative, science, dramatic play, and blocks. When center time is finished, the children have another outside time and lunch before they have one more large group activity before they go home.

What kinds of academic activities are offered? Our school is based on NAEYC's (National Association for the Education of Young Children's) developmentally-appropriate practice. We don't consider ourselves a traditionally academic preschool. However, children acquire some of the pre-reading and math skills by participating in hands-on, creative, open-ended activities.

What kinds of art activities are offered? Children participate in a variety of process-oriented creative art activities. Throughout the year, the children explore different kinds of materials including paint, scissors, glue, collage materials, etc. Our program is based on process-oriented, exploratory, creative art experiences as opposed to a more product-oriented philosophy. The children are encouraged to express themselves through their art experiences and to make the art experience truly their own.

Is the child's time structured or unstructured? Or a mixture of both? A mixture of both. Within the structure of a daily routine established by each classroom, the child has opportunity to participate in outside gross motor activities, inside free-choice center time, a time for snack and lunch, and a time for a large group activity (cooperative game, body movement activity, story, etc). The children are also involved in specialty activities such as music, library, and (for the pre-kindergarten children) physical education. While inside or outside, the children can make choices on which center they would like to participate in and how long they would like to stay before moving on to another activity.

If a child is not interested in a particular activity, does he/she have other choices or is he/she encouraged to try it anyway? The children are encouraged to participate in certain activities, however they are not required if they truly are not interested. The teacher will find another activity for the child or allow them to watch on the perimeter of the activity if that is what the child chooses to do.

How are disputes handled when they occur between the children? The two children are brought together to solve the dispute with the assistance of a teacher. Teachers help model for younger children (or any child needing guidance for that matter) the words and actions needed to help solve the dispute. At our school, we believe in natural consequences, if you knock someone's block tower down (intentionally or by accident) then you help rebuild it. If you grab a toy, you give it back and ask the child if you can have it when they are done. We also feel that each child should feel empowered. For example, the child that had his/her block tower knocked done, or the child whose toy was taken away, also has the opportunity to voice their displeasure to the other child.

When and for how long is nap time? Since most of our children are part-time, we don't require them to nap.

What kinds of beds do you use? No feedback received.

What do you do when a child is dropped off in the morning and is obviously not well? What do you do when a child becomes sick during the day? If a child is sick when they arrive, we ask the parents to take the child home. If a child becomes sick during the day, we call the parents to take the child home. If the parent cannot be reached or cannot come right away, the child is isolated from the other children yet is still in the company of an adult that the child feels comfortable with (teacher, assistant or Director).

Can you accommodate children with special needs? We can accommodate children with special needs, if we feel we can be of service to the child and the family.

KEEPING IT SAFE

Please describe your security measures for arriving and leaving the school. During formal arrival times, parents can either walk their child to the preschool yard or there is a preschool teacher at the carpool line to walk a child up to the yard. At dismissal time, parents pull through a carpool line and a teacher puts the child in the car. Regardless, parents are required to sign their child in or out of school with a full signature.

What medical supplies do you have on hand, and what medical experience does your staff have? Is your staff trained in CPR? Each classroom is equipped with a small First Aid kit that includes items to attend to small scrapes and cuts. There are full First Aid kits located throughout the campus. Every teacher and assistant is trained in CPR and First Aid.

Please describe your earthquake-preparedness plan, and what special equipment do you have on hand in the event of a disaster? All staff members are assigned a task in the event a disaster. We have several committees including First Aid, search and rescue, fire suppression, communications, well child (child care), and security. Each child brings in an earthquake kit to keep in our earthquake shed. The earthquake shed not only stores individual earthquake kits, there is also all the necessary items needed in the event of an earthquake including stretchers, First Aid kits, portable toilet, lots of water, blankets, fire extinguishers, etc.

SWINGS 'N THINGS

Please describe your playground. Does it have plenty of shade? Our playground provides opportunity for fast motor activity such as tricycles and scooters, as well as a climbing structure (age-appropriate for preschoolers) for climbing. We also have sand and water sources available. We have a balance of shady and sunny spots. We also like to provide opportunities for quieter activities such as painting, drawing or building with small manipulatives.

Do you put sunscreen on the children? We request parents apply sunscreen before coming to school, we will reapply if needed.

What kind of toilet training is available? We don't require the children to be toilet trained. However, if the teachers and parents are in agreement that a child is ready, the teachers will assist a child through learning to use the toilet.

HELPING OUT

What kinds of fundraising events are at your school each year? We have two main fundraisers; a silent auction/gala event and annual giving. There are several small fundraisers that parents can also participate in that change from year to year.

How much participation is required by each parent? We don't have a requirement for parent participation, however, we encourage each parent to help in whatever way they can.

KEEPING IN TOUCH

How do you communicate with parents? Is there a newsletter or phone tree? Each set of teachers send out a class letter about once a week. There is also a school wide newsletter that is distributed weekly and a seasonal publication called Connections. Each class also has a phone tree set up in case of emergencies.

Does the school publish an address book with all the parents' information in it? We have an all school roster/handbook that is given to each family once a year.

preschool

THE EARLY YEARS SCHOOL

302 Montana Ave.
Santa Monica, CA 90403
Phone: (310) 394-0463
See Map D on page 286

Contact: Joy Siegel and Tama Taub, Directors

- ACCREDITATION: NAEYC
- FOR-PROFIT
- FINANCIAL AID IS AVAILABLE
- NUMBER OF KIDS: 100
- TUITION: $8,700-$10,950 YEAR
- WE HAVE KIDS WITH SPECIAL NEEDS

WHEN TO APPLY: APPLICATIONS AVAILABLE ONCE THE CHILD TURNS ONE YEAR OLD. PARENTS MUST COME ON TOUR. APPLICATIONS ACCEPTED THROUGH DECEMBER.

On Montana Avenue, three blocks from the ocean, is a charming house built in the 1920s that now houses The Early School Years. Its two founders—Joy Siegel and Tama Taub—are still the Directors, and their calm energy seems to permeate the place.

As I arrived, parents (and some nannies) were dropping off their kids for the afternoon program and the fact that they have to enter Joy and Tama's shared office to sign in provides them with an opportunity to communicate with the top dogs. Despite the rain, the kids were mellow and eagerly participated in circle time. As a developmental program, "our priority is social and emotional growth for the children," Joy and Tama say. However, as I watched the kids, it was obvious that they definitely spend a lot of time on letters, numbers, shapes and colors.

In 1989, The Early School Years was one of the first early childhood programs to be accredited by the National Association for the Education of Young Children. Every class has team teaching (there are no aides) and all teachers attend workshops and conferences to further their education. There are about 40 to 50 open spots a year, and after leaving The Early School Years, the kids go on to a variety of private schools in the Santa Monica and Brentwood areas, as well as Franklin and Roosevelt, the two public schools located up the street on Montana.

BACKGROUND

The Early Years school was established in 1982 by Joy Siegel and Tama Taub.

Bird's Eye View

	Non-existent	Poor	Fair	Good	Excellent
Learning to Read — Children learn to explore the world of books				Good	
Dress-Up — Children experiment with different roles and imagination			Fair		
Hand-Eye — Children develop fine motor skills by using fingers and hands				Good	
Building Blocks — Children practice symbolic representation. They are developing an understanding of the relationships between size and shape, and the basic math concepts of geometry and numbers				Good	
Arts and Crafts — Children are developing small muscle control as well as creativity				Good	
Body Coordination — Children crawl through tunnels, climb and balance				Good	
Meeting Time — Gathering place to listen to the teacher and to stories				Good	
Weights and Measures — Water and Sand tables			Fair		
Beakers and Bunnies — Classroom pets, aquariums....planting...			Fair		
Counting 1-2-3 — A good preschool will stock basic early-learner software such as phonics or counting games				Good	
Outdoor Play — Encourage large muscle control and coordination				Good	

Q & A

HOW THEY LEARN

What is your school's teaching philosophy? We have a hands-on program based on Piaget, Erikson and Reggio.

How do you implement the philosophy? The teachers attend workshops, conferences, and take classes.

What specialty teachers are brought into the school? A music teacher comes in.

What is the teaching method? Developmental.

At what age do the children start? To what age is the school licensed? 2.9 to 6.

HOW TO GET IN

Are there open house dates? When are tours given? Tours are given a couple of times a month.

Is there an interview? With the child or without? No interview.

Is preference given to applicants whose siblings are alumni? Yes. We also give a preference to those enrolled in the parent-toddler group.

Are letters of recommendation encouraged? From what types of people? No.

How many applications do you receive each year? A couple of hundred.

How many open spots are there each year? 40-50.

**What are some of the schools that children

go on to after finishing their education at your preschool? Franklin Roosevelt, Palisades area, Warner.

PIGGY BANK

Apart from tuition, what other fees do you charge? There is no entrance fee. There is a $50 application fee.

How is tuition broken down? The morning sessions are $10,950 and the afternoon sessions are $8,700.

What are the different payment plans available? Three equal payments.

What is the fee schedule? First payment is due upon acceptance.

Is there a contract? Yes, there is a contract.

Do you have a tuition insurance program? No insurance program.

HELPING HANDS

What accreditation is necessary for the teachers to work at your school? Most teachers have a B.A. or 24 ECE units.

How many teachers are there? Twelve teachers—team teaching.

How many aides? No aides.

Do they come from other preschools? No feedback received.

IN THE 'ROOM

What's the adult-to-child ratio? 6:1 for the younger children, and 8:1 for the older.

What are the policies for initial separation between parent and child? Teachers do home visits. We ask parents to clear their calendar for two weeks.

Can you visit any time unannounced? Yes.

What are the hours? Monday through Friday from 9 a.m.-12 p.m.

Do you offer early bird or after-hours pick-up? If so, is there an extra fee? There is an option to stay until 2:30 p.m. on Tuesdays and Thursdays for an extra fee.

Please describe a typical day for a child at your school. The three hours involve inside and outside time, as well as snacks.

What kinds of academic activities are offered? Plenty (letters, numbers, shapes and colors), but our priority is social and emotional growth.

What kinds of art activities are offered? A number of different activities.

Is the child's time structured or unstructured, or a mixture of both? Structured, with lots of opportunities to choose.

If a child is not interested in a particular activity, does he/she have other choices or is he/she encouraged to try it anyway? No feedback received.

How are disputes handled when they occur between the children? Conflict resolution.

When and for how long is nap time? No nap time, because it is a half-day program.

What kinds of beds do you use? None.

What do you do when a child is dropped off in the morning and is obviously not well? What do you do when a child becomes sick during the day? Call parent right away and the child will stay in the assistant's office until the parent arrives.

Can you accommodate children with special needs? Yes.

KEEPING IT SAFE

Please describe your security measures for arriving and leaving the school. There are three gates; only one is unlocked.

What medical supplies do you have on hand, and what medical experience does your staff have? Is your staff trained in CPR? We have First Aid equipment and CPR-trained staff.

Please describe your earthquake-preparedness plan, and what special equipment do you have on hand in the event of a disaster? We have extensive earthquake supplies.

SWINGS 'N THINGS

Please describe your playground. Does it have plenty of shade? Climbing equipment and a sand area.

Do you put sunscreen on the children? Yes.

What kind of toilet training is available? Children don't have to be potty trained. We will work with parents.

HELPING OUT

What kinds of fundraising events are at your school each year? Garage sales, t-shirt/sweatshirt sales, dinner my silent auction. All money goes towards scholarship.

How much participation is required by each parent? None.

KEEPING IN TOUCH

How do you communicate with parents? Is there a newsletter or phone tree? Monthly newsletter, parent / teacher conferences, phone.

Does the school publish an address book with all the parents' information in it? School roster.

preschool-kindergarten

THE GROWING PLACE PRESCHOOL AND KINDERGARTEN

1049 S. Westlake Blvd.
Westlake Village, CA 91361
Phone: (805) 497-7064
www.growingplacewlv.org
See Map A on page 286

Contact: Diane Clarridge, Director

- ACCREDITATION: NONE
- NOT-FOR-PROFIT
- FINANCIAL AID IS AVAILABLE
- NUMBER OF KIDS: 232
- TUITION: $225-$450 MONTH
- WE HAVE KIDS WITH SPECIAL NEEDS

WHEN TO APPLY: PARENTS MAY CALL IN TO SET UP A VISIT AND GO ON THE WAIT LIST AT ANY TIME DURING THE YEAR. NO CUT OFF DATE.

Warm and inviting. Sound cliché? Maybe, but the caring feel permeates the visit I have with Diane Clarridge, who's been with the school for twenty-eight years. Set behind and in a building adjacent to the United Methodist Church of Westlake Village, the school has an ebullient feel. Diane Clarridge's gracious tour of the premises leaves me well informed of what a preschooler walks away with. For starters, this not-for-profit, non-denominational environment has a preschool license to enroll sixty-eight students, ages two through six. A kindergarten is housed in the same building, and the combined preschool and kindergarten enrollment is 239.

The teaching methodology used, according to Clarridge is, "developmentally academic, somewhat eclectic, using what is developmentally appropriate and able to be applied to our half day programs. The staff utilizes many ideas of Piaget, the Montessori, Reggio Emilia and High Scope methods." As insurance woes of present times prevent any organized school field trips, the solution has been to bring the areas of interest right to the doors of The Growing Place. An array of such programs for the students—arranged through fundraising activities—include Dr. Sue (the bug lady), Captain Karl (who educates on marine biology including bringing a baby shark for show and tell), and an internationally-renowned puppeteer is another of the attractions brought in by Clarridge and her staff. When these programs run, the school's body is divided into small groups to enrich the student experience.

Another example of an endearing show and tell is that snow is brought in during January or February to show it to students for the first time. The playground is shaded by a beautiful Eucalyptus tree and is spacious. In spite of toys being here and there, the play area is organized and clean. As we were leaving the playground on our tour, one of the students was doing the same, and as he slipped around my legs, he waved back, saying, "Bye, friends!"

BACKGROUND

The Growing Place was established in June 1976 as an outreach program of The United Methodist Church of Westlake Village. At that time, the Lutheran Church and Jewish Temple rented space from the church. It was determined that the school would be available to families of all faiths and would not include a religious component. The school remains a non-denominational, not-for-profit school.

BIRD'S EYE VIEW

	Non-existent	Poor	Fair	Good	Excellent
Learning to Read Children learn to explore the world of books				✓	
Dress-Up Children experiment with different roles and imagination				✓	
Hand-Eye Children develop fine motor skills by using fingers and hands				✓	
Building Blocks Children practice symbolic representation. They are developing an understanding of the relationships between size and shape, and the basic math concepts of geometry and numbers				✓	
Arts and Crafts Children are developing small muscle control as well as creativity				✓	
Body Coordination Children crawl through tunnels, climb and balance				✓	
Meeting Time Gathering place to listen to the teacher and to stories					✓
Weights and Measures Water and Sand tables				✓	
Beakers and Bunnies Classroom pets, aquariums....planting...					✓
Counting 1-2-3 A good preschool will stock basic early-learner software such as phonics or counting games				✓	
Outdoor Play Encourage large muscle control and coordination				✓	

Q & A

HOW THEY LEARN

What is your school's teaching philosophy? The Growing Place promotes learning through intentional, carefully planned learning experiences that enhance the social, emotional, physical and intellectual growth of each child in a nurturing environment.

How do you implement the philosophy? The school achieves this with its developmentally academic program. The children are grouped homogeneously. All teachers are highly accomplished in all areas of the curriculum.

What specialty teachers are brought into the school? There is an on-site Spanish teacher, and another on-site teacher for yoga. These are held after classes as extracurricular programs.

What is the teaching method? Developmental. Academic, somewhat eclectic, using what is developmentally-appropriate and able to be applied to our half-day programs. The staff utilizes many ideas of Piaget, the Montessori, Reggio Emilia and High Scope methods.

At what age do the children start? To what age is the school licensed? The preschool is licensed for 68 students from two to six year olds. The youngest that a child begins is 15 months, when they begin with the Parent and

Toddler Program. We currently have 60 students enrolled in this program. Since it is not a "drop-off" program, it is not required to be licensed. The school also has a kindergarten which follows state standards with a maximum enrollment of 20 students with two teachers. It also does not come under state licensing.

HOW TO GET IN

Are there open house dates? When are tours given? Separate open houses are not set aside. When parents are interested on going on the wait list, they sign up to come in for a tour.

Is there an interview? With the child or without? We recommend that the child accompanies the parent on the visit/tour.

Is preference given to applicants whose siblings are alumni? Only if that sibling will be attending school at the same time.

Are letters of recommendation encouraged? From what types of people? No.

How many applications do you receive each year? Approximately 350.

How many open spots are there each year? 246.

What are some of the schools that children go on to after finishing their education at your preschool? Local elementary schools in the Conejo Valley Unified District, Las Virgenes Unified School District, Oak Park Unified School District (the majority of them are "Blue Ribbon Schools"), View Point, St. Patrick's Episcopal Day School, Ascension Lutheran School, Hillcrest Christian School and Bethany Christian School.

PIGGY BANK

Apart from tuition, what other fees do you charge? There is no application fee. When a placement becomes available, an admission fee of $100 for preschool and kindergarten programs, and $25.00 for parent toddler programs, is required. At that time, the last month's tuition (at present, that is June 2005), is also due.

How is tuition broken down? Tuition is September through June is $225-$450 monthly.

What are the different payment plans available? Cash only. May be paid monthly or for the year. No discount is given for a ten-month lump payment.

What is the fee schedule? See above.

Is there a contract? Yes, it is titled an "Admission Agreement."

Do you have a tuition insurance program? No, we do not have a tuition insurance program.

HELPING HANDS

What accreditation is necessary for the teachers to work at your school? Lead teachers have BA/S in Early Childhood Education (E.C.E.). Some have MANS. Assistant teachers have AA in E.C.E. or almost completed. The Lead Kindergarten Teacher is a credentialed elementary school teacher.

How many teachers are there? There are 14 teachers.

How many aides? One aide.

Do they come from other preschools? Most of the teachers have been at The Growing Place more than ten years. The newer staff members have come from other schools.

IN THE 'ROOM

What's the adult-to-child ratio? The ratio is 7:1 for the two-and-a-half-year-olds; 8:1 for the three-year-olds; 9:1 for the four-year-olds; 10:1 for the kindergarteners.

What are the policies for initial separation between parent and child? Parents are welcome to stay in the classroom as long as it takes. This could be one day to as long as one month.

Can you visit any time unannounced? Parents may visit any time. Visitors must call and make an appointment.

What are the hours? Preschool is 9 a.m.-12 p.m. or 1-4 p.m. Parent and Toddler is one day a week from 9-11 a.m. Kindergarten is 9 a.m.-1:15 p.m.

Do you offer early bird or after-hours pick-up? If so, is there an extra fee? We offer 8-9 a.m., 12-1 p.m., 4-5 p.m. Cost $5 an hour.

Please describe a typical day for a child at your school. Welcome, choice time, circle time, choice time, clean-up, music time, wash hands, snack, outside play, wash hand, story time, goodbye.

What kinds of academic activities are offered? The teachers plan each week based on the needs of the class as a whole, but also taking into consideration many individual children's needs. Planning is done to encompass language, math, science and music concepts. These are all presented in a developmentally-appropriate way–hands-on, using all the senses where possible, and open-ended. Teachers do not use themes, rather they build on the children's interests and what is occurring in their lives.

What kinds of art activities are offered? Children are provided with a variety of media and allowed the freedom to be creative. The most structured part of the activities would be in discussing the proper use of the implements, empty the water and replace with clean water for the next person (water color painting), put the blue brush back into the blue paint, etc.

Is the child's time structured or unstructured, or a mixture of both? A mixture of both.

If a child is not interested in a particular activity, does he/she have other choices or is he/she encouraged to try it anyway? Yes, he/she has other choices. However, depending on the child, he/she may be encouraged to try.

How are disputes handled when they occur between the children? This is difficult to answer, since each instance is different. Corporal punishment, withdrawal of food or time-outs are never, ever used. Teachers provide modeling of the words for children to handle their emotions and ways to handle any future disputes.

When and for how long is nap time? Rest time is from 1:30-2:30 p.m. During this time, children are read to. Those who fall asleep are left to sleep until they wake themselves. All other children play in an adjacent enclosed outdoor play area.

What kinds of beds do you use? The children bring their own bedding and rest on floor mats.

What do you do when a child is dropped off in the morning and is obviously not well? What do you do when a child becomes sick during the day? No feedback provided.

Can you accommodate children with special needs? We presently have at least one autistic child in every class, as well as children with a variety of sensory motor and behavioral diagnoses. In the past we have had children with cerebral palsy, Down Syndrome and hearing loss.

KEEPING IT SAFE

Please describe your security measures for arriving and leaving the school. The toddler and preschool class families enter through double doors at the front of the building. The door automatically swings shut. This entrance can be seen from both offices. Children must be signed in and out by family members or persons designated and on file with the parents' permission. Teachers will not release children to someone they do not know. The transitional kindergarten and kindergarten have their own entrances. They also must be signed in and out as stated above for preschool students. All visitors must check into the school offices.

What medical supplies do you have on hand, and what medical experience does your staff have? Is your staff trained in CPR? Comprehensive First Aid kits are in every classroom, kitchen and director's office as well as a comprehensive kit is in each emergency evacuation backpack in each classroom and the office. All staff members and office staff are trained in First Aid and CPR. Training is renewed in both every two years.

Please describe your earthquake-preparedness plan, and what special equipment do you have on hand in the event of a disaster? Every class practices an earthquake and evacuation drill each month. Each classroom has a backpack complete with up-to-date class lists, individual student's emergency information, First Aid kit, CPR face masks, space blankets, AM/FM radio (with batteries), flashlights (with batteries), work gloves, crackers-and-cheese snacks, lollipops, paper, crayons, children's books, playing cards, trash bags, duct tape, and door tags. Our building has additional food, liquids, and clothing available for the whole school. The Alton Hall building has storage with additional first aid materials, diapers, and clothing. The Earthquake Shed on the exterior of the Youth Building has food and water for the whole school for four days, also portable potties, tarps, tents, plastic bags, garbage cans, etc. There is an earthquake plan which defines all staff members' roles.

SWINGS 'N THINGS

Please describe your playground. Does it have plenty of shade? The playground climbing equipment was replaced with new pieces that comply to the new national safety standards. We are fortunate to have many trees on the playground that provide more than adequate shade.

Do you put sunscreen on the children? We educate and encourage parents to apply sunscreen on their children prior to coming to school. If the parents provide the sunscreen, the staff will willingly apply it.

What kind of toilet training is available? Teachers work with the children on toilet training.

HELPING OUT

What kinds of fundraising events are at your school each year? Magazine drive in September, Book Fair in October, Sees Candies in November, t-shirt/sweatshirt in December, Photo Day in January, Sees Candies in February/March, Exploration Night in March/April and Book Fair in May. We make it clear that none of the fundraisers are to be door-to-door and that under no circumstances are they to feel pressured to participate in all of them. "Just pick the ones that are comfortable for your family."

How much participation is required by each parent? We ask for a minimum of two hours. All parents, however, participate at least ten hours. There are many ways in which parents can participate in the classrooms.

KEEPING IN TOUCH

How do you communicate with parents? Is there a newsletter or phone tree? Monthly newsletter. Letters home as necessary. Flyers. Posters. We have a phone tree for emergencies only.

Does the school publish an address book with all the parents' information in it? Each class has a class list with parent information.

preschool to 6th grade

THE NEIGHBORHOOD SCHOOL

11742 Riverside Drive
Valley Village, CA 91607
Phone: (818) 762-1212
See Map A on page 286

Contact: Gail Silverton, Director and Jeanne Silverton, Director

- ACCREDITATION: NONE
- FOR-PROFIT
- FINANCIAL AID IS AVAILABLE
- NUMBER OF KIDS: 82
- TUITION: $1,011-$1,596 MONTH
- WE HAVE KIDS WITH SPECIAL NEEDS

WHEN TO APPLY: APPLICATIONS ARE AVAILABLE ON TOURS, AND ENROLLMENT IS DONE ON A "FIRST COME, FIRST SERVE" BASIS.

From the school's philosophy literature: "First and foremost, we at the Neighborhood School believe that each child is an individual, a very valuable person with his/her very special needs, rate of development, temperament and method of learning." After my arrival to the school and as I waited for the school's director, Gail Silverton, I took a quick look around the comfortable lobby and was visually pleased by the bright primary colors, fish tank in the fireplace and comfortable seating. Later in the tour, I found out that the lobby is where parents are welcome to come in and take a seat. Parents are welcome to come unannounced at any time and (although not mandated to) are encouraged to participate when they can.

A telling piece of information in my conversation with Silverton was that she chooses her teaching staff based on their love of something, in addition to teaching—she favors an arts background. Surely all of the teachers have credentials as per state certification, but all of them are heavily predisposed to one aspect of the arts or another (theater, music, art, etc.). As well, students from diverse family structures are welcomed and encouraged here—single family homes, same-sex homes, grandparents as parents, etc. In other words, the typical mother/father model of family life isn't the only one our society deals with anymore, and none of the children coming from an "atypical" family life feel the worse for being "different." Diversity is acclaimed here.

Heavily arts-based, the playground has a large stage for student performances as well as the typical jungle gym. Plenty of shade is in order for the hot and sunny days. On the playground on the day of my tour, I saw a teacher mixing what looked like an edible batter but turns out to be wax for holiday candles that the kids were making as gifts. A small group was gathered around the teacher and the bowl and it looked as if they were eager to see this mix turn into the candles they would shape. The students are grouped by ages and are learning at the Neighborhood School through dramatic play and hands-on, developmental teaching. It seems to be a great place for both parent and child.

Background

The school was founded in 1989 by Gail Silverton and Patricia Ludwig. A second school was opened in 1993, and a third was opened in 1999.

Bird's Eye View

	Non-existent	Poor	Fair	Good	Excellent
Learning to Read Children learn to explore the world of books					✓
Dress-Up Children experiment with different roles and imagination					✓
Hand-Eye Children develop fine motor skills by using fingers and hands					✓
Building Blocks Children practice symbolic representation. They are developing an understanding of the relationships between size and shape, and the basic math concepts of geometry and numbers					✓
Arts and Crafts Children are developing small muscle control as well as creativity					✓
Body Coordination Children crawl through tunnels, climb and balance					✓
Meeting Time Gathering place to listen to the teacher and to stories					✓
Weights and Measures Water and Sand tables					✓
Beakers and Bunnies Classroom pets, aquariums....planting...					✓
Counting 1-2-3 A good preschool will stock basic early-learner software such as phonics or counting games				✓	
Outdoor Play Encourage large muscle control and coordination					✓

Q & A

HOW THEY LEARN
What is your school's teaching philosophy?
We embrace the idea of "the unhurried" child, each child passing through the same stages of development at their own rate. We also believe that to understand a concept, a child must be exposed to it using a hands-on method, visual exposure and also have an auditory experience as well. Unless the child has an interest or use for what is being presented it is not appropriate for pre-schoolers. Our curriculum is carefully planned every month, leaving plenty of room

for an emergent curriculum and other spontaneous events. We believe that we are part of a team, one that consists of the family, teachers and administration, all working towards the best interest of the child. Our staff is encouraged to bring their own interests and passions into the classroom generating enthusiasm, not only among the students, but with the staff themselves. Our aim is to turn every experience into one of learning.

How do you implement the philosophy? We hire a diverse and dedicated group of teachers who have an innate ability to understand the needs of children.

What specialty teachers are brought into the school? We bring in specialty teachers whenever we feel an area is lacking in our curriculum. In the past years we've had a physical education and a music teacher, a scientist and a specialist to guide the garden project. Whenever possible we use in-house talent.

What is the teaching method? We have a developmental/progressive philosophy.

At what age do the children start? To what age is the school licensed? Children begin approximately by two years, five months. The school is licensed from ages two years, five months to five-and-a-half years old.

HOW TO GET IN

Are there open house dates? When are tours given? Tours are given throughout the year by appointment, and applications are available at the tour.

Is there an interview? With the child or without? There is no interview but all prospective parents are required to attend a tour. We do not screen children, we assume our program is small and individual enough to accommodate most children.

Is preference given to applicants whose siblings are alumni? Yes.

Are letters of recommendation encouraged? From what types of people? Letters of recommendation help only if there is a long waiting list.

How many applications do you receive each year? We receive quite a few applications each year, but find that as families sign up so early for the program, that as the start date approaches many have moved or found their pre-school needs have changed. This opens spaces up very close to the start dates.

How many open spots are there each year? Openings vary. Kindergarten has about 15 (the child must turn five by December of the year they enter). First year has between 13 and 22, depending on whether we have two classes or one.

What are some of the schools that children go on to after finishing their education at your preschool? Oakwood, The Country School, Campbell Hall, Buckley, Laurence, Westland, Los Encinos, Wesley, Carpenter Avenue and Colfax.

PIGGY BANK

Apart from tuition, what other fees do you charge? A non-refundable $50 application fee is required with all applications. Upon acceptance to the program, a $300 registration fee for preschool, or $1,000 for kindergarten, is required.

How is tuition broken down? Tuition is $1,596 per month for five full days, and $1,011 per month for five half-days.

What are the different payment plans available? Monthly, annually.

What is the fee schedule? Contact school for details.

Is there a contract? No feedback received.

Do you have a tuition insurance program? One month's notice is required before withdrawing.

HELPING HANDS

What accreditation is necessary for the teachers to work at your school? Teachers must have 12 units of approved early child education courses, a bachelor's degree in a related field, two years teaching experience or a combination of the above. All staff is fingerprinted, and have a Department of Justice and Department of Social Service clearance.

How many teachers are there? Each classroom has two teachers.

How many aides are there? We have a roving aide on staff at all times, and some classrooms have the addition of an aide.

IN THE 'ROOM

What's the child-to-adult ratio? 6:1. or 7:1 in the older groups.

What are the policies for initial separation between parent and child? During the initial separation, we ask that the parent or a designated caregiver remain with the child until we jointly agree that the time is right to leave the child. All parties must be ready—the parent and teacher as well as the child.

Can you visit any time unannounced? Yes. Parents and teachers are welcome at any time. Visitors can observe unannounced but we cannot answer questions.

What are the hours? 8:45 a.m.-3:30 p.m. The kindergarten is from 8:45 a.m.-2:45 p.m. First year is 12:30-3:30 p.m., and second and third year are 9 a.m.-12 p.m.

Do you offer early bird or after-hours pick-up? If so, is there an extra fee? There is an option of staying until 3 p.m. for an additional charge.

Please describe a typical day for a child at your school. A typical day is divided between outdoor and indoor time. Six areas of curriculum (art, music, drama, language arts, math and science) are covered using a variety and ever-changing curriculum. The use of small and large motor skills is encouraged. There are usually two circle times, one more teacher-directed (stories, puppets etc.) and the other more child participatory and involved.

What kinds of academic activities are offered? Activities to encourage the use of language and expansion of vocabulary and expression of ideas. Math skills using manipulatives, counting games, cooking and sequencing activities.

What kinds of art activities are offered? Extensive art program. Collage, painting, ceramics (we have a kiln), wood work, open-ended projects with an emphasis on process rather than product.

Is the child's time structured or unstructured, or a mixture of both? A combination.

If a child is not interested in a particular activity, does he/she have other choices or is he/she encouraged to try it anyway? If a child is not interested in an activity, he/she will have other choices. If a child consistently avoids a certain activity, we will try and encourage them to try it and find out why they are avoiding it.

How are disputes handled when they occur between the children? No feedback received.

When and for how long is nap time? Rest time is from a half-hour to 45 minutes.

What kinds of beds do you use? The children lie on cots or on their own pillows and listen to stories read by the teacher.

What do you do when a child is dropped off in the morning and is obviously not well? What do you do when a child becomes sick during the day? Children must be fever and symptom free before returning to school. All sick children will be sent home. That decision is left to the discretion of the directors.

Can you accommodate children with special needs? These children are evaluated on an individual basis. The children must be ambulatory as the yard is sand and would be impossible to navigate with a wheelchair. Some children find it necessary to have a shadow teacher accompany them in order to fully benefit from the program. We have a room available for children that need special therapy during the school day, speech or sensory integration, but these therapists are provided by the family.

KEEPING IT SAFE

Please describe your security measures for arriving and leaving the school. There is a code on all the gates which is given out to the parents and guardians of the enrolled children. Children are signed in and out of the school on a daily basis and not allowed to be picked up by anyone that is not listed on a card filled out by the parent. If a child is going home with another family, the school must be notified in writing or the directors must be called on the phone that morning.

What medical supplies do you have on hand, and what medical experience does your staff have? Is your staff trained in CPR? We have basic First Aid supplies on hand and participate in an annual pediatric CPR/First Aid course. Parents must provide for special medications or supplies. We have experience dealing with children who have diabetes and are willing to monitor their blood sugar levels using the finger prick device provided by the parent. We have experience with seizures, but request the parent of an affected child to attend a meeting with all staff members prior to enrollment. The school has a "no nut" policy to protect those children with peanut allergies.

Please describe your earthquake-preparedness plan, and what special equipment do you have on hand in the event of a disaster? We have a closet designated for earthquake supplies, mainly food and water. The director lives directly across the street and has a full supply of camping equipment, including fuel and stoves. If it were necessary to evacuate, a phone tree would be activated and notes left on the premises as to our location. Woodbridge Park, on the corner of Moorpark and Elmer (one block east of Tujunga) would be our first destination, as it is possible to reach by foot. We would remain with and take full responsibility for the children until a parent or designated caregiver could be reached.

SWINGS 'N THINGS

Please describe your playground. Does it have plenty of shade? The Neighborhood School has a large yard with plenty of space and shade. There are enough covered areas to use the yard on the sunniest or rainiest days. We ask the parents to apply sunscreen at home and we will reapply if the children get wet. We have a tree house, stage area, chicken coop, garden, cement area for basketball, sandbox, as well as all the typical pre-school equipment. Art is done both in the classroom and in the yard.

Do you put sunscreen on the children? No feedback received.

What kind of toilet training is available? Children can attend the program in diapers, but these are provided by the parent. We will assist in toilet training at the request of the parent and will be guided by the practices used at home.

HELPING OUT

What kinds of fundraising events are at your school each year? There is minimal fundraising. Low-key, not mandatory. NO PRESSURE.

How much participation is required by each parent? Nothing is required. All families can participate whether they contribute or not.

KEEPING IN TOUCH

How do you communicate with parents? Is there a newsletter or phone tree? Each class receives a newsletter monthly as well as frequent notes and phone calls. There is a parent-staffed phone tree as well as an all-school email. The teachers are available every day before and after class. The directors are available whenever needed. Class meetings are held twice a year or at the request of a teacher.

Does the school publish an address book with all the parents' information in it? A roster is sent to each class with the address and phone number of the child's family.

preschool to 6th grade

THE NEW SCHOOL WEST

12731 Venice Blvd.
Los Angeles, CA 90066
Phone: (310) 313-4444
www.newschoolwest.com
See Map D on page 286

Contact: Roleen Heimann

- ACCREDITATION: NONE
- FOR-PROFIT
- FINANCIAL AID IS AVAILABLE
- NUMBER OF KIDS: 60
- TUITION: $775-$1,075 MONTH
- WE HAVE KIDS WITH SPECIAL NEEDS

WHEN TO APPLY: APPLY AT TOUR TIMES. WHEN REGISTRATION HAS BEEN FINALIZED, "OFFICIAL" NOTICES GO OUT IN MARCH BEFORE THE CHILD'S ENTRY.

The Reggio Emilia approach to education—"listen and value what children say and do," where the teacher is a facilitator rather than an instructor—has gotten an increased amount of press over the years. Although The New School West still considers itself developmentally-based, they have embraced and applied the Reggio approach and principles more than any other school I visited. As Director Roleen Heimann says, "When children and not teaching children becomes the focus, then the real learning happens." Located on Venice Boulevard in Culver City, The New School West is located in what used to be an apartment complex of little bungalows, so the classrooms flow nicely into a courtyard. According to Roleen, one of the Reggio principles is that "the environment is the third teacher," so the whole look and feel of the school is more home-like with natural colors, plants, mirrors and couches.

You do, indeed, feel like you're in someone's living room while visiting the school—while I was there, some kids cuddled up on one of the couches while a teacher read them a story, while a platter of pita bread and hummus (the morning's snack) sat on a table in front of them next to a vase of flowers. The older children were playing out in the yard while I was there, while inside the classrooms, children were drawing with markers and playing with blocks. There's a real communal feel to the school, which allows the kids to bond with everyone, and is helpful in many ways—such as when teachers go on maternity leave.

It's a very diverse group, and the idea of community is very important. The school is currently working on a "community book"—sort of a yearbook, with pictures and information about all of the teachers, kids, and their families—so everyone gets to know each other better. There's about 30 open spots a year, and almost all of the kids end up going on to public school. If you're looking for a more creative approach to preschool, the New School West is definitely worth a look.

BACKGROUND

Established in 1987 by Roleen Heimann and Happy Juma.

BIRD'S EYE VIEW

	Non-existent	Poor	Fair	Good	Excellent
Learning to Read Children learn to explore the world of books				✓	
Dress-Up Children experiment with different roles and imagination				✓	
Hand-Eye Children develop fine motor skills by using fingers and hands					✓
Building Blocks Children practice symbolic representation. They are developing an understanding of the relationships between size and shape, and the basic math concepts of geometry and numbers				✓	
Arts and Crafts Children are developing small muscle control as well as creativity					✓
Body Coordination Children crawl through tunnels, climb and balance					✓
Meeting Time Gathering place to listen to the teacher and to stories					✓
Weights and Measures Water and Sand tables				✓	
Beakers and Bunnies Classroom pets, aquariums....planting...				✓	
Counting 1-2-3 A good preschool will stock basic early-learner software such as phonics or counting games					✓
Outdoor Play Encourage large muscle control and coordination					✓

Q & A

HOW THEY LEARN

What is your school's teaching philosophy? The school is developmentally-based with five domains: social, emotional, physical, cognitive, creative and Reggio Approach-inspired.

How do you implement the philosophy? Teachers study together, workshops, collaborative work with colleagues.

What specialty teachers are brought into the school? No feedback received.

What is the teaching method? Developmental and Reggio Emilia Approach.

At what age do the children start? To what age is the school licensed? Children are 2.9 to five years of age.

HOW TO GET IN

Are there open house dates? When are tours given? Tours/open houses are usually six times a year.

Is there an interview? With the child or without? No.

Is preference given to applicants whose siblings are alumni? Yes.

Are letters of recommendation encouraged? From what types of people? Not required, but people do it.

How many applications do you receive each year? Over 100.

How many open spots are there each year? Around 30.

What are some of the schools that children go on to after finishing their education at your preschool? Public and private schools.

PIGGY BANK

Apart from tuition, what other fees do you charge? There is a $50 application fee, $200 annual materials fee and a $50 earthquake fee.

How is tuition broken down? Monthly tuition is full-time - 5x/week: $1075, 4x/week: $975 per month, 3x/week: $875 per month. Part time - 5x/week: $835, 4x/week: $835, 3x/week: $775.

What are the different payment plans available? Monthly.

What is the fee schedule? Due monthly.

Is there a contract? No.

Do you have a tuition insurance program? No.

HELPING HANDS

What accreditation is necessary for the teachers to work at your school? Almost all are from some early childhood education program and have been here a long time.

How many teachers are there? Nine teachers.

How many aides are there? No aides.

IN THE 'ROOM

What's the child-to-adult ratio? No feedback received.

What are the policies for initial separation between parent and child? Home visit prior to starting school, scheduled "play dates" prior to starting school. Each child has an individual plan.

Can you visit any time unannounced? Yes, but soon parents learn that is hard for their child.

What are the hours? 7:30 a.m..-5:30 p.m.

Do you offer early bird or after-hours pick-up? If so, is there an extra fee? A one-minute later charge goes directly to teachers.

Please describe a typical day for a child at your school. Inside free playtime, morning circle, snack centers open/free choice, outside time, lunch, rest time, circle time, snack, outside time.

What kinds of academic activities are offered? Focus on the whole child, with goals to strengthen all areas.

What kinds of art activities are offered? Children work with mixed media as expression of areas.

Is the child's time structured or unstructured, or a mixture of both? Both.

If a child is not interested in a particular activity, does he/she have other choices or is he/she encouraged to try it anyway? Yes.

How are disputes handled when they occur between the children? Look at behaviors, define them, work with the children to seek answers and take the time to problem-solve, not for them but with them.

When and for how long is nap time? Between 1 and 2 p.m.

What kinds of beds do you use? Mats.

What do you do when a child is dropped off in the morning and is obviously not well? What do you do when a child becomes sick during the day? They can't stay. We call parents.

Can you accommodate children with special needs? Every child has an individual plan in partnership with parents.

KEEPING IT SAFE

Please describe your security measures for arriving and leaving the school. Buzzer on door for parents to be identified.

What medical supplies do you have on hand, and what medical experience does your staff have? Is your staff trained in CPR? We have CPR and First Aid training. Supplies necessary for the unexpected.

Please describe your earthquake-preparedness plan, and what special equipment do you have on hand in the event of a disaster? Central phone number. Emergency release form. Monthly safety drills. Post-evacuation plan. Three days' supply of food and water.

SWINGS 'N THINGS

Please describe your playground. Does it have plenty of shade? Three yards, two large climbing structures, one that has room for trikes that's all sand.

Do you put sunscreen on the children? No feedback received.

What kind of toilet training is available? Accidents happen, but children need to be toilet trained.

HELPING OUT

What kinds of fundraising events are at your school each year? At least two a year, focused around social events and planned by the fundraising committee.

How much participation is required by each parent? We expect parents to be fully involved with the school.

KEEPING IN TOUCH

How do you communicate with parents? Is there a newsletter or phone tree? Verbal, written, email. There is a newsletter and a phone tree.

Does the school publish an address book with all the parents' information in it? Yes.

TOPANGA COOPERATIVE PRESCHOOL

1440 N. Topanga Canyon Blvd.
Topanga, CA 90290
Phone: (310) 455-3155
www.topangacooppreschool.com
See Map on D page 286

Contact: Volunteer Parents

- ACCREDITATION: NONE
- NOT-FOR-PROFIT
- FINANCIAL AID IS AVAILABLE
- NUMBER OF KIDS: 20
- TUITION: $275-$415 MONTH
- WE HAVE KIDS WITH SPECIAL NEEDS

WHEN TO APPLY: APPLICATIONS MAY BE SUBMITTED AT ANY TIME.

The hours are from 9 a.m.-1 p.m., because the public uses the playground and community building in the afternoons. The playground has an amazing view, and a tire bridge that requires great willpower not to run across it! There is also a large blacktop area for bikes, and children are not allowed outside without direct supervision.

Topanga Co-op's philosophy emphasizes developmentally appropriate learning, through play, music, and arts and crafts. They also strive to introduce children to activities and ideas that will inspire their creativity and help them develop a healthy concept of self. There is lots and lots of free-play and not a lot of structure. The instruction is all play-based. Helene D'Auria, one of the Co-op's volunteer parents says, "We don't have an issue with dirt or mess. As long as kids are happy, and not hurting anyone, it's okay!" Helene says what she loves about Topanga Co-op is, "the way the school respects the children, and respects the choices parents make about their children."

Current Director Cherie Nelson agrees that what makes Topanga Co-op unique is that "We are family-oriented. We can be flexible, and meet the needs of the family. We really work with the community to make this a comfortable place." As far as parent involvement, parents have a job with the school five times in a two-month period, and there is a required meeting once a month. Though the tuition is lower than other Canyon schools, you pay more at Topanga than other co-ops, but you work less. The good news is there's not a lot of fundraising! The L.A. Philharmonic Orchestra does a show once a year to raise money for the school. If you are a parent in the Valley, Topanga Co-op is expanding its reach to include Valley families.

BACKGROUND

The Topanga Co-op Preschool was originally founded by a group of progressive Topanga parents in the late 1960s. Classes were originally held in private homes. The school moved into the Topanga Community House in 1969, which has been its home ever since.

BIRD'S EYE VIEW

	Non-existent	Poor	Fair	Good	Excellent
Learning to Read Children learn to explore the world of books				✓	
Dress-Up Children experiment with different roles and imagination					✓
Hand-Eye Children develop fine motor skills by using fingers and hands					✓
Building Blocks Children practice symbolic representation. They are developing an understanding of the relationships between size and shape, and the basic math concepts of geometry and numbers					✓
Arts and Crafts Children are developing small muscle control as well as creativity					✓
Body Coordination Children crawl through tunnels, climb and balance					✓
Meeting Time Gathering place to listen to the teacher and to stories				✓	
Weights and Measures Water and Sand tables				✓	
Beakers and Bunnies Classroom pets, aquariums....planting...					✓
Counting 1-2-3 A good preschool will stock basic early-learner software such as phonics or counting games				✓	
Outdoor Play Encourage large muscle control and coordination					✓

Q & A

HOW THEY LEARN

What is your school's teaching philosophy? Our philosophy emphasizes developmentally appropriate learning through play, music, and arts and crafts.

How do you implement the philosophy? Our teachers reinforce our philosophy by providing the children with a variety of activity choices, lots of unstructured time, and modeling through role-playing, puppet shows, etc.

What is the teaching method? We stress learning through experience. Our teachers pro-vide activities and guide the children as they explore.

At what age do the children start? To what age is the school licensed? The school is licensed for ages two to six.

HOW TO GET IN

Are there open house dates? When are tours given? Tours are by appointment on an ongoing basis.

Is there an interview? With the child or without? No interview is required, however children under the age of three may be asked to spend some time with our director so that she can assess their readiness for preschool.

Is preference given to applicants whose siblings are alumni? Yes.

Are letters of recommendation encouraged? From what types of people? No letter of recommendation is needed.

How many applications do you receive each year? Varies year to year.

How many open spots are there each year? Varies year to year.

What are some of the schools that children go on to after finishing their education at your preschool? They attend excellent public and private schools in Topanga Canyon and the San Fernando Valley. We also have students who are home-schooled.

PIGGY BANK

Apart from tuition, what other fees do you charge? There is no application fee. There is a one-time registration fee of $100.

How is tuition broken down? Current tuition is $275 for two days a week, $338 for three days a week, and $415 for four days a week.

What are the different payment plans available? We have no special payment plans.

What is the fee schedule? Tuition is due at the beginning of each month.

Is there a contract? There is a simple contract.

Do you have a tuition insurance program? No.

HELPING HANDS

What accreditation is necessary for the teachers to work at your school? Teachers must be fully state and locally licensed.

How many teachers are there? We have two teachers working in the classroom each day. Our Director, Cherie Nelson, has an extensive background in co-op preschools, and teacher Timea Jakab is newly accredited with experience in several teaching methods.

How many aides are there? There are one to two parents who also work in the classroom each day.

Do they come from other preschools? No feedback received.

IN THE 'ROOM

What's the child-to-adult ratio? Co-op rules require a maximum ratio of five children to every one adult.

What are the policies for initial separation between parent and child? We respect the needs of both parents and children as they make this important transition. There are no enforced separation rules and no limits to the amount of time that a parent may stay with his/her child. While separation is the goal, and our teachers will work with parents to achieve it, no child is forced to separate before he/she is ready.

Can you visit any time unannounced? Yes. Parents are always welcome in the classroom.

What are the hours? We are open 9 a.m.-1 p.m.

Do you offer early bird or after-hours pickup? If so, is there an extra fee? There is no extended care.

Please describe a typical day for a child at your school. While we do have a simple structure to our days, we also value flexibility and following the children's lead. No two days are the same, but a typical day might look like this. The children arrive at 9 a.m. to a classroom full of color, activity, and opportunity. In addition to a large free play area, each day the teachers set up several different "stations" with more directed activities, which include arts and crafts, puzzles, games, nature and science activities, etc. The day starts with at least an hour of free play and the children can move freely from activity to activity or focus on one special project as they choose. Around 10 a.m., the staff and children tidy up the classroom and they may do some Yoga or have a song. Then they all come to the table for a healthy snack, which is provided by the school. After snack we have circle time, which can include stories, conversation, felt board activities, marking the day on the calendar, and short, simple pre-reading exercises. When circle time is over we all visit the bathroom and then head outside to the playground. Our kids have about an hour of free play on the playground. We have a variety of toys and activities and sometimes even bring out easels and have some art time outside. We love to take advantage of our beautiful weather and setting. Around noon the children come inside for lunch, or they may eat outside if it is nice. Lunch is usually followed by a group activity, perhaps a parade of musical instruments, or a bean bag game. Then the children have bike time until they come inside for closing circle at the end of the day.

What kinds of academic activities are offered? Although there is limited formal instruction, the children are surrounded by books, games, puzzles and art activities that incorporate letters, numbers, shapes and colors. Teachers reinforce basic skills through their playful interaction with the children.

What kinds of art activities are offered? Art is an extremely important part of our day, and our teachers are incredibly creative in the scope of their projects. Our children try everything from the classic (painting, coloring, collages, etc.) to nature art, food art, and even coffee filters have been used to make art.

Is the child's time structured or unstructured, or a mixture of both? We have periods of structure during the day, but we strive to ensure that the children have plenty of unstructured time.

If a child is not interested in a particular activity, does he/she have other choices or is he/she encouraged to try it anyway? Children are certainly encouraged to try activities. If a child isn't interested in participating in a structured activity, like circle time, then he/she will still be asked to stay with the group but will not be required to participate.

How are disputes handled when they occur between the children? When disputes occur, the children are encouraged to talk the issue out. If necessary, the teachers give the children the words to express their feelings.

When and for how long is nap time? We do not have nap time.

What kinds of beds do you use? No nap time.

What do you do when a child is dropped off in the morning and is obviously not well? What do you do when a child becomes sick during the day? Unwell children will not be permitted to remain at school. When a child becomes ill during the day, his/her parent will be called to pick them up.

Can you accommodate children with special needs? Yes.

KEEPING IT SAFE

Please describe your security measures for arriving and leaving the school. Children are delivered to and picked up from the classroom directly, and are signed in and out by their parents.

What medical supplies do you have on hand, and what medical experience does your staff have? Is your staff trained in CPR? We have all standard First Aid equipment and emergency kits. Our teachers are trained in basic First Aid and CPR.

Please describe your earthquake-preparedness plan, and what special equipment do you have on hand in the event of a disaster? In addition to personal earthquake kits for each child, the school keeps an emergency supply of food and water. Our building is also an emergency shelter for the Topanga area.

SWINGS 'N THINGS

Please describe your playground. Does it have plenty of shade? Our playground is large and shaded. We have a swing set, a large climbing structure with slides, fire poles, etc., a covered sandbox, and a playhouse. We also have one of the most spectacular views in Los Angeles, surrounded by the Santa Monica mountains.

Do you put sunscreen on the children? Our teachers do put sunscreen on the children as needed.

What kind of toilet training is available? Kids do not have to be toilet trained. Our staff will work with the families to support whatever level of toilet training has been achieved.

HELPING OUT

What kinds of fundraising events are at your school each year? Our major fundraising event is the Topanga Philharmonic Orchestra concert in the spring of each year. We do smaller fundraisers as needed. In the past, these have included garage sales, movie nights, candy bar sales, etc.

How much participation is required by each parent? All families are required to participate in the Topanga Philharmonic Orchestra event by serving on a planning committee and working at the actual event. Participation in other fundraising events is encouraged but not required. We are a parent-participation school and all parents are required to be involved in working in the classroom and fulfilling an administrative position. In the classroom, parents assist the teachers with all daily activities. Parents are required to work at the school an average of 2-4 days a month. There is a wide variety of parent jobs. We have snack parents, supply parents, maintenance parents, photography parents, cooking parents, etc. Aside from our teachers, the school is completely owned and operated by the parents and all of the day-to-day operations are conducted by parents.

KEEPING IN TOUCH

How do you communicate with parents? Is there a newsletter or phone tree? Email is our preferred method of communication. There is also a monthly parent meeting.

Does the school publish an address book with all the parents' information in it? Yes.

preschool to 8th grade

TURNING POINT SCHOOL

8780 National Blvd.
Culver City, CA 90232
Phone: (310) 841-2505
www.turningpointschool.org
See Map D on page 286

Contact: Deborah Richman, Director

- ACCREDITATION: AMS/CAIS
- NOT-FOR-PROFIT
- FINANCIAL AID IS AVAILABLE
- NUMBER OF KIDS: 72
- TUITION: $19,670-$20,430 YEAR
- WE HAVE KIDS WITH SPECIAL NEEDS

WHEN TO APPLY: APPLICATIONS ARE AVAILABLE THE FALL YEAR, ONE YEAR BEFORE ENTRY. DEADLINE TO APPLY FOR PRIMARY CLASSES IS IN DECEMBER. APPLICATIONS RECEIVED AFTER THE DUE DATE ARE WELCOMED AND CONSIDERED IF SPACE PERMITS. YOUNGER APPLICANTS ARE EVALUATED THROUGH THE SUMMER MONTHS.

Turning Point is absolutely stunning. However, I couldn't help thinking that it was almost too stunning—and a bit intimidating—as if the idea of making a mess, or getting paint anywhere but on the paper would not be encouraged. The school moved to its new location in Culver City three years ago and there's no arguing that it's a state-of-the art campus with very impressive (and stylish) teachers, all holding at least a Bachelor's degree. Frankly, at more than $15,000 a year for preschool tuition, it should be impressive. Families do not enroll in Turning Point just for the Early Childhood Program. Since Turning Point is a school that continues from Primary (early childhood) through Elementary and Middle School, a great deal of time is spent with prospective families to educate them about the school's philosophy. The school makes sure that Turning Point is a good fit for their family, and for their long-term commitment through eighth grade.

Montessori-based (in fact, the school's original name was Montessori of West Los Angeles), there are three preschool classrooms with 24 kids each from 2 years, 10 months through age five. The huge classrooms are colorful and gorgeous, with what seemed to be brand new everything—books, puzzles, blocks, tables and chairs. The rest of the school is equally beautiful, from its library with a storytelling center, to the auditorium, to the student garden. The only area that seemed lacking in abundance was the number of teachers, the adult to child ratio is 1:12. There are about 30 open spots a year and the school goes through eighth grade, after which most of the kids go on to the better private schools in town. The older kids remain very involved with the little ones. For instance, kindergarteners will come to the class to read to the primary kids once a week.

The Open House tour that I was given was by a fifth grader named Maya who had at been at Turning Point since preschool. If Maya is any indication of what the school turns out, she's a very impressive example—incredibly polite, articulate, and self-possessed. There's no doubt that the children at Turning Point are getting a wonderful Montessori-based education in a beautiful environment with very proficient teachers. However, if you're looking for a more down-to-earth nursery school experience, it's probably not the first place to visit.

BACKGROUND

Turning Point School is an independent, nonsectarian, coeducational school enrolling students in Primary (2 years, 10 months) through eighth grade. In February of 2001, Turning Point opened the doors to its new, state-of-the-art campus at 8780 National Boulevard in Culver City. The school was founded in 1970 as a nonprofit institution, originally named Montessori of West Los Angeles, by a group of educators and business professionals who strongly believed in the educational philosophy of Dr. Maria Montessori. In October of 1989, the name was changed to Turning Point to represent the series of turning points that children and schools experience as they grow and mature.

BIRD'S EYE VIEW

	Non-existent	Poor	Fair	Good	Excellent
Learning to Read — Children learn to explore the world of books					✓
Dress-Up — Children experiment with different roles and imagination					✓
Hand-Eye — Children develop fine motor skills by using fingers and hands					✓
Building Blocks — Children practice symbolic representation. They are developing an understanding of the relationships between size and shape, and the basic math concepts of geometry and numbers					✓
Arts and Crafts — Children are developing small muscle control as well as creativity					✓
Body Coordination — Children crawl through tunnels, climb and balance					✓
Meeting Time — Gathering place to listen to the teacher and to stories					✓
Weights and Measures — Water and Sand tables					✓
Beakers and Bunnies — Classroom pets, aquariums....planting...					✓
Counting 1-2-3 — A good preschool will stock basic early-learner software such as phonics or counting games					✓
Outdoor Play — Encourage large muscle control and coordination					✓

Q & A

HOW THEY LEARN

What is your school's teaching philosophy? It is based on the philosophy of Dr. Maria Montessori and incorporates as its foundation the concept of respect. All interactions, social and cognitive, are based on this underlying principle. Attention is given to each child's individual development needs and readiness levels. Our children are stimulated, challenged, and encouraged but not pressured or hurried.

How do you implement the philosophy? As our head teachers are Montessori trained, our school's philosophy is integrated in their daily interactions with the children and their curriculum planning. Additional faculty who work with our early childhood classes are given training by the Primary Division Head.

What specialty teachers are brought into the school? Starting in primary, specialty teachers work with students in music, Spanish and physical education.

What is the teaching method? In connection with our philosophy and mission, our classrooms are carefully prepared environments blending traditional Montessori materials, time-tested early childhood activities, and innovative learning materials. Children learn best when they are actively involved, therefore it is the process, not the product, that is the focus of our teacher-guided classrooms.

At what age do the children start? To what age is the school licensed? Two years and ten months by September is the guideline we use for Primary admissions. Our school continues through 8th grade. Students are 14 years or close thereto when they graduate.

HOW TO GET IN

Are there open house dates? When are tours given? Open house for Primary is in October. Tours are scheduled for selected Tuesday mornings October through January. Upon receipt of completed application, parents will attend an in-class observation and program overview on a designated Thursday. This is a full morning visit that includes presentations from key administrators.

Is there an interview? With the child or without? There is a parent interview with a key administrator (without the child). Small group evaluations are organized for children with or without parent as needed.

Is preference given to applicants whose siblings are alumni? Yes.

Are letters of recommendation encouraged? From what types of people? A Preschool Evaluation form is required for students already in a preschool program. Letters of recommendation from current/alumni families are accepted and sometimes helpful.

How many applications do you receive each year? It varies from year to year.

How many open spots are there each year? For students ages 2 years, 10 months through five-and-a-half, 25-30 openings are expected.

What are some of the schools that children go on to after finishing their education at your preschool? No feedback received.

PIGGY BANK

Apart from tuition, what other fees do you charge? The application fee is $75, and there is an entrance fee of $1,000 per student.

How is tuition broken down? Short Day (8:30 a.m.-1 p.m.) is $19,670. Primary Full day (8:30 a.m.-2:30 p.m.) is $20,430.

What are the different payment plans available? One payment, due on July 1st (May 1st if using a charge card).

What is the fee schedule? Fees are included in the tuition.

Is there a contract? Yes, there is a contract.

Do you have a tuition insurance program? No.

HELPING HANDS

What accreditation is necessary for the teachers to work at your school? All full-time faculty and staff at Turning Point School hold a Bachelor's degree. In addition Primary head teachers must have their Montessori certification; assistant teachers are required to have a minimum of twelve ECE units.

How many teachers are there? There are three head teachers and three full-time assistant teachers.

How many aides are there? There are two playground/daycare teachers and one additional lunch-helper aide.

Do they come from other preschools? Most teacher assistants come to Turning Point directly after graduating college and are mentored by the head teachers. Each primary class has one head teacher and a full-time teaching assistant in addition to the specialty teachers.

IN THE 'ROOM

What's the child-to-adult ratio? 12:1. The multi-aged setting and number of continuing students each year in a given class makes this an ideal balance.

What are the policies for initial separation between parent and child? There is a one week phase-in at the beginning of the school year. New Primary students come for a short visit in small groups for the first three days. For the last two days of phase-in of the class (new and returning students) come for three hours of school. After the phase-in week, primary students come for their regular day with individual accommodations for separation difficulties as necessary.

Can you visit any time unannounced? Yes, however appointments are encouraged so as not to disturb the class.

What are the hours? 8:30 a.m.-2:30 p.m.

Do you offer early bird or after-hours pick-up? If so, is there an extra fee? Before and after-school care is available from 7:30 a.m.-6 p.m. There is an extra cost of $10 per day ($8 per day for regular users) for after-school care. Before-school care is gratis.

Please describe a typical day for a child at your school. A typical day for a child would involve several group activities with their classmates, ample opportunity for individual choice of activities, guided group lessons, social interaction opportunities, and plenty of time for physical play, both structured with the athletic specialists and daily outdoor playground time. The afternoon offers a nap time and/or afternoon activity time as appropriate for each child's developmental readiness.

What kinds of academic activities are offered? Depending on the child's developmental readiness level, hands-on pre-reading and reading activities as well as manipulative math activities are introduced. Social studies and science are a part of the daily curriculum.

What kinds of art activities are offered? A full range of art activities and materials is available as free choice activities for the children on a daily basis. Projects are planned that integrate with thematic units of study, seasonal activities, and school-wide events.

Is the child's time structured or unstructured, or a mixture of both? A mixture of both.

If a child is not interested in a particular activity, does he/she have other choices or is he/she encouraged to try it anyway? Our children's day is filled with a combination of free choice and teacher directed activities. Respect for each child's interests is always given attention as well as the concept of sharing in group activities. This introduces the concept of compromise to the children in a developmentally appropriate way.

How are disputes handled when they occur between the children? Conflict resolution is taught to the children at their developmental level. Children are encouraged to use their words to solve problems with the adults as their support. Older children in our multi-age classrooms are proud to model the appropriate behavior for their younger classmates.

When and for how long is nap time? Nap time begins at 1 p.m. and lasts until 2:15 p.m. for the youngest children in the class. Older students rest for a shorter period and then resume activities in the afternoon.

What kinds of beds do you use? Cots are raised approximately three inches off the floor, and children bring their own nap blankets.

What do you do when a child is dropped off in the morning and is obviously not well? What do you do when a child becomes sick during the day? In both instances a parent is called to come and pick up the sick child. The child is isolated from his/her classmates until the parent arrives.

Can you accommodate children with special needs? Our facility is fully handicap accessible. We try to accommodate students' needs whenever possible without compromising our program.

KEEPING IT SAFE

Please describe your security measures for arriving and leaving the school. Primary students are signed in and out daily by a parent or authorized adult. A security guard is on campus whenever children are present. Ours is a gated community and doors remain locked to outsiders during the school day. Card keys are issued to faculty and staff for access to the building.

What medical supplies do you have on hand, and what medical experience does your staff have? Is your staff trained in CPR? Each classroom is equipped with First Aid and emergency equipment. The school maintains food and emergency supplies for 72 hours for all students and adults. All of the faculty and staff are trained in First Aid and CPR.

Please describe your earthquake-preparedness plan, and what special equipment do you have on hand in the event of a disaster? Teachers are required to conduct one-minute "drop and hold" exercises in the classroom from time to time. Teachers train their students to respond to the "drop and hold!" command by going into the "quake-safe" position under their desks. Teachers direct students away from windows and hanging fixtures. Emergency bags, supplied in all rooms, are stored accessibly.

Teachers assign related activities and projects to the students so they become familiarized with all aspects of this type of natural disaster, and encourage them to discuss this at home. Occasionally, the school will hold school-wide earthquake simulation drills.

SWINGS 'N THINGS

Please describe your playground. Does it have plenty of shade? Our primary/K-1 playground comprises one large climbing/activity structure with heavy duty padding underneath and around it. There are areas for students to ride tricycles, play in play houses, dig in the sandbox, and relax with friends. Large and small building blocks are available as well as basketballs and hoops. A drinking fountain is available for children's needs at all times and a bathroom is adjacent. The playground is cool from ocean breezes and shaded by peripheral trees.

Do you put sunscreen on the children? Parents are instructed to apply sunscreen daily as a preventative safety measure.

What kind of toilet training is available? None. We require our students to be potty trained before they start school at Turning Point. We do realize that three-year-olds new to school may have accidents and therefore a change of clothes is available in their cubby at all times.

HELPING OUT

What kinds of fundraising events are at your school each year? Our two major fundraisers are the Annual Giving Campaign in the fall and a Silent Auction/Dinner in the spring. Our student fundraiser is a Hoop-a-Thon. Funds from the Hoop-a-Thon are designated for a specific project each year. In the fall a book fair is held to create funds for our library and encourage book donations to the classroom libraries and the school library.

How much participation is required by each parent? Parents are expected to participate to the extent to which they are able. Attendance at the Silent Auction/Dinner is good and every student participates in the Hoop-a-Thon. We have a very supportive parent community with many different committees to be involved with. There is no requirement to volunteer, but most families do.

KEEPING IN TOUCH

How do you communicate with parents? Is there a newsletter or phone tree? The Wednesday Weekly is our vehicle to communicate with our families. Primary students use their lunchboxes to carry information from home to school and back. A newsletter is published about three times a year and circulated to the school and extended community. An automatic phone messaging service is used to relay more urgent/important information to our families. We have an out-of-state contact in the event of an emergency that affects local phone service.

Does the school publish an address book with all the parents' information in it? Each year, the school publishes a roster of families' addresses, phone numbers, and email addresses. Included in the roster is a listing of Faculty and Staff, along with Trustee and Parent Support Information. Class Lists with student birthdays are also published.

preschool

UCLA EARLY CARE AND EDUCATION

P.O. Box 951785 (Mailing Address)
101 S. Bellagio Way
Los Angeles, CA 90095-1785
(310) 825 5086
www.ece.ucla.edu
See Map D on page 286

Contact: Gay MacDonald, Executive Director

- ACCREDITATION: NAEYC
- NOT-FOR-PROFIT
- FINANCIAL AID IS NOT AVAILABLE
- NUMBER OF KIDS: 247
- TUITION: $1,225-$1,550 MONTH
- WE HAVE KIDS WITH SPECIAL NEEDS

WHEN TO APPLY: APPLICATIONS ARE ACCEPTED YEAR ROUND FROM UCLA-AFFILIATED FAMILIES AND CAN BE DOWNLOADED FROM THE SCHOOL'S WEBSITE. THERE IS A WAIT LIST.

The only possibly negative things I can say about the UCLA Early Care and Education Center is that there is a very, very long waiting list (if a space opens up and you get called, act on it immediately or the space will be filled!), and that it is exclusively available to UCLA Faculty, staff and students. The fact that UCLA offers this is a credit to the school, and might sway parents' decision to attend or work at the school. Gay MacDonald, Executive Director of all three current locations, took time out of her day to give me a very detailed two-hour tour. We started in the "infant garden" designed by the infant teachers. The garden supports socialization as well as language. In this lush garden, these infants are offered different levels, altitudes, textures, sand, a shallow stream (on hot days), very gradual hills to learn balance, and mini-mazes carved into the bushes for the feel of hide and seek. There is another garden geared towards the older children, created with just as much thought and planning.

As we walked into the first classroom, I caught a glimpse into what makes UCLA Early Care unique—male interns, not just females can play an important role in a young child's life. The children are encouraged to use gestures to communicate before they can speak. Instead of individual high chairs, specially made low chairs are used so the children's feet are on the floor. Croissant-shaped tables are used for meals, with five to six children "buttering" the outside edges, and the teacher in the middle. There is a full service nutrition program at the Krieger and University Village Centers, including personal chef and full kitchen. It is apparent why UCLA Early Care was chosen by the High Scope Educational Research Foundation and the NAEYC as an exemplary campus-based early childhood program!

The care and education is based on the philosophy that parents are the first and most important caregivers, and that early childhood teachers are parents' partners in child rearing. This is evident in the most gradual and organic approach to toilet training I have seen yet. This begins with the adult attitude to body function, starting with diaper changes, then "standing" diaper changes, so children get involved with the process of their diaper change. There is no pressure, and children develop at their own pace. The transition to using the potty is timed with the parents schedule as well, so the child gets total support. UCLA is a research school, primarily science research. Gay MacDonald explains, "Science is organized knowledge, which is what young children are doing. Children take what they know and make sense of it (organize it). It's very natural." The current three locations operate at a high level of consistency, but not conformity, leaving a lot of room for variation. I left the school more educated about early childcare, and this was after visiting for just a few hours!

BACKGROUND

UCLA Child Care Services was established in 1971 under the auspices of the Associated Student of UCLA. It is now known as Early Care and Education and is part of the Business and Administrative Services.

BIRD'S EYE VIEW

	Non-existent	Poor	Fair	Good	Excellent
Learning to Read Children learn to explore the world of books					🦉
Dress-Up Children experiment with different roles and imagination					🦉
Hand-Eye Children develop fine motor skills by using fingers and hands					🦉
Building Blocks Children practice symbolic representation. They are developing an understanding of the relationships between size and shape, and the basic math concepts of geometry and numbers					🦉
Arts and Crafts Children are developing small muscle control as well as creativity					🦉
Body Coordination Children crawl through tunnels, climb and balance					🦉
Meeting Time Gathering place to listen to the teacher and to stories					🦉
Weights and Measures Water and Sand tables					🦉
Beakers and Bunnies Classroom pets, aquariums....planting...					🦉
Counting 1-2-3 A good preschool will stock basic early-learner software such as phonics or counting games				🦉	
Outdoor Play Encourage large muscle control and coordination					🦉

Q & A

HOW THEY LEARN

What is your school's teaching philosophy? We believe that early learning is relationship-based. Our fundamental goal is to establish trusting relationships among children, teachers, and parents. Carefully constructed early education experiences promote exploration, critical thinking, cooperative play and the development of mutual respect.

How do you implement the philosophy? Each classroom is staffed by three full-time Early Childhood Teachers with Child Development Permits from the California Commission on Teacher Credentialing. Many of our teachers are working on advanced degrees.

What specialty teachers are brought into the school? UCLA Work-Study students provide additional staffing.

What is the teaching method? Implements a developmentally appropriate curriculum based on the view that children learn best when they are actively exploring a carefully constructed environment in the company of loving, professionally prepared teachers.

At what age do the children start? To what age is the school licensed? Infants start from 2-17 months. Toddlers are 18-33 months. Preschool is from 34-60 months, and kindergarten is 60-72 months. (University Village only).

HOW TO GET IN

Are there open house dates? When are tours given? Call the individual centers for information. The Fernald Center is run by Director Genie Saffren, (310) 825-4561. The Krieger Center is run by Director Sue Ballentine, (310) 825-5086. University Village Center is run by Director Gerardo Soto, (310) 915-5827.

Is there an interview? With the child or without? No interview.

Is preference given to applicants whose siblings are alumni? No, but there is a priority for siblings of currently enrolled children.

Are letters of recommendation encouraged? From what types of people? No recommendations needed.

How many applications do you receive each year? Several hundred.

How many open spots are there each year? The number varies based on ages of children leaving for kindergarten and on families moving away. We opened an expansion of five classrooms in 2006 that increased availability.

What are some of the schools that children go on to after finishing their education at your preschool? Many Westside and valley public and private elementary schools.

PIGGY BANK

Apart from tuition, what other fees do you charge? The application fee is $50 for staff and faculty; there is no fee for student families. There is a processing fee of $50.

How is tuition broken down? Tuition is $1,600 for infants, $1,550 for toddlers, and preschool and kindergarten tuition is $1,225. The fee includes diapers, formula and all food at Krieger and University Village. Parents send lunches at the Fernald Center.

What are the different payment plans available? Parents usually pay by the month, some by credit card, some by payroll deduction. There are occasional special arrangements responsive to individual needs.

What is the fee schedule? No feedback received.

Is there a contract? There is an annual contract.

Do you have a tuition insurance program? No tuition insurance.

HELPING HANDS

What accreditation is necessary for the teachers to work at your school? Our Child Care Resource Program provides individualized assistance, parenting and consumer information to over 1,000 families each year. We serve the diverse population of UCLA's student, staff and faculty families. Teachers must have a minimum A.A. or B.A. with child development units.

How many teachers are there? There are 52 full-time teachers (three in each classroom).

How many aides are there? There are additional student teacher assistants.

Do they come from other preschools? No feedback received.

IN THE 'ROOM

What's the child-to-adult ratio? The ratio is 3:1 for infants, 4:1 for toddlers and 8:1 for kindergarteners.

What are the policies for initial separation between parent and child? There is an individual plan for gradual separation from parents and attachment to primary caregivers over about a week or so.

Can you visit any time unannounced? Parents can visit unannounced.

What are the hours? Hours of operation are

7:30 a.m.-5:30 p.m., Monday through Friday, throughout the year.

Do you offer early bird or after-hours pick-up? If so, is there an extra fee? There are no extended hours. There is a late pick-up fee.

Please describe a typical day for a child at your school. We provide a daily schedule that balances active and quiet times, individual interactions with small and large group participation, child-initiated and teacher-directed activities.

What kinds of academic activities are offered? We offer "Preschool Pathways to Science"—a specialized, staff-developed curriculum that fosters children's critical thinking.

What kinds of art activities are offered? No feedback received.

Is the child's time structured or unstructured, or a mixture of both? No feedback received.

If a child is not interested in a particular activity, does he/she have other choices or is he/she encouraged to try it anyway? No feedback received.

How are disputes handled when they occur between the children? No feedback received.

When and for how long is nap time? No feedback received.

What kinds of beds do you use? No feedback received.

What do you do when a child is dropped off in the morning and is obviously not well? What do you do when a child becomes sick during the day? No feedback received.

KEEPING IT SAFE

Please describe your security measures for arriving and leaving the school. No feedback received.

What medical supplies do you have on hand, and what medical experience does your staff have? Is your staff trained in CPR? No feedback received.

Please describe your earthquake-preparedness plan, and what special equipment do you have on hand in the event of a disaster? No feedback received.

SWINGS 'N THINGS

Please describe your playground. Does it have plenty of shade? All the centers have great play spaces for children. There is plenty of shade.

Do you put sunscreen on the children? We use sunscreen.

What kind of toilet training is available? We start with diaper changes, then "standing" diaper changes so that children get involved with the process of their diaper change. There is no pressure, and children go at their own pace. The transition to using the potty is timed with the parents schedule as well, so the child gets total support.

HELPING OUT

What kinds of fundraising events are at your school each year? No feedback received.

How much participation is required by each parent? No feedback received.

KEEPING IN TOUCH

How do you communicate with parents? Is there a newsletter or phone tree? No feedback received.

Does the school publish an address book with all the parents' information in it? No feedback received.

preschool

UNIVERSITY PARENTS NURSERY SCHOOL

3233 South Sepulveda Blvd
Los Angeles, CA 90034
Phone: (310) 397-2735
www.upns.net
See Map D on page 286

Contact: Rachel Graves

- ACCREDITATION: NAEYC
- NON-PROFIT
- FINANCIAL AID IS NOT AVAILABLE
- NUMBER OF KIDS: 60
- TUITION: $278-$835 MONTH
- WE HAVE KIDS WITH SPECIAL NEEDS

WHEN TO APPLY: ON-GOING. CONTACT SCHOOL FOR MORE DETAILS.

Years ago, preschools run by parents who all took turns in the classrooms were called co-ops. These were usually ragtag affairs held in church basements staffed by well-meaning parents whose presence and opinions cycled in and out of their children's group life. Their reputations were always in doubt because of the turnover in staff and parental consensus.

UPNS is a stellar example of the new and improved abilities of parents to maintain quality in staff and facilities as well as to have a joyful, co-operative experience in the education of their children. The school is tucked away off a busy street in the heart of University Village. Be aware that there is another preschool directly opposite UPNS, which serves exclusively the diverse population of UCLA's student, staff and faculty families called UCLS Early Care and Education. UPNS also serves UCLA but is open to non-UCLA families.

Rachel Graves has been the director for 20 years. In any school setting this is a testament to her dedication, abundant skills and tenacity. She is the unifying force that promotes happiness, stability of staff and parent satisfaction. UPNS is a beautiful well-thought out, modern space. Very Californian in its architecture, the interior open walkways lead your eye to the play structures and classrooms. There is plenty of shade, which in our climate is a must. Outdoor shelves and toys are lined up neatly and there are even small-upholstered sofa chairs for outdoor book reading. The 3 and 4 year olds each have their own classroom and share this play area while the 2 year olds have their own classroom and play yard. I didn't see one "stray" child there during my visit, which is definitely worth mentioning.

Each classroom is visually exciting. One classroom was studying Africa and had a large hand-painted map of the continent along with African products, animals, topography etc. Another class was making fondue with a parent from Switzerland. Across the ceiling art/science/nature projects dangle. These are done in an aesthetically pleasing manner that shows child-generated effort aided by both parents and staff.

This parent participation school is as professional, clean, artistic and well-organized as any good preschool that I have visited, and as a parent you get to be part of the magical time of your child's preschool years. It is low-key only in that it is not running you ragged with fund raising. Whew!

BACKGROUND

The school was established in 1966.

BIRD'S EYE VIEW

	Non-existent	Poor	Fair	Good	Excellent
Learning to Read Children learn to explore the world of books				✓	
Dress-Up Children experiment with different roles and imagination				✓	
Hand-Eye Children develop fine motor skills by using fingers and hands					✓
Building Blocks: Children practice symbolic representation. They are developing an understanding of the relationships between size and shape, and the basic math concepts of geometry and numbers				✓	
Arts and Crafts Children are developing small muscle control as well as creativity					✓
Body Coordination Children crawl through tunnels, climb and balance					✓
Meeting Time Gathering place to listen to the teacher and to stories					✓
Weights and Measures Water and Sand tables				✓	
Beakers and Bunnies Classroom pets, aquariums....planting...				✓	
Counting 1-2-3 A good preschool will stock basic early-learner software such as phonics or counting games				✓	
Outdoor Play Encourage large muscle control and coordination					✓

Q & A

HOW THEY LEARN

What is your school's teaching philosophy? UPNS is founded on the belief that the preschool years are critical in a child's physical, intellectual and emotional growth. This is an exciting time for children, when they are busy discovering the world about them and how they fit into it. It is a time of experiencing life through the senses, and for children to explore their creative potential. A cooperative nursery school provides a bridge between home and this exciting outside world.

How do you implement the philosophy? Here, with the support of their parents, children learn how to treat others, how to get along in a social setting, and how to build a sense of assurance about themselves as individuals.

What specialty teachers are brought into the school? Music, gymnastics.

What is the teaching method? Developmental.

At what age do the children start? 2-5 years.

To what age is the school licensed? 5 years.

HOW TO GET IN

Are there open house dates? When are tours given? Monthly tours by appointment only.

Is there an interview? With the child or without? No feedback received.

Is preference given to applicants whose siblings are alumni? Yes.

Are letters of recommendations encouraged? From what types of people? No.

How many applications do you receive each year? 200.

How many open spots are there each year? 20.

What are some of the schools that children go on to after finishing their education at your preschool? Varies.

PIGGY BANK

Apart from tuition, what other fees do you charge? Application fee, enrollment fee.

How is tuition broken down? Full day program prices are from $320 to $835 per month. UCLA Affiliate rates are from $278 to $750 per month.

What are the different payment plans available? Check or cash.

What is the fee schedule? See our website.

Is there a contract? Yes.

Do you have a tuition insurance program? No.

HELPING HANDS

What accreditation is necessary for the teachers to work at your school? ECE units and experience.

How many teachers are there? Ten.

How many aides are there? One.

IN THE ROOM

What's the child-to-adult ratio? 1:5.

What are the policies for initial separation between parent and child? We have a detailed description in our handbook.

Can you visit any time unannounced? Yes.

What are the hours? 7:30 to 5:30.

Do you offer early bird or after-hours pick-up? If so, is there an extra fee? No.

Please describe a typical day for a child at your school? See our website.

What kind of academic activities are offered? None.

What kinds of activities are offered? Varies.

Is the child's time structured or unstructured or a mixture of both? Balanced.

If a child is not interested in a particular activity, does he/she have other choices or is he/she encouraged to try it anyway? Both.

How are disputes handled when they occur between the children? Redirection and communication.

What and for how long is nap time? 90 minutes to two hours.

What kinds of beds do you use? Cots.

What do you do when a child is dropped off in the morning and is obviously not well? What do you do when a child becomes sick during the day? We call the parents. The child should be excluded if they are unable to participate in normal activities, or if the child needs more care than can be provided by the child-care staff.

Can you accommodate children with special needs? Yes.

KEEPING IT SAFE

Please describe your security measures for arriving and leaving the school? For your child's safety, we require that you or other authorized adult (18 or older) bring your child into the program each morning and get them settled. Sign your child in upon your arrival. Be sure that staff is aware of your child's arrival before you leave.

What medical supplies do you have on hand, and what medical experience does your staff have? Is your staff trained in CPR? Yes.

Please describe your earthquake-preparedness plan, and what special equipment do you have on hand in the event of a disaster? We supply every necessity for a disaster.

SWINGS 'N THINGS

Please describe your playground. Does it have plenty of shade? Yes.

Do you put sunscreen on the children? Children should come with sunscreen. We will add it if needed.

What kind of toilet training is available? For two years olds, we work with the parents.

HELPING OUT

What kinds of fundraising events are at your school each year? Varies.

How much participation is required by each parent? Eight hours per month. All members are required to attend quarterly general meetings, and participate in fundraising activities in order to raise a minimum of $300 per year per family.

KEEP IN TOUCH

How do you communicate with parents? Is there a newsletter or phone tree? Yes, along with a Yahoo! Group online.

Does the school. Publish an address book with all parent's information in it? Yes, with their permission.

preschool-kindergarten

WAGON WHEEL SCHOOL

653 N. Cahuenga Blvd.
Los Angeles, CA 90004
Phone: (323) 469-8994
See Map C on page 286

Contact: Ruth Segal, Director

- ACCREDITATION: NONE
- NOT-FOR-PROFIT
- FINANCIAL AID IS NOT AVAILABLE
- NUMBER OF KIDS: 110
- TUITION: $1,400 MONTH
- WE HAVE KIDS WITH SPECIAL NEEDS

WHEN TO APPLY: THEY SHOW THE SCHOOL FROM SEPTEMBER THROUGH DECEMBER, THEN START REVIEWING APPLICATIONS AND MAKE SURE THEY HAVE A GOOD MIX ETHNICALLY, PROFESSIONALLY, ECONOMICALLY, BOY/GIRL RATIO.

Wagon Wheel doesn't have a brochure, a website or any other sort of advertising. It's completely word-of-mouth, but it's the name that comes up more than any other when discussing preschools east of Beverly Hills. Currently there are about 300 kids on the waiting list and 50 open spots a year. One visit to the school and you'll see why . As the daughter of a diplomat, owner/director Ruth Segal grew up living in many parts of the world so when she took over the school in 1977, providing a "sense of stability" for the children was a huge objective. Wagon Wheel kids get that stability, but it's set in an incredibly creative atmosphere, which is what makes it so terrific.

In fact, the whole Wagon Wheel experience seems to be about creativity and cultural awareness—whether it be the dance class I saw going on while I was there, the local area artists who come in to help the kids do long term arts and crafts projects, the magazine-quality photographs of Morocco taken by one of the parents that adorn the walls, or the world-renowned architect who was a recent guest speaker. The teachers seemed very relaxed, while their focus is definitely on the kids, they give them a great deal of room to explore and be independent. This creativity spreads outside as well. When designing the landscaping in the outdoor area, Ruth wanted the kids to be able to pretend they were in a jungle. For me it was more like a beautiful Mediterranean hideaway that I'd be reticent to ever leave. Amongst the exquisite landscaping, there's a mosaic wall made by the parents, art huts filled with top-of-the-line arts and crafts supplied by funds from the Friends Of Wagon Wheel foundation, and a Native American totem pole.

Set in what was originally a house, everything is very colorful and cozy, with the two- and three-year-olds in one facility and the four and five year olds in the other building. A multi-purpose modern design building was added. It was designed by Jay Vanos and a collaboration of many of the parents. As Ruth says, Wagon Wheel is a "home away from home with an education," and like a parent, Ruth is just as concerned with where the kids go when they leave her. To that end, she hosts Kindergarten Preview Nights where admission directors of various schools come to speak to parents. Some of the schools that Wagon Wheelers go on to include Third Street School, St. James, Willows Community School, The C.E.E., Echo Horizons, Campbell Hall, John Thomas Dye, Curtis, Turning Point, Wildwood, and Crossroads.

BACKGROUND

The school was established in 1946 by Tress Journey after identifying a need for pre-kindergarten learning that would prepare young children for the elementary grades by teaching them values, creative play and a love of learning.

BIRD'S EYE VIEW

	Non-existent	Poor	Fair	Good	Excellent
Learning to Read Children learn to explore the world of books					✓
Dress-Up Children experiment with different roles and imagination					✓
Hand-Eye Children develop fine motor skills by using fingers and hands					✓
Building Blocks Children practice symbolic representation. They are developing an understanding of the relationships between size and shape, and the basic math concepts of geometry and numbers					✓
Arts and Crafts Children are developing small muscle control as well as creativity					✓
Body Coordination Children crawl through tunnels, climb and balance					✓
Meeting Time Gathering place to listen to the teacher and to stories					✓
Weights and Measures Water and Sand tables					✓
Beakers and Bunnies Classroom pets, aquariums....planting...					✓
Counting 1-2-3 A good preschool will stock basic early-learner software such as phonics or counting games					✓
Outdoor Play Encourage large muscle control and coordination					✓

Q & A

HOW THEY LEARN

What is your school's teaching philosophy? We do not adhere to one particular teaching philosophy and are open to many. However, some of our methods include positive reinforcement, encouragement to express themselves, performances to enhance self-esteem, show and tell to teach them how to speak in front of groups. We encourage self-expression and have very independent children here.

How do you implement the philosophy? We teach through creative art, music, dance and cultural awareness. It's important for kids to know the world is eclectic.

What specialty teachers are brought into the school? A music teacher and a dance teacher come to the school once a week. Once a month we have a cultural visitor. We offer yoga, gymnastics and Spanish in the afternoon.

What is the teaching method? Because children are tested for elementary school between the ages of four and five, we teach them creatively through arts and crafts, phonics and games.

At what age do the children start? To what age is the school licensed? Ages two through five. There's also a kindergarten with 20 kids.

HOW TO GET IN

Are there open house dates? When are tours given? Parents can give tours to their friends after the November cutoff.

Is there an interview? With the child or without? There is no interview but four couples at a time come on tours with Ruth.

Is preference given to applicants whose siblings are alumni? Yes. Preference is also given to families in the neighborhood.

Are letters of recommendation encouraged? From what types of people? No.

How many applications do you receive each year? We receive about 150 applications a year. Currently, there are 300 children on the waiting list.

How many open spots are there each year? The number varies based on ages of children leaving for kindergarten and on families moving away.

What are some of the schools that children go on to after finishing their education at your preschool? Third Street School, St. James, Willows, The Center For Early Education, Echo Horizons, Campbell Hall, John Thomas Dye, Curtis, Mirman, Lawrence 2000, Turning Point, Wildwood, Crossroads, Oakwood.

PIGGY BANK

Apart from tuition, what other fees do you charge? The application fee is $75, and the entrance fee is $200.

How is tuition broken down? Tuition is $1,400 a month, which includes music and dance teachers, snack, holiday parties, and a graduation party.

What are the different payment plans available? Payment is due every month.

What is the fee schedule? Monthly payments.

Is there a contract? Yes, there is a contract.

Do you have a tuition insurance program? No tuition insurance program.

HELPING HANDS

What accreditation is necessary for the teachers to work at your school? They have to have all their child development units completed, which takes about two years of study.

How many teachers are there? There are eight teachers.

How many aides are there? There are four aides and two housekeepers.

Do they come from other preschools? Some of the teachers come from other preschools.

IN THE 'ROOM

What's the child-to-adult ratio? 15:2 with an aide.

What are the policies for initial separation between parent and child? The program begins in July. Parents can stay the first week and then individually we let the parents leave.

Can you visit any time unannounced? Yes, there is an open door policy.

What are the hours? Hours of operation are 7:30 a.m. - 3 p.m.

Do you offer early bird or after-hours pickup? If so, is there an extra fee? No early bird or late hours.

Please describe a typical day for a child at your school. From 7:30-8:30 a.m., children play inside at tables with puzzles, etc. Playground time is 8:30 a.m., and 9 a.m. is when the teacher starts the program (arts and crafts, then outside, music, outside, story time, outside). Children go outside every 30 minutes for a half-hour. Lunch is from 11:30 a.m.-12:30 p.m. From 12:30 p.m.-2:30 p.m. is nap time for the younger kids.

What kinds of academic activities are offered? Games with phonics. Pasting/gluing/cutting letters and numbers, weekly readers, messy art.

What kinds of art activities are offered? Tons of art activities. We have art huts in the backyard with clay, beads. We also invite people from LACMA and area artists to come in and teach the kids and we also do long-term arts and crafts (i.e. building a city, puppets).

Is the child's time structured or unstructured, or a mixture of both? A mixture of both.

If a child is not interested in a particular activity, does he/she have other choices or is he/she encouraged to try it anyway? We do encourage them to try, because we don't want them to be afraid to touch and experience.

How are disputes handled when they occur between the children? Get them to express what happened. Tell them they "need to use their words." Ask them, "What do you think you'll do next time?"

When and for how long is nap time? Two-hour nap time, and the three- to four-year-olds have one hour.

What kinds of beds do you use? They have cots and mats. Each kid has their own drawer with a sheet, blanket, any special toy they've brought from home. Music is always playing in the background during nap time.

What do you do when a child is dropped off in the morning and is obviously not well? What do you do when a child becomes sick during the day? Call parents to have them picked up. The child stays in Ruth's office until the parent arrives.

Can you accommodate children with special needs? No.

KEEPING IT SAFE

Please describe your security measures for arriving and leaving the school. Security at the school is extensive. It's walled and gated with security cameras.

What medical supplies do you have on hand, and what medical experience does your staff have? Is your staff trained in CPR? First Aid kit.

Please describe your earthquake-preparedness plan, and what special equipment do you have on hand in the event of a disaster? We do earthquake and fire drills monthly. We have approximately 70 earthquake kits. We also have an agreement with the Los Angeles Tennis Club down the street that we can bring the children there in case of emergency. The fire department knows to come to us right away as well.

SWINGS 'N THINGS

Please describe your playground. Does it have plenty of shade? One large sand area with structures, one grassy area with gorgeous landscaping to resemble a jungle.

Do you put sunscreen on the children? No feedback received.

What kind of toilet training is available? We work with parents and usually by mid-year the kids are trained.

HELPING OUT

What kinds of fundraising events are at your school each year? There are not a lot of fundraising events. However we do host a Gala where half the proceeds go to the teacher's bonuses funds and half goes towards school improvement.

How much participation is required by each parent? It's not required, but it is encouraged. Parents put out the newsletter and serve take care of preparing the hot lunches on Fridays.

KEEPING IN TOUCH

How do you communicate with parents? Is there a newsletter or phone tree? We see them every day and the school is small enough that we're always in contact. Teacher send an arts and crafts package home each week with the student with a letter as to what was done that week.

Does the school publish an address book with all the parents' information in it? No feedback received.

preschool to 6th grade

WALDEN SCHOOL

74 South San Gabriel Blvd.
Pasadena, CA 91107
Phone: (626) 792-6166
www.waldenschool.net
See Map B on page 286

Contact: Matt Allio, Director

- ACCREDITATION: CAIS, WASC
- NOT-FOR-PROFIT
- FINANCIAL AID IS AVAILABLE
- NUMBER OF KIDS: 40
- TUITION: $15,150 YEAR
- WE HAVE KIDS WITH SPECIAL NEEDS

WHEN TO APPLY: PARENT TOURS ARE OCTOBER THROUGH JANUARY. APPLICATIONS ARE DISTRIBUTED AT TOURS. APPLICATION DEADLINE IS IN FEBRUARY.

Walden School is located in Pasadena and the preschool occupies two rooms within the rest of the school. These rooms are large and well organized with lots of natural light thanks to the overhead skylights. The preschool has its own separate, well-equiped playground next to the older children's play area. This allows the older children to help out with the little ones, and quite often the sixth graders will "pop in" and read to the preschoolers. There are other advantages such as the little ones joining in with the older children in school assemblies.

Tina Riddle, the Director of the preschool program, explains that her students enjoy all the same privileges that the elementary school offers. This includes specialist teachers in spanish and music twice a week. They take physical education and dance classes each week and make regular visits to the local library to encourage a love of books. All these varied activities plus three field trips a year, makes for a very interesting time at school for these children!

Ms. Riddle and I went out onto the playground to watch the children as they played under the supervision of a couple of watchful teachers. A young boy wearing a helmet, zoomed towards us on his bicycle and braked right in front of us to say hello. He was having a wonderful time as were the other children. As I ended the tour, I said goodbye to Ms. Riddle and left feeling that this environment would certainly help in producing bright and confident young people. I was reminded of a quote from the Walden's school literature which pleasantly sums up the school's philosophy: "We strive to fix ideas in understanding, rather than words in memory." This school certainly has a lot to offer. Do take a closer look.

BACKGROUND

Founded in 1970 by Marilyn Fiedler as an alternative progressive school for pre-kindergarten through sixth grade.

Bird's Eye View

	Non-existent	Poor	Fair	Good	Excellent
Learning to Read Children learn to explore the world of books					✓
Dress-Up Children experiment with different roles and imagination					✓
Hand-Eye Children develop fine motor skills by using fingers and hands					✓
Building Blocks Children practice symbolic representation. They are developing an understanding of the relationships between size and shape, and the basic math concepts of geometry and numbers					✓
Arts and Crafts Children are developing small muscle control as well as creativity					✓
Body Coordination Children crawl through tunnels, climb and balance					✓
Meeting Time Gathering place to listen to the teacher and to stories					✓
Weights and Measures Water and Sand tables					✓
Beakers and Bunnies Classroom pets, aquariums....planting...					✓
Counting 1-2-3 A good preschool will stock basic early-learner software such as phonics or counting games				✓	
Outdoor Play Encourage large muscle control and coordination					✓

• • • • • • • **Q & A** • • • • • • • •

HOW THEY LEARN

What is your school's teaching philosophy?
At Walden, we nurture a child's natural wonder and personal dignity. We provide a personalized, developmentally appropriate program that encourages responsibility, initiative, child-led inquiry, ethical behavior and excellence. We promote positive conflict-resolution skills, understanding, and creativity in problem solving. Children learn academic skills and concepts through experience and Socratic discussion, as well as through direct instruction and practice. We teach children to value and respect diversity. We strive, therefore, to lay the foundation for wisdom, to encourage the spirit of Renaissance learning, and to teach that we all have stewardship for the world in which we live. Walden is dedicated to fostering intellectual, social and personal growth for each child, using both traditional and innovative methods within a developmentally appropriate curriculum. We believe in whole-child education, and recognize grade-level developmental milestones in establishing curricular goals and expectations. When children are appropriately challenged, the excitement and joy of learning are more likely to be retained. In addition to laying a firm academic foundation, Walden encourages disciplined and imaginative thinking and strives to help students see the inter-relatedness of all that they learn. Also stressed is the importance of self-esteem, of graciousness and generosity, and the appreciation of differences among people as well as the responsibil-

ity each of us has as members of a school community. Walden hopes to instill a love of learning in its students, as well as an understanding of the importance and skill of making choices and decisions.

How do you implement the philosophy? A Walden pre-kindergarten classroom provides a thoughtfully prepared environment that contains materials and activities chosen to foster intellectual, physical, personal, and social growth. Play is recognized as children's "work" and is respected as a medium through which children learn. Children are given rich, hands-on opportunities for experimentation and manipulation of materials. Child-led inquiry and spontaneous learning opportunities are encouraged in a collaborative setting, as teachers respond to students' interests with open-ended questions that foster the development of critical and analytical thinking skills. While the development of academic skills is an integral component of the program, an emphasis is given to the development of habits—work habits (responsibility, tenacity, striving to do your best) and habits of being (conflict resolution strategies, manners, caring for the environment). Another emphasis is the development of a strong social consciousness, with many aspects of the curriculum contributing to the creation of a caring community. All-school assemblies, buddy classes, sixth grade mentors, recycling and composting help to ingrain a sense of self in relation to others and the world.

What specialty teachers are brought into the school? Specialty classes in music, physical education, dance, Spanish, and library are integrated into the curriculum, enriching and deepening children's understanding. The school is particularly proud of its unique Storytelling Program, which provides children with valuable perspectives on personal and global relationships. Walden maintains a storyteller-in-residence who works in the classroom helping children develop confidence, language, effective oral communication skills, and an appreciation for oral traditions through out many cultures. Field trips and guests speakers are planned to enhance the children's experience.

What is the teaching method? Walden's teaching is grounded in the educational and philosophical theories of Piaget, Socrates, Thoreau, and Montessori among others, while informed by current educational research and teaching strategies such as N.A.E.Y.C.'s Developmentally Appropriate Practice.

At what age do the children start? To what age is the school licensed? We are licensed for three- to six-year-olds. Children must be three years old by the first day of school.

HOW TO GET IN

Are there open house dates? When are tours given? Parent tours are October through January. Prospective Parents' Open House is in early January.

Is there an interview? With the child or without? Children visit on a Saturday morning in January or February for an hour and a half.

Is preference given to applicants whose siblings are alumni? Yes.

Are letters of recommendation encouraged? From what types of people? Teacher recommendation from prior school.

How many applications do you receive each year? 60-80.

How many open spots are there each year? 15-25.

What are some of the schools that children go on to after finishing their education at your preschool? Most continue at Walden through sixth grade.

PIGGY BANK

Apart from tuition, what other fees do you charge? The application fee is $70, and there is a legacy fee of $500.

How is tuition broken down? Call school for breakdown.

What are the different payment plans available? One, two and ten payments.

What is the fee schedule? No fees.

Is there a contract? There is an annual contract.

Do you have a tuition insurance program? Yes, we have a tuition insurance program.

HELPING HANDS

What accreditation is necessary for the teachers to work at your school? B.A. degree with a minimum of 24 units in E.C.E.

How many teachers are there? There are two lead teachers and six specialty teachers.

How many aides are there? Three assistant teachers.

Do they come from other preschools? No feedback received.

IN THE 'ROOM

What's the child-to-adult ratio? 7:1.

What are the policies for initial separation between parent and child? There are no written policies. We work with the parents to serve the needs of the individual child.

Can you visit any time unannounced? Yes. We have an "open door" policy, parents may visit at any time.

What are the hours? School hours are 8:30 a.m.-3 p.m.

Do you offer early bird or after-hours pick-up? If so, is there an extra fee? Extended day hours 7-8:30 a.m., at an additional cost.

Please describe a typical day for a child at your school. 8:30 a.m.-12 p.m. involves morning group circle (morning greeting, attendance, calendar, share, read-aloud, class discussions), inside time (combination of children independently choosing materials and teacher-directed activities), and specialty classes (Spanish, P.E., dance, music, storytelling, library, snack, outside time). Lunch is from 12-12:45 p.m. Read-aloud/transition is from 12:45-1 p.m., rest time and outside time is from 1-2:30 p.m., and Group Circle (read-aloud, music, class discussions) is from 2:30-3 p.m.

What kinds of academic activities are offered? Materials are chosen and activities planned that enhance language/reading, math, science, and social studies concepts and skills within a wide range of developmental abilities.

What kinds of art activities are offered? Art materials are available for the children to use every day - paint, water colors, pastels, colored pencils, collage materials, etc. Additionally, there are teacher-directed art activities that allow the children to express themselves creatively while developing their skills.

Is the child's time structured or unstructured, or a mixture of both? A mixture of both. Walden is a child-led environment, we have a schedule for the day, but that changes with the needs and interests of the students.

If a child is not interested in a particular activity, does he/she have other choices or is he/she encouraged to try it anyway? Children are encouraged, not forced, to participate in all activities. If he/she chooses not to participate, other activities are available from which the child may choose.

How are disputes handled when they occur between the children? We foster the development of conflict resolutions strategies—the ability to identify a problem, express your needs, and negotiate solutions in a kind and respectful manner.

When and for how long is nap time? Children listen to stories and music. Those who do not sleep get up after 30-45 minutes and go outside or to another room. Children who do sleep wake-up by 2:30 p.m.

What kinds of beds do you use? We use floor mats at nap time, each child has his/her own mat.

What do you do when a child is dropped off in the morning and is obviously not well? What do you do when a child becomes sick during the day? Call his/her parent or someone on the emergency pick-up list.

Can you accommodate children with special needs? Our ability to accommodate a child with special needs is determined by the type of need the child has, and the resources we have available to support that child.

KEEPING IT SAFE

Please describe your security measures for arriving and leaving the school. Children are either dropped-off/picked-up in the classroom or in carline. All pre-kindergarten children are signed in and out by a parent or guardian. Children are not allowed to leave with anyone other than their parent or guardian unless given written permission. Arrival and dismissal gates are locked from the outside and are self-closing.

What medical supplies do you have on hand, and what medical experience does your staff have? Is your staff trained in CPR? All staff/faculty are trained in CPR and First Aid. Each room has a full First Aid kit. More extensive medical supplies are kept with the emergency equipment.

Please describe your earthquake-preparedness plan, and what special equipment do you have on hand in the event of a disaster? We have an extensive earthquake/disaster preparedness plan. All employees at the School have disaster training and we conduct an annual disaster drill. We have materials, supplies, and equipment stored on site. We have enough food and water for every person for three days.

SWINGS 'N THINGS

Please describe your playground. Does it have plenty of shade? Climbing structure with slide, monkey bars, and "tree house." Sandbox, dramatic play area, bike paths, basketball hoop, gardening area, shade tree with benches, tables for outside eating and activities, areas for manipulative play and art.

Do you put sunscreen on the children? We ask parents to apply sunscreen before school, and it is available for teachers to reapply during the day.

What kind of toilet training is available? Children must be toilet trained before they enter school.

HELPING OUT

What kinds of fundraising events are at your school each year? Annual Fund, Endowment, Parent Guild Spring Fundraiser, Book Fair, Walden t-shirt and sweatshirt sales, e-scrip, SchoolPop.com, foundation and corporate grants.

How much participation is required by each parent? Ten hours of parent volunteer service to the school per child.

KEEPING IN TOUCH

How do you communicate with parents? Is there a newsletter or phone tree? Monthly classroom newsletters, Walden Weekly school newsletters, Connections Newsletter three times a year, and e-mail news bulletins. "Buddy Families" are established for all new incoming families.

Does the school publish an address book with all the parents' information in it? A Parent Handbook is published each year with up-to-date information on the school and the families.

preschool

WESTMINSTER CHILD CENTER

4848 Eagle Rock Blvd.
Los Angeles, CA 90041
Phone: (323) 256-8086
See Map B on page 286

Contact: Rhonda Sihler, Director

- ACCREDITATION: NONE
- NOT-FOR-PROFIT
- FINANCIAL AID IS NOT AVAILABLE
- NUMBER OF KIDS: 85
- TUITION: $180-$475 MONTH
- WE HAVE KIDS WITH SPECIAL NEEDS

WHEN TO APPLY: CHILDREN CAN START AT ANY TIME OF THE YEAR IF THERE IS AN OPENING. REGISTRATION LETTERS FOR CHILDREN GO OUT IN APRIL AND MAY FOR SUMMER/SEPTEMBER ENROLLMENT. CALL THE SCHOOL FOR A TOUR.

Located in Eagle Rock Presbyterian Church on busy Eagle Rock Boulevard, amongst an unending row of auto parts businesses, the Westminster Child Center is deceptively big with a huge play area. As the former Director Carolyn Harris says "nothing succeeds like success," which is why the school is dedicated to helping children have as many successful experiences as possible.

The children and teachers in the five classrooms seemed rather quiet. One class was learning about circles, and one class was dancing—but even that seemed a bit low-key. Parents that choose this school are largely from the Eagle Rock area, with others from nearby Highland Park and Mount Washington.

There's fifteen minutes of chapel time on Tuesdays and Wednesdays, where the kids sing songs and say some "thank you" prayers. Accommodations can be made for those parents who don't feel comfortable with their child attending. While the classrooms may be somewhat utilitarian the play area is incredibly impressive. It's huge, with a bike path and lots of new equipment.

BACKGROUND

Westminster Child Center was established in 1962 by a group of woman from the Eagle Park Presbyterian Church. Over the past 42 years, there have been four Directors. The current director, Carolyn Harris, is in her 20th year as a director.

BIRD'S EYE VIEW

	Non-existent	Poor	Fair	Good	Excellent
Learning to Read Children learn to explore the world of books				✓	
Dress-Up Children experiment with different roles and imagination				✓	
Hand-Eye Children develop fine motor skills by using fingers and hands				✓	
Building Blocks Children practice symbolic representation. They are developing an understanding of the relationships between size and shape, and the basic math concepts of geometry and numbers				✓	
Arts and Crafts Children are developing small muscle control as well as creativity				✓	
Body Coordination Children crawl through tunnels, climb and balance				✓	
Meeting Time Gathering place to listen to the teacher and to stories				✓	
Weights and Measures Water and Sand tables				✓	
Beakers and Bunnies Classroom pets, aquariums....planting...			✓		
Counting 1-2-3 A good preschool will stock basic early-learner software such as phonics or counting games				✓	
Outdoor Play Encourage large muscle control and coordination				✓	

Q & A

HOW THEY LEARN

What is your school's teaching philosophy? Children learn best by doing, describing and exploring the world around them. All children learn every minute of the day and in a variety of ways. We believe in providing as rich a background as possible to facilitate that learning directed at their multiple intelligences in ways that are developmentally appropriate.

How do you implement the philosophy? All of our teachers are expected to address cognitive, social, emotional and physical development of each child.

What specialty teachers are brought into the school? We do from time to time bring in specialty teachers for music, movement and yoga.

What is the teaching method? We primarily use a discovery model method though some directed teaching is done at circle time, in learning songs and playing games.

At what age do the children start? To what age is the school licensed? We are licensed for children aged 2-6. We prefer children to be two years old by September when school starts.

HOW TO GET IN

Are there open house dates? When are tours given? Tours are available at any time.

Is there an interview? With the child or without? There is not a normal interview.

Is preference given to applicants whose siblings are alumni? Yes.

Are letters of recommendation encouraged? From what types of people? Not needed.

How many applications do you receive each year? No feedback received.

How many open spots are there each year? No feedback received.

What are some of the schools that children go on to after finishing their education at your preschool? No feedback received.

PIGGY BANK

Apart from tuition, what other fees do you charge? There is no fee to go on the waiting list, and there is no application fee. Registration fee is $200, non-refundable, one-time.

How is tuition broken down? Monthly tuition is $475 for preschool (two-to three-year-olds), and $180 for three-and four-year-olds.

What are the different payment plans available? Bills go out every month in the 20th and on due no later than the 10th. We bill two months in advance for preschool tuition and one month in advance regularly scheduled child care.

What is the fee schedule? See above. Scheduled childcare from 7:30-8:30 a.m. and 11:45 a.m.-6 p.m. is on an hourly basis. Unscheduled is a slightly higher hourly rate.

Is there a contract? Parents sign an admission agreement.

Do you have a tuition insurance program? No tuition insurance program is in place.

HELPING HANDS

What accreditation is necessary for the teachers to work at your school? Teachers must have a minimum of 12 ACE units. I have teachers with A.A. and B.A. degrees in early childhood education.

How many teachers are there? There are ten qualified teachers.

How many aides are there? No aides.

Do they come from other preschools? No feedback received.

IN THE 'ROOM

What's the child-to-adult ratio? 5:1 for two-year-olds (14 children, three teachers), 8:1 for three-year-olds (15 children, two teachers), and 9:1 for four-year-olds (18 children, two teachers).

What are the policies for initial separation between parent and child? Parents may stay with the child until the parent feels comfortable leaving the child.

Can you visit any time unannounced? Yes.

What are the hours? Hours are 7:30 a.m.-6 p.m.

Do you offer early bird or after-hours pick-up? If so, is there an extra fee? There is an extra fee for early and late pick-ups; cost is $3.50 per hour scheduled, and $4 per hour unscheduled.

Please describe a typical day for a child at your school. Early arrival is 7:30-8:30 p.m., 8:45-11:45 a.m. is preschool, lunch is from 11:45 a.m.-12:30 p.m., 12:30-2:30 p.m. is nap time. Outside play is 2:30-3:30 p.m., and snack time and daycare activities are from 3:30-4 p.m.

What kinds of academic activities are offered? Children learn shapes, numbers and letters.

What kinds of art activities are offered? Most activities are focus and express-oriented. There are different activities every day but equipment such us blocks, water, sand, wheel toys, swings climbing structure as always available. Easels for deriving and painting are always available.

Is the child's time structured or unstructured, or a mixture of both? There are always some open play and some structured time, singing and table activities every day.

If a child is not interested in a particular activity, does he/she have other choices or is he/she encouraged to try it anyway? No.

How are disputes handled when they occur between the children? Teachers will talk to children and help them solve disputes. We play with the children so they can learn how to say what they want. Hitting, biting, throwing sand are not okay. The basic rules are do not do anything to hurt yourself or another child or the environment. That really cover everything and every situation.

When and for how long is nap time? Nap time is two hours, from 12:30-2:30 p.m.

What kinds of beds do you use? We use cots.

What do you do when a child is dropped off in the morning and is obviously not well? What do you do when a child becomes sick during the day? We ask parents to take the children home.

Can you accommodate children with special needs? We have children with special needs each year, but don't have special facilities.

KEEPING IT SAFE

Please describe your security measures for arriving and leaving the school. We have a security gate at the front (Eagle Rock Boulevard entrance) and a self-closing gate at a parking lot entrance. There are only two gates open during the day.

What medical supplies do you have on hand, and what medical experience does your staff have? Is your staff trained in CPR? The teachers have both CPR and First Aid training on a regular basis.

Please describe your earthquake-preparedness plan, and what special equipment do you have on hand in the event of a disaster? We keep earthquake hits on hand for each child, and have additional food and water available as well as first aid equipment. We do both fire drills and earthquake drills.

SWINGS 'N THINGS

Please describe your playground. Does it have plenty of shade? We have a wonderful large playground with shade, trees, water, grass, a sandbox, swings, a large climbing structure, sand area, basketball hoops, and a cement bike path.

Do you put sunscreen on the children? No feedback received.

What kind of toilet training is available? Children must be toilet trained before they enter school.

HELPING OUT

What kinds of fundraising events are at your school each year? In September there is a back-to-school night-orientation to parents, Halloween Carnival and a Christmas Program. Teachers also plan field trips. Open house in May.

How much participation is required by each parent? Participation in fundraising is encouraged but not voluntary.

KEEPING IN TOUCH

How do you communicate with parents? Is there a newsletter or phone tree? Monthly newsletter, flyers and letters for special events. Parents also serve in our school committee.

Does the school publish an address book with all the parents' information in it? No.

preschool to 6th grade

Westminster Presbyterian Church Preschool

32111 Watergate Road
Westlake Village, CA 91361
Phone: (818) 889-1493
www.wpcwestlake.org
See Map A on page 286

Contact: Judy Hightower, Director

- ACCREDITATION: NAEYC
- NOT-FOR-PROFIT
- FINANCIAL AID IS NOT AVAILABLE
- NUMBER OF KIDS: 250
- TUITION: $225-$480 MONTH
- WE HAVE KIDS WITH SPECIAL NEEDS

WHEN TO APPLY: COME ON TOUR IN THE FALL

Thirty-four years ago, three mothers who attended the Westminster Presbyterian Church founded this preschool, which had its start as a community outreach program. Its success as a non-profit, non-denominational organization has allowed it to grow to its current size, with a teacher to student ratio of 1:8. The classrooms are located on either side of a beautiful courtyard with a towering maple tree right in the center. The architecture is white adobe Spanish Mission style and in the quiet and clean air of Westlake Village, it seems quite idyllic.

On the other side of one of the classroom buildings is the playground, complete with a raised garden in the center that the kids cultivate with the help of teachers or parents. It houses a climbing structure, trains, Legos, a sensory table, a wooden playhouse, large block building, swings and a slide. Partly covered in shade, it is large and I can imagine it to be a great stomping ground for any preschooler. Social and emotional growth is a big part of the play-based, developmentally appropriate teaching methodology in use here. As summed up in some of the school's literature, "The curriculum is developmentally-appropriate for the specific ages of the children and is based on proven theories by modern educators and psychologists. In other words, the specific activities that the children are engaged in during the day and the environment of the classroom have been specifically planned by the teacher to stimulate and challenge their young brains, and are based on the stage of their development."

In one of the classrooms there is a piano, and I'm told that music and art are a big part of the school activities. All toys are out and the students have access to all that is theirs to play with and get their hands on. From Westminster Presbyterian Church Preschool, approximately 75% of the students go on to public school and the remaining 25% to private schools.

Background

The school was started 34 years ago as a community outreach by three moms, who were also church members at Westminster Presbyterian.

BIRD'S EYE VIEW

	Non-existent	Poor	Fair	Good	Excellent
Learning to Read Children learn to explore the world of books					✓
Dress-Up Children experiment with different roles and imagination					✓
Hand-Eye Children develop fine motor skills by using fingers and hands					✓
Building Blocks Children practice symbolic representation. They are developing an understanding of the relationships between size and shape, and the basic math concepts of geometry and numbers					✓
Arts and Crafts Children are developing small muscle control as well as creativity					✓
Body Coordination Children crawl through tunnels, climb and balance					✓
Meeting Time Gathering place to listen to the teacher and to stories					✓
Weights and Measures Water and Sand tables					✓
Beakers and Bunnies Classroom pets, aquariums....planting...					✓
Counting 1-2-3 A good preschool will stock basic early-learner software such as phonics or counting games				✓	
Outdoor Play Encourage large muscle control and coordination					✓

• • • • • • • **Q & A** • • • • • • • •

HOW THEY LEARN

What is your school's teaching philosophy? The curriculum is developmentally appropriate for the specific ages of the children, and is based on proven theories by modern educators and psychologists.

How do you implement the philosophy? The specific activities that the children are engaged in during the day and the environment of the classroom have been specially planned by the teacher to stimulate and challenge their young brains and are based on the stage of their development.

What is the teaching method? Play-based, developmentally appropriate.

At what age do the children start? To what age is the school licensed? Two years, nine months of age to five years.

HOW TO GET IN

Are there open house dates? When are tours given? Our open house is for our enrolled families. Tours are scheduled as needed.

Is there an interview? With the child or without? No.

Is preference given to applicants whose siblings are alumni? Yes, and also to church members.

Are letters of recommendation encouraged? From what types of people? No.

How many applications do you receive each year? No feedback received.

How many open spots are there each year? No feedback received.

What are some of the schools that children go on to after finishing their education at your preschool? Local public schools, St. Jude's, Viewpoint, Carden.

PIGGY BANK

Apart from tuition, what other fees do you charge? There is a non-refundable yearly registration fee of $125.

How is tuition broken down? Monthly, tuition is $225 for two days, and $312 for three days, and $480 for five days.

What are the different payment plans available? Contact school for information.

What is the fee schedule? No feedback received.

Is there a contract? No feedback received.

Do you have a tuition insurance program? No feedback received.

HELPING HANDS

What accreditation is necessary for the teachers to work at your school? No feedback received.

How many teachers are there? There are 17 teachers.

How many aides are there? No feedback received.

IN THE 'ROOM

What's the child-to-adult ratio? 8:1.

What are the policies for initial separation between parent and child? Individual plans.

Can ou visit any time unannounced? Yes, and by law.

What are the hours? 8:30 a.m.-3:30 p.m.

Do you offer early bird or after-hours pick-up? If so, is there an extra fee? No feedback received.

Please describe a typical day for a child at your school. Music and art, playing with toys.

What kinds of academic activities are offered? Academics are integrated into all aspects of the classroom's activities.

What kinds of art activities are offered? Art activities are open-ended and child-directed.

Is the child's time structured or unstructured, or a mixture of both? A mixture of both.

If a child is not interested in a particular activity, does he/she have other choices or is he/she encouraged to try it anyway? Children have many other choices. They are always encouraged to try all activities.

How are disputes handled when they occur between the children? Accountability.

When and for how long is nap time? No nap time.

What kinds of beds do you use? No nap time.

What do you do when a child is dropped off in the morning and is obviously not well? What do you do when a child becomes sick during the day? No feedback received.

Can you accommodate children with special needs? Yes. We work in partnership with all three school districts that surround us.

KEEPING IT SAFE

Please describe your security measures for arriving and leaving the school. No feedback received.

What medical supplies do you have on hand, and what medical experience does your staff have? Is your staff trained in CPR? No feedback received.

Please describe your earthquake-preparedness plan, and what special equipment do you have on hand in the event of a disaster? We have worked with our local DART, fire department and urgent care facility and have provisions for three days.

SWINGS 'N THINGS

Please describe your playground. Does it have plenty of shade? They playground has plenty of shade. There is a climbing structure and raised garden, wooden playhouse, sensory table, swings and slides.

Do you put sunscreen on the children? We apply sunscreen as necessary.

What kind of toilet training is available? No feedback received.

HELPING OUT

What kinds of fundraising events are at your school each year? No feedback received.

How much participation is required by each parent? None.

KEEPING IN TOUCH

How do you communicate with parents? Is there a newsletter or phone tree? We have school newsletters and phone trees, as well as a parent advisory newsletter, room parent volunteer coordinator, classroom bulletin boards and teacher flyers.

Does the school publish an address book with all the parents' information in it? Not formally. Class lists are distributed.

preschool-kindergarten

WESTSIDE JEWISH COMMUNITY CENTER

5870 W. Olympic Blvd.
Los Angeles, CA 90036
www.westsidejcc.org
Phone: (323) 938-2531
See Map D on page 286

Contact: Ellen Greene, ECE Director

- ACCREDITATION: NONE
- NOT-FOR-PROFIT
- FINANCIAL AID IS AVAILABLE
- NUMBER OF KIDS: 120
- TUITION: $4,650-$13,200 YEAR
- WE HAVE KIDS WITH SPECIAL NEEDS

WHEN TO APPLY: APPLICATIONS ARE AVAILABLE IN LATE FEBRUARY OR EARLY MARCH AND ARE ACCEPTED UNTIL CLASSES ARE FULL. COME ON TOUR TO RECEIVE APPLICATION.

Despite its name, the Westside JCC Preschool is actually located in the Carthay Circle area, right across from Midway Hospital. Like its Silverlake counterpart, it could stand a facelift, but its inner beauty shines through once you manage to actually enter the building (a security guard escorts you in, and you have to go through two coded doors). "Homey" and "down-to-earth" with a "real sense of community" are the phrases that come up a lot when people talk about the school. As director Ellen Greene explains, "Our parents really get our philosophy. They understand it, and they want it." That philosophy is simply to develop a child's self-esteem and to promote positive feelings towards learning in a warm and nurturing environment.

With 130 students, the school is quite big—eight classrooms, an auditorium, a gymnasium, and various play yards. The classrooms themselves are amongst the largest I've seen, and each is very colorful and clean with a loft area. The teachers all seem to have years of experience rather than being straight out of school, and they deal with the kids in a loving but firm way. While I was there, one class was enjoying some accordion music by the teacher, while another took turns sharing family photos. Despite the rather gray day, another class happily played outside while upstairs in the gym, others participated in movement class.

Like the Silverlake JCC, Shabbat is celebrated on Friday, and while there is "respect for cultural diversity," it's not necessary to be Jewish to attend. Most of the kids come from the neighborhood and upon leaving, sixty percent go on to public school while 40% go on to private school.

BACKGROUND

The school was established in the early 1950s by Rose Engel. The Early Childhood Center began over 60 years ago and many of today's students are second or third generation attendees.

BIRD'S EYE VIEW

	Non-existent	Poor	Fair	Good	Excellent
Learning to Read Children learn to explore the world of books					●
Dress-Up Children experiment with different roles and imagination			●		
Hand-Eye Children develop fine motor skills by using fingers and hands				●	
Building Blocks Children practice symbolic representation. They are developing an understanding of the relationships between size and shape, and the basic math concepts of geometry and numbers				●	
Arts and Crafts Children are developing small muscle control as well as creativity				●	
Body Coordination Children crawl through tunnels, climb and balance					●
Meeting Time Gathering place to listen to the teacher and to stories				●	
Weights and Measures Water and Sand tables				●	
Beakers and Bunnies Classroom pets, aquariums....planting...				●	
Counting 1-2-3 A good preschool will stock basic early-learner software such as phonics or counting games				●	
Outdoor Play Encourage large muscle control and coordination					●

Q & A

HOW THEY LEARN

What is your school's teaching philosophy? Our primary goals are to develop a child's self-esteem, promote positive feelings towards learning, and to encourage social interaction within a Jewish preschool.

How do you implement the philosophy? Our classes integrate active learning to promote cognitive, social, emotional and physical growth and creative development. We provide a rich Judaic environment.

What specialty teachers are brought into the school? There is a music specialist (half-hour for all classes) and a bi-weekly movement specialist (half-hour every other week). Intergenerational programming takes place with our senior adults at the JCC, usually with art and music.

What is the teaching method? Active learning through a developmental approach. We have environments (centers) where children choose their activities.

At what age do the children start? To what age is the school licensed? Two years, four months by September of the school year. We are licensed through kindergarten.

HOW TO GET IN

Are there open house dates? When are tours given? Tours are arranged and done mornings between 9:30 a.m. and 11:30 a.m.. Tours are done on an individual basis.

Is there an interview? With the child or without? There is no interview process or registering over the phone. We at least want to meet with the family.

Is preference given to applicants whose siblings are alumni? Yes.

Are letters of recommendation encouraged? From what types of people? No.

How many applications do you receive each year? No feedback received.

How many open spots are there each year? No feedback received.

What are some of the schools that children go on to after finishing their education at your preschool? No feedback received.

PIGGY BANK

Apart from tuition, what other fees do you charge? There is a non-refundable $500 deposit, applicable to the first month's tuition. There is no entrance fee.

How is tuition broken down? Tuition depends on the age of the child and hours of attendance. From $4,650 to $13,200 per year.

What are the different payment plans available? First and last payment (one month's tuition equals one payment) are due prior to the beginning of the school year, then eight payments go from October through May. In May, pay in full and receive a 1% discount.

What is the fee schedule? See tuition costs above. We offer 1 p.m. and 3 p.m. enrichment classes for an additional fee (nine classes), and also offer vacation programs for winter, spring and summer (the summer program is a camp); contact the center for prices.

Is there a contract? Yes.

Do you have a tuition insurance program? No tuition insurance. Families can withdraw with 30 days' notice in writing.

HELPING HANDS

What accreditation is necessary for the teachers to work at your school? Teachers must meet minimum requirements of the state (our staff exceeds minimum licensing standards) and have experience. They are encouraged to continue their education. Teachers are reimbursed for school tuition and receive salary increments.

How many teachers are there? There are eight teachers.

How many aides are there? There are ten aides.

IN THE 'ROOM

What's the child-to-adult ratio? 5:1 for the two-year-old classes and 8:1 for the three-, four- and five-year-old classes.

What are the policies for initial separation between parent and child? The parent stays until the child is comfortable in the classroom—as long as it takes. Parents are encouraged to be in the background and leave for brief periods until the child adjusts.

Can you visit any time unannounced? Yes.

What are the hours? 9 a.m.-6 p.m.

Do you offer early bird or after-hours pick-up? If so, is there an extra fee? There is an early drop-off from 8-9 a.m., an extended day from 12:45-3 p.m., and Rainbow Crew and extended care are from 3-6 p.m.

Please describe a typical day for a child at your school. A consistent routine enables children to anticipate what happens next. The day consists of small and large group experiences and outside play. Art and music are included daily. Some older classes take field trips.

What kinds of academic activities are offered? None, really. Children learn best by playing and following their own curiosity.

What kinds of art activities are offered? Art is provided every day.

Is the child's time structured or unstructured, or a mixture of both? Unstructured with a routine. The child is able to choose activities from centers that change regularly.

If a child is not interested in a particular activity, does he/she have other choices or is he/she encouraged to try it anyway? No, but the child will be encouraged to try.

How are disputes handled when they occur between the children? We encourage conflict resolution and problem solving between the children, and teach them appropriate words to use. We use behavior modification. This approach helps children to become more aware of the impact of their actions upon others.

When and for how long is nap time? Nap time is 90 minutes for two-and three-year-olds, 45 minutes to one hour for four-year-olds, and 30 minutes for kindergarteners.

What kinds of beds do you use? We provide cots for the younger children (parents send bedding) and mats for the kindergarteners.

What do you do when a child is dropped off in the morning and is obviously not well? What do you do when a child becomes sick during the day? The parent or the emergency contact is called and the child is isolated until they are picked up. We require a child to be fever-free for 24 hours before returning to school.

Can you accommodate children with special needs? We have been including some special needs children for the last five to six years. Usually autistic children, some with therapeutic companions.

KEEPING IT SAFE

Please describe your security measures for arriving and leaving the school. We have a 24-hour security guard, key pad entries with special codes for school families, and video surveillance.

What medical supplies do you have on hand, and what medical experience does your staff have? Is your staff trained in CPR? No feedback received.

Please describe your earthquake-preparedness plan, and what special equipment do you have on hand in the event of a disaster? Emergency procedures are posted. We have water and food for three days, flashlights, blankets, etc. Children bring an earthquake kit with a change of clothes, underwear, socks, sweatshirt and flashlight/batteries. Children will stay at the center (or Midway Hospital) until picked up by a parent or guardian. Staff are instructed to stay with the children.

SWINGS 'N THINGS

Please describe your playground. Does it have plenty of shade? We have a large, tree-lined playground. There are many activities to choose from including climbing, sand, water play, trikes, etc. Water pitchers are brought out for drinking, and tables are available for snacks and lunch. Snacks are provided in the morning; all food is kosher, and fruit, milk and a carbohydrate are served at each snack.

Do you put sunscreen on the children? No feedback received.

What kind of toilet training is available? Children are encouraged to begin toilet training if they show signs of readiness. Our toilets are child-sized for comfort.

HELPING OUT

What kinds of fundraising events are at your school each year? Selling entertainment books, wrapping paper, family festival with silent auction, family dinners in restaurants.

How much participation is required by each parent? Fundraising is strongly encouraged but not required.

KEEPING IN TOUCH

How do you communicate with parents? Is there a newsletter or phone tree? Newsletters twice a month, room parents who communicate via phone tree and email.

Does the school publish an address book with all the parents' information in it? Yes.

preschool to 8th grade

WALDORF EARLY CHILDHOOD CENTER

1441 15th Street
Santa Monica, CA 90272
Phone: (310) 260-2708
www.wswaldorf.org
See Map D on page 286

Contact: Gita Labrentz, Academic Director

- ACCREDITATION: AWSNA
- NOT-FOR-PROFIT
- FINANCIAL AID IS NOT AVAILABLE
- WE DO NOT HAVE KIDS WITH SPECIAL NEEDS
- NUMBER OF KIDS: 80
- TUITION: YEAR
  $10,125-$13,500 (preschool)
  $15,375-17,500 (K-8)

WHEN TO APPLY: APPLICATIONS MUST BE RECEIVED BY JANUARY FOR EARLY DECISIONS IN MARCH. OTHERWISE, THERE IS A ROLLING ENROLLMENT.

As I entered the gate of the Westside Waldorf School, I joined about 40-50 other adults (mostly couples) for a meet-and-greet and continental breakfast. We were given color-coded name tags, to be separated into tour groups. The school was established in Santa Monica in 1988, and was founded by parents seeking Waldorf education for their children. I found the methodology and philosophy of Waldorf quite unique to other schools I have visited. At the heart of the Rudolf Steiner or Waldorf method is the conviction that education is an art. Whether the subject is arithmetic or history or physics, the presentation must live-it must speak to the child's experience. To educate the whole child, the heart and will must be reached, as well as the mind. My tour guide explained that the goal is to assist the child's development according to each child's way of learning and innate interest. Their imagination, intuition and inspiration are ignited through a innovative curriculum that is based in European thinking.

As we toured through the various classrooms, instructed to be absolutely non-intrusive, and not to interact with the children, it felt a little like observing animals in their natural state! There is soft, natural lighting; unfinished wood, pale, soothing colors. Simplistic toys, made with natural materials, are imagination inspired. In every room there are lounge areas for reading and relaxing. Rhythm is the basis for much of the activities. Rhythm in the early childhood is fairly routine. The three R's: rhythm, repetition and routine-explained Sumaiya, the school's coordinator. There is circle time in each classroom. It is moving song and verse, almost a theatrical performance. The theme/topic changes seasonally. Another part of the routine is cooking. Children help bake bread in each classroom, and prepare for the day. The room is filled with that warm, comforting smell of freshly baked bread. Today the children help prepare soup, which is cooked during class. Then they spend one hour in the playground, put on their slippers and come back inside to partake in the fruits of their labor.

The playground is noteworthy, primarily because of its size. It's huge! There is a shed, with tools for digging and building. Large wooden structures, including a bridge, and a rock-climbing wall, provide ample opportunity to explore large motor skills, balance, and imagination! Children can transfer to Waldorf schools in other cities, if you relocate. There are over 800 Waldorf schools nationwide. After finishing at Westside Waldorf, many students go on to Highland Hall (continuing Waldorf education), Crossroads, Windward, Wildwood, Archer School, Westchester Neighborhood School and various public schools.

BACKGROUND

The school was established in 1988 by several parents seeking a Waldorf education for their children. The first campus was on Pearl Street and 16th Street. The Waldorf Early Childhood Center is located at 1441 15th Street in Santa Monica.

BIRD'S EYE VIEW

	Non-existent	Poor	Fair	Good	Excellent
Learning to Read Children learn to explore the world of books					✓
Dress-Up Children experiment with different roles and imagination					✓
Hand-Eye Children develop fine motor skills by using fingers and hands					✓
Building Blocks Children practice symbolic representation. They are developing an understanding of the relationships between size and shape, and the basic math concepts of geometry and numbers					✓
Arts and Crafts Children are developing small muscle control as well as creativity					✓
Body Coordination Children crawl through tunnels, climb and balance					✓
Meeting Time Gathering place to listen to the teacher and to stories					✓
Weights and Measures Water and Sand tables					✓
Beakers and Bunnies Classroom pets, aquariums....planting...					✓
Counting 1-2-3 A good preschool will stock basic early-learner software such as phonics or counting games				✓	
Outdoor Play Encourage large muscle control and coordination					✓

Q & A

HOW THEY LEARN

What is your school's teaching philosophy?
To educate the whole child. Their imagination, intuition and inspiration are ignited through a genius curriculum that is based in European thinking.

How do you implement the philosophy?
Through the arts, all main lesson subjects are reinforced by music (strings program), singing, drawing, movement, handwork, crafts, woodworking, foreign languages. These are integral to the main subject lessons beginning in the

first grade.

What specialty teachers are brought into the school? There is one Spanish, one Japanese, one eurhythmy, one woodworking, one games, and one handwork teacher.

What is the teaching method? Natural development-oriented to each child's way of learning and their innate interest in all things. Waldorf, Rudolf Steiner. A social and artistic education.

At what age do the children start? To what age is the school licensed? Two years of age for Parent-Toddler. Two years, nine months for preschool. We are licensed up to Grade Eight.

HOW TO GET IN

Are there open house dates? When are tours given? January 13th, February 10th, March 17th, and April 21st. An RSVP is required for attendance and no children of any age are asked to come. This is a PARENT EVENT ONLY.

Is there an interview? With the child or without? The interview is done with the class teacher, parents and the child.

Is preference given to applicants whose siblings are alumni? Yes.

Are letters of recommendation encouraged? From what types of people? Letters of recommendation are asked for Grades applicants. We ask the applicant's current teacher to complete a confidential teacher recommendation form. The acceptance of the applicant is provisional until all paperwork has been reviewed.

How many applications do you receive each year? Approximately 65.

How many open spots are there each year? No feedback received.

What are some of the schools that children go on to after finishing their education at your preschool? Highland Hall (continuing Waldorf education), Crossroads, Windward, Wildwood, Archer School, Westchester neighborhood schools, various public schools.

PIGGY BANK

Apart from tuition, what other fees do you charge? A non-refundable and non-transferable $150 application fee. There is an entrance fee for all families entering all grades.

How is tuition broken down? Tuition is $10,125-$13,500 for nursery programs, $15,375 for kindergarten, and $17,500 for grades one through eight.

What are the different payment plans available? There is an annual payment with a 10% discount, or a ten-month payment plan (August-May).

What is the fee schedule? See above.

Is there a contract? There is a legally binding contract, where after May 1st the contract is under the Tuition Refund Plan.

Do you have a tuition insurance program? Tuition adjustment is available in the grades on a need-only basis only.

HELPING HANDS

What accreditation is necessary for the teachers to work at your school? Teachers must have Waldorf credentials.

How many teachers are there? There are six grade teachers, and five early childhood teachers. Other teachers include one Spanish, one Japanese, one eurhythmy, one woodworking, one games, and one handwork teacher. All faculty come from Waldorf schools.

How many aides are there? There are five early childhood assistants.

IN THE 'ROOM

What's the child-to-adult ratio? The preschool ratio is 15:2.

What are the policies for initial separation between parent and child? There is a lengthy discussion with parent(s) and teacher with regards to separation. Each teacher is different in his/her methodology as children as different, too. Some instances may show the child is able to transition easily, while another child may have a higher difficulty. Parents are invited to stay in the classroom during their child's separation, as long as there is no interaction between teacher and child.

Can you visit any time unannounced? NO.

What are the hours? Drop-off is at 8:30 a.m. Pick-up for the two-day program is 12:30 p.m. Pick up for the three, four and five-day program is 2 p.m.

Do you offer early bird or after-hours pick-up? If so, is there an extra fee? Early pick-up can be arranged with a conversation with the Class Teacher. There is no reduction in price if you pick up before naptime.

Please describe a typical day for a child at your school. Development activities and art.

What kinds of academic activities are offered? All activities in the early childhood program are primarily development.

What kinds of art activities are offered? Watercolor painting, finger knitting, sewing, arts and crafts, beeswax molding, cooking, baking, etc.

Is the child's time structured or unstructured, or a mixture of both? Rhythm in the early childhood is fairly routine. The three R's: or–rhythm, repetition, routine.

If a child is not interested in a particular activity, does he/she have other choices or is he/she encouraged to try it anyway? There are always other choices. The teacher may need assistance with another task that needs to be completed.

How are disputes handled when they occur between the children? No feedback received.

When and for how long is nap time? About an hour. Children do not necessarily have to nap, as it can be rest time.

What kinds of beds do you use? Cots, and families provide their own bedding.

What do you do when a child is dropped off in the morning and is obviously not well? What do you do when a child becomes sick during the day? We have an emergency contacts folder. The teacher may directly call the child's parents, or the office does. If we do not hear from the parental guardians within 20 minutes, we start calling the people they have listed as emergency contacts. If that is the case, then we get back in touch with the parental guardian to let him/her know whom the child is going home with.

Can you accommodate children with special needs? No feedback received.

KEEPING IT SAFE

Please describe your security measures for arriving and leaving the school. There is a full-time security guard at the crossing at all times.

What medical supplies do you have on hand, and what medical experience does your staff have? Is your staff trained in CPR? No feedback received.

Please describe your earthquake-preparedness plan, and what special equipment do you have on hand in the event of a disaster? Each class has an emergency preparedness kit. Regular fire drills are performed in compliance with local rules. We have an emergency contact list and an arrangement with Portland Waldorf School as a remote contact point.

SWINGS 'N THINGS

Please describe your playground. Does it have plenty of shade? No feedback received.

Do you put sunscreen on the children? No feedback received.

What kind of toilet training is available? We require that all children be toilet trained and weaned.

HELPING OUT

What kinds of fundraising events are at your school each year? We have an annual giving campaign, a silent auction, Capital Campaign, special dinners and festivals.

How much participation is required by each parent? As much as can be given (we have set a target of $5000 per family). Parents are required to contribute at least 20 hours of volunteer work through the school year.

KEEPING IN TOUCH

How do you communicate with parents? Is there a newsletter or phone tree? Weekly newsletter, email, lots of events for entire family (pajama party, pizza and ice cream social).

Does the school publish an address book with all the parents' information in it? We have a school directory.

Fiona Whitney Now Offers One-On-One and Group School Selection Counseling!

Fiona Whitney is pleased to offer a counseling service designed to help guide parents through the often confusing and time-consuming process of finding the right school for their child.

Fiona Whitney offers this most important service to parents who need help making a decision on which school to send their child to. Often after having sifted through mountains of materials a parent can find themselves even more confused than they were before! There are so many choices, but don't worry she can help you.

Here are some of the topics that will be covered during your consultation, which comes with a short list of schools that will be recommended for you to take a closer look at:

- What are the definitions of the various school teaching methods?
- Which one is right for your family? Will the right preschool lead to the right grade school?
- Are there "feeder" schools and which ones are they?
- What are your Kindergarten/Elementary/Middle and High School options?
- Should my child attend public or private school?
- What is the difference between a charter school and a magnet school and how do you apply to attend either?
- Have you added up the 'total' costs of a private school?
- How far are you willing to commute?

Consultation Fees:

- 1/2 Hour Phone Consultation: $150.00
- 3/4 Hour Phone Consultation: $225.00
- 1 Hour Phone Consultation: $295.00
- 1 Hour in person Consultation at your home: $325.00
- Group Consultation (4- 8 people): $95.00 per person
- Extra hours billed in 1/2 hour increments

Additional consultation help in visiting schools, helping with school applications and more by request.

Comments from some of the clients that we have worked with in the past:

"Loved it! Really gave me some guidelines on this long journey! Thank you."

"I'm very glad I spent the money. It saved us thousands and thousands of dollars since we decided to send our child to our local public school on your recommendation."

"Wonderfully helpful. My husband and I feel very empowered about the choices for schooling, now and in the future."

After a short interview (via email or telephone), Fiona Whitney will compile a short-list of her findings and then meet in person or via telephone conferencing to present the best school options, based on individual needs and interests.

"I want to hear what you want, and to help you find the right "fit" for your child. How can I be of service?"

Fiona Whitney

MAP OF LOS ANGELES COUNTY

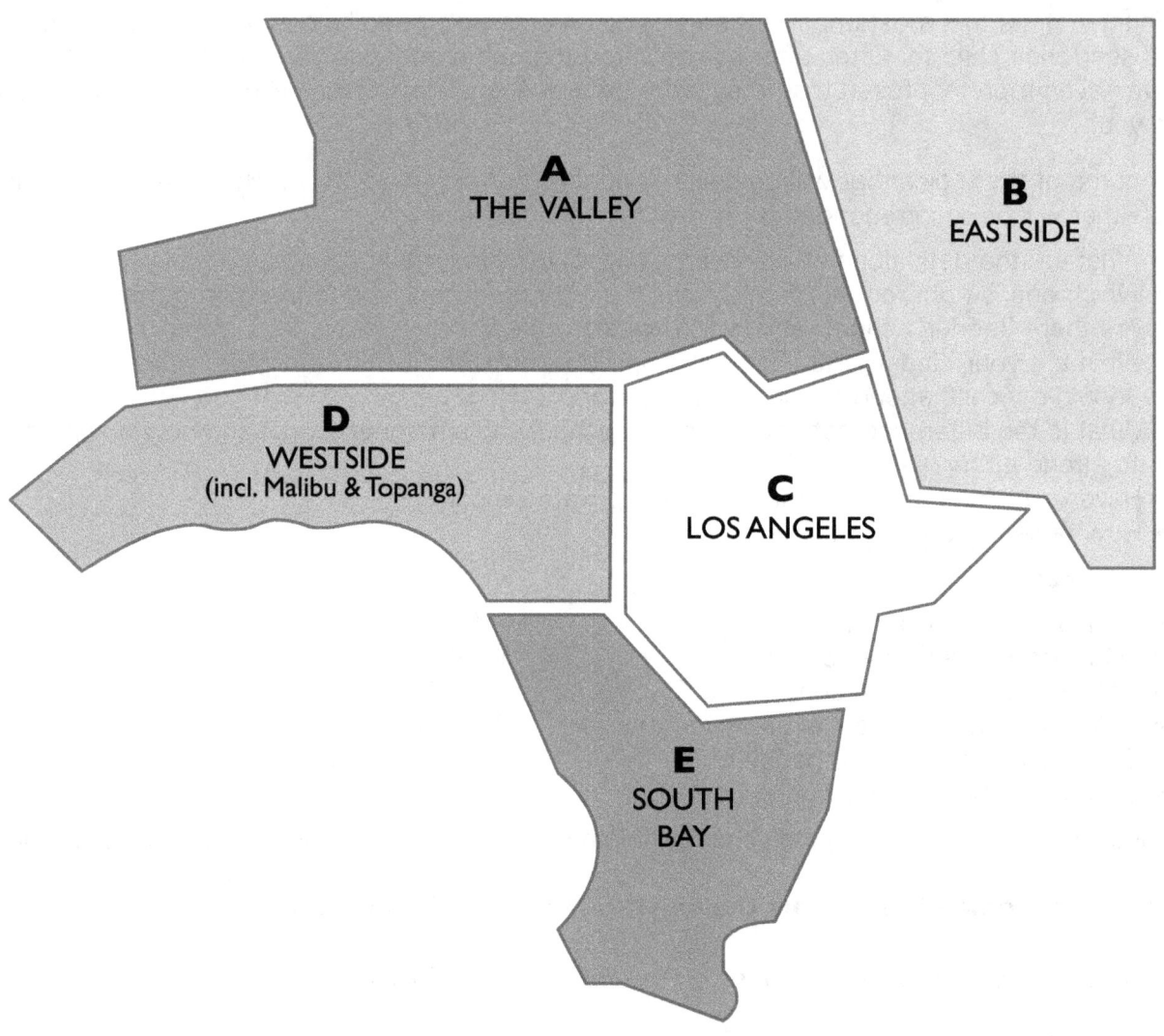

ACCREDITATION/MEMBERSHIP CODES

AMI . . . . American Montessori International

AMS . . . . American Montessori Society

AWSNA . . . . American Waldorf Schools of North America

CAIS . . . . .The California Association of Independent Schools

NAES . . . . .The National Association of Episcopal Schools

NAEYC . . . . .The National Association for the Education of Young Children

NAIS . . . . .The National Association of Independent Schools

NCME . . . . .National Center Montessori Education

WASC . . . . .The Western Association of Schools and Colleges

www.ingramcontent.com/pod-product-compliance
Lightning Source LLC
Chambersburg PA
CBHW051208290426
44109CB00021B/2383